Steam City

HISTORICAL STUDIES OF URBAN AMERICA

Edited by Lilia Fernández, Timothy J. Gilfoyle, Becky M. Nicolaides, and Amanda I. Seligman

James R. Grossman, Editor Emeritus

A complete list of series titles is available on the University of Chicago Press website.

Steam City

Railroads, Urban Space, and Corporate
Capitalism in Nineteenth-Century Baltimore

DAVID SCHLEY

The University of Chicago Press
Chicago and London

The University of Chicago Press, Chicago 60637
The University of Chicago Press, Ltd., London
© 2020 by The University of Chicago
All rights reserved. No part of this book may be used or reproduced in any manner
whatsoever without written permission, except in the case of brief quotations in
critical articles and reviews. For more information, contact the University of Chicago
Press, 1427 E. 60th St., Chicago, IL 60637.
Published 2020
Printed in the United States of America

29 28 27 26 25 24 23 22 21 20   1 2 3 4 5

ISBN-13: 978-0-226-72025-8 (cloth)
ISBN-13: 978-0-226-72039-5 (e-book)
DOI: https://doi.org/10.7208/chicago/9780226720395.001.0001

Library of Congress Cataloging-in-Publication Data

Names: Schley, David, author.
Title: Steam city : railroads, urban space, and corporate capitalism in nineteenth-
    century Baltimore / David Schley.
Other titles: Historical studies of urban America.
Description: Chicago : University of Chicago Press, 2020. | Series: Historical studies
    of urban America | Includes bibliographical references and index.
Identifiers: LCCN 2020004121 | ISBN 9780226720258 (cloth) |
    ISBN 9780226720395 (ebook)
Subjects: LCSH: Baltimore and Ohio Railroad Company. | Railroads—Maryland—
    Baltimore—History. | Capitalism—Maryland—Baltimore.
Classification: LCC HE2781.B35 S35 2020 | DDC 385.09752/6—dc23
LC record available at https://lccn.loc.gov/2020004121

♾ This paper meets the requirements of ANSI/NISO Z39.48-1992 (Permanence of
Paper).

For Jessica

Contents

Maps, Figures, and Tables

Maps and Figures

Tables

Introduction

The Cornerstone

The railroad age in America kicked off with a grand parade through Baltimore. On the morning of July 4, 1828, thousands of people lined the streets and leaned out of windows to watch a procession of tradesmen, sailors, farmers, and politicians as they marched toward the western fringes of the city, where construction on a new "rail-road"—the first of its kind in the United States—was to begin. The celebrants anticipated that this enterprise, dubbed the Baltimore & Ohio (B&O) Railroad, would in due course connect their city to the fertile Ohio River valley. First, though, it would have to cross hundreds of miles of mountainous, sparsely populated terrain, an engineering challenge of unprecedented dimensions. To commence work on this audacious project, the company's founders tapped ninety-year-old Charles Carroll of Carrollton, the last living signer of the Declaration of Independence and one of the B&O's principal investors. Carroll sat in a horse-drawn open carriage near the head of the column making its way through the city. He had agreed to dig the first shovelful of earth for the railroad, an act that he asserted to be the second-most important of his life, eclipsed only by his signature of the declaration fifty-two years earlier. When the parade reached the designated site and Carroll sunk his spade into the ground, he inaugurated another kind of revolution.[1]

Nineteenth-century writers recognized the significance of this undertaking immediately. By running fossil-fueled steam engines on straight iron rails, the B&O and the many railroad companies founded in its wake promised to liberate overland travel from the age-old constraints of inclement weather and muscle fatigue. Pundits wrote of the "annihilation of time and space" as they marveled at the social and economic changes wrought by railroads and other novel modes of communication within their lifetimes. Generations later, these transformations seem no less profound. Historians have documented the important role played by railroad enterprise in the making of industrial capitalism. Whether excoriated as the tools of rapacious robber barons or praised as models of rational organization, railroad companies have long been recognized as the progenitors of the corporate forms and practices that structured the American economy after the Civil War.[2]

In some ways, this end point—the postbellum rail corporation, its iron bands spanning the continent, its smoking locomotives hauling industrial products, its middle managers coordinating a large and diffused workforce, its bosses cutting backroom deals with congressmen—seems prefigured in the ceremony that launched the B&O. Speeches by the fledgling company's leaders in 1828 stressed the power of this new technology to level mountains and shrink the continent, rhetoric that railroad boosters continued to deploy with little modification half a century later. When it came time to break ground, however, the founders revealed a vision for the railroad very different from the modern corporate enterprise it was to become. Carroll did not till the earth to clear space for a rail or a golden spike—he instead made room for a *cornerstone*, a squat slab of marble embossed with the words "FIRST STONE of the BALT & OHIO RAIL ROAD." Inaugurating the company with a cornerstone ceremony figured the B&O as a civic undertaking, akin to a new public building or monument. Even as the railroad prepared to stretch hundreds of miles beyond the city limits, the stone grounded it in Baltimore, marking it as a public initiative with a distinctly urban character.[3]

The B&O was not unique in this regard. Other early railroads, founded in an era wary of corporate power, reflected a limited vision of private enterprise and an expansive vision of urbanism, in which cities—that is, urban publics acting collectively, often through their mayors and city councils—set in motion initiatives intended to reshape economic geography. At the dawn of the railroad age, writers described the B&O as an urban project, launched by "Baltimore," that would bolster the city's lagging economy by capturing a hinterland in the trans-Appalachian West. Boosters from other eastern entrepôts—Philadelphia, New York City, Boston, and Charleston—likewise conceived of railroad corporations as instruments of urban development. In the 1840s, many of these state- and city-sponsored internal improvements failed amid a general depression, and most subsequent railroads incorporated as private enterprises, but even then, the B&O and many other major railroads remained dependent on municipal aid and subscribed to an urban mission.[4] Public ends warranted public investment. The state government of Maryland and the municipal government of Baltimore provided the bulk of the political and financial capital that launched the B&O and, by extension, the American railroad industry as a whole. In an era of urban governance characterized by paltry poor relief and minimal municipal tax rates, when city councils sought to keep expenditures as low as possible, Baltimore's elected officials incurred unprecedented debts to build a rail line that spanned mountains and crossed rivers hundreds of miles from the city limits. Periodic cash infusions from the Baltimore city government, eventually totaling $10 million, sustained the oft-imperiled B&O for twenty-five years as the railroad struggled to complete its tracks to the Ohio River. The municipal government paid this price because it considered the B&O an appendage of the city: an agent of urban growth and a source of civic pride.[5]

Steam City explains how this ambitious urban project became a modern capitalist enterprise. In doing so, it tracks the changing role of the city—as a place and as a polity—within the development of American capitalism. It suggests that the development of the nineteenth-century corporation and the growth of the nineteenth-century city were interconnected in ways that scholars have not yet recognized. Historians have long acknowledged that urban ambitions played a critical role in the earliest stages of railroad enterprise, but they characterize this as a fleeting phase, truncated by the Panic of 1837 and all but forgotten by the time of the railroad construction boom of the 1850s. Instead, historians have framed the spread of railroad networks and the rapid urbanization of nineteenth-century America as complementary, even symbiotic phenomena. Rail lines, after all, extended the reach of urban markets and concentrated trade in urban centers. Railroad corporations feature in such narratives as the agents and urban centers as the sites of such changes.[6]

The B&O's cornerstone, though, reveals that this order of things—the powerful, boundary-crossing private corporation and the passive, investment-seeking municipality—was itself a historical construct. Starting in the 1830s and continuing well into the 1860s, company executives, private investors, railroad employees, city and state politicians, and urban citizens' groups participated in a protracted contest to define how railroad corporations should operate and whose interests they should serve. Municipal officials and a large swath of urbanites envisioned the railroad as an instrument of urban development, an engine of growth designed to bring trade to their doorsteps and give work to mechanics. By the 1850s, private investors and railroad executives, eager to expand their operations and maximize dividends, argued that this perspective was hopelessly outdated. They held that railroads should function instead as independent, profit-seeking entities that competed with one another for traffic, untethered by obligations to the urban public. Their position prevailed: by the end of the Civil War, American railroads took an unmistakably private form, even as they continued to receive municipal support.

This privatization emerged not from institutional maturation or in response
to market pressures, but through a political process, a public fight over the
role the city would play in railroad management. Before railroads could become modern business enterprises, models for the large-scale corporations
that remade the late nineteenth-century economy, they had first to shed their
urban origins.

This was, at its core, a spatial process, a struggle over the physical form of
the city itself. In Baltimore, the fight to set the railroad's objectives started as
a conflict over control of the street. In the 1830s, the B&O pioneered the practice of laying tracks through urban thoroughfares in order to bring goods to
the port and forge connections with other rail companies. Rail lines in other
major cities followed suit. But whereas railroads enjoyed virtually unfettered
license to remake the spaces of the countryside, the city street became a particularly problematic component of their infrastructure. Railroad corporations found their powers challenged and delimited when they entered the city,
as the presence of a dense urban population subjected their traffic to interruption, protest, and regulation. Some urbanites complained that the tracks
whisked coveted western merchandise straight through the city without benefiting the local public and called for municipal policies that would instead
encourage trade to accumulate in town. Many more contended that urban
rail infrastructure imperiled citizens' lives and limbs, and accordingly they
demanded speed limits, restrictions on steam power, and the removal of the
track itself. Opponents of privatization favored traffic policies and infrastructural projects that, by subjecting the movement of rail traffic through urban
space to safety and trade regulations, framed the city as an entrepreneurial
entrepôt and made railroads answerable to the urban public.

Advocates of a privatized B&O responded with their own visions for the
city. Instead of an economic agent, they saw Baltimore as a site for investment and argued that goods should circulate as freely within the city limits
as they did without. In addition to laying tracks in the streets, they sought
to realize this vision by building specialized port and depot facilities, lobbying for unrestricted use of steam power, and ultimately routing rail traffic
around the urban core through a system of tunnels and harbor ferries. As
they did so, they converted the nineteenth-century walking city into a site of
mechanized movement. The B&O led the way in many of these efforts, but
it was not alone—remaking urban space and revising municipal policy so as
to accommodate rail traffic was a project undertaken by many rail lines. The
material work of building infrastructure that could funnel steam-powered
trains through the city opened up new ways of thinking about urbanism, the
corporation, and capitalism itself. Laying street tracks and digging urban tun-

nels promised to realize the railroad boosters' boasts of spatial annihilation and helped redefine the city as a node in a privately controlled railroad network. Reinventing the railroad as a private corporation meant making the city a place of transit.[7]

Transformations of the urban landscape thus served the privatization process in more ways than one. Public and private were moving targets in the nineteenth century; the boundaries of the public good and the limits of private power looked very different at the dawn of the railroad era from how they did by the Gilded Age. As private stockholders and municipal officials wrangled over railroad policy, the city street emerged as a critical testing ground for new configurations of these categories. Fights over the use of city streets led directly to questions concerning what the public could expect from the railroad corporation and how to define the scope of private enterprise. In their efforts to build urban infrastructure, stockholders developed arguments they later deployed when calling for unfettered private control of the company. As they reoriented urban space to prioritize through travel, stockholders and their allies formulated a new spatial logic for corporate capitalism, one that tied the free movement of goods to the free flow of capital in a system that located competition and economic agency in private enterprise. In Baltimore, seemingly abstract questions about rate structures, dividend payments, and procurement policies were in fact wrapped up in public debates over the railroad's material presence in urban space. For the stockholders, urban space was at once the locus of their operations, a tangible illustration of economic principles, and a catalyst for institutional change.[8]

Examining the twinned transformations of the B&O and Baltimore thus offers a street-level perspective on the development of American capitalism. *Street-level* is no metaphor: this book contends that the institutions, ideas, and infrastructures of capitalism were made, negotiated, and assembled from the ground up. Examining the history of capitalism from the street makes decisions that seem technologically determined or economically logical when surveyed from on high appear instead political and perhaps even contingent. The construction of crosstown railroad tunnels reflected not simply a need for rapid through travel but the triumph of a new vision of the city; the implementation of rate structures favoring long-haul shipments over local traffic stemmed less from the ineluctable economics of rail than from a new conception of railroad enterprise. Viewed from the street, capitalism appears to evolve less through an internal logic than through acts of political will that only later were enshrined as laws of trade or economic principles. Adopting this vantage point expands the number and type of actors involved in creating this system, as well. Readers will be unsurprised to find a great deal of atten-

tion devoted to railroad presidents and mayors in this book, but the story of
Baltimore and its railroad is also the story of action and activism by draymen and carters, freight conductors and machinists, pedestrians and escapees
from slavery, and an array of other citizens, employees, visitors, investors,
and clients.

Steam City tells this story by combining the sources and methodologies
of urban history, economic history, and cultural geography. It draws on corporate records, municipal archives, and Baltimore's printed media. Material
from the B&O's archives illuminates the challenges associated with conducting railroad operations in the city streets, chronicles company agents' vexed
interactions with local merchants, and reveals the infighting on the board of
directors between the city government's representatives and those chosen by
the private stockholders. Minute books and memoranda reveal how railroad
executives came to insist that the company's survival demanded smooth, uninterrupted passage through the city. In the Baltimore City Archives one can
find letters from cartmen, grocers, and industrialists documenting the railroad's effects on their daily lives. As they do so, they insist that the railroad's
distinctive powers of movement must stop at the city limits and yield to the
ad hoc traffic patterns of the city streets. Examined alongside newspapers,
manuscripts, maps, and pamphlets, these archives reveal some of the otherwise forgotten contests that accompanied the spread of railroad networks in
the United States.

Nineteenth-century capitalism was a practice, something made on the
ground. This book argues that the rise of the private corporation as an economic agent and the spatial configuration of the industrial metropolis were
structurally intertwined: the development of modern capitalist institutions
and ideologies was predicated on the cultivation of new understandings of
economic geography and the production of new types of urban space. Making
corporate capitalism meant making the capitalist city—a space for investment
and movement, its political powers contained by its borders.

Capitalism, Geography, and the Railroad

Scholarship on nineteenth-century capitalism has burgeoned in the past
two decades as historians have detailed the ways in which industrialization
and economic integration altered social structures, reconfigured the natural
world, and mapped selfhood onto market relations. Recent histories of capitalism apply the methodologies of cultural history to unpack the meanings
of exchange in a social world shaped by contract.[9] The overriding goal of this
historiography is to denaturalize the operations of an economic system that

in popular representations appears inevitable and self-sustaining. To do so, historians of capitalism reconstruct how and by whose agency capitalist ideals and practices took hold in American society.[10]

This historiography has tended to approach space and geography through the lens of commodification. Readers learn of the ways in which capitalist commodification transmuted land and resources into plats on a map or figures on a balance sheet.[11] Yet while this literature is attentive to the power of capitalism to transform particular spaces, at times it can overlook the ways in which capitalism ordered space itself. This is starting to change. Much of the recent work on the history of nineteenth-century capitalism comes from scholars of American slavery, who have shown that the Cotton Kingdom relied on constant territorial expansion to defuse cyclical environmental, financial, and political crises. These claims build on work by scholars in urban studies and geography like David Harvey, who contends that investment of surplus capital in urban property and infrastructure constitutes a "spatial fix" for crises of overproduction.[12] Despite this debt to urban scholarship, the city—as both a political entity and as a site of circulation and investment—remains understudied in the historiography of nineteenth-century American capitalism. This book, by paying close attention to stockholders' and railroad executives' attempts to transform urban space and redefine the role of the city within the American economy, frames capitalist development as a spatial process that entailed material and political shifts in urbanism. Attending to the machinations and arguments of the B&O's directorate, Baltimore's city council, and the citizenry as a whole reveals how controversial changes in the production of space helped new definitions and new understandings of capitalism take hold. Corporate capitalism, as it developed in the nineteenth century, involved not only new modes of organizing work and ownership but also new forms of mobility and novel configurations of urban space. Conflicts over the use of city streets helped produce corporate capitalism as we know it today.[13]

In these conflicts, both the B&O's supporters and its critics deployed the language of geographic scale—terms like *local* and *national*—to advance their political agendas. Private stockholders, for example, characterized the uninterrupted flow of railroad traffic as a matter of national concern while shrugging off protest over conditions in the street as petty local obstructionism. In doing so, they engaged in what cultural geographers refer to as the social construction of scale, justifying their preferred policy outcome by suggesting that it occupied a higher plane than their opponents'. Historians, already accustomed to thinking critically about geographic scales as categories of analysis by questioning, for example, the primacy of the nation-state as a framework for research, can benefit from close attention to such rhetoric. In nineteenth-century Baltimore, everyone from draymen to railroad magnates worked to locate spaces, organizations, and events in a scalar hierarchy. Such sorting was critical to the creation of a corporate capitalist spatial order. Municipally sponsored projects in the early republic like the B&O reflected a conception of the urban that stretched far beyond the city limits and identified the railroad corporation as an adjunct to that polity's interests. For this reason, privatizing the railroad entailed constricting the agency of the urban public, defining the urban as local and the corporation as national.[14]

This book also offers an opportunity to revisit the history of the American railroad. The bulk of railroad historiography focuses on the period after the Civil War, once a national railroad network had taken shape. Many works in this field have identified the late nineteenth-century railroad as the embodiment of modern capitalist enterprise and documented its power to reorder American geography. Yet shifting our attention from the heyday of American railroading to its beginnings helps us see the railroad corporation in a new light. Historians looking at the postbellum railroad have characterized controversial policies like discriminatory rate structures as logical responses to the capacities of the locomotive or the economics of transportation, but when viewed from antebellum Baltimore, these same policies appear not only contested but also contingent. The transcontinental railroads and other late nineteenth-century rail companies that became the focus of populist ire were working from a playbook written in the formative early years of the American railroad.[15]

The View from Baltimore

Both the city and the company under examination here played important roles in nineteenth-century America. The B&O was one of the four major trunk rail lines that spanned the Appalachian Mountains before the Civil War and one of the most prominent corporations of its day. Baltimore was the third-largest city in the United States for much of the period covered in this book; its population as enumerated by the census grew from 80,620 in 1830 to 332,313 in 1880. Baltimore hosted more than a dozen national political conventions and witnessed the first experiments in telegraphy.[16] Baltimore also stands out for its demographic and political characteristics. It was a major urban center in a slave state, a place where enslaved and free, native-born and immigrant, worked uneasily side by side.[17] These conditions make Baltimore fascinating terrain from which to examine the spatial dynamics of capitalism, as in the nineteenth century the city became a testing ground for competing ideas and practices.[18]

Baltimore's position within American political economy had significant effects on the twinned transformations of railroad and city. The urban public that lost its oversight of the B&O's operations was a narrow and exclusionary one, a fact that will frustrate any efforts to read this story as a declension narrative pitting public-minded heroes against narrowly self-interested villains. By the late antebellum period, advocates for municipal regulation of railroad practices often framed their efforts as a fight against "northern" incursions, thus placing local control of the railroad's policies and the fight against abolitionism in the same framework. Nor did Baltimore's African American community have many allies among the advocates of privatization. Many leaders in the B&O enslaved people themselves and identified as Southern Democrats. While Baltimore had the largest free black community in the United States, African Americans were all but absent from the city's voter lists and the B&O's employment rolls until after the Civil War.

Black Baltimoreans found themselves marginalized in the political fights over the fate of the railroad and the city, but they experienced acutely both the liberating possibilities and the devastating dislocations that the railroad brought to the city. The years between the incorporation of the B&O in 1827 and the Great Strike of 1877 witnessed profound transformations in the urban landscape, changes closely connected with the rise of new modes of communication and new economic and political orders. How people worked, the neighborhoods they inhabited, the houses they built, and even the way they crossed the street all changed in this period as the railroad brought rapid communications, fossil fuels, and new modes of corporate organization to the city. Baltimoreans watched—and protested, and participated, and intervened—as advocates for an economic system that emphasized rapid travel, unrestricted circulation, and individualistic profiteering reshaped their city. For the stockholders and executives of the B&O, creating corporate capitalism meant producing a new spatial order for Baltimore. The consequences of this order, whether favorable or adverse, were not shared evenly. For some, the tracks, tunnels, depots, wharves, and smokestacks in place by 1877 represented the fulfillment of the railroad's founding promise to the city. For many others, they did not. As the century progressed, popular anger mounted against the railroad company and the economic shifts it spearheaded; this book begins with a parade, but it ends with a riot.

The city at the heart of this book did not ultimately become one of the command centers of the global economy. Baltimore's trajectory from an urban public capable of projecting a major rail line to a place of transit whose economic fortunes are determined by forces beyond its control presaged the contemporary spatial logic of globalization. Today the city is bounded, a political entity defined by its geographic parameters. Its field of legitimate action is circumscribed territorially. The private corporation, by contrast, floats above political jurisdictions, transcending municipal, state, and even national boundaries. While the corporation's physical operations are necessarily grounded in the built environment, it is not defined by its physicality and owes little allegiance to place. This relationship to geography is central to the spatial order of global capitalism; capital is mobile and corporations can shift the site of production as costs of labor or tax burdens warrant. Today cities wrangle for investment and infrastructure, sports games and concert venues, but the scope of local public action has diminished as that of corporate power has expanded.[19] Turning our attention to nineteenth-century Baltimore can help us understand why.

The Urban Origins of the American Railroad

Five years into the job, the strains of leading the first railroad in the United States were starting to wear on Baltimore & Ohio president Philip E. Thomas. In 1832, Baltimore congressman Benjamin C. Howard, one of Thomas's frequent correspondents, asked Thomas to furnish information on railroad technology for a curious friend who had succumbed, Howard playfully suggested, to the railroad "mania." Thomas was not amused. In his reply, he took exception to his friend's joshing:

> I hope I may be permitted to remark that I consider it to be rather an irreverent manner of speaking in reference to us Rail Road advocates to say, when we manifest a laudable zeal in support of this incomparable system, or even shew an inclination 'to obtain some information about Rail Roads' that we 'are bitten by the Mania[.]' I however take some consolation in the reflection that reformers and improvers in all Countries have been suspected *by their wiser neighbours* of being more or less out of their heads. As regards myself, to tell the truth, when I reflect on the trouble I have brought on myself—the sacrifices I have made—the obstinate adherence I have maintained, and the little good I have gained, I am almost tempted to suspect that I am a great fool, if not actually cracked, and 'sans badinage[.]' I ought perhaps not to think hard of my friends for giving me a limit of it.[1]

Thomas's exasperation reflected the challenge of launching an infrastructure project of unprecedented scale. With only stubby, thirty-mile-long British railways to serve as models, the B&O had been tasked with laying double-tracked iron rails across four hundred miles of rugged terrain. The company's well-publicized experiments in railroad construction led the *American Railroad Journal* in 1835 to dub the Baltimore & Ohio "the Railroad University of the United States," because other start-up rail companies learned from its example—and its mistakes.[2] There were plenty of the latter. By 1832, when Thomas wrote to Howard, his company was four years into a construction process already marred by unexpected costs, legal challenges, and labor unrest, and it had yet to reach even the Potomac River, some sixty miles from Baltimore.

Under such circumstances, the railroad's ultimate destination, the Ohio River, likely seemed more distant than ever. Yet these early struggles coincided with a wide-ranging public discourse about railroad transportation that emphasized its transformative potential: the "mania" to which Howard alluded. The B&O's pioneering role in American railroading in the 1820s and 1830s placed it at the forefront of a transatlantic conversation about the social and economic potential of this new technology. Newspaper editors and railroad promoters reported daily on advances in locomotive technology and track-laying techniques while speculating about the long-term ramifications of railroad travel. Seasonal constraints, irregular terrain, and imperfect roadways meant that overland journeys had always been slow and strenuous ordeals, but the railroad, by placing mechanized engines on frictionless rails, promised to make travel over mountain ranges no more exhausting than sitting in a chair. Railroad futurists anticipated that such changes would reconfigure the public's experience of time and alter its understanding of space, leveling mountains and dissolving barriers.[3]

Thomas thus found himself mediating between faltering practices and grand expectations in the railroad's early years. Yet on one point, early B&O supporters spoke with one voice: the purpose of the railroad, all agreed, was to bolster the stagnating economy of its terminal city, Baltimore. For all the visionary qualities of early railroad ventures, Philip Thomas and the other merchants and financiers on the company's board of directors conceived of this enterprise as an instrument of urban development. In fact, they framed the railroad as an effort to restore, rather than disrupt, the commercial status quo. In the 1820s, improvements in transportation such as the introduction of steamboats along the Mississippi and Ohio Rivers and the opening of the Erie Canal in New York diverted western trade that had formerly found a market in Baltimore to New Orleans and New York City. The B&O was to recoup this trade by smoothing the path over the mountains, rendering Baltimore once again the most convenient eastern market for western goods and affirming the city's natural advantage of proximity to the trans-Appalachian West.

The railroad project constituted an intervention within an economic geography centered on cities and a political economy governed by "natural laws." The B&O's founders believed that trade flowed like water along the path of least resistance, seeking the shortest outlet to the sea. The task of directing this flow fell to cities—that is, incorporated urban publics acting and imagined as coherent entities—which, in concert with state governments and private investors, funded improvements that channeled trade into their markets. The B&O would thus serve the interests of Baltimore as internal improvements in Pennsylvania served Philadelphia. If Baltimore did not complete its line, it would represent a failure of political will and the city would stagnate; conversely, the fruits of a completed B&O would accrue to the city as a whole.[4] Baltimoreans discussed the trade the railroad would generate not in abstract terms but as a physical presence that would reshape the city. By investing in this novel enterprise, they invested in Baltimore's future.

During the B&O's early years, then, public discourse on the railroad centered on visions of how the completed line would shape the city's development and help it win a contest for commercial supremacy with Philadelphia, New York, and Boston. Concerns about how to manage and how to fund the rail line sparked controversy in these years, but a broad consensus that the railroad would operate to Baltimore's benefit marked it as a public project, which in turn justified extensive public investments. The city and state governments assumed most of the risk associated with launching the world's first long-distance railroad. Although Thomas complained of his sacrifices on behalf of the company, it was sacrifices by the urban public that turned the railroad from a popular craze into a practical reality.

The Talismanic West

"The West—the far, the mighty West!" wrote the *Baltimore American* in 1838. "What a host of anticipations are conjured up in the mind of an American by the bare mention of that of that talismanic word." When internal improvement advocates in Baltimore and other eastern cities thought of the future, they looked west. Whereas in Europe, turnpikes, canals, and early railroads linked well-developed markets, the internal improvement initiatives launched from eastern cities in the 1820s and 1830s were speculative exercises, wagers on the future development of the vast and fertile region across the Appalachian Mountains.[5]

Rarely acknowledged but ever present in such anticipatory writings were the geopolitics and imperial militarism by which the West had entered the jurisdiction of the United States. Although on paper the nation's borders had extended beyond the Appalachians since independence, the political fate of the Ohio River valley remained uncertain even a decade before the opening of the Erie Canal; only the military defeat of pan-Indian forces in the War of

1812 cemented U.S. sovereignty in the region.[6] Few writers noted this recent history in their descriptions of the internal improvements now projected across the mountains, and those who did elided the violence of this acquisition with the language of racial destiny. The *American* wrote bloodlessly of the region's development: "Where, a little time ago, the Aborigines enjoyed uninterrupted possession, and where the foot of a white man had never trodden, has sprung up, as if by magic, community after community."[7] Most commenters simply adapted the language of imperial conquest to a new context: cities, not soldiers, would now vie for control of the West. A Cincinnati paper noted that the "trade and productions of the inexhaustible and fertile plains of the West have become the grand object of contest for our Atlantic cities," and that "the palm of victory will be splendid; they who achieve it will be placed on the flow tide of fortune, and boundless wealth and influence will be the natural result." Such claims embedded narratives of urban expansion into the metanarrative of Manifest Destiny.[8]

Aside from Baltimore, the players in this contest for the West were Boston, New York City, and Philadelphia. These cities, arrayed along the seaboard in a northeasterly axis, had served during the colonial period as hinges linking nearby agricultural and maritime producers with Atlantic markets. With independence, merchants and municipal officials in each of these cities began to turn their attention to the interior, hoping to enlarge their respective hinterlands by funding turnpike and canal projects. They argued that such efforts would, if successful, place their home cities at the top of the new nation's still-malleable urban hierarchy. Boosters in these eastern cities, like boosters in small western towns, claimed that their metropolises possessed natural advantages that would make them centers of prosperity, so long as those advantages could be realized through active, public-spirited campaigns of improvement. East Coast boosterism differed from its western counterpart, though, in that eastern urban elites sought not to will a city into existence but to position their city as an entrepôt. Even at the cusp of an era of industrial expansion and financial innovation, they envisioned urban development principally in terms of the collection and exchange of commodities. Trade formed the economic base that would drive economic growth, facilitate the expansion of urban services, stimulate a lively cultural scene, and, of course, bolster the value of their collected property. And although in retrospect the dominance of New York City in American commerce appears to have been all but assured by the late 1820s, many writers in Philadelphia, Boston, and New York itself believed that active exertion could yet reshape the nation's economic geography.[9]

Compared with Boston, New York, and Philadelphia, Baltimore was a newcomer, the last of the major East Coast cities to attain prominence. Baltimore first developed in the 1750s as a port serving wheat farmers from northern and western Maryland who sent their produce to markets in Europe and the West Indies. The city grew rapidly during the Revolutionary War by acting as a provisioning center for American troops. Baltimore merchants enriched themselves further during the Napoleonic Wars, sending wheat to famished Caribbean islands cut off from mercantilist lines of supply. The growing city exerted considerable energy and capital to improve the harbor, extending wharves and opening streets to facilitate the transfer of cargo from wagon to ship. Public funds and hours of labor went into the unpleasant work of dredging silt from the harbor in order to preserve the city's maritime link to distant markets. Although Baltimore served as an ocean outlet for trans-Appalachian goods from at least the 1810s, the city did not match these harbor improvements with symmetrical investments in the infrastructure serving its western hinterland. As of 1818, the federally funded National Road helped smooth the way for farmers and merchants traveling from the Ohio River port of Wheeling, Virginia, to the Potomac River town of Cumberland, Maryland. From there, poorly maintained turnpikes served the wagons bringing goods to Baltimore's market. The National Road reinforced the city's favorable geographic position for western trade relative to other Atlantic ports—Baltimore sits 150 miles closer to the Ohio River valley than Philadelphia and 200 miles closer than New York City. In the first half of the nineteenth century, writers in Baltimore were as likely to describe those competing metropolises as "eastern cities" as they were to frame them as "northern." Baltimore's boosters identified their city's western perch as its principal natural advantage in the interurban competition for trans-Appalachian trade.[10]

By the 1820s, though, Baltimore was in the midst of a profound commercial downturn prompted by a series of geopolitical, economic, and infrastructural changes. Internationally, the end of the Napoleonic Wars eliminated the need for illicit trade from Baltimore to the West Indies. Domestically, the introduction of Bank of the United States branches in the trans-Appalachian West gave the region's merchants more stable lines of credit and thus the ability to choose their markets, making their established relationships with Baltimore wholesalers less important. And in New York, the opening of the Erie Canal provided a faster and cheaper route for goods previously hauled arduously over the Appalachian Mountains. The canal transfigured America's economic geography by making New York the preferred eastern market for western goods, closer by time, if not distance, to the fertile lands of the West.[11]

Even before the opening of the Erie Canal in 1825, Baltimoreans began to fret about the possibility of losing western commerce to their northeastern neighbors. In 1818, the state legislature asked William Hollins, a civil engineer, to collect information on Maryland's turnpike companies. Hollins, alarmed by his findings, published a pamphlet advising his fellow citizens to take action if they wanted to retain their western trade. Hollins called for the creation of "a Great Highway" to the West to reinforce the city's natural advantage of proximity to the Ohio River valley. Philadelphians had already initiated improvements designed to subvert these advantages. If the people of Baltimore retaliated by building a roadway to the West, it would undercut Philadelphia's maneuverings and guarantee the city's prosperity. Conversely, should the city fail to undertake such a project, Hollins warned, "the grass will ere long grow in some of her streets."[12]

In the 1820s many in Baltimore's municipal government likewise came to see internal improvements as matters of existential import. As the Erie Canal neared completion, some city officials pushed for investment to improve navigation on the Susquehanna River, which feeds into the Chesapeake approximately fifty miles northeast of Baltimore, in order to tap the Erie Canal.[13] Others felt, though, that to capture western trade, Baltimore needed a western canal of its own. They called for the city to fund a branch that would intersect the nascent Chesapeake & Ohio (C&O) Canal, incorporated in 1825, at its terminus in Washington, DC. The politician and military officer Robert Goodloe Harper drew lines on a map to show that such a canal would place Baltimore's harbor at the mouth of a vast watershed stretching from the Blue Ridge Mountains in Virginia west to Chicago and north to Upper Canada (fig. 1.1).[14]

Enticed by the prospect of capturing such a vast hinterland, Baltimore's merchants and public officials had committed themselves by 1826 to the prospect of forging a direct link with the western waters. Mayor John Montgomery pressed in his annual address for an improvement that would effect the "union of the Ohio, the Potomac and the Patapsco." Hezekiah Niles's nationally influential Baltimore-based paper *Niles' Weekly Register* opined, "A spirit is abroad to favor the making of roads and canals."[15] Cost estimates for a canal through the Alleghenies soon dampened that spirit. The mountainous terrain between Baltimore and the West would require a series of time-consuming and expensive locks, and early projections put an $8 million price tag on the C&O Canal.[16] This realization led Baltimoreans to conceive the B&O Railroad.

The Origins of the B&O

John H. B. Latrobe, who served as general counsel for the B&O from its inception until the 1880s, later recalled that railroads first entered polite

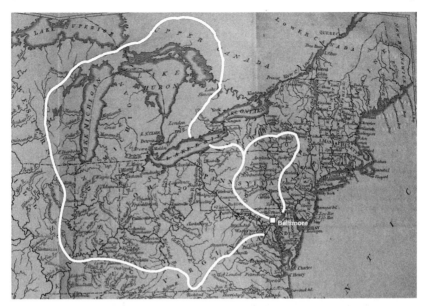

FIGURE 1.1. General Harper's map, 1824. The white lines demarcate the Ohio River hinterland to Baltimore's west and the smaller Susquehanna River hinterland to the north, as Harper indicated them on the map. Courtesy of the Peabody Library, Johns Hopkins University, Baltimore.

conversation at a dinner party held in the house of Baltimore politician John Eager Howard, most likely late in the summer of 1826. Latrobe's memory may have been fuzzy on that point—the legislatures of Pennsylvania, New York, and even Maryland had looked into funding rail ventures as early as 1825 following the success of experimental single-use lines like the Granite Railway in Quincy, Massachusetts (founded in 1823). In Latrobe's reminiscence, though, tales of upstart British railroads held the listeners at Howard's soiree spellbound. One of the guests, a merchant named Evan Thomas, had recently returned from England, where he had observed the operations of the world's first steam-powered rail line, the twenty-five-mile-long Stockton & Darlington Railway. His animated account piqued the curiosity of those assembled in Howard's home, particularly his own elder brother, Mechanics' Bank president Philip E. Thomas. Evan was, according to Latrobe, "not a man to lead in any undertaking." His brother was a different story: Latrobe described Philip Thomas as perceptive and clearheaded. The brothers, sons of an abolitionist Quaker minister, had come to Baltimore at the turn of the nineteenth century. In 1800, Philip set up shop in the city as a hardware merchant and brought his brother on board as a partner. Soon Philip entered banking and took an active role in Baltimore's civic affairs. He was a founding trustee of the new almshouse, established in 1823, which implemented a system of compulsory labor, surveillance, and corporal punishment that quickly reduced municipal public expenditure on poor relief. He next turned his attention to the city's connections with the West, serving as Maryland's representative to the C&O Canal before he grew disillusioned with that project. Now, in 1826, the fifty-year-old banker was well positioned to persuade others to entertain a seemingly audacious proposition: that the same young technology then moving coal across twenty-five miles of relatively flat English terrain could help Baltimore overcome a mountain range hundreds of miles wide.[17]

Philip Thomas found one early ally in the financier George Brown, who worked in the Baltimore headquarters of his father's firm, Alex. Brown & Sons. George's father, Alexander, was already a wealthy man when he immigrated to Baltimore from Ireland in the late 1790s, and the linen business he founded in 1800 quickly morphed into a transatlantic financial institution, with branches in Philadelphia and Liverpool run by his sons. George Brown remained in Baltimore, where he handled a brisk business in foreign exchange, tobacco and cotton consignment, and shipping. Although the conservatively managed firm weathered the uncertainties of war and the economic slump of the 1820s, father and son could not help but note with concern New York's commercial ascendance. For both Alexander and George, building a railroad to the West seemed like an opportunity to revive their adopted city's fortune—and perhaps profit from the iron trade as well.[18]

On February 12, 1827, George Brown hosted at least twenty-five of Baltimore's most prominent merchants, attorneys, and bankers at his house to discuss the prospects of building a railroad over the mountains. That night, a committee consisting of the Thomas brothers, George Brown, Benjamin C. Howard, and three other men agreed to investigate the idea. Their report, presented a week later, argued, with a logic that would have been familiar to William Hollins nine years earlier, that the city's future prosperity required the construction of a double-tracked railroad from Baltimore to the Ohio River. A transmontane rail line would affirm Baltimore's natural advantage of proximity to the West and restore commercial ties recently broken by the rise of steam navigation on the Mississippi and the opening of the Erie Canal in New York. The authors conceded that Baltimore would have to share western trade with New Orleans, but they maintained that a railroad would make their city the principal eastern entrepôt for western merchants, beyond the reach of northern competitors. Rapid white settlement of the Mississippi valley augured rapid growth in trade, and they calculated that the railroad would bolster land values along its route by $40 million, including a forecasted $20 million increase in the valuation of Baltimore real estate. Such anticipated gains dwarfed the railroad's cost, at least by their estimates. The authors observed that the Granite Railway in Quincy had cost around $11,000 per mile to build, and they figured optimistically that construction expenses would diminish with experience and economies of scale. Thus, they declared that a railroad from Baltimore to the Ohio River would cost around $5 million in total, a down payment that would return to investors in the form of accelerated commerce, rising land values, and stock dividends.[19]

The meeting endorsed the report unanimously and formed a new committee to make this proposal a reality. As its first act, the committee ordered the printing and circulation of 1,500 copies of the railroad report. The discussion to that point had taken place in private, in a home instead of a hall, without the advance notice in the press that preceded ward meetings or public demonstrations. Now the time had come to take the proposal public. The title of their published report, *Proceedings of the Sundry Citizens of Baltimore*, cast the founders not as private investors but as civic-minded urbanites. They portrayed the railroad as a project to be undertaken by the city itself. "Whilst the Cities of Philadelphia and New York are making such great and efficient exertions to draw to themselves the trade of the West," said the *Proceedings*, "Baltimore must soon lose the comparatively small portion which remains to her of this trade, should she continue inactive." Depicting the city as an actor helped turn "Baltimore" into a coherent entity, unifying the fates, interests, and character of urbanites around a common place of residence. But this was more than a rhetorical exercise; personifying the city reflected the authors' expectation that the urban public, represented by the city government, would contribute to the formation and operation of this railroad. The railroad's ends would be public, and so, too, would its means.[20]

The "sundry citizens" had no intention of handing control of the proposed enterprise to the city government, however. Even as they anthropomorphized Baltimore, the railroad's initiators identified several groups within the city that would have to cooperate in order to launch the project—including first and foremost the men at Brown's meeting themselves, a mercantile elite who embodied the city's entrepreneurial spirit. To many early observers, the railroad promoters' collective reputation offered the surest evidence of the project's feasibility. But while the "character, energy and enterprize of the highly respectable gentlemen who have undertaken the business" made it likely to succeed, said the *American*, they still needed "proper legislative aid and the co-operation of the citizens." Only with mutual understanding between Baltimore's mercantile elite, the city and state governments, and the urban citizenry would Baltimore complete its railroad and "again assume that high stand in the estimation of the people of the West."[21]

The citizenry in this construction did not represent Baltimore's populace as it existed but rather a white male artisan and industrial class. Even though the *Proceedings* personified Baltimore with a female pronoun, actual women played no role in their analysis. And while Baltimore had the largest free black population in the United States, the document rendered them invisible as well. Perhaps the most striking absence of all was slavery. By 1827, the enslaved population of Maryland was already shrinking as the tobacco industry stagnated and planters manumitted their workforces or sold them south to the cotton frontier. Many of the B&O's founders, as some of the richest men in Baltimore, were themselves large-scale enslavers, but the report tied the city's future to the growing "white population" of the West. Slavery was not part of the story the railroad's founders told about themselves or their enterprise; however, as we will see, the new railroad hardly sat outside of Baltimore's slave labor system.[22]

The vision of Baltimore's future articulated by the *Proceedings of the Sundry Citizens* was one that many in Maryland were happy to embrace, and the men at George Brown's house had the connections necessary to speed their proposal through the legislature. Just nine days after they agreed to publish their report, the Maryland legislature passed an act incorporating the Baltimore & Ohio Railroad Company. In the 1820s, all corporations needed special legislative charters that enumerated their rights and privileges, a requirement designed to ensure, at least in theory, that they operated for the commonweal. The B&O's charter, modeled on those of turnpike companies, passed in both houses of the legislature with little debate scarcely more than a day after the Baltimore delegation presented it. The charter granted the company significant powers, including eminent domain and—distinct from turnpike companies—exclusive right to the use of its tracks. Most importantly, the charter exempted the railroad from taxation by the city and state. Rather than taxing its profits, the city and state were to benefit as investors in the new line. The act of incorporation defined the company as a private entity that would draw on public funds and advance public ends.[23]

The founders asked not whether the state and city should contribute start-up capital, but rather how much and in what proportion to private investment. Investments from the State of Maryland and the City of Baltimore provided necessary credit and bolstered public confidence that the project would serve the common good. Practically speaking, public investment ensured that representatives of the city and state would have seats on the board of directors alongside the private investors' representatives. The charter capitalized the B&O at $3 million and reserved half of the shares for public investment— ten thousand for the state government and five thousand for the city. Fifteen thousand remained for private investors to purchase (or "subscribe" for, in nineteenth-century parlance).[24] Baltimore's city council quickly bought up its designated shares, a $500,000 investment premised on the notion that it was "the duty and interest of the city of Baltimore liberally to contribute to a project so vitally important to its present increase."[25] Only a handful of critics expressed concern over this public investment in railroad enterprise, worrying that a speculative fervor would overtake government.[26]

Private investors matched the local government's enthusiasm. More than a quarter of Baltimore's populace—around twenty-two thousand people— bought a piece of the railroad, some acquiring as little as a fraction of a share of the oversubscribed stock. Installment payment put the $100 shares within the reach of investors whose means were more modest than the "sundry citizens," although the wealthiest Baltimoreans still captured the bulk of the company's private equity.[27] Even private citizens' investments took on a public character. The *Baltimore Gazette* newspaper defined stock ownership as an act of local patriotism; one of its correspondents went so far as to call for "a general distribution of the stock among the citizens of Baltimore," albeit more out of a desire to avoid free riders than any democratic impulse.[28] In any case, the company embedded itself in Baltimore's economy long before it reached the Potomac River, much less the Ohio. Banks accepted B&O stock certificates as collateral for loans and likewise lent money to the company to cover its debts.[29] Many of the company's founders had been financiers and brought those connections to the new railroad. Philip E. Thomas resigned the presidency of the Mechanics' Bank in order to lead the Baltimore & Ohio, but he did not immediately have to alter his commute—the railroad held its first meetings in the upper floors of that bank.[30]

These financial considerations implicated the company in Baltimore's system of unfree capitalism. Philip Thomas's Quaker faith led him to ban the use of slave labor in the construction and operation of the line. Yet while enslaved people did not lay the rails or run the trains, the B&O's early capital was inextricably linked to slavery. The wealthy enslaver James Carroll, a distant relative of Charles Carroll of Carrollton, carved off ten acres of his Mount Clare estate and donated it to the company as a depot in 1828, selling an additional fifteen acres to the B&O two years later; land that had been maintained by forced labor for generations thus served as the company's first depot and eventually housed its vast machine shops. Likewise, the railroad's earliest capital came at least in part from profits extracted from the uncompensated labor and sale of enslaved people. Many of the B&O's initial investors counted human beings among their property, including the infamous slave trader Austin Woolfolk, who maintained a home and slave pen on Pratt Street, scarcely half a mile from the Mount Clare depot.[31]

"The enactment of this bill has justly been considered as the commencement of a new era in the history of Baltimore," wrote the *American* shortly
after the governor signed the B&O's charter into law. On this matter, the city's
often fractious press spoke in unison, praising the leaders who had created
the company and expressing pride in their city and state for taking the nation's first steps toward railroad transportation. Writers both local and distant
cast the B&O as an urban project with an imperial scope. A newspaper in
Ohio recorded its astonishment "that a single City . . . very little older than the
independence of our country, should from the interprize [*sic*] and resources
of her own citizens, have projected a public work" that would be worthy of
"the oldest and most powerful empire in Christendom." The press declared
that the railroad project would, by reaffirming the city's natural advantage
of proximity to the interior, make Baltimore the premier Atlantic entrepôt
of western trade, "beyond the reach of competition."[32] The wisdom, audacity,
and assured success of the B&O quickly became a trope in local public discourse, reproduced faithfully in newspapers and guidebooks.

Financing the B&O

The company's representatives began retelling the story of the B&O's creation only a few years after the fact. In 1830, the published proceedings of the
board of engineers included preliminary remarks on the origins of the railroad. While the rest of the nation was engrossed with canals, the authors
wrote, "a few enterprising and influential citizens of Baltimore conceived the
magnificent project of constructing a Rail-road from the City of Baltimore to
the Ohio River," the product of a "conviction that some effectual effort must
be made to sustain the declining wealth and importance of this City." What
sounded like a boastful affirmation of the wisdom of the company's founders was actually a plea for public funds. The railroad could usher in a new
era of prosperity for Baltimore only once it was complete, and the company
quickly found that its cash in hand would not suffice for that task. Rather
than turning to private citizens for further investment, the company's leaders
looked first to public sources to finance its westward progress. Recounting the
company's origins story—reminding the public of the crisis that spurred the
B&O's incorporation and celebrating the men whose initiative had launched
the enterprise—helped define the railroad's responsibilities to the city and
vice versa, justifying repeated claims on the public purse.[33]

The B&O's executives did not limit their financial ambitions to municipal
and state funding. The company's board of directors asked Congress for federal investment in 1828, 1829, and 1831, each time insisting that the railroad

be understood as a "national" operation meriting national funds. Company president Philip E. Thomas lobbied his connections in Washington, including Maryland's representatives in Congress, but to no avail. The recent election of Andrew Jackson made this an unpropitious time to request federal assistance, and the president's veto of the Rockville Turnpike Bill, which contained funds for Baltimore's improvement, depressed any hopes of aid from Washington. The federal government never granted direct support to the B&O, although the U.S. Army Corps of Engineers did conduct and pay for the initial surveys that charted the railroad's path to the West.[34]

As Thomas bemoaned the diminishing odds that Jackson would support his company, he wrote, "Our own state will we hope also do something for us[,] as will the City of Baltimore."[35] He hoped for state aid, but he knew he could count on the city. Unable to obtain federal patronage, the mayor and city council became the B&O's means of first resort. In 1831 the railroad turned to the city council to provide the investment it had sought from Congress, and Hezekiah Niles assured the readers of Niles' Weekly Register that municipal largesse would furnish the capital necessary to push the project forward.[36] Recourse to local public aid became a recurrent feature of the company's first twenty years. Asking the city council for an additional $500,000 in 1832, the board of directors wrote, "No where can your memorialists apply for this [aid], with more hope and prospect of success, than to your honorable body." Although the sum they asked for was "large in itself, [it was] but small in comparison with the value, which the work that it will foster, must, when completed, give to every description of property in Baltimore." Few questioned this logic, and the city government acceded to almost every request for an advance, loan, or subscription in order to ensure the continued operations of the railroad.[37]

To make these investments, the city and state governments assumed sizable new debts. Both Maryland and Baltimore issued bonds in support of the B&O, first to pay for stock purchases and later to shore up the company's shaky finances.[38] By 1830, installment payments on B&O stock constituted by far the costliest single item in the city's budget, representing more than a quarter of municipal expenditure for 1829 (table 1.1). The cost of interest payments on debt soon overtook the installments. Niles' Weekly Register commented in 1835 that the city stock (i.e., municipal bond) debt had reached nearly $1 million. The paper nonetheless reassured readers that this investment would "pay a good dividend, in time—or, at least, advance the value of property in the city, so that its owners can well afford to pay the interest on these loans."[39] Such expenditures on railroad installments and interest represented a considerable outlay at a time when municipal governments strove

TABLE 1.1. Principal items of expense in the 1829 Baltimore city budget

Principal expenditures in 1829	Cost
B&O installments	*$75,000*
Damages for opening streets	$40,752
Watching and lighting	$26,743
Deepening/preserving harbor	$26,257
Interest paid on stock	*$21,956*
City's poor	$17,500
To commissioners to reduce debt	$16,798
City court	$12,000
Fire companies	$4,990
Diary of City Council	$4,160
Extending Bowley's Wharf	$4,000
Rent of offices, council chamber	$1,000

Source: Adapted from *NWR*, 27 March 1830, 85–86.

Note: Railroad-related items are italicized.

to limit taxation as much as possible. After 1835, debt service accounted for anywhere from one-third to half of the city's annual budget. Where in 1830 Baltimore's outstanding bonds amounted to slightly more than half a million dollars with an annual interest obligation of $25,000, by 1844 the city's debt stood at $5.5 million, with an interest burden of more than $300,000, an increase almost entirely attributable to municipal support for internal improvement projects.[40]

Yet as the city government's aid to the B&O increased, its influence over the company's affairs did not expand proportionally. In 1836, the B&O's board of directors asked the municipal government to invest an additional $3 million in the company to help push the line beyond Harpers Ferry, and the state legislature passed a law authorizing the city to borrow the money necessary to purchase B&O stock. The bill provided that the city could appoint an additional representative to the board of directors for every 5,000 shares subscribed.[41] But as the city council pointed out in voting fourteen to ten against this subscription, this arrangement would further the already-problematic underrepresentation of the municipal government on the board of directors. Private stockholders had a representative for every 1,250 shares, whereas the city and state governments each selected one director for every 2,500 shares owned. Of the eighteen directors, twelve represented $1.5 million in private investment, four represented $1 million in state investment, and two represented $500,000 in city investment.[42]

The press immediately excoriated the city council for raising objections, suggesting that councilmen hoped to turn the railroad enterprise into an instrument of partisanship and patronage. The *American*, a business-oriented

Whig paper, printed the most elaborate critique of the council's action, artic-
ulating a sharp division between public and private in questions of management. If the rates of representation continued as the councilmen suggested,
the paper noted, the board would ultimately become larger than the city
council itself. Municipal models of government would not work for a railroad
corporation: "Rail roads are not to be made by speeches and committees and
reports and resolutions and all the paraphernalia of parliamentary pomp."
City directors would never work with the earnestness of directors with "a
pecuniary interest in the success of the work." The deliberative powers of a
democratic government were capable of determining but not executing objects of public investment.[43] The city council reluctantly rescinded opposition
to the $3 million loan in the face of these critiques, and the B&O thanked the
city for its contributions in its 1836 annual report: "Cost what the road may,
however, it will be a cheap road to Baltimore; as, restoring to her the trade of
which the great works of rival cities have deprived her, it will place her in possession once more, and forever, of all the advantages to be derived from her
geographical proximity to the west."[44] The city needed only to keep putting
money in the railroad enterprise; nature would take care of the rest.

"What Do the People Mean by Rail-Roads?"

Debates in Baltimore's press over the political consequences of public funding represent one strand of a wide-ranging discussion in the 1820s and
1830s about the implications of rail travel for American life and democracy.
For nineteenth-century railroad promoters, rail travel promised to reorient
humans' relationship to the natural world, allowing commercial affairs to
proceed unhampered by the vicissitudes of climate or geography. This power
originated not in the novel artifice of the steam locomotive but in the simpler
mechanics of the rail. The fundamental principle of the railroad, as described
by British engineer Thomas Tredgold, was "to form hard, smooth, and durable
surfaces for the wheels of the carriages to run upon." These surfaces would be
"parallel rails of iron," and the carriage wheels would be outfitted with guides
(called flanges) to keep them in line on the rails. By reducing friction, rails
amplified power; the same horse could haul eight times as much weight on a
railroad as on a turnpike. Tredgold analogized movement on rails to "a body
impelled on the smooth surface of ice."[45]

The physics of rail travel were not necessarily intuitive to early nineteenth-
century audiences. Some insisted that railroads represented only a slight
improvement over ordinary roads, or that steam engines could work as effectively on turnpikes as on rails. In 1829, the author of a juvenile reader

attempted to remedy these misconceptions by inventing a young character named Elizabeth McDermott who struggles to comprehend the idea of a "rail-road." "What do the people mean by rail-roads?" she asks her father. "You know in the country, our fences are made with rails; and I'm sure if a road was laid over with rails, it would be so rough that it would break the horses' feet, the carriages and our bones, to drive along it." Her father tries to explain, but it takes a trip on the railroad in Baltimore for Elizabeth to finally understand: "As soon as I saw the road itself, all became plain enough. . . . The things they call rails, are long and smooth, and straight pieces of timber. They have wheels made on purpose, which runs length-wise along the rails, and turn round with no more noise or jolting, than would be made by a book moved on a table."[46]

Most observers trying to understand the new technology did so by contrasting it with that of the canal. "Railways promise to be one of the greatest triumphs which man has ever achieved over nature," wrote one enthusiastic journalist shortly after the B&O's incorporation. "Canals are but the diversion of one of the principal elements."[47] Canals required large supplies of water and extensive locks, whereas railroads' iron pathways enabled them to ascend slight grades and thus adapt to varied terrain.[48] This made railroads comparatively economical, at least in theory; even as per-mile construction expenditures shot upward in the B&O's early years, head engineer Jonathan Knight insisted that building a canal would cost nearly twice as much.[49] Moreover, railroads' mechanical operations promised to eliminate long-standing seasonal limitations on commerce. Canals froze in the winter, interrupting the flow of trade for months on end, and in the summertime, their stagnant and shallow channels of water could abet the spread of malaria and cholera; railroads appeared the more convenient and salubrious mode of travel.[50]

The most remarked-upon advantage of the railroad, though, was its speed. Engines tested in England in the late 1820s already traveled at a clip of twenty to twenty-five miles per hour—fast enough to go from Baltimore to Wheeling or Pittsburgh in one day. As one B&O supporter noted, the side-by-side construction of the C&O Canal and the B&O Railroad on the banks of the Potomac River meant that someday a canal boat would float along at three miles an hour while a train zoomed by at nearly seven times that pace.[51] In effect, by liberating travelers from the constraints of foul weather, seasonal variation, and mountainous terrain, railroads would more closely approximate movement through open water than canals could. Niles' Weekly Register predicted in 1827 that crossing the Appalachians would soon be functionally the same as crossing the Chesapeake: "Little travelling palaces will be prepared [on the railroad], in which persons may eat, drink, sit, stand or walk, and sleep, just as they do in steam boats."[52]

Canal supporters defended their interests against this upstart technology, pointing to potential problems in the physics and the political economy of rail travel. They disputed both the advantages of and need for railroads, somewhat myopically assuring the public that the speed of "six miles an hour, is very satisfactory," and somewhat less myopically predicting that the cost of railroad construction would exceed projections. Although it may be tempting to scoff at such objections and attribute them to a timeless dread of innovation, the canal advocates' retorts reflected at least in part a concern for how the railroad's particular patterns of movement would alter the rhythms of American commercial and political life.[53] If the movement of goods on rails could be analogized to steady river transport, the mechanics and economics of rail travel could not. Defenses of canals doubled as ruminations on political order, pointing out that the railroad's monopolizing power threatened to undermine both individual freedoms and yeoman self-sufficiency while enriching a large corporation. Whereas travelers directed their own movement on a canal or turnpike, the railroad would transform movement into a service provided by a company, placing those travelers at the mercy of corporate schedules and prices. Unlike canals and turnpikes, railroads retained exclusive rights to the use of the paths they created. In so granting this "monopoly" on travel, the state opened up fears of corporate power. Josiah White of the Lehigh Coal and Navigation Company in Pennsylvania noted that one could enter or exit a canal at any point, but the railroad required special locations to stop and unload: "By canal, every boatman may choose his own motion, within the maximum motion; by railroad, every traveller must have the same motion." This restricted motion made railroads "vastly inferior" to canals "as a public work, and in a republican country."[54]

One of the most extensive articulations of these concerns was a pamphlet decrying Maryland's subscription to Baltimore & Ohio Railroad stock in 1827 written by William Hollins—the same man who nine years earlier had published a report on the necessity of linking Baltimore to the West. Hollins argued that railroad technology did not merit state investment because, unlike a canal or a turnpike, the railway was not "*a free highway* for every one choosing to travel it." More troubling still was the fact that the state's investment did not leave it with a controlling interest in the railroad, meaning the public would not be able to direct its future actions. To give money to a corporation outside of state control would be akin to placing "the *very sinews of government* in the hands of a company."[55]

Some Marylanders who found themselves in the B&O's path expressed more self-interested concerns, objecting to the company's expropriation of land and its use of a largely immigrant workforce. The earliest stretches of track proved some of the most challenging to build, both because the terrain immediately west of Baltimore required extensive digging and because the techniques for laying rail lines remained largely untested. The engineers believed that the route needed to be as level as possible, which meant that the road mostly hewed to winding river valleys—from the Patapsco valley near Baltimore to the Potomac River, and then up the Potomac to Cumberland. Where the terrain was not already flat, workers made it so. The company hired independent contractors to work on construction, and by 1829, around two thousand laborers worked at the dangerous business of digging a path for the B&O. Some work crews consisted of native-born whites and free blacks from Baltimore, but the majority were recent immigrants, particularly from Ireland.[56] They built the new line through farmland, small towns, and mills. Many farmers welcomed the tracks, as they meant proximity to depots from which to ship their crops. A few, though, objected to the imperious process by which the railroad's engineers seized land for the tracks, intersecting arable plots without first consulting their occupants. Even more troublesome in farmers' eyes was the large number of laborers suddenly camped out on their land. One rural landowner charged that Irish workmen pillaged his trees to sell in Baltimore. When the company tried to suppress the practice, a number of workers quit their railroad jobs to focus on poaching lumber full-time.[57]

Reports of violent behavior within the workforce alarmed some Baltimoreans as well. As construction got under way, the newspapers periodically buzzed with stories about "outrages" and "riots" on the railroad. In some cases, violence erupted between Irish and African American work camps; others were intra-Irish conflicts that dated back to the old country. Some in the press blamed liquor, and the B&O prohibited the consumption of alcohol in its contracts for construction after July 1829, but these were not all aimless brawls. Worker violence often targeted contractors who failed to pay back wages or absconded with weeks' worth of employees' earnings. The press downplayed the seriousness of such instances, stressing that ringleaders had been caught and brought to justice and reassuring readers that only railroad workers had been harmed in the affrays.[58]

This suite of concerns, including monopoly power over transportation, impositions on property, and the introduction of immigrant labor, did little to dull popular enthusiasm for the B&O in its earliest days. Locals and visitors gathered daily to watch construction on the new line, and their curiosity produced the B&O's first revenues. In January 1830, five months before the railroad commenced its first regular operations with a route to Ellicott's Mills, thirteen miles west of Baltimore, the company began charging twenty-five cents for novelty rides along a short, completed stretch of track. Those eager to experience the new technology firsthand could walk to Mount Clare Station at the outskirts of West Baltimore and board a horse-drawn railcar for a trip out of the city and back again. Although the line would soon adopt steam locomotives, a few guests experienced more short-lived experimental efforts, such as a sail car that with a fresh gust of wind could reach speeds of twenty miles per hour.[59] Many early visitors commented on the smoothness of the ride, including one New Yorker who signed his letter to the *New York Journal of Commerce* "De Witt Clinton." "I know of no manner of travelling more pleasant than on the rail road," he reported. But by choosing the principal supporter of the Erie Canal for his nom de plume, "Clinton" signaled that he had not come to Baltimore to joyride. Having witnessed firsthand the viability of railroad transportation, he urged New Yorkers to invest in a railroad of their own to counter the project in Baltimore. The first great railroad construction boom was under way.[60]

Spatial Annihilation and Political Economy

"It is complained of by persons at a distance, that too much room, in some of the Baltimore papers, is given to accounts of rail roads, engines, and cars," wrote *Niles' Weekly Register* in 1830. Niles insisted that this emphasis was only sensible, as Baltimore was at the center of momentous changes that would soon profoundly reorient people's relationship with the world around them. Long before scholars resurrected the phrase to describe the effects of globalization, nineteenth-century commentators like Niles referred to the "annihilation of time and space" when talking about transportation on the railroad. Each early experiment with the railways prompted enthusiastic writers to celebrate the triumph of human ingenuity over natural impediments. Steam power in particular heralded the dawn of a new epoch. "It seems as if *space* and *gravity*, though not to be wholly conquered by the ingenuity of man, are to be subjected to his dominion," wrote Niles. In time, entire mountain ranges would "sink . . . beneath the pressure of unconquered steam."[61] These predictions were just the starting point for wide-ranging reflections on the steam-powered future. As locomotives leveled mountains, the North American continent would become as a neighborhood. Eliminating space promised to extend the reach of cities. For Baltimoreans, the B&O promised to bring "an empire to our doors."[62]

One way to grasp these changes was to frame them in terms of everyday life. A corollary of the collapse of space was the geographic expansion of time—one would soon breakfast in Baltimore and take afternoon tea in Philadelphia, as routine habits unfolded over vast distances.[63] A newspaper correspondent in 1828 told the readers of the *Gazette* that he had fallen asleep and dreamed a vision of Baltimore's future circa 1837. In that year, less than a decade after its commencement, the B&O had reached the Ohio River. The railroad had transformed the city, the dreamer wrote. One could now leave Baltimore at five o'clock in the morning and after the smoothest of journeys arrive in Cumberland, Maryland, by nine o'clock at night. Baltimore had grown by nearly 45 percent since 1830, and connections between Maryland and Great Britain proliferated as enterprising citizens established packet lines from Baltimore to Liverpool. More fancifully, the dreamer reported that a "Dr. Vapour" had improved rail travel by redirecting steam through a series of pipes connected to an organ in the passenger car, enabling riders to entertain themselves with music—perhaps playing the hit tune of 1837, "Railroad Sonata."[64]

Yet for all the rhetoric of transformation and spatial collapse, the B&O's founders and early supporters assumed that commerce would continue to operate according to predictable laws of trade. They embedded one of their key presumptions in the name of the company itself—the O in B&O stands not for the state of Ohio but for the river, the channel that would supply goods and passengers for the railroad to funnel into the Chesapeake. The railroad's founders took for granted that navigable waterways would remain the principal conduits of trade into the future and characterized the railroad as a means to supplement rather than supplant riverine commerce.[65] In their description the railroad often became akin to a river itself, a way to neutralize topography so that trade could "flow" from the Ohio River valley into Baltimore's harbor. This characterization reflected a mechanistic understanding of commerce that cast trade as the movement of goods through space. Laws of trade, they held, dictated that goods would travel to market along the path of least resistance. As one correspondent to the *Gazette* put it, "Trade like water, seeks its conveniences and its level, and will find them."[66] Merchants, the B&O's founders assumed, would ship their products to the closest market because that would be the cheapest destination. B&O representatives and the city's press asserted repeatedly that the railroad, once completed, would provide the shortest and most convenient outlet for western merchants, thus making Baltimore the premier entrepôt for western goods.[67]

The principal objective of the B&O was, therefore, not to transform commercial practices but to restore Baltimore's "naturally" ordained primacy in western trade. To be sure, its supporters expected the B&O to forge a new

hinterland; the company's engineers reconnoitered possible routes and reported back enthusiastically about new and enhanced supplies of minerals
and agricultural products, particularly coal, to be hauled by the railroad.[68]
Yet for all the changes it would induce, railroad officials saw the company's
mission as restoring a natural balance, giving back to Baltimore the proximity that had been taken from it by artifice. The board of directors claimed,
"It has required all the assistance of art, and all the efforts of skill and enterprise, overcoming the natural inferiority of their position, to give to the cities
of New York and Philadelphia that traffick with the west which they now
possess, and which once seemed the exclusive birth right of Baltimore." By
effectively eliminating the mountains as a barrier to travel, the completed railroad would return Baltimore, New York, and Philadelphia to the same relative
positions they occupied prior to the opening of the Erie Canal.[69]

These characterizations of the laws of trade reflected a circumscribed
vision of human economic agency. If the movement of trade followed physical
laws, one could funnel commerce like a stream of water. As the engineer
Charles Ellet Jr. put it, the course of trade could be predicted with equations
"more worthy of reliance, than . . . many of physics." As physicists had derived the formulas that governed the material world through observations
of nature, so political economists might predict the movement of goods and
people through careful readings of the landscape. The railroad would simplify
these efforts. Its iron rails and steam locomotives would connect sites in a
manner that removed undulations of terrain and variations of the seasons
from these calculations, making distance the principal factor in the shipping
merchant's ledger.[70]

The B&O's founders were hardly the first to frame economic activity as a
natural process. This metaphor was central to the history of political economy,
as eighteenth-century thinkers such as Adam Smith applied the self-regulation
and balance of nature to the conduct of human activity in order to legitimate the pursuit of private interest.[71] The B&O's advocates veered sharply
from the classicists' noninterventionist economic worldview in their support for a government-funded railroad, however. Although merchants and
farmers, collectively, could be expected to ship their products in predictable
ways, cities—that is, urban publics—and states, as the progenitors of internal improvement initiatives, could remake the landscape and alter the flow
of trade. Internal improvement advocates in neighboring states shared Baltimoreans' belief that natural laws governed commercial practices; they disagreed, though, on the question of which internal improvement processes fit
consistently with natural patterns and which were abominations of artifice.
Thus when, in 1828, the Maryland legislature incorporated the Baltimore &

Susquehanna Railroad (B&S) to connect Baltimore with York, Pennsylvania, along a route paralleling the Susquehanna River, Philadelphia newspapers cried foul. The government of Pennsylvania had devoted millions of dollars to internal improvement projects designed to foster growth in that region. An editorial in Philadelphia's *Pennsylvania Gazette* warned, "We are to labour to fill the cask, and Baltimore is to tap the bottom of it."[72] Baltimore's papers responded that the B&S only complemented the Susquehanna River's current, and that natural advantages necessarily superseded state boundaries. The flow of the Susquehanna directed its trade to Baltimore; Philadelphians' political connection to the river valley was "but a rope of sand in comparison."[73]

These conflicts revolved around control of hinterlands that would in turn foster urban growth. Yet what form that growth would take or how it would shape the spaces and economy of the city remained open questions. Some writers quickly incorporated the railroad into the political economy of the "American System" of internal manufacturing and high tariffs. In Baltimore, supporters of the American System, most notably Hezekiah Niles, saw the railroad as a tool that would transform the political economy of the city and the nation. The B&O would facilitate increased circulation and movement of goods and people, speeding up the pace of the economy and spreading wealth to many different Baltimoreans. *Niles' Weekly Register* printed a joke in which a befuddled father explains to his son that the American System was "something that goes on rail, kind o' somehow." Niles said that the comparison was not bad. The root of public wealth, he held, was the transfer of goods between hands. Each transaction accrued a modest profit to the individual handling the goods, and each profit—each increase in price—ultimately benefited the local economy by diffusing wealth and ensuring greater general prosperity. The railroad would abet this process by reducing the cost of transportation; savings would pass into general circulation, and more money would be available to pay workers and purchase ever-greater quantities of manufactures. "The facility of *transportations* is closely a-kin to the facility of *transformation*," Niles concluded—not only for goods but for the city itself.[74]

The railroad—and the transactions it facilitated—represented for Niles movement toward an industrial future for Baltimore under the American System. The first step in this new direction was reducing the city's reliance on foreign trade. Daniel Raymond, the Baltimore-based political economist, argued in 1823 that national wealth should be understood as a country's capacity to provide for its citizens. This capacity derived from the industriousness of the people, and it increased when transactions occurred within a nation so that both beneficiaries were national citizens. By this logic, foreign trade generated less wealth than domestic.[75] Niles adopted a similar position.

The railroad would facilitate the circulation of value *within* Baltimore, enabling citizens to grow rich off each other's productions, using exchange to constantly transform, in effect, one good into another. Foreign trade—the dominant economic function of Baltimore before 1825—was a highly visible exercise, with many ships sailing into and out of the harbor and workers hauling goods on and off the decks. But it always involved one transfer. An export was consigned in Baltimore and then sent abroad; the profits did not return.[76]

This analysis of the comparative effects of domestic and international trade highlighted the tangibility of trade as Niles and other railroad supporters conceptualized it. Although they often deployed abstract language to characterize the effects of commerce, it was an irreducibly material phenomenon, characterized by the physical movement of goods. Railroad supporters anticipated that the B&O's salutary effects on Baltimore would come in the form of increased movement through the city as the railroad poured western goods onto its streets. Indeed, the very language they used to describe urban decline—"grass growing in the street"—linked the city's commercial fortunes to its street-level traffic. The decline of traffic meant the decline of business, and without wagon wheels to beat down vegetation sprouting up between cobblestones, nature itself would overtake the city.

The railroad was to restore the whirlwind of commercial activity that had characterized Baltimore's formative years. The *Gazette* argued that the B&O would "throw into our city, such a vast increase of business, as will *immediately* set in motion its entire manufacturing, mechanical and laboring population."[77] The movement of the railroad would beget motion in the city, and the city would in consequence grow outward, developing the valuable shoreline for shipping and filling in the grid with workers' housing and warehouses.[78] In 1828 the *American* discussed plans to open Lombard Street, a new east-west avenue that the paper's editors believed would clear out and beautify an area that had grown dense with vice and overcrowding. The newspaper argued that such improvements had to take place before land values increased, as this would make changes in the urban landscape more difficult to implement. The article concluded, "The advantages of Baltimore are great and striking: but a main source of her prosperity is that active spirit of her inhabitants, which has even gone beyond her rapid growth, and put her on enterprises [i.e., the B&O] of a magnitude worthy of states and kingdoms."[79] The movement in one article from the opening of a city street to the launch of a railroad was not an act of juxtaposition but an assertion of continuity. In the editors' view, both of these changes reflected the urban scale at which commercial development would occur: street traffic and railroad shipments alike contributed to economic growth.

For Hezekiah Niles, visions of an industrialized Baltimore were also visions of a white Maryland. By moving the city and the state to the American
System, the railroad would accelerate the demise of slavery in Maryland
and point the state toward a white, free labor future. Niles, a Delaware-born
Quaker, saw in the South an economic system that enriched a handful of
planters while impoverishing white laborers. Just as foreign trade removed
wealth from the nation, so the southern reliance on cotton exports slowed
the pace of circulation and thus the growth of wealth in that region.[80] Reliance on slavery also hindered economic development by undermining free labor. Free white laborers and agriculturalists abandoned Maryland for distant
places that valued labor more highly, he argued. States like Maryland would
either have to cast off slavery or watch as their economies and political power
gradually declined. In the B&O, Niles saw a powerful weapon against slavery.
The same cost savings that allowed the railroad to accelerate the circulation
of values also worked to reduce the value of manual labor and therefore undercut the viability of slavery as a system. Thus, as workers toiled to lay the
first miles of track west of Baltimore, Niles opined that "every shovelfull of
earth, cast from the bed of a canal or rail road constructing, [does] something
towards the abolition of slavery, in the reduced value of slaves."[81]

This was decidedly not an egalitarian outlook—Niles and others of a like
mind-set aligned railroad modernity with whiteness. The demise of slavery,
Niles held, would have to be accompanied with forced removal of African
Americans from Maryland, as free blacks had the same "general bad effects
as slaves" and were "less worthy and moral." On this point, at least, Niles had
prominent allies within the B&O itself. Philip E. Thomas raised funds and
organized on behalf of the colonization movement that sought to remove the
state's free blacks to Africa in the 1810s and 1820s. John H. B. Latrobe, B&O
counsel, played a still more active role, serving as president of first the Maryland Society and then, from 1853 until well after the Civil War, the American
Colonization Society.[82] Others joined Niles in tying the railroad to Maryland's racial destiny. A correspondent to the *American* identified the B&O
as a crucial project for the development of Baltimore's "back country," and
exhorted white agriculturalists to move to Maryland to make their fortune.
With "white cultivators in Maryland, and a good rail road to the west, Baltimore would flourish and increase," said the anonymous writer.[83]

Niles devoted an unusual amount of ink to political economy and racial
theory. Most commenters who celebrated the B&O project made no mention of slavery or race at all, save for remarks about the white population
of the West whose trade Baltimoreans sought to capture. B&O shareholders
dependent on enslaved labor for their livelihoods and personal comfort likely

opposed this particular vision of the railroad's effects. Later, railroads in states to Maryland's south showed that railroad technology could indeed coexist with and even help sustain the institution of slavery. Some railroad corporations hired enslaved laborers and others owned people outright.[84] In the early years of the B&O, however, the railroad was an elastic project, capable of sustaining interpretations ranging from benign predictions of mobile tea times to racist anticipations of a white future.

As other rail lines threatened to overtake the B&O, the public conversation around the company began to change, losing some of its celebratory tone and acquiring an anxious edge. Locally, the launch of the aforementioned Baltimore & Susquehanna Railroad in 1829, the construction of the B&O's Washington Branch to the nation's capital starting in 1831, and the incorporation of the Baltimore & Port Deposit Railroad (later the Philadelphia, Wilmington & Baltimore Railroad) in 1832 helped shift the discourse from one of western bonds to one of geographic centrality. In this account, the Baltimore & Ohio became the most important link within an extensive transportation network and a symbol for Baltimore's ambitions as a commercial center.[85]

More troubling for Baltimoreans was the quick movement by citizens of Philadelphia, New York, and Boston to overtake the Baltimore & Ohio with railroad projects of their own. Boston papers praised the gumption of Baltimore's citizens while suggesting that a railroad west from their own city might offer similar advantages; in 1835, the heavily state-funded Western Railroad started plotting a course to Albany to tap the Erie Canal.[86] Philadelphia papers likewise saw the trade of the West as an object of great competition among eastern cities and told their readers that their city would need to take action to reinforce its natural advantages; eventually, their response to the B&O would materialize as the Baltimore company's archrival, the Pennsylvania Railroad, launched with support from the municipal governments of Philadelphia, Pittsburgh, and other cities.[87] Even New Yorkers did not take their city's commercial dominance for granted. An editorial in the *New York Spectator* warned its readers, "Baltimore and Philadelphia press her [New York] on one side and Boston on the other:—all seeking to divert from her a portion of that commerce which has placed her at the head of American cities." The solution was to invest state money in a rail line through the southern portion of the state that would funnel this commerce to Manhattan—the New York & Erie Railroad.[88]

If the Baltimore & Ohio ever enjoyed first-mover advantage in American railroading it was already a distant memory by the mid-1830s as these new projects to the northeast (along with a rail line starting from Charleston, South Carolina, funded in part by the state and city governments) set out to capture western trade. By 1837, far from witnessing the B&O's triumphal completion to the Ohio as the *Gazette*'s correspondent had dreamed nine years earlier, Baltimoreans watched anxiously as other lines threatened to overtake their own. From the outset, the company's founders had warned that the city's natural advantages would be rendered meaningless if the citizenry succumbed to sloth or petty bickering and allowed Philadelphia and New York to cement their ties with the West.[89] Political failure—an inability of the body politic to act as one in pursuit of its interests—could thus undo natural advantage. Years of delays and cost overruns made this prospect very real, and commentators urged the company to push forward aggressively. A series of letters published pseudonymously by statesman John Pendleton Kennedy argued that Baltimore possessed greater natural advantages than Philadelphia, but that natural advantages had to be maintained: "Rail Roads and Canals, in effect, shorten distances. When other cities, therefore, shorten their distances from the sources of trade, Baltimore must shorten hers, or she will be left behind." The Baltimore & Ohio was essential, but it was not enough. "Baltimore should imitate the spider," wrote Kennedy, "spread her lines towards every point of the compass, and lodge in the centre of them." This call to action was in fact a call for funds; it would take money from the state and city coffers to safeguard Baltimore's place on the spider's web.[90]

A Popular View of the Railroad: July 4, 1828

Contemplations of the railroad in print were the province primarily of the elite, from the commercial leaders who proposed the project in *Proceedings of the Sundry Citizens* to the newspaper editors who marveled at the locomotive's capacity to shrink distances. This does not mean, though, that the broader urban public remained silent. In 1828, the B&O's board of directors chose to mark the company's transition from printed speculation to physical reality by organizing a grand parade to celebrate the start of construction on the new line. The parade, scheduled for the anniversary of national independence, was to pass through Baltimore from east to west, culminating with a cornerstone-laying ceremony to commemorate the symbolic start of construction. For the board of directors, the parade presented an opportunity to affirm their vision of the company, positioning the B&O as a project of public significance while lionizing the men at its helm. The municipal government and groups such as the Freemasons signaled their assent to this vision by contributing money and organizational prowess to the event. Yet the parade also afforded a larger urban public a chance to express their own perspective on the new project that their labor and taxes would do so much to support.

The scope of participation in the parade speaks to a popular appropriation of the event to ends perhaps unintended by the organizers. Here manifested, however subtly, a counternarrative to elite political economy, as an ebullient urban public claimed its own place in the railroad's origins story.[91]

The largest component of the parade was a procession of the city's workers engaged in activities representing their various industries. Months before the parade started, members of the various professions arranged for spots on the parade and outfitted their floats with tools and costumes befitting their positions and activities.[92] Baltimore's workers and artisans took advantage of the opportunity to express some of their own concerns. Parade planning took place in the wake of a minor controversy stemming from the B&O's efforts to import iron from Britain free of duty instead of sourcing iron locally.[93] In light of this controversy, a committee of blacksmiths wrote to Philip E. Thomas, volunteering to furnish a pick, a spade, and a hammer for the cornerstone laying. They added, passive-aggressively, "Will you have the goodness to inform us if these articles have been provided from abroad or if not, if they would be acceptable to the Company." Thomas cordially accepted the blacksmiths' offer and assured them that importation of materials was necessary only for the iron rails.[94]

The parade began before eight o'clock on the morning of the Fourth, moving west along Baltimore Street from the Merchants' Exchange Building to the site of the ceremony. The night before, thousands had converged on Baltimore to witness the historic event, and as the procession made its two-hour march through the city, an estimated fifty thousand people cheered on the participants.[95] At the head of the parade marched a series of military and symbolic figures, followed shortly by a number of notables connected with the company, including the directors of the Baltimore & Ohio, the engineer corps, and, most resplendently, a horse-drawn barouche bearing the aged Charles Carroll of Carrollton. After this initial wave came the workers' floats. The order of the parade broadly reflected a narrative of society's progress from subsistence to complexity, starting with the fundamentals of life and ending in the flourishes of urbanity and commerce. Farmers went first, followed by the makers of agricultural implements, bakers, and brewers. Next came metalworkers, weavers, stonecutters, fancy chair makers, coopers, sugar refiners, and glass cutters, to name a few. At the back of the parade of professions marched ship makers and riggers, pilots, sea captains, and sailors, followed finally by the draymen and carters. This ended the parade of workers; behind them were government officials at the local, state, and national levels; military officers; clergy and public teachers; merchants and traders; and near the end, "Citizens, Mechanics, and Artizans not included in the above arrangement."[96]

When they reached the site of the ceremonial cornerstone laying around ten o'clock, marching gave way to speeches, all of which turned on the promise of the railroad to transform space and revive economic fortunes, and all of which celebrated the ingenuity and industry of "man" in undertaking such a project. At the conclusion of the principal address, "two boys dressed as Mercuries" brought a copy of the remarks to a mobile printers' station, where it was reproduced for distribution among the audience.[97]

The speeches and ceremony constitute the bulk of the official written record of this event, but for those watching from Baltimore Street, the workers' procession—the largest component of the parade—must have been the most memorable feature. The people of Baltimore did not merely witness the beginning of a grand project launched by the city's luminaries but asserted their role in its creation. The workers adorned each float with messages and decorations expressing their trades' contributions to public welfare. In doing so, they also positioned themselves in relation to the new enterprise. Some trades, such as the blacksmiths, the stonecutters, and the printers, demonstrated their stake in the B&O's success by contributing directly to the ceremony.[98] Still others, from farmers to draymen to sailors, by marching constituted themselves as the public that the railroad was to serve. Some rendered this point explicitly. The float most widely remarked on was that of the ship captains, mates, and seamen, who created a mock ship called the *Union*, fully rigged and outfitted in Fells Point, the hub of Baltimore's maritime trade. After the captain of this ship pledged to use the railroad to sail over the mountains, he and his crew broke ranks in the parade and overtook Charles Carroll and the railroad officials. The boisterous crew then started singing, to the tune of "Hail to the Chief":

> Hail to the road which triumphant commences
> Still closer t'unite the east and the west;
> Hail to the hope in our vision that glances,
> With prosperous commerce again to be blest;
> . . .
> [C]heerily together our efforts uniting,
> Let's help this great work in advancing.
> O dear and glorious be the day,
> Which causes all this grand display;
> O long remember'd may it be,
> Through Baltimore's prosperity.[99]

The *Union* and its crew pledged to help the railroad, but they also defined it as an instrument of urban growth, one that would enhance, not supersede, the city's maritime interests. In the parade, they and the other professions banded together to trumpet their contribution to the city's well-being and to tie their own professional ambitions to the project under way. If they accounted for the bulk of the population, then it was their ends that the railroad would serve and their labor that would make it possible.

Conclusion

Baltimoreans never embraced the railroad unanimously, and as the Baltimore & Ohio project began, the reality of its operations began to overtake the imagination of its possibilities. Baltimore's elected officials clearly believed that public funding for the B&O would ultimately redound to the commonweal, but the city's investments nonetheless constituted, from the start, a transfer of public wealth into the hands of the elite. Questions about who would control the enterprise, and to what ends, surfaced even before train service began. Nevertheless, the company appears to have enjoyed widespread support among the citizens of Baltimore in its early years. Although railroad technology remained unproven, the B&O's founders argued that it would work according to recognizable laws of trade, drawing on an understanding of commerce that was simultaneously physical and abstract.

When the B&O's founders and supporters conceptualized trade in terms of movement across space, they assumed that sheer distance was and would remain the deciding factor in merchants' shipping patterns. This accounts for the seemingly paradoxical relationship between the project's transformative powers and conservative goals—for all its projected ability to collapse time and space, the railroad remained an adjunct to established natural patterns of trade. This static interpretation of trade and geography foresaw the quickening of communications but did not account for the way that new speed would change merchants' calculations. The railroad was created to serve a political economy that it would ultimately undermine.

Tracks in the Streets

Among the earliest supporters of the Baltimore & Ohio was Philip Uhler, who purchased stock in the fledgling company as soon as it became available in 1828. A civic-minded businessman with deep roots in Baltimore, Uhler had every reason to favor building a rail link to the West. For starters, the railroad could bolster his prospects. Uhler sold groceries (mostly liquor) out of a house on Pratt Street that he shared with his wife and four other people; very likely he expected that the B&O would facilitate his dealings with western whiskey suppliers. Beyond dollars and cents, though, backing the railroad project fit with Uhler's larger interest in Baltimore's political and social development. Around forty years old by the time the "sundry citizens" sought their charter, Uhler was a veteran of ward-level politics and charitable efforts, an occasional (unsuccessful) candidate for city council, and an active supporter of John Quincy Adams and the American System. Uhler embodied the admixture of self-interest and public spirit that the B&O's founders said would fuel the railroad's success.

Yet as abstract conversations about natural advantage gave way to practical questions about tracks and trains, Uhler's views on the company and its management curdled. When the B&O announced in 1829 that it planned to build its terminus at the waterfront in East Baltimore, Uhler argued that doing so would deprive his West Baltimore neighborhood of its rightful share of the railroad's trade. Later, in 1830, he spearheaded public opposition to the placement of tracks in the center of Pratt Street, warning that railcars would disrupt traffic patterns and endanger lives on his busy home street. The B&O's managers dismissed his concerns and went forward with their plans, but living with a railroad at his doorstep did not assuage Uhler's apprehensions;

in 1835 he circulated a petition that pronounced the rails in Pratt Street a dangerous impediment to the "ordinary use of the street" and called for their removal. The tracks remained, however, to Uhler's personal misfortune. In September 1837, merchants unlocked a B&O car parked on a steep incline on Howard Street in order to load it with flour. They lost control of the car and it rolled downhill, striking Philip Uhler's wife as she crossed the street. Both of her legs were crushed, and she died of her injuries two weeks later.[1]

Philip Uhler's progression from railroad supporter to railroad adversary and finally to bereaved widower exemplifies both the opposition to and the effects of placing railroad infrastructure within the urban built environment. Baltimore stood at the forefront of this process, not only in the United States but also in the world: major European cities deliberately barred rail infrastructure from the urban core. Observers in American cities from Boston to Charleston closely monitored and ultimately emulated Baltimore's experiment with urban rails.[2] Questions raised in Baltimore about how best to accommodate railroad travel within a bustling urban streetscape were never merely technical matters. In disputes over where to place the B&O's depot, whether the railroad should take up a carrying trade formerly handled by draymen and carters, and how pedestrians and drivers should move through city streets now laid with iron rails, Baltimoreans articulated competing normative visions for the street and the city.

At issue were new patterns of movement. Fluid and frictionless, train travel fit uneasily with existing traffic patterns and blurred the line between the spaces of the city and the countryside. In doing so, it raised questions about the meaning of urbanism itself. What made a city distinct from other forms of settlement? If the railroad was to annihilate space, did it matter if that space was rural or urban? Track supporters contended that mechanizing movement within the city would, by accelerating the pace of transactions, position Baltimore at the center of a national economic system. To track opponents, though, this vision threatened the urban way of life as they understood it, sacrificing public space and public safety for the benefit of a few. Such arguments tied Jacksonian concerns about monopoly to tangible practices of mobility and framed equal access to public space as a democratic prerogative. Yet the track debates reflected more than partisan fighting; Philip Uhler, after all, was no Democrat. Nor do the substantial material and financial stakes that various participants had in these questions fully explain their positions. Various parties made arguments designed to advance special interests or reinforce property regimes, but when aired in public, their claims took on new salience and became the basis for broad-based political action on questions of urban form and movement. Through the track debates of the 1830s, thousands of Baltimore's citizens asserted their own stakes in the planning process and participated in the conversation over what the city was to become.

This conversation reflected the structural limitations on political action in antebellum America. The debate over the place of railroad tracks in the city streets cut across class but not racial lines. Similarly, the absence of Mrs. Uhler's given name from newspaper accounts of her death is a telling omission; with few exceptions, women appeared in these controversies only as symbolic shorthand for ideas about progress. But while white women and African Americans of both sexes did not (openly) pen editorials or write legislation, they did take action on the subject, signing petitions for or against the tracks and using them for personal enrichment or self-liberation. More generally, all Baltimoreans shared in the experience of the rails. Long before the B&O reached the Ohio River, the citizens of Baltimore got a preview of the mechanized future. Not everyone liked what they saw.

The "Wealth-Diffusing Railroad"

John H. B. Latrobe, looking back on the B&O's early days from a remove of forty years, recalled that in the 1820s and 1830s his fellow Baltimoreans thought of the company as the "wealth-diffusing railroad . . . the rose of a vast watering pot, the smallest of whose tricklings was to fertilize the spot it fell on, whatever its previous desolation and aridity."[3] The B&O's founders encouraged this manner of thinking by insisting that the completed railroad would initiate a new golden age for Baltimore. As citizens began to think through the implications of this anticipated growth for their own districts, though, the same visions of prosperity that helped unite Baltimoreans in support of the B&O led them to fracture into acrimonious neighborhood rivalries. Questions over where to place the railroad's principal depot within Baltimore animated particularly anxious debates, since everyone assumed that the area around the station would become a focal point for commercial activity while neighborhoods left at a far remove would languish. Property owners drew on the rhetoric of natural advantage to argue that their neighborhoods constituted the most favorable sites for a terminus. West Baltimoreans pushed for the retention of Mount Clare Station as the primary point of deposit while their East Baltimore counterparts insisted that the line extend to the deep-water wharves of Fells Point (fig. 2.1).

No less pressing than the depot question was the matter of how, where, and whether the B&O would convey its tracks through the city. If depots concentrated trade, tracks promised to disperse it, connecting various warehouses

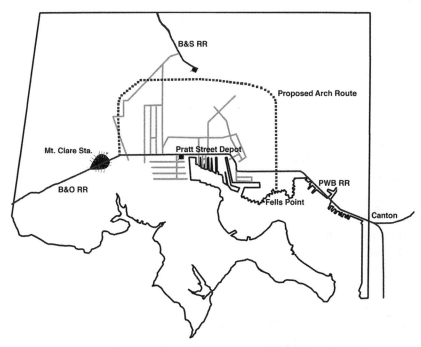

FIGURE 2.1. Baltimore's railroad infrastructure, ca. 1839. The dark-gray lines that run from west to east and from the north depict tracks built by the railroad companies; the dotted line approximates the route of the proposed arch plan. The light-gray lines in the city center represent likely locations of the privately owned branch lines. Map by Tracy Leung. Adapted from G. W. Boynton, *Map of Baltimore, 1838* (Massachusetts, 1838).

and wharves with the company's main line to the west (called the Main Stem). At the same time, urban tracks threatened to disrupt established practices and destabilize property relations. Months before work began on the Main Stem, the state and municipal governments issued guidelines for the company to follow when laying rails for its City Division, the stretch of track that would run trough the built-up parts of Baltimore. In 1828 the Maryland legislature amended the B&O's charter so as to grant the company the right to run tracks through Baltimore's streets, although this was subject to municipal approval and had to be in such a manner as not to "interfere with the free use and travelling on said streets."[4] The city government added its own provision in an effort to forestall interneighborhood rivalries: the company must set its urban route "with a view *alone* to the best interests of the *present City* of Baltimore, as it is now built." The council thus attempted to ensure that the anticipated real estate boom would serve current property owners, not speculators buying up land on the city's outskirts.[5]

The state and city government set the conditions, but the company undertook the work. Building a railroad through a city was no less novel an undertaking than building one over a mountain; as of the late 1820s, the only localities that had attempted to integrate rail infrastructure with urban space were English towns much smaller than Baltimore.[6] The size and scale of the B&O made it a new type of actor in the urban landscape. Typically, property owners opened Baltimore's streets and wharves piecemeal, collaboratively, but such ad hoc methods would not suffice for an institution conducting coordinated operations across a route extending hundreds of miles beyond the city limits.[7] Railroad operations demanded consistent street grades and smooth interchanges, and realizing these conditions within Baltimore's uneven topography required systematic planning of a sort not commonly seen in antebellum cities. Although the municipal government authorized rail construction within the built portion of the city, the specialized technical knowledge needed to lay tracks meant that B&O engineers Jonathan Knight and S. H. Long, acting at the behest of the board of directors, orchestrated these interventions in the urban landscape.

The board tasked the engineers with balancing three mandates as they plotted the railroad's path through the city: the city's instruction that the tracks distribute trade evenly through town, the state's requirement that the tracks not interfere with the free use of the streets, and the company's need to bring goods to tidewater for transshipment. The engineers decided that to realize all three of these goals, they would have to isolate the tracks from "the bustle unavoidable in a densely populated city." Placing a "*great leading* [*rail*]*road* along a thickly settled street," they wrote in 1828, would pose "an insurmountable barrier" to ordinary traffic, leading to costly delays for the company and fatal accidents for the citizens.[8] They singled out Pratt Street, the east-west thoroughfare that formed Mount Clare's northern boundary, as a particularly unsuitable approach. The heavy business done there and the "crowds with which [it is] almost incessantly thronged . . . utterly preclude the expediency and feasibility of introducing a Rail-road."[9]

Working from these principles, the engineers devised a plan in 1829 to bring the railroad tracks to tidewater while separating their right-of-way from street-level traffic. They called for the railroad to approach Baltimore from the southwest and arch over the northern edge of the built portion of the city. Tracks would form a parabola, bridging over major thoroughfares and then tunneling through Lexington Hill before curving down to reach the wharves at Fells Point. Smaller, single-track lines could branch off of this horseshoe-shaped railway artery and run to various locations throughout town. This plan called for significant changes to street grades only in undeveloped portions of the city and allowed most extant buildings to remain undisturbed.

But it also committed the B&O to a set of expensive and intricate interventions in the urban landscape at a time when the company had not completed even a single section of its route to the West.[10]

This roundabout plan generated debates among citizens who questioned its implications for Baltimore's finances, infrastructure, and property values. A number of writers disputed the engineers' calculations and offered their own assessment of the technical merits of the proposed route, predicting that this costly system would constrain the growth of the city and ultimately prove impracticable. In doing so, they asserted their right to have a say in the city's future development; one Baltimorean went so far as to argue that there should be an election to decide on the plan, as the city council should not give "carte blanch[e] to the Rail Road Company" to remake the urban environment without first receiving popular consent.[11] The proposal also set off a vociferous debate between partisans of West and East Baltimore. Advocates of a West Baltimore terminus claimed that the circuitous tracks deprived their neighborhood of its natural rights. James Carroll was particularly vocal on this point; having donated ten acres for the B&O's Mount Clare depot in 1828, he had no intention of seeing trains roll past his doorstep to an eastern end point. Carroll argued that roads ought to take the straightest path possible, and that the abrupt right turns and expensive tunneling called for in this plan indicated foul play on the part of the company's managers. Carroll and his West Baltimore neighbors blamed an East Baltimore conspiracy for this deviation from the railroad's "natural" route.[12] Supporters of an eastern terminus shot back with their own invocation of natural rights, in their case the superior capacity of East Baltimore port facilities. Only Fells Point, they said, could accommodate the deepwater ships that would soon crowd the harbor to receive the B&O's trade.[13]

Both sides cautioned that rejecting the naturally ordained terminus would lead to the establishment of a new city beyond Baltimore's borders. A depot outside of Baltimore would attract new development and cause the city itself to decline as a market and entrepôt—the ultimate irony for a railroad founded to revive the urban economy. One observer warned that if the road failed to reach Fells Point, the B&O's private stockholders would instead build a new harbor outside the city limits. The railroad would thus foster the growth of a new city, "to the great and irreparable injury, perhaps ruin, of [Baltimore] as now improved."[14] West Baltimoreans responded to this hypothetical with a more concrete example in their favor—a newly founded industrial and residential development along the waterfront just east of the city limits called Canton, financed in part by investors from New York City. The Canton Company's charter gave it the right to build tracks connecting with rail lines in Baltimore. West Baltimoreans warned that if the B&O terminated in the eastern part of the city, outside capitalists would use this provision to siphon the city's hard-won western trade.[15]

In light of these objections and wary of the heavy cost of the engineers' proposed route, the B&O delayed making a decision on how to enter the city until 1831, when it adopted a radically different approach. Rather than go around the built portions of the city, the board of directors decided to place tracks directly through the heart of Baltimore. After two years of clandestine surveys, the company presented its new plans to the city council in February 1831. Whereas three years earlier the engineers had declared Pratt Street particularly unsuited to railroad operations, they now reversed their judgment. The best route through Baltimore, they said, went along Pratt Street past the Basin (today's Inner Harbor) to a patch of municipally owned land just west of Fells Point, which the city provided to the railroad company gratis. From this route, branches could extend to every neighborhood, and depots at various points in the city could diffuse the incoming trade throughout town.[16]

The proposal to run the railroad down one of the busiest streets in the city sparked outcries that dwarfed the terminus controversy of three years earlier. Urbanites, organizing at the neighborhood level, fractured into clusters of support and opposition. From February to early March 1831, ten of the twelve wards in the city called meetings to discuss the proposed extension and announce their opinions.[17] Although east and west remained geographic fault lines in the controversy, wards did not speak with one voice; in a few cases, a single ward held multiple meetings representing different viewpoints.[18]

The flood of ward announcements in Baltimore's newspapers drew the attention of local satirists, who published fake notices that ridiculed the self-seriousness and pomp of these gatherings. As the participants in one imagined meeting put it, "We had rather the whole scheme of connecting Baltimore with the West should be defeated, than that our portion of the town should be made to share equally the anticipated benefits, with the other portions." Satirists found the form of these meetings—the appointment of officers, the lengthy preambles and resolutions, and the self-important speeches—as ripe a target as their message. An account of the meeting of one fictitious ward described the appointment of a chairman, assistant chairman, secretary, and assistant secretary, and the "liberal bestowment of the complimentary but empty title of Esq. on most of the gentlemen named." By focusing on the meetings' tone and rituals, the articles mocked track opponents for presuming to voice their opinions on this matter in public. For these writers, railroad policies lay beyond the scope of ward-level politics.[19]

Opponents of the plan did question the railroad company's authority to remake the built environment, but their critique was wider ranging than the satires allowed. Track opponents drew connections among practices of movement, economic justice, and community life. The most substantial criticism took shape in an eight-page pamphlet composed at a meeting of citizens from western and southwestern Baltimore, chaired by Philip Uhler. The participants at this meeting echoed many of the property-based concerns about the loss of business and violation of "natural advantages" that had been voiced in the debate over the arched route the year before. Now, though, facing the prospect of a rail line down Pratt Street, they added fearful anticipations of the negative influence the railroad would have over the city's built and social environment.[20] The unprecedented nature of this proposal meant that Uhler and his neighbors could only predict what would happen if a railroad passed through their street. Still, the pamphleteers' understanding of railroad technology led them to believe that tracks on Pratt Street threatened urban life as they knew it.

The pamphleteers argued that railroad infrastructure would upend the ordinary use of the street. Steam engines, for example, posed an inherent danger in a dense urban environment; the sound of hissing steam would startle horses, and sparks from engines could ignite fires. The most pointed objections in the pamphlet, though, concerned the tracks and cars themselves. Iron tracks—embedded in public space but used exclusively by a private company—would impede free movement even when no trains were running; jutting up from the roadbed, they would catch wheels and limit vehicles' ability to maneuver, effectively halving the usable space of the street. Train traffic would amplify this disruption: because rails reduced friction and fixed the train's path, railcars would not be able to stop quickly or swerve out of the way of other traffic, thereby forcing all other vehicles to yield. This dominance ran counter to the ad hoc negotiation Uhler and his fellow citizens associated with street traffic. The street accommodated a range of uses: farmers unloaded their wagons, draymen hauled their packages, and parents sent their children on errands. Train tracks subordinated all of these to the movement of railcars, undermining the spatial order of the street. Uhler offered a hypothetical example: if "a six horse wagon loaded with wheat, should meet a Rail Road car filled with passengers riding for pleasure," the wagon, though conveying the principal product of Baltimore's market, would nonetheless have to yield to the railcar, business "giv[ing] way to pleasure." The likelihood of this scenario was beside the point—even the possibility of such an exchange showed that the railroad's fixed path and rapid movement upended the basic equality with which vehicles met one another in the street. The same perverse logic would apply to the city as a whole. Ultimately, the passage of trains along

Pratt Street would create a physical and mental boundary cutting the city in two, "a frightful barrier . . . [making] communication between the two districts north and south of Pratt street . . . vastly inconvenient, embarrassing and unpleasant." Serving the imperatives of long-distance travel threatened to upend the very meaning of the street, turning a space that had once bound the city together into a site of dislocation and peril. Uhler framed the railroad as a danger to urbanity itself: an instrument that would speed communications but cleave community.[21]

B&O officials and their advocates in the press responded to such charges by promising that railroad tracks would alter commercial and social uses of space in Baltimore minimally, if at all. They precluded some objections by acceding to them: horses, not locomotives, would pull cars within the city. They pledged as well that the rails would protrude only slightly above the roadbed, enabling all vehicles to cross without difficulty. They conceded that rail traffic might obstruct other vehicles but assured the public that railcars could stop quickly if needed to avoid accidents.[22] The board promised the municipal government "less interruption and danger from the passing of the Railway Cars along a street than from the passing of Drays and other Vehicles now in common use."[23]

The mayor and city council approved the B&O's plan and authorized the company to run tracks along Pratt Street to the waterfront, but subject to municipal oversight and stipulations. The city's ordinance specified that tracks were to be placed down the middle of the street and forbade the use of steam power within the built portions of the city, requiring the company to exchange its locomotives for horses at Mount Clare Station. To ensure that the railroad did not violate established patterns of movement within the city, the ordinance imposed a speed limit for trains of three miles per hour, which the council characterized as "a walking pace." Most importantly, section 10 of the ordinance stated that if the mayor and city council should later find that the street railways constituted "an obstruction or impediment to the ordinary use of any street or streets," they could compel the B&O to remove them and "replace the street or streets in the same condition in which they were before the railway was laid down."[24] In practice, though, once installed, the rails proved difficult to remove.

Street Traffic

Frederick Douglass's earliest memories of Baltimore centered on its streets. Born into slavery on Maryland's Eastern Shore, Douglass—at the time called Frederick Bailey—was sent to Baltimore at the age of seven or eight to labor in the household of Hugh Auld, who lived in Fells Point. The streets of that neighborhood became a key point of reference in his later recollections as he contrasted the big city with his earlier rural environs. In Baltimore, he strode over pavement baked by the summer sun that burned his unshod feet, finding himself "walled in on every side by towering brick buildings." Initially a site of danger and confusion, the street soon became a place of work, since much of his employment consisted of running errands and keeping Auld's son Tommy from "getting in the way of carriages" as they walked through the city. Later, Douglass's earliest reading lessons took place in the street as well, as he used his white playmates as teachers and perused Webster's spelling book while out on errands.[25]

Douglass thus experienced the street as a place of both danger and opportunity, a site of work, leisure, and even education. He shared this space and this experience with many other Baltimoreans. Even the busiest streets of Baltimore accommodated a range of uses and users. In a city marked by sharp stratifications along racial, class, and gender lines, the street was one place where all citizens met one another, albeit not on equal terms—city law tasked the night watchmen with dispersing what Mayor Jacob Small in 1831 termed the "hord[e]s of colored persons and boys, who prowl about the streets, [and] take possession of the foot-ways" in the evening hours. Drays and carts shared space with pleasure carriages while genteel pedestrians brushed against Baltimore's interracial cohort of notoriously profane hackmen. In this environment, drivers improvised their traffic patterns; vehicles used verbal cues or hand gestures to negotiate right-of-way as they passed. The street was also a site for business transactions. Hucksters, often African American women, walked the streets selling strawberries and oysters while teamsters used the street to load and unload their vehicles. Drivers maneuvered around parked wagons and carts of vegetables as they made their way through the city. As they did so, they dodged not only other moving vehicles and pedestrians but animals as well—horses, pigs, dogs, and occasionally cattle.[26]

Laying railroad tracks in a major thoroughfare like Pratt Street thus set the stage for a confrontation between the coordinated schedule and frictionless movement of the railroad and the ad hoc spatial order of the city street. Where observers like Philip Uhler looked at these conditions and saw impromptu patterns, the B&O's managers saw chaos. Practices of movement premised on negotiation and exchange meshed poorly with the precise operations of a railroad, and the company quickly set about rearranging urban practices to fit its needs. Within half a year of opening the tracks on Pratt Street, the B&O's board of directors asked the city council to pass a series of ordinances regulating the use of the street so that trains could run without

interruption from joyriders or traffic jams, deeming such laws essential for
the operation of an urban railroad.[27]

The city government complied, and the legislation that followed from these
requests defined how individuals could interact with the new mode of transit.
The city government did not absolve the railroad company of legal burden;
any railcars sitting in the street for more than an hour had to be chained up
or the city would fine the board of directors, for example. Most of the laws,
though, applied to private citizens or individual agents of the railroad. The city
banned unauthorized use of railcars and instructed all vehicle drivers to pass
only on the right-hand side when traveling on railed streets.[28] Ordinances penalized obstruction of foot pathways, which had acquired a new importance
for circulation now that tracks occupied a portion of major thoroughfares.[29]
Consignees or agents of the railroad could load or unload a car only at designated depots or by the express permission of nearby property owners.[30]

The impact of these regulations reached beyond Pratt Street thanks to
branch lines extending from this central route that connected various warehouses, wharves, and places of business with the railroad's City Division. Although the B&O endorsed the construction of branch lines in principle, the
board of directors refused to pay for or maintain such tracks. Instead, the city
government allowed private property owners to request track extensions in
their streets.[31] Once the city council approved an application for a branch line,
property owners could hire a contractor to build a railroad extending from
Pratt Street, adjusting street grades as necessary.[32] The challenges posed by
urban operations led a Baltimore engineer to invent a special curved girder
in 1831 that allowed railcars to make sharp turns around streets and into warehouses. Austrian observer Franz Anton Ritter von Gerstner noted that this
design enabled American cities to be "crisscrossed in all directions by railroads." By 1839 no fewer than fifteen branches extended from Pratt Street onto
other roads, turning the entire city into a rail yard.[33]

The B&O's supporters praised this growing network of tracks for disci-
plining the traffic and business practices of the city as a whole. In 1835 a city
council committee credited the railroad with standardizing the city's once-
chaotic traffic patterns, finding "even less confusion & disorder now than
before the track was laid down" at one busy downtown intersection. Wagon
drivers who had once parked their vehicles perpendicular to the pavement to
load them now, thanks to the tracks, had no choice but to park them parallel
to the side of the road, thus removing one persistent obstacle to free movement on the street. Furthermore, the tracks compelled streams of traffic to
keep to opposite sides of the street as they passed in different directions.[34]
Dividing the street had forced movement into orderly patterns.

This is not to say that the railroad alleviated crowding—quite the opposite. During a six-day period in June 1832, 413 B&O cars brought 1,490 bar-
rels of flour, 86 tons of granite, 48 tons of paving stone, and 22 hogsheads of
tobacco to Baltimore, and conveyed 1,014 passengers to and 1,252 passengers
from the city. The B&O's business amounted to nearly seventy cars moving
through the city daily in either direction. But streets crammed with vehicles
and boxes of merchandise appeared to many as signs of progress in a city
that had been ailing since the end of the War of 1812. A number of observers
commented approvingly on the increase in traffic congestion and attributed
it to an escalation in travel between Baltimore and other cities facilitated by
the city's railroad lines. Some conceded that the railroad impeded mobility
within Baltimore but framed this inconvenience as the price of prosperity.
One municipal report questioned those who fretted over traffic: "Why Complain of the obstruction produced by Bringing Business to t[he] City—when
but for that Business we should have no City[?]"[35]

The counterpart to an uptick in street traffic was a surge in construction,
particularly in the western part of the city near Mount Clare Station. The
Patriot marveled that warehouses and buildings rose up in the area almost
instantaneously, "as it were by the touch of the magician's wand."[36] Real estate
transactions, not magic, produced this sudden burst of development; the railroad had a buoyant effect on property values. As early as 1828, advertisements
for lots near a projected depot pledged that the railroad would soon make the
area "a scene of active business," increasing the value of the land.[37] Two people
owned much of the rural land surrounding the new Mount Clare depot—the
aforementioned James Carroll, and Anna McHenry Boyd. Boyd, like Carroll,
saw the railroad project as an opportunity to put her landholdings to more
profitable use: she sold patches of land south of Pratt Street to the B&O for
use as car shops and a passenger station, then turned to her remaining plots
on the north side of the street, which she leased to speculative developers who
erected narrow row houses for the company's rapidly growing workforce.[38]
In addition to these new swaths of working-class housing, West Baltimore
began to emerge as a commercial and financial district, with genteel homes
and businesses—including specialized brothels located near the principal depots of the B&O and Baltimore & Susquehanna Railroads that catered to elite
travelers and locals.[39]

Observers in other cities monitored the results of Baltimore's experiment
closely. In the early to mid-1830s, pro-track factions in New York, Charleston,
and Philadelphia pointed to the B&O's example to assuage citizens who were
wary of granting rail companies the use of public streets. The New York &
Harlem Railroad, looking to extend its line into the heart of Manhattan in

1832, declared that, in doing so, it hoped to emulate "the triumphant success" of the B&O's City Division. To critics' concerns about disruptions to the ordinary use of the street, the New York company and its advocates argued that the safety precautions instituted in Baltimore—the use of horsepower, the strict speed limit, and the municipality's right to remove the tracks—allowed trains and street traffic to coexist peacefully.[40] The South Carolina Canal and Rail Road Company likewise promised to follow Baltimore's precedent as it urged the state government to authorize the construction of tracks through Charleston. Citing reports of the B&O's effects in Baltimore, the company argued that a railroad would serve as an engine of urban growth, filling up the city's warehouses and boosting property values.[41] Philadelphia saw the fiercest opposition to urban rails, and here, too, Baltimore's pioneering experience served as a guide. In 1835, as residents of the inner suburbs in Philadelphia undertook violent extralegal efforts to remove the tracks, Philip E. Thomas personally intervened in their debates. In Baltimore, he said, opposition to the railroad's path had been roused by "certain individuals in the two western wards" and was not the result of "any real inconvenience occasioned by obstructions caused from the Rail tracks."[42]

With Baltimore leading the way, the gradual extension of rail lines within and between cities created possibilities for connection that had been unthinkable a decade earlier. Laying tracks through Pratt and other streets gave Baltimoreans a front-row seat for the railroad's promised annihilation of space. By 1838, a traveler could leave Baltimore at 6:30 a.m. and arrive in Philadelphia for dinner, moving from Pratt Street to Chestnut Street in the course of a day on a $2 ticket.[43] Newspapers reported enthusiastically as travel times shrank from days to hours. "What anticipations! what changes!" wrote the Charleston, Virginia, *Free Press* in 1835 as the B&O approached the nearby Potomac River town of Harpers Ferry: "Why, it seems but a short time since it was considered a grand achievement to have travelled from Baltimore to this place within twenty-four hours." Soon, the townspeople would make the same trip in well under ten hours.[44]

The implications of placing rapid travel at Baltimoreans' doorsteps were not lost on Frederick Douglass. Writing in the *Colored American* in 1840, Douglass appropriated the rhetoric of spatial annihilation to the cause of self-emancipation: "A few years since, when elopements from slavery were fewer than they now are, the poor slave . . . [who] would flee from his chains . . . had to wind his way by a circuitous route, on foot, sleeping by day, and walking by night, and after a week's time, he might, if not overtaken, as was frequently the case, reach New York. . . . Now so extensive are our railroads . . . that a poor fugitive may leave Baltimore in the morning, and the third night following, may find himself safely in Canada."[45]

Douglass knew well of what he spoke: the Philadelphia, Wilmington & Baltimore Railroad provided his path out of the city and out of bondage. It was a rapid but perilous journey. The state subjected the movement by rail of free black travelers, unlike white passengers, to close oversight and regulation, requiring them to carry papers that described their appearance and certified their freedom, and mandating that they travel only by day. Douglass had to work within these constraints as he made his escape. On September 3, 1838, Douglass jumped on a train as it pulled out of the station. By prior arrangement, a hackman had dropped him off at the very last minute; Douglass predicted correctly that amid the jostle of a crowded departing train, he could slip on board undetected. In lieu of free papers, he borrowed from a friend a document identifying him as a free American sailor, and, as he did not look much like his friend, he wore typical sailors' clothing provided by Anna Murray, a free woman of color whom he would soon marry, to assuage any suspicions. His gambit worked; the conductor barely glanced at his papers. But he was not out of danger yet. The route to Philadelphia at that time involved river crossings by steamboat, the most perilous of which was in Wilmington, Delaware, slavery's northernmost outpost in the East and a place teeming with slave catchers. For someone traveling in these circumstances, time, rather than collapsing, seemed to expand. "The train was moving at a very high rate of speed for that time of railroad travel," Douglass recollected over half a century later, "but to my anxious mind it was moving far too slowly. Minutes were hours, and hours were days during this part of my flight." Finally, "after an anxious and most perilous but safe journey," Douglass found himself walking the streets of New York as a free man. The railroad placed Pratt Street and Broadway in proximity to one another, but gaining freedom in this way required much more than a $2 ticket.[46]

Douglass's method was not unique; in 1840 the *Sun* complained that "the loss of slaves in this city" via railroad had increased of late and pointed to cooperation between free and enslaved African Americans in purchasing tickets out of Maryland.[47] The state legislature in 1839 took action to stanch the losses felt by enslavers due to escapes by railroads and steamships: a new law forbade any railroad, steamboat, or other vessel to transport an unaccompanied slave. Companies that violated this law would forfeit $500 and reimburse the erstwhile owner for the cash value of the escapee.[48] The B&O, once completed, passed through two slave states, but at points its tracks came within three miles of the Pennsylvania border. The creation of a deputized company police force in 1853 implicated B&O employees in the maintenance of slavery by authorizing them "to arrest any colored persons whom they shall find on the line . . . without a legal pass."[49] Board members grumbled at the extra expenses incurred by these laws but acquiesced to the state's authority until a new state constitution mooted the question by abolishing slavery in 1864.[50]

Even as the tracks revolutionized interurban mobility, they represented obstructions and dangers to many other Baltimoreans, particularly the city's fleet of draymen, hackmen, and carters. The street was their office; short-distance haulers solicited customers, loaded and unloaded goods and passengers, and traveled through the city streets. They paid the municipal government for the right to do so—the city used the sale of licenses to regulate the hauling trade. As the haulers saw it, the license implied a mutual obligation: they paid a tax for the privilege of using the street, which in turn meant that the city could not adopt measures restricting their mobility (and hence their livelihood). The railroad tracks, use of which was the sole prerogative of the B&O, surrendered space in the public street to an untaxed private interest. And as trains began depositing goods directly at the harbor, draymen and carters watched the much-anticipated western trade pass by without benefiting any in the community, save the railroad's officers and the shipping merchants. In an era obsessed with the politics of monopoly power, the railroad corporation and its well-connected, wealthy benefactors seemed to Baltimore's haulers to embody illegitimate privilege. As one petition put it, the Pratt Street tracks infringed "the right of labour" because they put local trade under the control of a company that compensated its executives generously but used its "complete monopoly of the transportation thro' the streets" to establish its "own price for labour."[51]

The B&O's monopoly was at once spatial and economic—the company's exclusive right to use its tracks both hindered the draymen's and carters' use of the street and gave it exclusive control over the shipment of goods to the harbor. Poor men who had paid taxes to run carts over the streets now found those streets blockaded by a tax-exempt railroad.[52] When railroad agents unloaded goods on Pratt Street, for example, they occupied up to two-thirds of the space in the street, causing traffic jams as other vehicles maneuvered through the narrow passageway remaining.[53] As Philip Uhler had predicted, though, the height of insult for haulers came when their vehicles encountered a train in motion. A city commission tasked with investigating the effects of the street tracks found that the infrastructural requirements of the railroad made it a unique and commanding presence in the street. Ordinarily two vehicles meeting each other would "mutually give way . . . to allow each other to pass," but the railroad car, "confine[d] to the rails by the flanges of its wheels," could not "give way; every thing else must yield to it," thus monopolizing the road and denying the community its right of "ordinary use of a street." Drivers often had to hurry to clear the track as an approaching railcar "hurried" along the tracks "with irrisistible [sic] force to the demolition of every thing which obstructs its passage."[54] Where the railroad's supporters looked at the congested condition of the streets and saw chaos giving way to order and prosperity, the draymen and their allies saw something more ominous: the imposition of a monopolistic spatial order within the ostensibly public space of the street, heralding the breakdown of street-level democracy.

Draymen were not the only Baltimoreans with cause to complain about the tracks. Laying tracks sometimes entailed tearing up streets or removing pipes, and contractors frequently failed to repair damaged infrastructure.[55] The rails interrupted the flow of wastewater through the gutters crossing Pratt Street, flooding basements during heavy rains and generating a powerful stench in hot weather. In winter, snow piled up between the rails and the curb, blocking carriage access to houses on the street.[56] Most noteworthy, though, were the frequent and often fatal accidents that increasingly showed up in the pages of the daily press in the 1830s. The victims of accidents included vehicle drivers whose wheels became stuck in the track and, disproportionately, railroad employees tasked with handling the cars in the freight yards.[57] But it was the opportunities and dangers that the railroad generated for the city's children that garnered the most attention. The cars' constant movement created an ersatz transit system whereby children (and, often, inebriated adults) could hop on passing cars to get around the city. Rail depots, with their idle cars and stacks of loosely guarded merchandise, also became sites for play and petty crime.

Such behavior could quickly become dangerous. In 1837, for example, a fourteen-year-old orphan named John Ball was running an errand when, despite warnings from the conductor, he jumped on a railroad car passing through Pratt Street to hitch a ride. As he dismounted, he slipped and fell under the car, losing a leg. Ball was fortunate to survive; in another instance, Lanchart Machey, the thirteen-year-old son of a German immigrant shoemaker, was crushed between two cars at a depot. His father had sent him to take work to their Pratt Street home, but he had, said the Sun, "taken the opportunity of playing upon the cars, by which act of indiscretion he lost his life." To the Sun, the lesson of this and other accidents was clear: "His dreadful fate should be a warning to the heedless boys who are daily in the habit of playing about the depot, to the annoyance of the persons employed and at the risk of their own lives."[58]

News reports of such accidents usually emphasized the carelessness of the injured party and the quick restoration of order. The brief articles often took care to absolve the railroad company of any blame and to remind readers that the citizenry must remain vigilant when moving through railed streets.[59] The implicit argument—that the railroad's promise of prosperity warranted the risk to the city's vulnerable populations—occasionally became explicit when citizens debated whether to extend tracks into a new street. In one such case, the *Patriot* reported that as property owners in East Baltimore "calculated" the benefits that would accrue from increased rents once the railroad reached their streets, some "shrewd old dames . . . calculated over their tea cups how many infant victims are to suffer under the wheels of the new Juggernaut"—and "consequently resolved on additional watchfulness."[60] Likewise, the *Sun* disdainfully reported that citizens opposed efforts to introduce B&S tracks on High Street because "inconveniences must occur, and many children will be killed—'oh, horrible.'"[61] Such arguments contrasted a masculinized interest in progress with feminized concerns about public safety. The profits of the railroad justified occasional fatalities.

Urban accidents were one cost of doing business for the B&O. The company was careful to pay indemnities to victims of street collisions in a way that avoided litigation without conceding liability. In Philip Uhler's suit against the company for the death of his wife, the board instructed counsel to devise a compromise without setting a precedent. When the attorneys failed to reach a settlement with Uhler, the matter went to court. The suit drew the attention of newspapers in other cities that were experimenting with urban tracks, although ultimately it did not establish meaningful case law. While the jury accepted Uhler's argument that the company had not exercised "ordinary care" in entrusting its car to an unaffiliated merchant, it awarded him only $500 in damages out of the $20,000 he sought. The low award, the *Sun* speculated, was likely because he had remarried in the two years since his wife's death.[62]

The Track Removal Campaigns

A few years of experience with urban rails convinced some citizens that the tracks did more harm than good to Baltimore and that they should be removed so as to restore the city to its prior condition. As early as 1833, a candidate for city council pledged "to support the Mechanics' and Working Mens' [*sic*] Interest, by using his endeavours to remove that worst of all nuisances from the city, the Baltimore and Ohio Rail Road."[63] The city council's Joint Committee on Railroads took up the cause in 1834–1835. In a pair of reports, the committee condemned the Pratt Street tracks for interfering with the ordinary use of the street and blamed them for concentrating trade in the hands of a few.[64] Soon after the Joint Committee published its first report in 1834, several wards in West Baltimore called meetings that demanded the restoration of the pre-railroad status quo.[65] The campaign to remove the tracks escalated in the March 1835, when Solomon Etting, who had formerly been one of the city's representatives on the B&O's board of directors, circulated a petition of Pratt Street residents complaining that the railway interfered with their use of the street and demanding its removal.[66]

Etting's petition and the Joint Committee's report roused public attention on this matter, and mass petitions began to circulate advocating either the removal of the tracks or their permanent retention. Some 2,354 Baltimoreans signed the petitions. Track removal advocates placed more petitions in circulation but only narrowly surpassed the track retention petitions in total signatures, 1,183 to 1,171. Some trends emerge from a close examination of these documents. Overall, thirty-five illiterate Baltimoreans signed the petitions by indicating their mark, twenty-three of whom supported track removal. Furthermore, although not every petition indicated the signatories' home wards, those that did confirm the impression that track opposition was more common in West Baltimore, whereas support for the tracks was concentrated in the eastern part of the city.[67]

Two distinct petitions opposed the urban tracks. One, signed by hackmen, called for the removal of the rails for the good of their profession. The other (for which Philip Uhler was a principal signatory) identified the tracks as unfair impositions on the public. These petitions called for the restoration of the street to its "original" condition. Counterpetitions answered these demands by claiming that the tracks benefited the city more than they harmed it and by condemning the selfishness of those who would tear them up. But they did not stop there; in order to forestall future debate on the subject, they asked the municipal government to declare the rails permanent fixtures in the urban environment, not subject to removal.[68]

Track retention advocates argued that this proposal followed logically from the rights of property and the special nature of a railroad system. By consenting to the construction of private branch lines, they insisted, the city voided its right to remove the tracks on Pratt Street. An ad hoc city council committee favorable to this cause explained the reasoning: branch tracks depended on their connection to a wider railroad network, so returning Pratt Street to its former condition would render them useless, impairing the exercise of an array of existing contracts. Thus, track removal constituted a threat not only to private property but also to private enterprise more broadly. The tracks had, by this logic, changed the nature of the street itself; streets no longer existed independent of one another but as subarteries within a system centered on Pratt Street that stretched as far as the railroad itself.[69]

A minority on this committee countered that this line of argument threatened the very concept of public space and, with it, urban democracy. The minority's report warned that making the tracks permanent fixtures violated the council's obligation to maintain the public thoroughfares of Baltimore for all citizens. It would, in effect, pass control of the streets into private hands, allowing the "moneyed corporation" and private warehouse owners to do as they pleased in public space. The likely end point of this act would be the demise of Baltimore as a self-governing community; after all, outsiders could someday commandeer the B&O by cornering its stock, placing control of the city's streets in the hands of strangers.[70]

The city council embraced the majority's vision and moved quickly to declare the rails permanent fixtures on the city streets by a combined vote of thirty-two to thirteen. Mayor Jesse Hunt vetoed the measure, however, stating that while it was inappropriate and unnecessary to remove the tracks at present, he did not wish to relinquish the right to do so unless so instructed by a clear majority of Baltimore's citizens.[71] Both the tracks and the right to remove them remained, opening the door for subsequent rounds of debate. Petitioning for track removal in Pratt and other streets continued for the next several decades. As the issue recurred, both sides recapitulated their basic arguments; in each case, the tracks remained.[72]

In the mid-1830s, though, before the track debates became a regular feature of Baltimore's public life, the conflict over removal and retention revealed fissures in the city's body politic deep enough that participants in a ward meeting in East Baltimore warned their fellow citizens of the danger of "present[ing] to the world the Strange spectacle of a 'city divided against itself.'"[73] These divisions were more than neighborhood rivalries—they reflected incompatible understandings of the nature of urban space and public authority. For those who called for track removal, urban democracy demanded the restoration of public space to its former condition. For those invested in retaining the tracks, the rail lines running through the city bound streets together in a way that precluded community intervention. Buried in these competing conceptions of the street were diverging notions of the city's role in the national economy, which came to the fore in debates over railroad through traffic.

"A Mere Place of Transit"

The question of how to handle through traffic was one of the principal points of contention in the track debates of the 1830s. Through traffic included passenger travel or freight shipment that moved through Baltimore but did

not begin or end in the city. As the conversation around railroad depots invoked concepts of natural advantage, so the through-trade debate applied the
political economy of railroad enterprise to urban space. Draymen and carters and many opponents of track extension (and, later, proponents of track
removal), drew on Hezekiah Niles's version of the American System when
they argued that keeping transshipment slow would build wealth within the
community. Niles himself favored building rail lines through Baltimore, but
this was a difference only of scale; where he strove to consolidate transactions
within the nation, track opponents hoped to do so within the city. By holding
tracks at the city's western edge, draymen, hackmen, and carters could find
employment hauling shipments and passengers bound for Philadelphia or
elsewhere to warehouses, wharves, and depots on the other edge of town. In
this way, even transient goods would pass through many hands and sustain
many livelihoods. But if street tracks deposited fully loaded trains at the waterfront, they would concentrate exchange at just one site and enrich just one
party. One writer warned that if railroad cars went straight to the docks, they
might as well continue directly to Philadelphia—in which case, "We become
a mere place of transit."[74] By 1835, proponents of track removal argued that
this was precisely what had happened.[75]

The B&O's representatives and East Baltimore businessmen countered
that the long-term commercial viability of the city depended on its ability
to attract trade and capital. By this logic, it made sense to provide for the
rapid transfer of goods even if they were bound to other destinations. They
held that the railroad should bring goods and passengers traveling onward
straight to the point of transfer, with as little delay as possible, and the gains in
efficiency would encourage capital accumulation in Baltimore. Failure to do
so would in effect act, the company explained, as "an onerous and unnecessary tax," working ultimately to the advantage of Baltimore's urban seaboard
competitors in the competition for western trade.[76] One writer reasoned that
if the object of the rail line was to bring western commodities to Baltimore's
port, it made no more sense to stop one mile from the docks than it did ten
miles away—an argument that dismissed any qualitative difference between
urban and rural space for the purpose of rail travel.[77]

These competing views on through trade surfaced repeatedly during the
controversies over urban tracks, but they collided most forcefully in 1836
when the B&O announced plans to share a depot with the Baltimore & Port
Deposit Railroad (later the Philadelphia, Wilmington & Baltimore, or PWB)
on Pratt Street.[78] In early March 1837 the board of directors received a memorial signed by many Baltimoreans decrying the joint depot proposal. The

memorialists worried that the plan would reduce Baltimore to the status of a waypoint and recommended instead the location of several depots around the city, so as to "give opportunity to the citizens generally, to reap advantage from your great work of internal improvement." The company in its response assured the public that the interests of the Baltimore & Ohio Railroad and its terminal city were "identical." Uniting the depots would not make Baltimore a mere place of transit. "The only difference between the two arrangements," the B&O explained, was "that a passenger arriving here and wishing to continue his journey, will in the one case, have to remove himself and his baggage from one car to the other, and that in the other, the same transit must be made, by means of an omnibus." As the company expressed it, the prosperity of the city stemmed from "permanent causes" that could not be alienated simply by making it easier to leave the city. Baltimore enjoyed an all-weather harbor and proximity to the trans-Appalachian West, benefits tied to the transit of merchandise into and out of the city. The city would prosper because of its mercantile advantages, the low prices of its goods. The real threat to its prosperity lay in the exertions of cities like New York and Philadelphia, whose internal improvement projects threatened to override Baltimore's advantages. If the city government added delays or impediments to through travel, it would undermine Baltimore's superior geographic position and encourage its adversaries.[79]

The city directors pressed the company's case further in their own report by taking a broader geographic perspective. They characterized the B&O as "only an important link in the great chain of internal communication between the east and west," and Baltimore as but one node within this larger network. The city had no more right to arrest the passage of trade than any other town along the B&O's route. The railroad would in time realize Baltimore's natural advantages, they said, but not if confounded by "local views, sectional interests or selfish motives."[80] The city council, surprised to hear such a statement emanate from its own representatives on the board, reacted sharply, deeming this argument an affront to Baltimore's citizenry. A municipal committee resolved that the joint depot proposal (and the city directors' rhetoric) threatened to subvert Baltimore's status as the eastern terminus of the B&O.[81]

Both arguments reflected the power of the railroad to reorient the public imagination of the city and of urban space. Through trade was at the heart of the B&O's founding mission, which was, after all, to make Baltimore the clearinghouse for western trade, facilitating shipments between the Ohio River valley and the Atlantic markets. After only half a decade of operations, though, the railroad started to undermine the commercial logic that had prompted its creation, leading Baltimoreans on both sides of these debates to rethink the role of the city as an economic actor. In defending the joint depot plan, the B&O's board of directors suggested that municipal attempts to regulate the movement of goods and passengers through town might undercut the city's position in an emerging national market. To the long-standing concept of natural advantages, which held that the city's prosperity depended on securing a hinterland beyond the reach of other locales, they added the notion of competitive advantages, factors like market conditions that encouraged merchants to do business in Baltimore. While the urban public took an active role in cementing natural advantages by investing in the railroad, measures by that same public to distribute trade or protect public safety within Baltimore represented a threat to competitive advantages. As Philip Uhler had conjured the injustice of a wheat wagon waiting for a train to pass in 1830, so the board now imagined a hypothetical traveler dragging his luggage onto an omnibus; in each case, infrastructure policy interfered with rights of mobility. The board, though, tied the mobility of the traveler to the mobility of capital— hinder the former, and capital would flee to a place that offered, to borrow a twentieth-century turn of phrase, "a more favorable business climate."

In effect, the board appropriated citizens' concerns about obstructing traffic and applied them to obstructing capital by shifting the geographic scale of the conversation. The B&O and its allies contended that railroad enterprise must be understood within a national framework, and they used the rhetoric of scale to trivialize their opponents' concerns, claiming that the narrow interests of a few aggrieved citizens stood in the way of progress. The importance of city streets lay in their ability to connect a national market rather than to foster local prosperity. The city council's response invoked scalar rhetoric as well in order to categorically differentiate the spaces of a major terminal city from those of "villages" along the railroad's route. The city directors' claim that the requirements of a national communications network trumped the privileges of urban space "plac[ed] Baltimore entirely below the rank she deserves," said the council, and threatened to reduce the city—in popular imagination and in fact—to "a mere place of passage." A metropolis like Baltimore had every right to compel travelers to pass through its streets.[82] Such arguments about the implications of rail travel for understandings of urbanism would continue for decades. More immediately, the debate over the Pratt Street Depot revealed a shift in power: the city council, having authorized the placement of the tracks, found itself unable to stop the B&O from sharing its station with the railroad to Philadelphia. The B&O and PWB ignored these protests and held their depot in common for the following thirteen years.[83]

Conclusion

The debates over the passage of the railroad through Baltimore in the 1830s reflected distinct understandings of how and to what ends the city should function. Imposing the complex operations of a railroad on the crowded urban
environment prompted questions that illustrated a rift along class and geographical lines. Railroad opponents expressed concerns about the equitable
distribution of trade, the safety and openness of the streets, and private monopoly control of public space. They saw the welfare of the city as rooted in
the collective well-being of its citizens and neighborhoods. Railroad supporters characterized these priorities as parochial and restrictive. They were concerned not with which Baltimoreans would transport goods locally but with
whether the goods would start with the B&O or take the Erie Canal; fears
about safety in the street paled in the face of desire for efficient and speedy
transactions.

This was not a conflict between traditionalists and innovators, but a clash
between two visions of urban modernity. Nearly all Baltimoreans—including
the draymen and carters—supported the idea of a railroad from their city to
the Ohio River and accepted its promises of economic revival at face value.
They were not Luddites, and even in a decade that saw multiple instances
of popular violence in the face of economic corruption, the track removal
efforts proceeded through officially sanctioned channels.[84] It remained a civic
protest, marked by appeals to the mayor and city council rather than sabotage
of the iron rails, as in Philadelphia. But the track debates reflected divergent
ideas about who had the right and the authority to enact changes in public
space. Draymen, carters, and their allies envisioned a city in which long- and
short-distance travel were sharply divided, privileging urban space as a place
of commerce and sociability; the railroad company countered with the notion
of a mechanized place of movement, extending the efficiencies of rail travel
into the urban street. These fault lines over urban space would remain broadly
intact over the following half century.

3

The Rise and Fall of the B&O Note

In January 1842, a crowd of "mechanics and working men" assembled in Baltimore's Monument Square to rally support for a new type of money then circulating in the community, known variously as railroad notes, stock orders, or B&O notes. This currency had served as the principal medium of exchange for ordinary transactions in Baltimore since 1840 but had entered an inflationary spiral early in 1841 when the city's bankers refused to accept it on deposit. The bankers defended their actions by arguing that the railroad notes could not truly function as money because they were not backed by gold. The crowd at Monument Square rejected this logic and countered with its own definition of value:

> In the opinion of this meeting the stock orders now in circulation in Baltimore, are essentially the currency of the People.
>
> Because they are based upon the people's property, wealth and labor.
>
> Because their value can be understood and appreciated by the people, far better than that of any other paper issues of corporations or individuals.
>
> Because they constitute that which all the business intercourse of the people is carried on, and any attempt to depreciate them is an act of hostility against the people's interests.

This was a radical departure from standard economic principles and practices. The value of money, the protestors said, could inhere in the strength of the local economy rather than the aura of precious metals. The government could furnish the basis for transactions instead of depending on the whims of a moneyed elite. And the strength of the currency could be determined in open squares rather than in speculators' secluded chambers.[1]

The B&O notes represented Baltimore's response to a widespread currency crisis in the 1830s and 1840s. Andrew Jackson's war on the Bank of
the United States decentralized the American monetary system: from the
late 1830s until the Civil War no fewer than 7,000 distinct banknotes issued
by 1,600 different banks circulated within the country. The most respectable
notes promised redemption in specie, especially gold, but the conceit that a
banknote represented an equivalent quantity of so-called hard money was a
well-known fiction: American banks issued notes far in excess of the gold in
their coffers, trusting that their customers would not attempt to redeem every
outstanding note at once. Even these inflated banknotes proved insufficient
to fuel the increasing volume of transactions in the antebellum American
economy, and notes of more dubious provenance filled this currency vacuum.
Companies and private citizens printed bills that promised redemption not
in specie, but in banknotes—writers dubbed these compound notes "shinplasters." What's more, a wide variety of fraudulent notes circulated that
mimicked the appearance of legitimate banknotes. The result was that, in a
given city, three different $10 bills might have three different exchange values.[2]
Things got more complicated when one left town; the difficulty of redeeming
notes issued by faraway banks made distance a structural limitation on the
value of currencies. In this fractured, localized system, travelers had to change
currencies as they moved from one place to the next, negotiating exchange
rates along the way. If a note retained its value when removed from its point
of origin, this suggested the economic vitality of that *place* as well as the respectability of its issuer.[3]

Such irregularities posed challenges for the conduct of even basic transactions in nineteenth-century America. Uncertainty about the means of exchange reflected a broader discomfort with the increasingly anonymous economic relations proliferating in an expanding capitalist system. In the best
of times, this uneasiness manifested in complaints about financial operators,
confidence men, and forgers: people who manipulated the complexities of
the urban economy to swindle honest citizens.[4] But the fragmented monetary system was prone to shocks and crises that went far beyond individual
transactions, undermining the very foundations of economic exchange. This
was never more evident than in the Panic of 1837. The Panic started as a collapse in the European market for American securities such as state and local
bonds. As London bankers tightened their belts, they called on U.S. banks
to repay their debts in bullion. The banks responded by suspending specie
payments: they declared unilaterally, and in breach of their legal obligations,
that they would no longer redeem their notes in gold. Once banks stopped
paying specie to notes-bearing customers, the bottom fell out of the entire

financial system. If banknotes could not be redeemed, they became nearly worthless, leaving Americans without a functional currency with which to pay their bills. These straitened conditions prompted many to rethink basic assumptions about the economy and their place within it.[5]

The currency experiment in Baltimore had practical aims but far-reaching implications. The B&O note represented a solution to two distinct problems: the railroad company's inability to finance westward construction and the citizenry's need for a viable medium of exchange. The municipal government agreed to entrust its bonds to the railroad company, and the railroad company agreed to print a currency for general use based on those bonds. Though framed in the press as a temporary expedient, the B&O notes represented something bolder: an urban monetary policy that reformulated principles of exchange in the hopes of protecting and stimulating the city's economy.[6] By securing the notes in municipal bonds rather than the supposedly intrinsic value of specie, the new currency's promoters argued that the city's collected wealth could serve as a basis for transactions, effectively monetizing Baltimore's built environment.

The few scholars who have examined these notes have deemed them a flawed and exploitative financial scheme. This is a sound evaluation: in issuing this currency, the B&O took municipal bonds that could not command face value on the market and tried to pass them at par among impoverished citizens by slicing them into denominations as small as 6.5 cents. Such arguments cannot account for protests like the one at Monument Square, however. Attending to the popular political activism around the B&O notes reveals an intellectual history that is missing from positivist assessments of the currency's viability.[7] Debates over the B&O note in Baltimore reflected wider arguments about the nature of exchange, the value of money, and the limits of government action. As proponents of the new currency gathered in ward meetings, currency conventions, and street protests, they characterized the economy as a political construct, subject to review and intervention at public meetings. They rejected the specie standard and suggested that their own collected property could furnish a populist source of value instead. Their opponents responded that municipal bonds could not provide a stable basis for exchange and argued that a community's choice of currency served as an index of its integrity.

For twenty-eight months, from late 1839 through early 1842, the B&O note served as the principal medium of exchange in Baltimore and its environs. As it passed through people's hands, into and out of shops, the new currency came to stand in for larger concerns about the meaning of value. Conflicts over the B&O note thus reflected the broader struggle in the 1830s and 1840s to settle the principles and politics of an emerging capitalist system. The outcome was not as straightforward as it may at first appear.[8]

The Circulation of Money

Given the era's obsession with scam artists, a surprising number of antebellum political economists readily admitted that capitalism itself was, in effect, a confidence game. Accepting paper money from a stranger constituted an act of faith: the recipient trusted that the note received would later pass current. Hezekiah Niles forthrightly declared that as long as a community sustained this confidence in its media of exchange, it would prosper. His theory of development stressed the importance of frequent exchanges for economic growth, and credit allowed far more exchanges to take place than specie ever could. Currency was the instrument by which credit circulated; paper money bridged the gap between the abstractions of political economy and the material conditions of urban life. Thus, Niles found it distressing to learn in 1834 that notes from Virginia banks had suffered a sudden discount in Baltimore's markets. Only days before, the same notes changed hands by the thousands at par, enabling working people to acquire the necessities of life; now, he said, currency brokers had cast doubt on the notes' value, throwing the system into tumult. Niles pinned the depreciation on conscious decisions by greedy individuals to gut the means of ordinary transactions. He shuddered to imagine the effect of such acts on what he termed "the continually moving business of the people."[9]

The sudden discount on Virginia notes marked the beginning of a currency crisis that plagued Baltimore and other American cities for a decade. The want of a stable circulating medium intensified during the Panic of 1837. Historians debate whether this crisis stemmed from Jacksonian monetary policies, grew out of capitalist overexpansion, or reflected some combination of the two. Regardless of the initial cause, its effects were clear: a collapse in the European market for American securities, the calling in of U.S. banks' transatlantic debts, and the subsequent suspension of specie payments by bankers who feared a run on their limited holdings of gold.[10] Following the path of these suspensions illustrates an increasingly interconnected financial system. New York banks, fearing overdrafts from London, closed first; Philadelphia banks, fearing New Yorkers would come to collect their debts in specie, followed. Baltimore banks protested that they had no choice but to do the same. With northern banks conserving their specie, Baltimore's failure to follow suit could result in the loss of the city's gold.[11]

These cascading suspensions took place within a political system in tumult.

For the past decade, questions about how best to constitute and control a rapidly changing economy had precipitated party formation and realignment. In the mid-1830s, activists within a nascent urban labor movement argued forcefully that the decline of artisanal production and the rise of finance capital had enabled the ascendance of a self-interested elite bent on subverting the American political and economic systems. Paper money stood at the center of their grievances—they held that commercial banknotes, administered by unaccountable institutions, drove the wild inflation that made life in major urban centers increasingly precarious for working-class people. With its fluctuating exchange rates and proliferating forms, paper money did not offer a straightforward index of value, which in turn allowed bankers and bosses to deploy it for speculation and fraud, in the process depriving wage earners of the true value of their labor. By 1837, this critique of paper currencies and the banks that issued them found a home in the antimonopolist Locofoco wing of the Democratic Party, which called for the use of "hard money"—specie—in lieu of paper as a means to avoid the price swings and exploitation associated with banknotes.[12]

Baltimore, like other eastern cities, saw spirited debates over banks' role within the community. As the Second Party System took shape, Baltimore emerged as a largely Democratic city, although this did not prevent an occasional Whig majority in the city council or the election of Whig mayors. Whigs enjoyed disproportionate representation in the city's press; until the Democratic-leaning *Sun* opened its presses in 1837, only one of the city's major dailies—the *Republican*—pronounced for Jackson and his followers. Regardless of affiliation, Baltimore's papers regularly devoted column space to the politics of banking at the local, state, and national levels. At times, such questions spilled outside the editorial pages and onto the streets, most notably in 1835, when malfeasance and maneuverings at the Bank of Maryland triggered three days of rioting.[13]

In the late 1830s, the suspension of specie payments gave questions of commerce and currency new urgency. The staid, Whig-supporting *American* cast the banks as neutral indices of economic conditions, "thermometers of the commercial atmosphere," powerless to alter the financial climate and forced by circumstance to suspend specie payments.[14] The *Sun* sat on the other extreme, characterizing bank suspension as a deliberate and pernicious abdication of legal responsibility set in motion by Nicholas Biddle, president of the Bank of the United States. To the *Sun*'s editors, banks' obligation to redeem their notes overrode all other considerations, even if it meant losing every ounce of gold to New York.[15] Between these two grim assessments of Baltimore's financial realities—one insisting that local institutions had no agency and the other subordinating the financial health of the community to legal principles—lay a spectrum of public opinions on banks' roles within the urban economy. Correspondents to the *Gazette* and the *American* called for banks to cooperate in order to sustain a sound circulating medium.[16] The editors of the *Clipper* argued for bank policy that placed the interests of the citizenry above legal abstractions, asking readers "to look at home, and to consult the interests of the people among whom we were born and raised, and with whom our lot is cast, probably for life."[17]

Baltimoreans had plenty of occasions to rehearse such arguments about the economics and ethics of bank policy; bankers resumed and suspended specie payments repeatedly over the next four years. From 1837 to 1842, Baltimore banks often announced target dates for resumption, and sometimes even began, tentatively, to redeem their notes in specie. But these moves were always contingent on the implementation of similar policies in Philadelphia and New York, and once banks in those cities resuspended specie payment, Baltimore banks followed suit.[18] The seaboard cities' still-novel rail connections allowed the news of suspension to spread quickly and forced bankers to act fast. Baltimore bankers convened an emergency meeting early in the morning of October 10, 1839, when they learned that Philadelphia banks had suspended specie payments the previous day. Before opening their doors, they decided to follow suit. Sure enough, at the start of business later that morning they were greeted by "several brokers from the Eastern cities, who had arrived the night before by the late rail road train." The *American* said that in consequence of the suspension the "city yesterday was exceedingly quiet."[19]

The "quiet" that the *American* reported highlights the overlap between the health of a city's currency and its economic vitality in the nineteenth century. Baltimoreans drew explicit links between the financial health of commercial centers and the movement of goods and people. It is no coincidence that both vehicular traffic and paper notes were said to "circulate"—they represented two types of movement (one of bodies, one of credit) that together sustained the city's economy. Bereft of a strong circulating medium, business slowed, and the consequences manifested in the built environment: less traffic, less construction, fewer exchanges.[20] Cutting off specie payments meant that banks no longer redeemed their notes in gold, which in turn undermined their function as a store of value. The money supply stagnated; no new notes entered circulation, and those that remained on hand depreciated.

The people most adversely affected by the specie suspension were not those who held accounts in the banks but those unable to afford such accounts. Because state law in Maryland and elsewhere prohibited the issue of banknotes for sums below five dollars, many of the poorest Baltimoreans rarely handled paper currency. Instead, in good times at least, the primary circulating medium for low-end transactions was specie, in the form of small silver coins called "fips" or "levies." But the currency vacuum caused by specie suspension quickly sucked up the city's supplies of small change. Banks refused to circulate the change they had in their vaults, and hoarders stockpiled any coins they could get their hands on.[21] This shortage affected Baltimore's retailers and the poor most directly, and they turned to the municipal government for assistance. The city council took such requests seriously, fearing that in the absence of public action, trashy shinplasters might flood the city's channels of circulation, further degrading the local economy. Mayor Samuel Smith announced in 1837 that the city would, following practice in other cities when local banks suspended specie payments, issue its own scrip to provide for community needs.[22]

The city backed its new currency with municipal bonds, meaning that its exchange value would be determined by the city's credit, which rested on the size and vitality of the tax base. This made the city itself the source of value for its circulating medium. A correspondent to the *Gazette* pointed out that banks held some $700,000 in specie while the city housed taxable real estate valued upward of $40 million: "The public can judge from this statement how ridiculous it is to consider specie as the only correct representative of the value of property."[23] In effect, supporters of the new currency argued, city scrip activated value that otherwise sat dormant in Baltimore's buildings, turning it into an engine for growth and circulation so that the city could again, in the words of another correspondent to the *Gazette*, "see the active pick and spade of the industrious laboring man employed and hear the busy hum of the various mechanical branches."[24]

These notions sat poorly with those Baltimoreans who championed specie as the only legitimate source of value—including, most vocally, the editors of the *Baltimore Sun*. The *Sun* countenanced no distinction between city scrip and shinplasters.[25] The editors saw the quality of a city's circulating medium as a reflection of the community itself. To the *Sun* as to other hard-money supporters, nature endowed specie with an inherent value that no human effort could erase or replicate. As such, deviations from the specie standard reflected not just faulty economic reasoning but also defective moral character. Degrading the medium of exchange degraded Baltimore as a market and a polity.[26] The *Sun* illustrated the ties between personal character and the character of exchange when it warned the public about mock notes circulating in 1839, including one that could be "redeemed" with rum. The paper deemed this note "a good currency for 'loafers and suckers,' as it promises to pay in that which is to them more valuable than specie."[27] By proposing a source of value outside of the gold standard, the city demonstrated the moral acumen of a drunkard.

The *Sun*'s protests notwithstanding, scrip from the municipal government circulated within Baltimore as currency from 1837 to 1839, but in neither the volume nor the denominations that banknotes had during more prosperous times. There remained a dearth of money for ordinary transactions, particularly in small change.[28] Rather than issue more of its own notes, however, the city council chose to use this crisis to meet another pressing need—funding the construction of the B&O Railroad.

The Origins of the B&O Note

Popular wisdom in the 1830s held that the fortunes of the B&O and its terminal city were closely intertwined. The success of one would reinforce the other, as Baltimore's growth would draw more traffic to the railroad and increased rail traffic would foster urban growth. By the end of the decade, though, the fortunes of the two entities had become interdependent in a more practical way, through the mechanisms of finance. The municipal government and local citizens' sizable investments in the railroad tied the city's immediate economic fortunes to the B&O's stock price. Banks accepted B&O stock as collateral for loans, helping to propel other investments in the city. *Niles' Weekly Register* noted in 1834 that the company's stock, when at par or above, "add[s] to the circulation of values, and serve[s] all the great purposes of money." Conversely, though, when its value ebbed much of the city's money was "locked-up" in the railroad, "a severe check to 'forward' industry." Improving the railroad's business could transform Baltimore's commerce in more than the obvious ways.[29]

Thus, the railroad's slow progress in the late 1830s compounded fears of economic decline and stagnation in Baltimore. From 1828 to 1832 the B&O laid sixty-nine miles of track from Baltimore to the Potomac River at Point of Rocks, only to stand in place for the next five years, stymied by legal and financial difficulties. The C&O Canal, making its own way west from Georgetown, objected to sharing right-of-way with the railroad along the river valley and issued injunctions against the B&O that held up construction for two years. Once the canal and the railroad arranged to share space in the riverbed, the B&O quickly extended its line to Harpers Ferry at the juncture of the Shenandoah and Potomac Rivers, but here, too, it stalled, this time for want of funds.[30] The state of Maryland and the city of Baltimore each authorized loans of $3 million to pay for westward construction, but neither could sell bonds in European markets amid the depression. The situation appeared dire. The line would yield no substantial returns until it could at least connect with the National Road at Cumberland and profit from the coal trade there.[31] Yet the city's bonds, for want of a buyer, sat idle, unable to provide the capital needed to continue laying track.

The weight of the public's disappointment in the B&O fell on an increasingly dyspeptic Philip E. Thomas, and in 1836 he resigned the presidency. To replace him, the board of directors looked outside of Baltimore, selecting the Delaware-born diplomat and statesman Louis W. McLane. "With a President so marked as Mr. McLane for talent, resources, and energy, the day is not distant when all our most sanguine expectations will be realized," enthused the *Baltimore Republican*. McLane's résumé advertised him as someone with friends in high places. He had represented Delaware in both houses of Congress before serving successively as minister to the United Kingdom, secretary of the Treasury, and secretary of state in the administration of Andrew Jackson. As the B&O struggled to finance its construction, the board hoped that McLane's political acuity could help the company sell its bonds overseas. John H. B. Latrobe, though, found his new boss's attitude as haughty as his connections, characterizing him later as a man who did not brook dissent. This might not have been such a problem had Latrobe trusted McLane's business instincts, but in the lawyer's view, at least, McLane demonstrated neither sound judgment nor much interest in his new position.[32]

Still, this was not McLane's first foray into the private sector; before coming to the B&O, he enjoyed a profitable and productive stint as president of the Morris Canal and Banking Company in New Jersey. McLane had taken this position in no small part to secure the promised $6,000 annual salary, a massive sum for the time that helped him provide for the education of his twelve children. To lure him to Baltimore, the B&O had to match McLane's former salary, which exceeded the $4,000 per annum afforded to Thomas. In any event, after a stint in New York, McLane appears to have been ready to return south. Breaking from his abolitionist father, McLane had become an enthusiastic enslaver, owning ten people by the time of his death. His political instincts told him that he had better secure a position below the Mason-Dixon line in anticipation of conflict between the North and the South.[33]

Nonetheless, McLane's arrival in Baltimore in mid-1837 was not a happy homecoming; when he examined the company he helmed, he did not like what he saw. "Public confidence, not only in the extension of the work westward, but in the working of the existing road, appeared to be entirely withdrawn," he later recalled. He could regain that confidence only with a ready supply of cash.[34] His most recent employer, which had combined canal-building and banking operations, offered one model for how an internal improvement company could take on financial responsibilities, but he opted for a different solution. In November 1839, he laid a proposal before the board of directors that deployed a novel means to make use of the $3 million in municipal bonds (known as "city stock") that had sat unsold since 1836. Rather than receiving cash from the sale of the city stock, the B&O would take the bond certificates and store them in the company's headquarters. The railroad company would then print notes in varying denominations that, when presented to the company in sums divisible by $100, could be redeemed for the equivalent number of $100 interest-bearing city stock certificates. (Though unremarked upon at the time, this provision ensured that the notes would serve as a convertible currency for only the wealthiest Baltimoreans). By paying its employees in these notes and accepting them for all debts owed to the company, the B&O could not only continue its westward progress but also provide a functional medium of exchange for its terminal city. The company's Committee of Finance endorsed McLane's proposal enthusiastically. Acknowledging that some in the community might object to paper money in principle, the committee maintained that currency ought to be understood as "merely the medium of exchange of the products of Capital and labor." The notes' security in municipal bonds meant that the urban public would gain a circulating medium far safer than any shinplasters.[35]

The company revealed its plan to the public in December. Mayor Sheppard Leakin, a Whig, endorsed the program a month later, predicting that the citizens of Baltimore and the surrounding areas would quickly adopt this medium of exchange. The majority-Democratic city council likewise favored the new currency.[36] Despite this bipartisan support, not everyone shared Mayor Leakin's optimism; voices of dissent came from the press, the statehouse, and within the board of directors. Before the company's announcement, the *Sun*, predictably, denigrated the proposal as a means to displace specie as the basis of value. "We advise the public not to touch one of them [railroad notes], even with a pair of tongs," wrote the *Sun* in 1838.[37] Governor William Grason, a Democrat, apparently shared the *Sun*'s concerns, warning that these issuances would introduce "complete confusion" to Maryland's economy.[38] On the board of directors, too, questions about the legality of creating a new circulating medium troubled two city directors, but they were voted down.[39]

A number of Baltimoreans took to the press to respond to these complaints, and in doing so, they characterized the B&O notes as a new kind of money. The new currency, wrote a correspondent to the pro-Democratic *Baltimore Republican*, held a higher purpose than "the emolument of any monied or private Banking Corporation." It was, rather, a "scheme" to complete a "great public improvement." In a financial landscape already ravaged by controversies over bank regulation and the uncertainties of an increasingly complex economy, the notes reflected a way to secure a stable source of value by insulating the currency from fluctuations abroad. In part, they did this by bypassing the central problem posed by banknotes—the danger that the paper in circulation would surpass stores of specie. B&O notes were not promissory but instead were commodities in their own right: small-denomination city bonds. A bank run to cash in B&O notes was unlikely, if not impossible, because each one represented an equivalent value in city stock.[40]

More fundamentally, though, the B&O notes' basis in municipal bonds offered a new way to think about exchange. The value of city bonds rested on the city's ability to meet its interest payments, which in turn stemmed from the size and vitality of the tax base. This tax base included all of the real and personal property held in the city—including property in human beings. Maryland's constitution prescribed a uniform tax rate for all forms of property in order to forestall efforts by the state's non-slaveholding majority to tax slavery out of existence. In practice, assessors routinely underestimated the market value of the enslaved by as much as 70 percent, making investments in slavery a tax haven for white city dwellers. Nonetheless, even in this attenuated form, anchoring the B&O notes in municipal bonds helped turn the bodies and labor of the enslaved into the basis for everyday transactions.[41]

Most writers who defended the B&O notes stressed another foundation for the notes—real estate. Unlike personal property or specie, real estate constituted an inalienable source of value and served as the bedrock of municipal tax revenues. Writers who defended the new currency thus argued that it secured its value in the built environment of the city itself. In the judgment of the *Clipper*, this made these notes preferable to "any other paper currency, because, unless Baltimore be destroyed by an earthquake, or totally consumed by fire, (very improbable events,) it is impossible that the guarantee for their redemption can fail." That the city stock could not sell at par on the open market was irrelevant; although bond prices rose and fell according to short-term stimuli, their value resided in the viability of the community. The B&O note took Baltimore's future growth as the starting point for exchange, assuming that increased circulation would ultimately drive urban expansion. As property values went up, so, too, would the value of the municipal bonds. Confidence in the note meant confidence in the city.[42]

Transferring the bonds to the B&O rather than selling them in London benefited the public in another way as well. As long as the bonds remained in the B&O's possession—that is, as long as the notes circulated as currency—they did not accrue interest, which meant that the city government could avoid collecting taxes to meet the interest obligation. As the B&O put it in a communication to the Maryland legislature in 1841, the notes served the public both as a convenient currency and as a mechanism that made the public subscription to the railroad available—and at seemingly no cost.[43]

Managing the Currency

The B&O started engraving plates to print five- and ten-dollar certificates on December 11, 1839, adding one-dollar bills a week later. In the absence of specie-paying banknotes, these "railroad notes" quickly became the principal currency of the city. Their number and denominations proliferated. By the end of summer, 1840, the B&O had placed $505,000 in circulation (table 3.1).[44] The B&O's $1, $2, and $3 bills circumvented legal restrictions on notes below $5, but the city's most pressing monetary need remained a small-note currency in the sub-$1 (or "fractional") denominations that had previously circulated as silver fips and levies, which could facilitate the minor transactions that comprised the bulk of ordinary commercial life.[45] Both retailers and their customers continued to complain about a shortage of small change.[46]

At the council's request, in February 1841 the B&O began issuing notes worth less than a dollar. The company explained to the state legislature that their notes drove out inferior currencies and gave the citizens of Baltimore "a small note circulation which depends for its value not upon the produce or ability of the board or individual that issues it, but upon the wealth and resources of the commercial emporium of Maryland."[47] The *Sun*, of course, objected, insisting that maintaining the ban on sub-$1 notes would eventually force hoarders to circulate the silver fips presently stashed in their vaults.[48] But for news outlets like the *Clipper*, an insistence on metal change placed a misguided faith in the value of specie over the interests of the community. After all, the B&O notes helped the community avoid a tax, and forcing the resumption of specie payments might undermine their value. Proposals like

TABLE 3.1. B&O notes in circulation, fall 1840

Denomination	Number of notes	Nominal value
$100	100	$10,000
$5	6,800	$34,000
$3	13,000	$39,000
$2	39,000	$78,000
$1	354,000	$354,000
Redeemed		−$10,000
Circulating (as of 30 September 1840)	412,900	$505,000

Source: Adapted from *AR* 14 (1840): 11.

the *Sun*'s threatened the public good just "to give a few grasping individuals the power to jingle specie in their pockets."[49]

Specie had at least one tangible advantage over paper money: coins held their shape as they passed from hand to hand. The new notes, by contrast, quickly became damaged or defaced as they entered widespread use. This posed a problem for the B&O, which served as a clearinghouse for the new currency, exchanging worn bills for clean copies. Acting in this capacity forced the company to exercise judgment on matters far removed from transportation. Clerks had to decide, when confronted with a "mutilated" bill, whether to replace it or not. When the company began offering fifty cents in exchange for badly damaged notes of any greater denomination, it only confused matters further.[50]

The B&O offered this compromise to hedge against fraud. The layout of the notes proved a tempting target for counterfeiters, who had perfected a system for manipulating the notes by August 1840. It worked like this: counterfeiters obtained several high-value bills and one similar-looking note of a lower value. Then, after carefully cutting out the numbers from the high-value notes so as not to sacrifice their viability for exchange, they pasted those numbers onto the lower-value note. This subterfuge meant that notes had to be read carefully—one needed to know that, for example, the left-hand vignette of the fifty-cent note represented the goddess Minerva, and the 12.5-cent note's vignette featured the goddess of liberty and another female figure.[51]

In some ways, theft (and its prevention) helped establish the legitimacy of this new currency. In October 1840, a swindler exploited uncertainty about the value of the notes to defraud laborers on the Main Stem of the B&O, convincing them to exchange their wages for what turned out to be fictitious banknotes. Many workers lost more than a year's worth of savings.[52] In other places and times, shinplasters' questionable legal status meant that such depredations did not necessarily violate the law. In 1841, though, the city council asked the state legislature to make theft of B&O notes a felony, as was the case with banknotes.[53] The notes came to parallel banknotes in other ways as well. In the summer of 1841, the *Sun* reported with astonishment the appearance of compound shinplasters—notes redeemable in B&O notes, designed to resemble them so as to confuse the unwary.[54]

The stock orders did not circulate in Baltimore alone. B&O notes proliferated along the rail routes. The Philadelphia, Wilmington & Baltimore Railroad accepted the stock orders as currency, thus giving them passage up and down the northeastern United States. The B&O brought them south to Washington and west to Harpers Ferry and beyond.[55] By the summer of 1840, the notes constituted the predominant small-denomination currency in the nation's capital, and as of November 1841, they were ubiquitous in Maryland, Virginia, Delaware, and Pennsylvania as well.[56] Few people outside of Baltimore showed any enthusiasm for the currency. Public officials in other cities attempted ineffectually to drive the B&O notes out of circulation.[57] As the *Sun* had feared, the railroad notes assumed metonymic significance for Baltimore's commercial integrity. The Philadelphia *Ledger* wrote in August 1841 that Baltimoreans "really appear to take all that is offered to them [as currency] with the greatest indifference, and evince no little surprise that a stranger should intimate that a bag full of the worthless trash in any other community would fail to purchase him a single meal."[58]

Gouge's Journal of Banking, a staunch advocate of hard-money principles, made the comparison between Baltimore and Philadelphia even more explicit in an 1842 article chiding the former city for disobeying the "*natural law*" of currency: that currency of lesser value drives out that of greater. The B&O's decision to issue bills in denominations as small as six and one-quarter cents had directly caused the present scarcity of silver small change in Baltimore, the *Journal* wrote. Less than a hundred miles away in Philadelphia, by contrast, strictly enforced laws prohibiting such notes, and in consequence, enough silver remained in circulation to answer the needs of retail.[59] The people of Baltimore had arrayed themselves against laws of trade that were beyond the power of humans to nullify.

Diagnosing Depreciation

In Baltimore, though, the currency worked, at least for a while. By 1841, the B&O notes came to perform almost every function fulfilled by specie-backed banknotes during better times (fig. 3.1). The *Sun* complained that the railroad's "'stock orders' have filled nearly, if not altogether, all the ordinary channels of circulation here."[60] All channels but one; the city's banks, though delinquent in supplying their own circulating media, neither accepted B&O notes on deposit nor paid them out. Many in the press and within the railroad company assumed that this refusal stemmed from bankers' doubts about the legality of such payments and thus suggested that the state legislature permit banks to accept B&O notes on deposit. Such a measure would not require banks to redeem notes in specie but merely to aid in their circulation. The B&O's directors considered this essential to the notes' success and figured (or at least hoped) that bankers' interest in public welfare would lead them to embrace such a plan. In a memorial to the state legislature, the company characterized

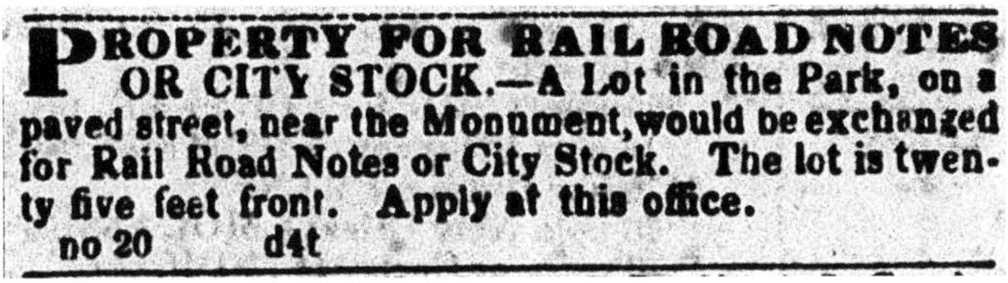

PROPERTY FOR RAIL ROAD NOTES OR CITY STOCK.—A Lot in the Park, on a paved street, near the Monument, would be exchanged for Rail Road Notes or City Stock. The lot is twenty five feet front. Apply at this office.
    no 20   d4t

FIGURE 3.1. Ad from the *American*, 20 November 1841. Courtesy of the Periodicals Department, Enoch Pratt Free Library, Maryland's State Resource Center.

banks as actors embedded in an interconnected local economy, dependent on "the prosperity of the community," which in turn hinged on the success of the railroad. This long-term view of the city's economic prospects surely superseded any short-term profits bankers stood to earn if their institutions issued their own small notes, they reasoned.[61] The legislature concurred and authorized Maryland banks to receive and pay out the stock orders.[62] Having obtained legislative license, the company arranged a meeting with the bankers at which they offered to pay the difference between market value and par price of city stock held by any institution that accepted the orders.[63]

Shortly after the bill passed, though, the *Clipper* reported a 5 percent discount on the B&O notes. The sudden downgrading of the city's circulating medium baffled the editors, especially because banks had been authorized to take these notes at par. Some writers figured that the depreciation had to be attributable, at least in part, to fears that the B&O had printed too many notes, but even with approximately $63,000 worth of new stock orders entering circulation every month, the nominal value of the currency as of March 1841 had not yet reached half of the $2.3 million in bank paper that had fueled Baltimore's economy before the specie suspension (table 3.2). The *Clipper* surmised that the "sudden reduction in value is the result of misrepresentation and trickery."[64]

Some blamed, in the familiar language of antebellum moral economy, the city's "brokers and shavers" for this rapid decline, but most soon pinned the sudden discount on another culprit: the city's banks. Although by then legally entitled to circulate the B&O currency, the banks chose not to do so. The *American* diagnosed the problem at once: "If the Banks would agree to receive these notes they would rise at once to par. There is no unwillingness on the part of the community to receive them." The community did not need banks to legitimate the currency, as its value was innate, and railroad notes continued to change hands at par for ordinary transactions in Baltimore. People who owed money to the banks, though, could not pay their debts in these

TABLE 3.2. B&O notes in circulation, spring 1841

Denomination	Value in circulation
$100	$10,000
$5	$34,000
$2 and $3	$234,000
$1	$563,000
$0.50, $0.25, and $0.125	$3,000
Circulating (as of 27 February 1841)	$844,200

Source: Adapted from Sun, 11 March 1841.

notes, and because banks provided credit and stored funds for the city's businesses, their refusal to handle the railroad currency limited its utility and thus
depressed its value.[65]

The banks refused the notes, the press speculated, in order to force
their own paper currency on the citizens of Baltimore. The depreciation of
what one writer called "the people's circulation" thus stemmed from an act
of private malfeasance against the public good, an exercise of power by the
bankers over the community.[66] The Clipper anticipated that bankers' insis-
tence on receiving their own non-specie-paying notes would lead ultimately
to a flood of unredeemable shinplasters, the withdrawal of railroad notes
from circulation, a tax hike as the city started paying interest on its bonds—
and a tidy profit for the banks.[67] The normally even-keeled American warned
bankers that such narrow self-interest did not make for sustainable public
policy. If they continued to ignore the needs of the community, they were
courting a public response that went beyond the realm of print. A letter from
"The People" in the Clipper ominously cautioned "our would be masters, the
'Banks'" to "remember that the physical strength resides in the governed."
Such warnings bore extra weight in light of the bank riots six years prior.[68]

Banks drew the preponderance of blame in 1841, but the B&O did not escape criticism. A few writers characterized the currency scheme as a mechanism by which the company could further its expansion westward while shifting the sacrifice onto the community. One went so far as to reject pious claims
that the railroad would serve the common good, as its traffic offered scant
benefit "to the great mass of the retailers and smaller business-men, who are
now made to bear the whole burden which has grown out of this mad policy
[i.e., stock orders.]"[69] As this comment suggested, laborers, retailers, and
other working-class Baltimoreans had the most to lose as these notes declined
in value. Bankers could refuse to take B&O notes, but shopkeepers had no
choice—the notes had become the "retail currency" of the city.[70] One critic—
John M. Gordon, president of the Union Bank of Baltimore, who wrote under

the pseudonym "Vindex"—maintained that only the city's "aristocrats" prof-
ited from the currency. Rich men used B&O notes to pay wages as employers,
only to turn around and demand rent in bankable currency as landlords.[71]

The city council recognized the problem Vindex posed even as it disagreed
with his diagnosis of the cause. Councilmen maintained that the public as a
whole shared a responsibility to sustain the stock orders (and, in so doing, to
sustain the B&O) and took it upon themselves to bolster the city's medium
of exchange in February 1841. They enlisted the city treasury in their cause,
resolving to accept B&O notes in payment of city taxes and to remit the same
to meet city expenses.[72] In sanctioning a new use for the notes, the council
hoped to counter an already-palpable decline. But the *Sun* suggested later
that this move only spurred further inflation. The notes, after all, represented
municipal bonds, which constituted a sound investment so long as the city
government could pay interest. But because the council had voted to take
the notes in payment for its taxes, it would have to sell more bonds to raise the
money to meet its interest obligations. This glut of municipal bonds on the
market would reduce their value and thus depreciate the currency.[73]

"It Is Time for the People to Act"

In November 1841, the Baltimore weekly *Argus* wrote of a man who walked
into a bank and offered railroad paper to pay his debt, which the teller refused. He then drew "from his pocket three hundred dollars in the money of
the identical bank" and demanded specie for it, saying: "If you do not receive
my railroad notes, I will proceed to the magistrate and issue a warrant on each
note I have in my possession in your bank. They hesitated not long . . . but
brought forward the note, which was paid by the railroad orders just refused.
Will not everyone act thus? It is time for the people to act decidedly."[74] The editors of the *Argus* were not the only ones who believed that the currency situation warranted decisive action, individually and collectively. Louis McLane
argued in October 1841 that Baltimoreans themselves could "do much to sustain or depress the standard of these orders,—to quiet or spread alarm."[75] He
wrote amid a growing push for a public solution to the currency depreciation,
as the press buzzed with reports of meetings between railroad directors, city
councilmen, and bankers.[76] The *American* published a variety of proposals
designed to raise the B&O notes to par, most of which involved mandating
that banks accept them on deposit, interest payments for deposited notes, and
a reduction of the number in circulation.[77]

As these correspondents suggested proposals, citizens organized a "Currency Convention" in the late fall of 1841. The convention, comprising rep-

resentatives elected from each ward, sought to mediate between the banks, the B&O, and the city council. When it met in November, the convention declared that as Baltimore's banks had abandoned the citizenry, the citizenry must now abandon the banks. It proposed reviving the Franklin Bank, a savings bank that had failed the previous January, as a bank of deposit for the B&O notes.[78] The city council approved this plan and the Franklin Bank's directors agreed to pay 5 percent interest on B&O note deposits. At first the arrangement seemed poised to restore the notes to their former strength. The notes' market value increased slightly, the discount falling to between 5.5 percent and 6.5 percent.[79] But in the long run these incentives did not stop the notes' decline. Even with $250,000 in orders on deposit at the Franklin Bank, the mayor reported in January 1842 that too many remained in circulation to prevent depreciation.[80]

Meanwhile, representatives from the city's other banking institutions did not let the public criticism they received go unanswered. Many of the city's bankers communicated with the citizen committees and the city council, the most vocal being the head of a bank closely connected with the B&O—the Mechanics' Bank of Baltimore. The Mechanics' Bank had served as the bank of deposit for the railroad's early funds, and Philip E. Thomas had been the president of that institution before heading the railroad. The man at the helm of the bank in 1841 was John B. Morris, who had been the youngest founding director of the railroad and had given the keynote address at the cornerstone-laying ceremony in 1828. Morris announced that the directors of his bank were "unable and unwilling" to handle notes selling at a 15 percent discount.[81] City stock could not substitute for gold. The notes' "purpose as a circulation is merely conventional, depending on the discretion of those who receive them, and cannot be used by a Bank as a set off for any liability it may have incurred." As these orders would vary in value with the market price of city stock, receiving them would be equivalent to investing in depreciated bonds.[82]

The Currency Convention reacted sharply to this logic. Pronouncing the nation's banking system "radically wrong," the convention proposed an avowedly public solution. Its report declared that "these orders are emphatically the currency of the *people of Baltimore*—brought into existence by them—created for their benefit *as a whole*—and that honor, patriotism, and interest all combine—to unite all in sustaining them." Because the notes continued, despite the banks' efforts, to serve the public's day-to-day needs, the convention framed the central problem facing the citizenry as a choice between a sound public medium of exchange and the proliferation of dubious private notes. The convention called for decisive political action: interest payments for notes in circulation, a municipal buyback of several hundred thousands of dollars' worth of them, and mandatory resumption of specie payments regardless of the consequences for the city's banks.[83]

Nothing came of these proposals, but the public debates over banking policy and currency adjustment drew critical notice in northern cities. The *United States Gazette*, based in Philadelphia, declared Baltimore "a Loco foco Anti-Bank city" and mocked efforts to impose by "force" new burdens on the banks by asking them to deal in railroad notes.[84] Although Philadelphia's currency had itself suffered as creditors in New York and Boston drained its specie, papers in that city tut-tutted the Baltimore public for violating, as one put it, "every rule of banking."[85] By late 1841, more than a few of Baltimore's own citizens took to the press to warn their neighbors that the currency question had brought their city into disrepute.[86]

Many Baltimoreans, though, considered the "rules of banking" subordinate to the interests of the community, and they took to the street to demonstrate their views in large public meetings from the autumn of 1841 to the spring of 1842. These meetings depicted monetary questions as a matter of public policy rather than economic law and said that banks' specie suspension had created room for experimentation. One meeting resolved that, under trying circumstances, "the public has a right to adopt . . . that [currency] which it may deem the preferable."[87] Many defended the railroad notes as something more than a necessary evil. When the city's butchers met in January 1842 to pledge their collective commitment to the currency, for example, they celebrated it as an essential feature of working-class Baltimore life.[88] Not every meeting embraced a populist politics or economic vocabulary, though. Several of the gatherings brought the public together only to create committees led by businessmen, or else conducted smaller closed conventions of ward representatives who wrote resolutions that they then reported back to the public at large. And not every meeting sought to bolster the railroad currency—some looked to hasten its demise.[89]

Yet the economic elite who called these public gatherings quickly learned the limits of their authority. These were popular initiatives, subject to the approval or disapproval of the crowd. In late January 1842, W. I. Van Ness, a grocer, called a meeting at the Exchange Building to discuss the "propriety of reducing"—rather than increasing—"the current value of the Baltimore and Ohio railroad orders." The massive assemblage that greeted him at the Exchange undermined this goal. As Van Ness tried to call the meeting to order, he found himself shouted down. Contrary to the meeting's stated goals, the crowd resolved instead to sustain the B&O notes and to resist efforts to depreciate them. In the *Sun*'s account, after reading the first resolution, "The room being at this time excessively crowded, a general cry arose of, 'to the street! to the street!!' so to the street they went as they best could, crushing, rushing, crowding, jostling, &c." Van Ness made his way through the dense throng to a seat on the steps of a private house across from the Exchange, where he found himself presiding over a meeting whose attendees vowed to advance the B&O notes to par.[90] Removing the mass meeting from the Exchange Building to the street underscored the power of the people as a body and highlighted the significance of public space as a site of deliberation and popular action. Standing in the street, they asserted their prerogative to determine financial policy by insisting on a currency whose value rested in public economy rather than private power.

Critical observers both inside and outside Baltimore found such open-air declarations at once absurd and ominous. Dismissive writers in Baltimore's papers responded to the currency meetings as they had to the track protests a decade earlier—with satire. Newspaper correspondents lampooned the idea that currency fluctuations could be the subject of public policy.[91] A reporter for the *New York Herald*, on the ground in Baltimore, likewise found the demonstrations ludicrous. His coverage of a meeting from November 1841 featured comic-opera portrayals of incompetent speakers trying to sustain the inflated currency and sober but futile attempts by bankers to explain the folly of such efforts. As the value of the currency sunk further below par, the protests assumed a dangerous aspect in this reporter's eyes. A dispatch describing a rally held in March 1842 reflected his concerns about urban democracy. This meeting, convened through public notice by a "little man, hardly knee high to a duck, who sells lozenges," drew as many as five thousand people. The reporter found it disconcerting that a figure as ridiculous as "Ducklegs" could summon so large a crowd: "Such meetings have an inflammatory and dangerous tendency and should be suppressed," he concluded.[92] Whereas the open-air meetings defined currency matters as political questions subject to public action, such comic renderings sought to remove the state of the currency from the realm of public deliberation entirely.

As citizens gathered in the street—and wags mocked them in the press—the city government and the railroad corporation struggled to devise a plan to revive the sagging notes. Some argued that depreciation was simply a self-correcting market at work.[93] But the B&O did not trust the market in this instance. The company had already resolved in October 1841 to cease issuing stock orders until it could retire some of them from circulation. The board also refused to continue accepting the city's $3 million subscription in stock orders, insisting instead on bankable paper.[94] The company continued to take the stock orders in receipt for fares and pay them out to employees at their nominal value through the end of the year, but it attempted to hand the management of the stock orders over to the city.[95] The company's creditors increasingly refused payment in stock orders even as the notes remained the predominant currency the railroad received from customers.[96]

As the company distanced itself from the orders, the city government scrambled to find a way to counter the depreciation. Mayor Samuel Brady framed this as a top priority in December 1841, but any legislative action entailed risks to the city's credit and income flow. A number of proposals were drafted but did not make it to a vote.[97] One bill, calling for the payment of 5 percent interest on the stock orders, did make it to Mayor Brady's desk, but he vetoed it, fearing it would add to the city's debt without necessarily improving the currency.[98] In lieu of paying interest on the notes, Brady suggested in his annual message that the city use any surplus in the 1843 budget to fund and retire the orders.[99] Brady was at odds with his city council on this matter, however; on January 10, frustrated at the "difficulty" he had encountered, he contemplated resigning his office.[100]

Unlike the municipal government—and much to its chagrin—the state evinced no inclination to improve the value of the stock orders. The currency's depreciation coincided with a broader shift in the state's relationship to the B&O: as the general depression continued, the state government found its heavy internal improvement debt increasingly difficult to bear. For Maryland, as for many other similarly indebted states, the early 1840s marked a turning point; after the state defaulted on its interest payments in 1842, it never again furnished financial aid for internal improvement companies, a decision later formalized in an 1851 constitutional amendment that barred such practices.[101] Straitened circumstances left the Maryland legislature in no mood to accept B&O notes in payment for taxes and fees, and it started to move against the currency it had previously authorized.[102] In March 1842, the state passed a new law to ensure that the railroad never again attempted such an issue, declaring that any officer of the B&O who authorized the circulation of notes worth less than five dollars could be fined or jailed.[103]

Public faith in the orders also deteriorated through the winter of 1841–1842. Unlike the butchers, who had resolved to take the stock orders at par value, one trade group after another convened meetings at which they determined to accept the notes only at a discount. The *Sun* used these occasions to call attention to its *"Prophecy Fulfilled"*—of all the daily papers, Democratic and Whig alike, only the *Sun* had objected to these notes. Dry-goods dealers moved first, announcing in February 1842 their intention to take B&O notes only at their market value (a 20 percent discount at the time). Grocers followed suit, and shoe dealers moved soon after.[104] Some protested that these efforts violated the spirit of the open public meetings that had acted to boost the B&O notes to par. After all, it had been a meeting of grocers to downgrade the currency that had poured out into the street and called for its elevation.[105] But retailers insisted they had a moral obligation to take the notes at their real value. Their solution was collective as well: "Let LABOURERS, MECHANICS, DEALERS, EVERYBODY, COMBINE to put an end to this" currency.[106]

As retailers began discounting the stock orders, workers began to refuse them. A number of watchmen petitioned the city for compensation in current funds.[107] Likewise, when the B&O attempted to boost the currency by mandating the payment of all employees in railroad orders, many of them protested. Contractors on the line requested company bonds in lieu of B&O notes, and several workers at the Mount Clare depot were fired for refusing to take the stock orders. Fearing a lawsuit, the board's Committee on Finance recommended paying wages in a stronger currency.[108] By late March, the company decided it was time to abandon the railroad orders. The board declared on March 21 that actions by the government and circumstances "wholly beyond their control" had "entirely deprived these orders of their character or utility as a currency," and resolved henceforth to receive only viable monies.[109]

This left the matter in the hands of the city government, which moved to retire the railroad notes. Withdrawing from circulation a currency so deeply embedded in the city's economy and municipal finances proved to be a delicate and controversial process. City authorities complained that they had worked hard to sustain the notes but without the aid of state or railroad authorities. After plans to raise taxes to fund the stock orders came to naught, the council rescinded its earlier resolution accepting them in payment of taxes and offered a 25 percent premium to any corporate body that would agree to fund up to $500,000 in the now-defunct currency. Ultimately, the city took on another $500,000 in debt to do the job itself.[110] The debacle produced at least one political casualty: Mayor Brady, who announced his resignation on March 11. He objected to the final measures the council had taken to retire the currency and relinquished his position so that the government could "harmonize."[111]

By the end of March 1842, the railroad notes were largely defunct (fig. 3.2).[112] "'The best currency in the world,' has suddenly disappeared from our view," wrote the *Sun* as the notes slid to a 50 percent discount, "but not without leaving numberless evils in its train."[113] The city burned $800,000 in stock orders in mid-April.[114] But the city's underlying currency woes remained: when the state mandated the resumption of specie payments in May 1842, banks sharply restricted their issuances, and a wave of bankruptcies ensued. Perhaps this is why, despite the B&O notes' rock-bottom valuation, a trace

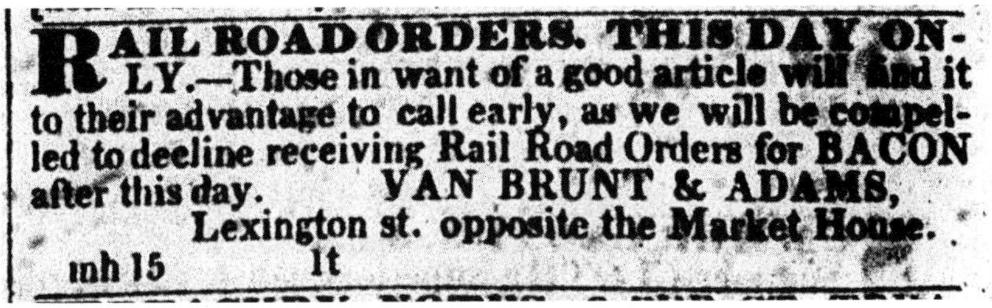

RAIL ROAD ORDERS. THIS DAY ON-
LY.—Those in want of a good article will find it
to their advantage to call early, as we will be compelled to decline receiving Rail Road Orders for BACON
after this day.   VAN BRUNT & ADAMS,
       Lexington st. opposite the Market House.
mh 15   1t

FIGURE 3.2. Ad from the *American*, 15 March 1842. Courtesy of the Periodicals Department, Enoch Pratt Free Library, Maryland's State Resource Center.

number of them lingered in circulation even into the next winter, leading the *Sun* to pronounce their death again in January 1843.[115]

Aftermath

The railroad notes went up in smoke, but they lingered for decades in public memory. Lawmakers in Annapolis grew more cautious when legislating for the B&O. An 1846 bill authorizing the company to issue corporate bonds contained an important caveat: "*Provided*, that nothing herein contained shall be taken to authorize the said company to issue any thing in the nature of a banknote, or other paper, to be used for circulation as currency."[116] The company's chroniclers came to regard the stock orders as a crafty and public-minded initiative, a means to make the most of a difficult financial market. The B&O's Transportation Secretary in the late 1850s, William Prescott Smith, wrote a history of the company in which he devoted several pages to the financial maneuverings of the McLane administration. He deemed the stock orders a "master-stroke of policy," one that enabled the city to comply with its obligations without sacrifice.[117]

For others, though, the stock orders indicated the railroad's abuse of power and public trust. In 1871, John M. Gordon—the former president of the Union Bank of Baltimore, who had signed himself "Vindex" in communications with the *Sun*—waxed bitterly about McLane's railroad orders. In a tract largely given over to Gordon's racist rants about postemancipation African Americans in Norfolk, Virginia, where he was living, he found space to complain of the "bright financial scheme" that had, thirty years earlier, "saturated" Baltimore's currency supply. Gordon's immediate objective in writing this pamphlet was to persuade Virginia to drive the B&O from its borders, but he drew another postwar parallel that indicated the position of these notes within the financial landscape. McLane's scheme, he said, had "since been copied, on a colossal scale, by the fraudulent, rebel government at Washington." The "railroad circulation and the greenback . . . are as little *a* and big *A*."[118] Gordon was a racist and a crank, but on this he may not have been wrong. The federal government's greenback money rested ultimately in public confidence in the strength and power of the nation, much as B&O notes drew their value from their security in the city's tax base.[119]

Although he did not allude to this in his writings, Gordon likely realized that the B&O had funded its first incursion into Virginia with those same funds. The currency accomplished its immediate goal—it turned the buildings and property of Baltimore into iron rails. Fueled by this municipal bond-backed currency, B&O workers laid tracks along the Virginia side of the Potomac River, finally reaching the coal mines of Cumberland in 1843. To this day, freight trains run along a route carved by labor funded with B&O notes. In the end, the real beneficiaries of this currency scheme were not the people of Baltimore but the railroad's executives.

Conclusion

The story of the B&O note is one of the powerful appropriating others' resources and labor to enrich themselves. The company financed construction for the crucial stretch of track from Harpers Ferry to Cumberland by shifting the risks to working people and the urban public at large, an almost improvisatory strategy that highlights the contingent origins of even the bedrock material structure of capitalist enterprise. The story also affirms the power of the railroad executives' temporary antagonists: the bankers. Perhaps the notes would have collapsed regardless of the bankers' resistance; indeed, the history of currency in antebellum America suggests that that was the most likely outcome. Still, it appears that the manner in which the notes failed owed as much to the political will of the city's banking institutions as it did to any instability intrinsic to the currency. Like many controversies in the Jacksonian period, the contest over the B&O note was metapolitical, an argument about what types of matters can be subject to public review. Bankers achieved their objectives by denying their agency, arguing that the rapid depreciation of the notes in 1841 followed inevitably from their departure from the intrinsic value of specie rather than their institutions' policies.

The rise and fall of the B&O note reminds us, though, that the meaning of value was still up for debate in the 1840s. Many saw "the currency of the People" as an opportunity to resolve the representational problems associated with paper money—the disjuncture between the value it proclaimed and the goods it could purchase—by binding the community's medium of exchange to something as tangible as the ground they walked on, using the promise of urban growth to foster exchange. Their rallies, conventions, and debates reflected a belief that collective action could sustain and develop the economic life of the community. Questions about how and whether to shore up the B&O note in the autumn and winter of 1841–1842 were thus also questions about political economy—who had the power to control the means of exchange, the legitimacy of monetary regulations, and the boundaries of public interest. When the mechanics and city officials who supported Baltimore's currency experiment argued that municipal credit could facilitate transactions and stimulate growth, they offered an urban antecedent to what would be, within the subsequent few decades, a major, global shift in monetary policy—the territorialization of currency by national governments, which seized control of the media of exchange within their borders.[120] In all likelihood, Baltimore City was too small and its borders too porous to pursue such initiatives successfully, yet this postscript also suggests that, for all the bankers' protests, the railroad currency may not have been as utopian as it appeared. Shifting the history of finance from the ledger book to the street underscores the political process by which controversial economic practices become foundational economic principles, beyond the reach of democratic oversight. The mechanics' protest at Monument Square and others like it challenged the notion that the world of commerce was governed by laws they were powerless to alter.

Straight Lines and Crooked Rates

In 1845, after more than a decade of track debates, financial struggles, and currency controversies, Louis McLane still promised an anxious public that, upon completion of the B&O, "Baltimore shall become, what nature originally intended her to be, second to none of the cities of the Union."[1] Those looking for evidence of nature's intent needed only to glance at a map; the railroad's mechanization of travel promised to neutralize the mountains and draw a straight line from the Chesapeake to the Ohio River valley, thus realizing Baltimore's natural advantage of proximity to the west. This logic had underwritten early support for the B&O; it would underwrite support for its completion as well.

By 1845, though, some readers questioned McLane's sanguine assessments of the railroad's promise and the city's future. For starters, the line remained stuck in place at Cumberland as the company's executives negotiated with unfriendly legislatures in Virginia and Pennsylvania to secure a path to the Ohio River; if the road could not reach its destination in a timely fashion, Philadelphia and New York would overtake Baltimore, and the city's natural advantages would expire.[2] More ominously, though, this report came at the cusp of dramatic changes in the railroad industry that unsettled the very premise of the B&O. From the late 1840s into the 1850s, track mileage in the United States more than tripled. During this construction boom, no fewer than four trunk railroads breached the Appalachian Mountains. The B&O, first to start, was the last to reach the western waters. The New York & Erie opened to the town of Dunkirk on Lake Erie in 1851, and the Pennsylvania Railroad completed an all-rail route from Philadelphia to Pittsburgh in 1852. A series of short rail lines paralleling the Erie Canal, in operation since 1842, consolidated under the aegis of the New York Central in 1853. Competition from these companies, coupled with the proliferation of shorter rail lines that increasingly superseded turnpikes and waterways as commercial channels, shook up practices within the B&O.[3] As this nascent rail network reduced shipping times from weeks to days, shipping merchants' calculations changed in ways that raised anew questions about how railroads worked and whose interests they served.

In Baltimore, the B&O's struggles in the wake of its 1853 completion to the Ohio River at Wheeling, Virginia, moved these questions to the center of public discourse. Far from initiating a new era of prosperity, the aftermath of the B&O's grand termination ceremony revealed a city suffering from an economic slump and a railroad with anemic traffic, defective infrastructure, and dissatisfied customers. The board of directors' request for a massive $5 million investment from the municipal government triggered a widespread discussion about the railroad's responsibilities to its terminal city. The most controversial question in this debate concerned rate policy: should a publicly funded railroad set rates that favored traffic to Philadelphia over traffic to Baltimore? Answers to this question reflected changing ideas about the nature of the public good and the limits of public action. Rate discrimination proved controversial for the B&O and for American railroads more generally in the decades to come; for now, company officials worked to secure municipal investment without incurring municipal oversight. After 1853, fewer citizens and public officials accepted that the objectives of the railroad company and those of the city government necessarily aligned.

Terminal Questions

Unlike rival companies based in Philadelphia or New York City, the B&O required the cooperation of a "foreign" state, either Virginia or Pennsylvania, to reach the western waters. By the 1840s, the charters those states had granted to Maryland's railroad in the 1820s had long since lapsed, and they both now had westbound internal improvement projects of their own that they sought to protect. Hostile state legislatures had the power to stop the B&O quite literally in its tracks. For five years, from 1843 to 1848, the Baltimore & Ohio idled at Cumberland as Louis McLane and other company officials undertook exhaustive negotiations in Richmond and Harrisburg to secure right-of-way to the Ohio River. The B&O's supporters fumed that this political recalcitrance violated the "spirit of the age." D. K. Minor's *American Railroad Journal*, reviewing the B&O's predicament from Philadelphia, lamented that the company's dependence "upon foreign legislation" gave it "difficulties, far greater than the *mountains* in their path, to overcome."[4]

Still, the crisis was largely one of the company's own making. Until 1845, most people inside and outside the B&O assumed that the line would terminate at Wheeling, Virginia. Located on the Ohio River approximately sixty miles southwest of Pittsburgh, Wheeling was an important site on the National Road, Baltimore's original route to the West. By the 1840s, though, two other cities had emerged as prospective termini for the B&O: Pittsburgh, at the mouth of the Ohio River, and Parkersburg, ninety miles downriver from Wheeling (fig. 4.1). Either of these outlets promised to cultivate distinct hinterlands. A Pittsburgh terminus would link Baltimore to the trade of northern Ohio and the Great Lakes while offering the advantages of a mature urban market at the head of river navigation. Terminating at Parkersburg would enable the B&O to tap the well-developed lower Ohio and Mississippi valleys

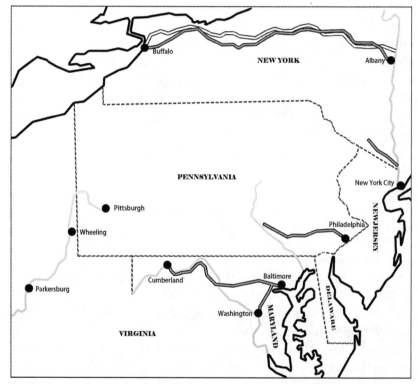

FIGURE 4.1. The B&O, its prospective termini, and other trunk lines, ca. 1845. As the B&O struggled to find an Ohio River terminus, other trunk rail projects were under way: the Pennsylvania Railroad, incorporated in 1847, from Philadelphia to Pittsburgh; the New York & Erie, running from the Hudson through southern New York State to Lake Erie; and the New York Central, which consolidated a series of short lines paralleling the Erie Canal in 1853. Map by Yiu Sze Ki. Adapted from *Sketch Illustrating the Positions of the Commercial Cities and Towns of the Eastern, Middle, and Western States with the Principal Existing and Proposed Lines of Communication* ([s.n.], ca. 1845).

and allow for easy extensions to Cincinnati and St. Louis.[5] Both presented political challenges, however. Pittsburghers eagerly sought a connection with Baltimore, but Philadelphians bristled at the prospect of permitting a rival city's railroad to siphon off trade that, they believed, rightly belonged to them. A Parkersburg terminus faced opposition from Wheelingites and from eastern Virginians then plotting their own internal improvement project westward from Norfolk.[6] Still, officials and stockholders in the B&O had grown dissatisfied with the small market and intermediate position of Wheeling. They decided to take their chances. In 1845 the stockholders summarily rejected the Wheeling terminus by a vote of 50,632 shares to 2—those two being the shares of a stockholder from Wheeling.[7]

This set the stage for two years of intra- and interstate wrangling as advocates of all three prospective termini made their case. Each claimed that natural advantage and the laws of trade favored their preferred city. Parkersburg's partisans said that one need only glance at a map to see the superiority of their preferred route: a horizontal line drawn from Baltimore to St. Louis passes through both Cincinnati and Parkersburg. The straight-line route promised to fulfill the railroad's founding mission of simplifying geography: by funneling traffic eastward without delay or deviation, the straight line would make Baltimore the uncontested eastern outlet for what were at the time the largest urban centers of the trans-Appalachian West.[8] The pro-Wheeling camp countered that the laws of trade just as readily served their route, because river trade would simply continue upstream if it did not find an outlet at Parkersburg. At Wheeling, moreover, the B&O could contend for the Great Lakes trade as well as that of the lower Ohio valley.[9] And both Virginia termini held at least one advantage over Pittsburgh: at Wheeling or Parkersburg the B&O would not have to compete with Philadelphia-based lines for traffic. Both would allow the B&O to intercept river traffic before it reached Pittsburgh, which would leave Philadelphia, said the *Sun*, "to feed, like the prodigal, upon the rejected husks of Baltimore commerce."[10]

The B&O question divided Pennsylvanians as well as Virginians. Representatives from eastern Pennsylvania wrangled with their western counterparts in the state legislature over whether and how the B&O would operate within the state's borders.[11] In 1846, the Pennsylvania legislature hatched a compromise measure that ultimately had significant consequences for the B&O and for the American railroad industry more generally. To mollify Pittsburghers anxious to gain a rail link to the eastern seaboard, the state agreed to incorporate a new railroad company to run from Philadelphia to Pittsburgh; if the new company failed to raise $1 million by July 1847, the state would permit the B&O to enter Pennsylvania and terminate at Pittsburgh. When private

investors proved reluctant to commit substantial resources to this new enterprise, Philadelphia merchants turned, as their Baltimore predecessors had,
to the city government. After a hotly contested election, Philadelphia's city
council pledged the necessary funds for the western railroad. The company
thus chartered became the Pennsylvania Railroad, the B&O's fiercest competitor and eventually one of the largest corporations in the world. In addition to Philadelphia and its suburbs, the City of Pittsburgh and other local
communities provided crucial assistance in the Pennsylvania's early years. By
1851, more than 70 percent of the company's capital came from municipal and
county governments, although state law dictated that government representatives could make up no more than 49 percent of the board of directors.[12]

As the new railroad, fueled by urban public investment, made its way west,
boosters in Pittsburgh and Baltimore attempted to circumvent the Pennsylvania legislature. Pittsburghers launched a new railroad, the Pittsburgh &
Connellsville (P&C), to run from their city to the Maryland state line, where
it could connect with the B&O. They sought investment from the Baltimore
railroad to make this happen, but the B&O's leaders found little to like in this
proposal. McLane pointed out that Philadelphia interests might commandeer
the company or intercept its route, and he demanded the right to determine
the P&C's path and control its branches as insurance against these possibilities.[13] These demands outraged Pittsburghers. Meanwhile, in Richmond, the
Virginia legislature continued to hold fast against a Parkersburg terminus.[14]

Barred from its preferred termini, the B&O remained in limbo at Cumberland until 1847. As the Baltimore press and national outlets like the *American
Railroad Journal* bemoaned the petty politics that kept the B&O from forging onward, some began to argue that the time had come for the railroad
to continue westward even if it meant choosing an inferior terminus.[15] In
the absence of permission to build to either Pittsburgh or Parkersburg, the
B&O's top officials suddenly changed their tune and endorsed Wheeling.
They couched this pragmatic decision in the language of natural advantage.
A committee declared that Baltimore's prosperity and the stockholders' interests required a terminus far enough downstream of Pittsburgh to capture
trade passing up the Ohio River and to avoid competition with Philadelphia
and New York. A Wheeling terminus would accomplish this goal.[16] Whereas
building to Pittsburgh would have benefited Philadelphia, said a correspondent to the *American*, with Wheeling, Baltimore would have "a Western city
of our own" that "owe[s] her prosperity to us."[17]

These optimistic appraisals of Wheeling's advantages papered over the
political struggles that precipitated the decision, but they nonetheless echoed
familiar claims about the laws of trade and geographic destiny. Not all were

convinced. A small but vocal contingent of Baltimore businessmen with commercial ties to Pittsburgh and investments in the B&O urged the railroad to invest in the P&C despite the clash over terms. This group included figures who would play major roles in the B&O in the years to come, such as the Quaker merchant and financier Johns Hopkins, who started buying up B&O stock in the 1840s and joined the board in 1847, and the Irish-born merchant Robert Garrett, whose son John later became a long-serving president of the B&O.[18] The pro-Pittsburgh group observed that market realities rendered Wheeling's downriver location moot; even though steamships reached Wheeling first, shipping agents charged the same price for deliveries to Pittsburgh further upriver. As the *American* put it, Pittsburgh was "a rich emporium of commerce," whereas Wheeling was "pretty nearly stationary and of no special importance in the world of trade."[19]

Louis McLane and a preponderancy of the directorate made it clear that this was a losing cause, however. McLane's rebuttal reiterated established principles of economic geography and natural advantages; he reminded his readers that Baltimore's position between north and south gave it a distinct and natural hinterland. "The city that should . . . grasp at that which fairly belongs to another," he wrote, "would be very apt to lose the whole." With a Wheeling terminus, the B&O could forge for Baltimore a backcountry beyond the reach of New York and Philadelphia's highly capitalized corporations.[20] Yet a major factor in the B&O's decision concerned an aspect of railroad business that operated independent of, if not contrary to, the welfare of Baltimore's market: through travel.[21] If the B&O built to Pittsburgh, it could surely offer merchants there the shortest route to the sea: Baltimore sits approximately 275 miles as the oriole flies from Pittsburgh, whereas the distance from Pittsburgh to Philadelphia exceeds 300 miles. Yet for travelers bound for Philadelphia or points north, a trip to Baltimore from Pittsburgh would only add unnecessary cost (three to four dollars) and time (five to six hours).[22] Already, company records showed that fully two-thirds of the passengers arriving in Baltimore from the Ohio River continued onward to Philadelphia and points north "without stopping in this city longer than to take a hurried meal."[23] It would make no sense for such passengers to board a B&O train at Pittsburgh when they wanted to reach Philadelphia. By contrast, passengers boarding at Wheeling would reach Baltimore by the time they would have reached Pittsburgh on the river and could then save nearly forty miles total on their trip to Philadelphia.[24]

Thus, if debates on the terminus question resounded with the language of natural advantage and the laws of trade, they also hinted at potentially destabilizing changes afoot in the commercial world. The pro-Pittsburgh camp,

which later became influential within the B&O, warned that distance no longer carried the paramount importance that the railroad's founders had assumed. And the rationale for building to Wheeling stressed the railroad's need
to capture trade bound for other cities, irrespective of Baltimore's market. The
competing railroads to the north making their way westward and the rise of
a new generation of merchants within Baltimore challenged long-standing
assumptions about economic geography even as the B&O lurched toward its
final stretch.

Completion

Not all the new voices within the company were so critical of Wheeling.
Thomas Swann, a lawyer with a penchant for oratory who joined the board
of directors in 1847, celebrated the selection of Wheeling and worked hard to
sell the terminus to the public. Alongside Johns Hopkins (who changed his
mind once the board ruled out Pittsburgh), Swann promised listeners that
"the moment" the B&O "touch[ed] the Ohio River," all the river trade bound
for New York would "concentrate at that natural outlet," Wheeling. The Ohio
River regained its talismanic quality; writers promised that any outlet there
would realize the city's destiny, fostering new trades and augmenting the
population.[25]

In 1848, Swann replaced Louis McLane as president of the B&O. He effectively inverted his predecessor's career trajectory; whereas McLane transi-
tioned from federal politics into the world of internal improvements, Swann
used his experience with the B&O as a launching pad for a political career
that saw him serve as a Know-Nothing mayor of Baltimore, a Unionist governor of Maryland, and a Democratic representative in Congress. Born to
a wealthy Virginia family in 1809, Swann married into a wealthy Baltimore
family in 1834, and he enslaved people on both sides of the Potomac until
shortly before the Civil War. In 1836 he joined his in-laws in Baltimore, where
he practiced law and invested in real estate around town; by 1842 he held
taxable property well in excess of $100,000, which may explain why as B&O
president he accepted a salary only half the size of McLane's princely $6,000
per annum. His assets included significant holdings of Baltimore & Ohio
Railroad stock, which had sunk to a mere $28 per share (from a $100 par
value) by 1848. Swann argued that to right the ship—or train, as it were—the
company needed to work arduously towards its chartered end: completion
to the Ohio River. In 1849, at Swann's initiative, the board of directors took
out contracts to extend the line all the way to Wheeling, a $6 million, two-
hundred-mile project.[26]

By 1851, the B&O's contractors employed 4,870 men in construction, spread out along a mountainous and sparsely populated stretch of terrain. Swann's push for construction coincided with the height of the Irish famine, and the company eagerly recruited desperate immigrants to labor on the line with promises that the "country between Cumberland and the Ohio River . . . is healthy—subsistence abundant—wages good, and employment certain." Those good wages amounted to 87.5 cents a day for eleven hours of work (eight hours for work in the tunnels), a sum that would have been even lower if not for strikes in March 1850 that secured a raise. The strikes also prompted the company to employ a private police force along the line. The chief engineer Benjamin H. Latrobe tasked the police with maintaining order in the labor camps, not least because of intra-Irish conflicts that periodically led to disruptive fighting. Tensions undoubtedly ran high, but the workforce collectively managed to blast, bridge, and bore their way through hundreds of miles of unforgiving terrain in the face of landslides, tunnel collapses, and other threats to life and limb. It took sixteen years for the B&O to complete the first two hundred miles of track from Baltimore to Cumberland; it took only four years to complete the second two hundred miles from Cumberland to Wheeling.[27]

Well before the construction crews finished the last leg, B&O executives started making arrangements for other termini. In 1850, only three years after McLane praised Wheeling as a safe haven from competition with northern cities, the Pennsylvania Railroad announced plans to extend a branch called the Hempfield Railroad from its main line to a point on the Ohio River south of the B&O's projected terminus.[28] Now, having committed itself to build to Wheeling, the B&O finally secured from Richmond permission to build a branch line called the Northwestern Virginia Railroad (NWV) from its Main Stem to Parkersburg as a way to preempt the Pennsylvania's maneuvers.[29] In Baltimore, observers inside and outside the company greeted the long-deferred prospect of a Parkersburg terminus with enthusiasm; whereas the Pennsylvania Railroad had easily subverted their Wheeling terminus, the NWV offered a direct path from Baltimore to St. Louis that would prove, they imagined, difficult to overcome.[30] To think otherwise was to doubt the manifest lessons of geography. Thomas Swann, addressing a public meeting, instructed his listeners "to look at the map in full. . . . There can be no such thing as mistaking a straight line." All the capital in Pennsylvania could not subvert this fact of geometry, he promised. Swann made these remarks at a rally held to convince the city government to invest $1.5 million in this branch line—a railroad that began and ended outside of Maryland.[31] The mayor and city council found the promise of a straight-line route to the West too enticing to pass up, and in April 1852 the state authorized Baltimore to purchase stock in the NWV. Construction began later that year.[32]

The prospect of this superior terminus did not dull enthusiasm for the completion of the Main Stem at Wheeling in 1853. For well over a decade, discourse about the B&O had reflected anxiety over the line's floundering performance, its stuttering progress, and the intensifying competition it faced from projects emanating from Philadelphia and New York. Now, though, as the labor camps moved ever further west over the mountains, the tone of public conversation lightened and for a time even recaptured some of the enthusiasm that had accompanied the B&O's earliest days. The press anticipated that completion to Wheeling would finally inaugurate Baltimore's golden age.[33] And, as in the late 1820s, voices inside and outside the company characterized this coming triumph as a public achievement. The B&O's annual report for 1852 praised Baltimoreans for the spirit and courage that had achieved this long-awaited union of east and west.[34]

This "courage" had taken the form of financial contributions that strained the municipal budget to secure future gain. "What originated in individual enterprize, and was sustained, at first, by private resources, has, from time to time, received the fostering aid of both city and State," wrote the editors of the *American* as the B&O neared completion. This account understated the public's contributions to the founding of the railroad, but it grasped a broader truth about the company's development—that the urban public had, at great sacrifice, propped up the line. Other American city governments invested in rail projects, but few as extensively as Baltimore. As of 1853, Baltimore City's internal improvement debt reached $5.5 million, with an additional $2 million in municipal credit wrapped up in loan guarantees for the B&O and other railroads. These commitments placed the city government in perpetually pinched circumstances. Interest payments on debt reached $360,000 per annum by 1845; in that year, the city taxed thirty-one cents of every hundred dollars to repay interest but only five cents to pay for public schools. American city governments were notoriously tightfisted in this period, but this debt made Baltimore's tax rates among the highest in the nation even as the city's mayors had to defer expenses they considered essential, such as additional night watchmen or street lighting. By 1851, the municipal budget faced a deficit of $75,000. No wonder the *American* "regarded the Baltimore and Ohio Railroad [not] as a *close-Corporation* designed for the interest of individuals exclusively, but as a great institution in which all sections of our State and City were deeply concerned."[35]

Many believed, though, that an end to this public hardship was at last at

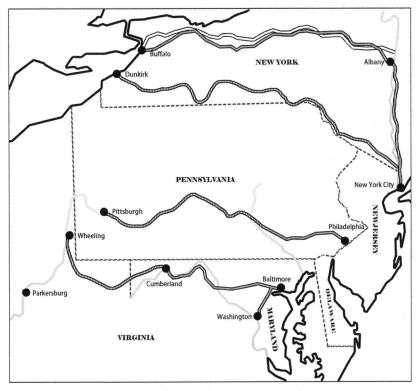

FIGURE 4.2. The east-west trunk rail lines as of 1853. By the time the B&O reached the Ohio River at Wheeling in 1853, the Pennsylvania Railroad and New York & Erie Railroad had already reached the western waters at Pittsburgh and Dunkirk, respectively. In 1851, the Hudson River Railroad opened, connecting the rail lines running parallel to the Erie Canal (which consolidated as the New York Central in 1853) to New York City; later, in 1869, Cornelius Vanderbilt merged them to form the New York Central & Hudson River Railroad. Map by Yiu Sze Ki. Adapted from *Sketch Illustrating the Positions of the Commercial Cities and Towns of the Eastern, Middle, and Western States with the Principal Existing and Proposed Lines of Communication* ([s.n.], ca. 1845).

hand. Workers laid the final link in the track from Baltimore to Wheeling on Christmas Eve of 1852 (fig. 4.2). A ceremonial trip over the rails brought company officials, politicians, and other notables from Baltimore to Wheeling. They celebrated on arrival with a grand banquet, at which guests enjoyed twenty-eight different dishes while listening to oratory from company officials and politicians. Philip Thomas's health did not permit him to make the trip, but George Brown was on hand to recount the creation of the company at his house in 1826.[36] President Swann, never shy about speechifying, spoke as well, proclaiming that failure to complete the railroad would have led to ruin for Baltimore. Yet in enumerating Baltimore's advantages, Swann did not suggest that the railroad alone could realize the city's promise. "Baltimore can no longer remain a mere place of *transit*," he said. "She must become an *original* market."[37] How to achieve this goal soon became a pressing political question.

Reassessing Railroad Operations

Having seen the line at last reach the Ohio River, Thomas Swann considered his task complete; he tendered his resignation within months of opening the road to Wheeling. As he prepared to leave Baltimore for a European vacation, the B&O's board of directors saluted him for writing human ingenuity into the landscape: "Human skill and boldness, under your decisive management, pierced the hills and spanned the ravines."[38] A similar triumphalist spirit resounded throughout Baltimore upon completion of the B&O, and the earliest reports hinted at an uptick of revenue for the rail line.[39] The *Sun* eagerly cast good commercial news as evidence that the "laws of trade, which are generally immutable" had finally convinced those western merchants who had decamped for the more "pretentious" cities to the north to once again bring their business to Baltimore.[40]

The *Sun*'s boast arrived the same day as a less-than-enthusiastic annual report from the B&O. Wheeling still lacked rail connections, and low water on the Ohio that year prevented large boats from venturing upriver. As a result, reported new president William G. Harrison, most of the business the B&O had done so far was local. Although the total number of passengers increased by more than 25,000 from 1852 to 1853, the number of through travelers actually fell (table 4.1).[41] The steep decline in through travel for 1853 was likely anomalous, but the haste to complete the line meant that substantial portions of the track remained in poor condition. With some tunnels yet unfinished and others alarmingly prone to collapse, trains often had to run circuitously around mountains, where sharp curves and steep inclines slowed the engines. These defects made the route expensive to operate, and western merchants complained about the high rates levied to cover these costs. Furthermore, the most heavily trafficked portion of the line, the stretch between Baltimore and the Cumberland coal mines, had only a single track, which limited the number of trains that could run and ensured that problems at any point disrupted travel up and down the line. Passengers encountered frequent delays as massive coal trains overturned on the serpentine track. Such experiences belied the once-prevalent metaphors of water travel that had shaped Baltimoreans' early conceptions of locomotion. Iron rails and steam-powered engines had not eliminated the vicissitudes of terrain as thoroughly as boosters had anticipated.[42]

TABLE 4.1. Passenger through and way travel on the Main Stem, 1850–1853

	Local passengers	Through passengers	Local passenger miles	Through passenger miles	Through passengers as % of travelers	Through passengers as % of miles
1850	146,021	34,885	6,625,550	6,209,441	19.28	48.38
1851	141,764	23,498	6,477,060	4,182,633	14.22	39.24
1852	173,673	11,704	7,777,786	2,083,401	6.31	21.13
1853	208,562	2,313	16,922,858	413,714	1.10	2.39

Source: All data from Transportation Report Tables, table L, in ARs 24–27.

Note: Some tables, without explanation, list half passengers; I have truncated those figures here.

The citizens of Baltimore likewise failed to see the immediate returns that the boosters had conditioned them to expect; if anything, the city's economic prospects worsened after the B&O opened to Wheeling. Swann's frenzied push to complete the line had catalyzed a building boom in Baltimore in the late 1840s and early 1850s, which, coupled with an influx of European immigrants, precipitated industrial development and dramatic changes in the built environment. From 1840 to 1860 the city's population doubled as Germans fleeing political repression and Irish fleeing famine immigrated to Baltimore. Many of the new arrivals—particularly the Irish—found work in the B&O's Mount Clare shops building cars and forging track, and they settled in the hundreds of row houses built in West Baltimore and other neighborhoods. The work required to complete the railroad fostered industrial growth as well, as workers labored in new steam-powered factories (fueled by Cumberland coal) to build parts and supplies. People found it easy to hope that the B&O's completion would open up new avenues for Baltimore-built products and stimulate further development. Even Baltimore's street grid reflected this enthusiasm with the opening of an Ohio Street in 1851.[43] Through the first quarter of 1853, locals and northern investors sank money into Baltimore real estate as construction crews erected warehouses and extended wharves, all in anticipation of a torrent of trade that was to accompany the spring thaw.[44] Instead, completion to Wheeling brought a sharp contraction in the city's labor market. With its tracks in place, the B&O could reduce its Mount Clare outputs, and the number of workers in its employ declined. The company would meet much of its subsequent demand for equipment and track in new shops located in Wheeling and the railroad town of Martinsburg, Virginia.[45]

The mechanics at Mount Clare registered their disappointment with these returns in February 1853 with Baltimore's first major industrial strike. They observed that their wages remained static while their bosses and the top executives received raises. When the B&O's managers ignored their protests, employees of the B&O and Baltimore & Susquehanna workshops, joined by workers from other manufacturing establishments around Baltimore, struck for higher pay. In mass gatherings at Monument Square and in processions that stretched a mile long, upwards of four thousand men pledged solidarity with their fellow mechanics, hoping to bolster wages across the city. The workers took to political channels to gain support, and in response the second branch of the city council instructed the city directors in the B&O to use their influence to augment the mechanics' wages. The company complied and the B&O's employees ended their strike, setting aside a portion of their salaries to support those who remained on the picket lines. By April, almost all the strikers returned to work at higher wages than before.[46] The strikers had called on the municipal government to mediate between an enfranchised workforce and a municipally funded employer in the name of justice and the public good. By casting its influence in favor of the workers, the city government made the company's employment practices a matter of public policy. Not all, though, embraced this model for industrial labor relations. One correspondent to the *Sun* signed "TAX-PAYER" wrote angrily that only the "unerring laws of supply and demand" should settle wage disputes. The city had used its position as the largest stockholder in the B&O to force a decision contravening the "laws of political economy."[47]

Facing disappointing returns, labor unrest, and an interventionist city council, the company sent assistant master of transportation William Prescott Smith on a tour of the West in May 1853 to diagnose the cause of its difficulties. Smith found there a nascent national market for transportation—one in which, he said, both the B&O and Baltimore stood poorly equipped to complete. Passenger trade languished for want of customers—the B&O met no railroads and only one steamship line at Wheeling, and barely twenty passengers a day transferred for passage eastward.[48] But the problem clearly ran deeper than that, as even people bound for Baltimore often went by northern routes. Travelers complained about inconvenient timetables, meager connections, and B&O employees' surly attitudes.[49] Inadequate maintenance had caused a serious accident on the road a little over a month before Smith's trip—two cars overturned on a broken rail, killing eight and seriously injuring many others. This and other problems generated what Smith called a "fear that pervades the whole West about the safety of our Road," which deterred "nervous old ladies (and stout men besides,)" from taking the Baltimore route.[50]

Freight traffic also languished amid complaints about high rates and antiquated business practices. The western merchants Smith spoke to complained that the B&O charged too much for shipments to Philadelphia or New York and that Baltimore itself offered an undesirable market for their goods. Smith wrote, "I find a general complaint out West among the heavy dealers, of what they call the 'old fogy,' 'one horse,' or 'picayune' way of doing business in Baltimore."[51] Such disparaging remarks reflected both Baltimore's paltry international connections and the uncompetitive commission charges levied by the city's merchants; shipments took longer to reach Philadelphia and New York than Baltimore, but they could be handled in those cities to greater advantage. Unless the company reduced its rates to Philadelphia and New York, Smith warned, the B&O would find itself limited to the business the Baltimore market alone could sustain.[52]

This represented one facet of a broader overhaul of the company's operations that Smith proposed. Natural advantages played little role in his program for commercial success. In fact, the railroad's promised annihilation of space and time had undercut the benefits of Baltimore's position. As the president of a Kentucky railroad put it, although the B&O would be the "*first Road to the Seaboard his Road will strike,*—there are *three other great lines of communication with which they can just as readily connect.*" The rise of railroad travel, Smith suggested, had subordinated distance and travel time to other, less tangible factors in determining which route people took. Rather than reducing transportation to a calculation governed by abstract laws of trade, breaching the mountains had in his estimation elevated the importance of face-to-face communication. In addition to changing the B&O's rate structure, Smith recommended cultivating personal business relationships. Company agents in major western markets, for example, could negotiate rates with shippers and drum up new business, while in Baltimore, B&O managers could wine and dine visiting newspaper editors, merchants, and railroad presidents to leave them with a favorable impression of the company.[53]

The publication of Smith's travelogue in pamphlet form allowed his assessment to circulate beyond the B&O's offices and helped lay the groundwork for a broader redefinition of the company's goals and operations. Yet while the railroad's executives ultimately took up many of his suggestions for institutional and policy changes, they initially attributed the line's failures to deficiencies in infrastructure, including unfinished tunnels and sharp curves in the track. Company officials began to push for new equipment and a double track on the line even before completion; some argued that even though it had reached the Ohio River, the railroad was not yet truly "finished."[54] In light of such shortcomings, the B&O appealed to the municipal government for aid, requesting an infusion of cash to fund improvements to infrastructure and rolling stock that became known as the $5 million loan. This call for public support ignited a confrontation between the B&O and the municipal government over the company's relationship to the city.

Rate Discrimination and the $5 Million Loan

The track debates of the 1830s demonstrated that railroads' pursuit of through trade had ambiguous implications for urban prosperity. Whereas the B&O competed with other trunk lines for shipments bound for Philadelphia or New York, its executives quickly found that local trade could bear nearly any rates they set and thus could cover the brunt of the company's operating expenses.[55] In 1853, after opening its tracks to the Ohio River, the B&O adopted rate structures that differentiated fares for long- and short-distance travel—a practice known as rate discrimination—in the hopes of capturing a greater share of competitive traffic. Rate discrimination entailed either charging less to ship to places beyond than to Baltimore (absolute discrimination) or charging through freight and passengers a lower rate per mile than local traffic (proportional discrimination). Either way, with discriminatory rates in place, distance did not determine fares. This threatened to convert Baltimore's location west of its competitors into a natural *disadvantage* by encouraging eastbound shipments to move straight through Pratt Street on their way to other markets. Although Baltimoreans had particular grounds for concern, merchants up and down the eastern seaboard looked on warily as publicly funded railroad companies established discriminatory rates that penalized local markets. In 1851, for example, Philadelphia-based merchants on the Pennsylvania Railroad's board of directors rejected proposals to establish fares that favored trade to Baltimore, arguing that doing so would undercut the railroad's developmental mission; only in 1854 did the Pennsylvania lower its prices to encourage high volumes of traffic, regardless of destination.[56]

The size of its investment and the scale of its representation within the company led Baltimore's city government to play a more active role than most municipalities in monitoring these practices. In the summer of 1853, the city council investigated B&O rate policy. William Parker, the company's general superintendent, framed discrimination as a necessary business practice. He explained to city director Joshua Vansant, "We must meet the Pennsylvania Railroad in Philadelphia & offer our transportation on equal terms—this strikes us as an axiom." Parker admitted that under this policy the B&O occasionally charged lower rates to Philadelphia than to Baltimore, but he argued that this lay beyond the B&O's power to prevent.[57] Here Parker confessed to absolute discrimination, but proportional discrimination also undercut Baltimore's position. A through ticket from Columbus to Philadelphia in July 1853, for example, cost $13.30, of which $7.40 went to the B&O and the balance to other lines. At the same time, the ticket from Columbus to Baltimore cost $12.30, of which the B&O received $7.70. If Baltimore enjoyed the same rates as Philadelphia, the total cost to travel to Baltimore would have been just $11.57—that is, $0.73 less than the company charged.[58] Discrimination meant that a shipper sending two identical packages would pay the B&O less for the one bound for Philadelphia than the one bound for Baltimore, even though the same engine moved them the same distance over the same rails. This rate structure penalized the B&O's home city and bolstered its prime competitor.

The city council report published in August condemned these practices; it resolved that charging anything other than equitable rates subverted the B&O's founding mission and threatened to reduce Baltimore to a mere place of transit. In response to this outcry, the B&O's managers promised in August to set rates so as "to make our city the great centre of the trade and travel."[59] But they did not concede the principle underpinning rate discrimination— William Parker's "axiom" that the B&O had to match the Pennsylvania Railroad's rates to Philadelphia—and the principle was the crux of the matter. A half decade earlier, the rhetoric of the terminus debates resounded with the language of interurban competition: McLane, Swann, and even Hopkins had argued that the key factor in selecting an Ohio River outlet was Baltimore's ability to compete with other cities for trade. Now, the site of competition shifted from the urban to the corporate realm, and the object of competition shifted from trade to traffic.

The B&O's concession to the city's interests temporarily tabled these debates, but when the company requested a loan of $5 million from the city government to fund improvements on the line a month later, rate discrimination returned to the forefront of public discourse. In September 1853, the B&O's managers called for a major renovation of the infrastructure from Baltimore to Wheeling and looked for an infusion of cash to build 218 miles of double track along the eastern portion of the Main Stem. They found little interest among private investors in the midst of a tight money market, and so they turned to the city to endorse the company's bond issue. The company's annual report for that year promised investors that they would have no difficulty securing this commitment from the municipal government. After all, what was good for the B&O was good for Baltimore.[60]

At first there seemed little reason to doubt this prediction. A city council committee reported favorably on the proposed endorsement, reasoning that the railroad's central place within Baltimore's systems of capital, credit, and commerce made it too big to fail. Refusal to endorse the bonds would

intensify the B&O's embarrassed financial state to the city's detriment because B&O stock, held primarily by Baltimoreans (including, of course, the
municipal government itself), accounted for much of the city's commercial
capital and credit. Conversely, helping the road operate more efficiently would
bolster Baltimore's property values and business prospects. The committee
thus recommended endorsing $5 million of the B&O's bonds—a move that
would double the municipality's financial commitment to the company.[61] The
editors of the *American* endorsed this proposal and characterized the B&O as
a civic institution. "We consider the Railroad just as much a part of the city
as its streets or its churches," wrote the editors, "and would just as soon . . .
open a profit and loss account with the monument, with Jones' Falls, or the
harbor . . . as to abandon the Baltimore and Ohio Railroad."[62]

Affirmations of the B&O's centrality to local interests and the need for
public funding had become commonplace over the previous quarter century
in Baltimore, but by 1853, a weary citizenry received them with an unprecedented level of skepticism. For secondhand furniture dealer James P. Kennedy,
the $5 million request represented the latest affront to an overwhelmingly
Democratic urban electorate; he reminded the city council in a petition that
the B&O, like "all incorporated Companys," took "wealth from the manny
and heaps it on the few." He encouraged the majority-Democratic council
to cease imposing Whig policies on their voters and instead to submit the
matter to the people as a referendum in accordance with "sound demogratick
doctran."[63] Yet even people who had once supported public funding for the
railroad found that this new request strained credulity. President William G.
Harrison's pleas for money came less than a year after Thomas Swann's boasts
of the company's bright future. Cynical observers characterized this request
as a shakedown. The B&O, wrote one correspondent to the *Sun*, would
always be in dire financial straits "as long as it knows that the city of Baltimore . . . has always millions at her command for the mere asking."[64] And
where the *American* cast the $5 million endorsement as a patriotic move, the
Sun claimed that the improvements these funds would pay for offered no
benefit to the city. The railroad's extant capacity served Baltimore's market
adequately, said the editors. The proposed improvements instead served the
needs of through trade. The ultimate goal of this renovation, said the *Sun*,
was to bolster the B&O's profit margins and allow it to pay dividends to its
stockholders.[65]

Some, though, saw an opportunity in this request. A memorial to the council from 104 firms and individuals urged the municipal government to make
any public assistance for the B&O contingent on its pledge to carry freight
to Baltimore at rates no higher than those charged for other destinations—

that is, to forestall discrimination against Baltimore.[66] Supporters pointed out that antidiscrimination policy did not mean bestowing Baltimore with any particular perks. "We want no discrimination in our favor," one writer had pointed out in August. "All that we claim for our market is this, that the merchant can reach us as quickly and as comfortably . . . [as] other cities."[67] The proposed proviso looked only to place Baltimore *"on the same footing"* as its neighbors, wrote one correspondent to the *Sun*, whereas encouraging the movement of trade to Philadelphia consigned Baltimore to second-class status.[68]

These proposals reflected a vision for the future of railroad enterprise quite different from that advanced by assistant master of transportation William P. Smith in his report earlier that year. Smith had stated that the B&O could not compete with other trunk lines without imposing discriminatory rates; advocates of antidiscrimination provisions countered that for a publicly funded line, competition with other trunk lines for through trade was irrelevant if it did not serve the public interest. Pursuit of municipal funding, they suggested, exposed the company to municipal oversight. This was not in itself a new idea—the city and state representatives on the board of directors ostensibly fulfilled this function. But the city's representation never matched the scale of its investment, and city directors had proved all too prone to side with their stockholder-appointed colleagues on sensitive issues. More fundamentally, the results of the railroad's completion to the Ohio manifestly undercut claims that tapping the river would foster economic growth and that the B&O's policies necessarily aligned with the interests of the public at large. As they entered a new age of railroad operations, a subset of Baltimore's population called for greater public control over the line, to make sure that, at the very least, its policies did not actively discourage Baltimore's development as a market. The company could compete for traffic to Philadelphia as much as it liked—it just couldn't do so by raising rates to Baltimore.

The city council heeded these suggestions. A bill extending $5 million in municipal credit to the B&O passed on December 14, 1853, and it contained a provision barring discrimination against traffic to Baltimore.[69] President Harrison flatly rejected this offer. He characterized antidiscrimination measures as unwise political interference with business practices and said that the B&O could not accept legislation that undermined control of its tolls.[70] Yet he had no intention of withdrawing his request for municipal aid. As such, Harrison and his allies had to explain why Baltimoreans should fund a company that wished to discriminate against them.

One response was to insist that the interests of the B&O's wealthy investors necessarily aligned with those of the city as a whole; as they had personal

stakes in Baltimore's prosperity, surely they would take no action that undermined its commercial standing. Johns Hopkins, the wealthy merchant and
private director, came to personify this approach. One correspondent to the
Sun wrote sarcastically that after investing in local securities and property,
Hopkins now, "as if bent on his own destruction," acted as a director to "DIS-
CRIMINATE against Baltimore, thereby driving the trade away from our city
and destroying not only the value of his immense investment in warehouses
but also his stock and bonds."[71] This line of argument did not so much defend discrimination as insulate the company's leaders against charges of bad
faith while casting doubt on the competence of the city government to set
such policies in the first place. Many in the business community accepted
this logic (which, after all, equated wealth with wisdom and public spirit) and
circulated a petition calling for municipal endorsement of the B&O's bonds
without rate restrictions.[72]

The B&O's defenders also advanced a more counterintuitive claim: that
antidiscrimination laws actually hurt Baltimore's competitive prospects. The
American Railroad Journal, by this time helmed by Henry Varnum Poor and
published out of New York, monitored the debate unfolding in Baltimore and
chided the city's politicians for following the example of provincial "southern
communities" that sought "to increase the business of a particular place by
throwing impediments in the way of free movement of persons and property."
Antidiscrimination and physical obstruction alike contravened the spirit of
the age: "There is no doubt that the interests of every town or city . . . are
best promoted by the unembarrassed and untaxed movement both of persons
and property through it."[73] These invocations of free movement clearly resonated: the *American*, despite having condemned discrimination months earlier, chided antidiscrimination Baltimoreans for their "old fogyism," against
which the paper's editors "contended for free intercourse, without local stoppage or restriction."[74]

Such arguments recapitulated the logic of the track debates twenty years
prior; then, too, the B&O's defenders had argued that impeding the movement of people and goods in the hopes of fostering development would cause
potential investors to flee Baltimore for less restrictive cities. But the parallel
of antidiscrimination and track obstruction obscured the fact that municipal
rate policies did not seek to prevent the B&O from transporting goods to any
given destination. The railroad could make any through trade arrangements it
saw fit, match any rates offered by other trunk lines—so long as shipments to
Baltimore enjoyed the same privileges. The very awkwardness of this analogy
evinced the central place of movement within a capitalist ideology still in formation. The railroad's allies transmuted principles of unrestricted movement

first developed in the 1830s into a broader conviction that municipal regulation represented an affront to freedom. Calls for "untaxed movement" and "free intercourse" showed the legacy of earlier clashes over movement in Baltimore's streets; the track debates offered an intellectual framework and key metaphor for those who sought to constrict the boundaries of public action.

And, as in the track debates, foes of regulation characterized the railroad company as a national enterprise and used the language of scale to constrain the scope of municipal policy. The *American* defined the problem as a "*local stoppage*." The *American Railroad Journal* dismissed out of hand the B&O's founding goal of promoting the "trade, commerce, and general welfare of Baltimore." Baltimoreans had "lost sight of the importance of making their road the most convenient through route between New York, say, and the west."[75] The task of Baltimore's government and its citizens in this logic was not to make their city the "arbitrary terminus" of this national rail line but to cultivate what one writer termed "local advantages." Some, for example, praised the B&O for allowing through travelers transferring in Baltimore to linger in the city before hurrying on; perhaps merchants would discover the city's charms while passing through and choose to do business there instead of continuing to New York.[76] This was a remarkably passive program of action for a city government that only a quarter century prior had sought to bolster its economy by projecting a railroad over the mountains.

Even in the face of such arguments, though, the notion that the railroad and the city remained responsible to one another persisted. The same writer could, for example, characterize discrimination as "simply and alone a business question" beyond the reach of municipal scrutiny while praising the B&O for bringing "the riches of the West to our doors," affirming the railroad's role in economic development.[77] Likewise, the editors of Baltimore's newspapers simultaneously embraced a privatized understanding of the railroad's rate policy and contended that the railroad served public ends and warranted public support. Whereas in the summer much of Baltimore's press had condemned the B&O for discrimination, all but one newspaper now came down against municipal rate limits. Even so, they hedged their bets, insisting that regulation was unwarranted because the B&O discriminated very little anyway.[78] In any event, the protests had the desired result. Several days after the B&O rejected the first bill, the council passed new legislation in its stead. The second bill eliminated provisions concerning discrimination and changed the form of the city's aid—rather than endorse the company's bonds, the new bill offered a direct loan of $5 million to the B&O so that it could double track the Main Stem.[79]

The aftermath of the $5 million loan suggests that the economic geography of natural advantage and laws of trade remained powerful well into the 1850s. The market for municipal bonds proved as poor as the market for corporate bonds, and thus by the end of 1854, the B&O had received little of the promised money.[80] In 1856, the company decided to take the funds it had received to date—about $550,000 of the $5 million eventually lent—and pass them on to the struggling Northwestern Virginia Railroad, headed by Thomas Swann, back from Europe. Doing so meant abandoning efforts to double track the Main Stem, and some in the city council called this a "breach of faith," instructing the commissioners of finance to withhold further payments until the company complied.[81] Swann, in an open letter to the mayor, protested that the city could not counter the pernicious effects of the Hempfield Railroad without supporting the NWV.[82]

Swann need not have worried about opposition from Baltimore's mayor. He assumed that position himself later that year, rising to the mayoralty on the Know-Nothing ticket after an uncommonly violent election. On resigning the presidency of the NWV to enter politics, the board of directors for that company wished him luck in governing a city that was "reaping the fruits of his indefatigable and intelligent administration" of both the B&O and Northwestern Virginia.[83] The NWV opened in early 1857, and Swann in his mayoral address for that year noted that it held the "key in all future time to the rich products of the Ohio and Mississippi valleys." The City of Baltimore was by then a first mortgage holder in the branch line.[84] Yet even the NWV could not secure Baltimore's advantages beyond the reach of competition: in May 1857, the *Sun* reported that Philadelphians had launched a new railroad project to connect their city to Parkersburg.[85]

Conclusion

"The student of nature, seeking a true history of the world's material progress, reads [it] in the hills, mountains, valleys, and rivers . . . written with unerring accuracy, by a mightier hand than man's." So begins *The Book of the Great Railway Celebrations of 1857*, a fulsome account of the festivities that accompanied the opening of the Northwestern Virginia Railroad, published in 1858. The author was William P. Smith, who five years earlier had authored a pamphlet downplaying the significance of Baltimore's natural advantages. Now he revisited the question of geography, but in a different register, placing it within the sweep of human history. Populations, Smith wrote, "grow and increase, wherever located to advantage, until sufficiently developed to fulfil their destiny, and then overflow the bounds which circumscribed them." Physical barriers like oceans and mountains only inspired efforts to facilitate their breach. Such it was, Smith wrote, with the Alleghenies—the mountains had impeded expansion, forcing Americans to develop in one location into a mature commercial people until their numbers swelled to the point "that the waves of population would not be restrained." Then, "man," unwilling to confine himself to the use of rivers for travel, created the locomotive, eliminating mountain barriers to travel.[86]

Smith placed the B&O within a teleology dictated by the natural ebb and flow of populations. Just as railroad boosters a decade earlier had asked their readers to take a glance at the map, Smith argued that the fates of the city and of the nation could be read in the landscape. But neither individual nor collective will shaped the geography he described. Smith's impersonal formulation of the railroad's role in geographic expansion made the B&O an agent of world-historical change while it situated Baltimore as an incubator—not an initiator—of progress. If railroad projects followed inevitably from natural processes, then the B&O owed little to its city of origin. Baltimore represented merely one point on a timeline of human progress, just as it was one point on a line of railroad infrastructure.

Smith's account of providential design belied the B&O's prolonged difficulties selecting a terminus, though. The process of moving westward was not a simple matter of charting a course or conquering nature. The company had to contend with and mollify competing localisms, popular demands, and hostile state legislatures. A variety of actors participated in this process—elected officials, corporate executives, newspaper editors, and citizens gathered in public meetings. And Smith's vision of economic geography—both his call for reformed business practices in 1853 and his theory of human expansion—received sustained challenges from Baltimoreans who advanced an understanding of the railroad corporation as an instrument of the municipality, subject to its oversight. This included mechanics employed by the B&O, who used the city government's leverage over the company as a bargaining tool to secure higher wages, and the merchants and citizens who protested rate discrimination. The expansion of American railroad networks in the 1840s and 1850s undermined Baltimoreans' ability to speak confidently about invariable laws of trade, the certainty of straight lines, and the expansive agency of urban publics, Thomas Swann's rhetoric notwithstanding. But a corporate-controlled landscape of unrestricted movement and untrammeled rate setting was not the only understanding of economic geography vying to replace it.

The Smoking, Puffing Locomotive

When the Baltimore & Susquehanna Railroad (B&S) proposed running steam engines down North Street to the newly opened Calvert Station in 1849, John J. Frisby anticipated dire consequences. In a memorial to the city council, cosigned by more than two hundred fellow petitioners, he warned, "The terror inspired in the horse by the War Elephant in ancient times, was as nothing contrasted with his horror in the presence of the smoking, puffing locomotive." The iron horse, he believed, could not coexist peacefully with its flesh-and-blood namesake. Frisby, a general commission merchant who lived and worked downtown, had no reason to fear that this chaos would impinge on his livelihood or disrupt his daily routines. Nonetheless, he found it hard to countenance the presence of steam engines on a thoroughfare like North Street (today known as Guilford Avenue)—a major route out of town, a popular venue for carriage riding, and, most importantly, a principal corridor for funeral processions headed to the romantic rural grounds of Greenmount Cemetery, a resting place for Baltimore's elite since 1839. Frisby's plea to the council painted a harrowing scenario: "Imagine yourselves, gentlemen, with your families, mournfully escorting some beloved friend's remains to the tomb. Suddenly an alarm is raised that a train is approaching. All is noise and confusion. The terror, the dashing and plunging of the horses, the shrieks of the females, and your own hurried and impotent efforts to rescue, present an appalling scene!"[1] Eighteen pastors and church officials concurred in a separate petition that steam engines would profane this sacred rite. In such circumstances, the locomotive threatened the dignity of human life—and death—itself.[2]

With these memorials Frisby and his fellow petitioners added their voices to a conversation about locomotives and urban space then unfolding in city halls and courtrooms across the United States. In the 1840s and 1850s, as the nation's track mileage increased tenfold, questions concerning the place of cities within emergent railroad networks took on new urgency. Railroad executives bristled at the municipal locomotive bans they encountered in large cities like Baltimore, Philadelphia, and New York. They contemplated a steam-powered future in which locomotives ran from point to point unhindered by such restrictions. Efforts to realize this vision in the courts yielded mixed results. Some suits, particularly in the West, proved fruitful; in 1839, for example, the Kentucky Court of Appeals affirmed the right of railroad companies to run steam engines through Louisville's Main Street, deeming locomotives "the offspring, as they will also be the parents, of progressive improvement." The spirit of the age, ruled the court, demanded that municipal safety regulations give way to technological advancement. Other courts, though, held that population density made urban restrictions on steam power sensible. Thus, when in 1843 the New York State Supreme Court upheld Buffalo's right to bar locomotives from its streets, the judges ruled, "We need no other proof than what may be derived from our own observation and the experience of the times, that a train of cars impelled by force of steam power through a populous city, may expose the inhabitants . . . to unreasonable perils."[3]

These two decisions, four years apart, succinctly framed the parameters of the debate: progress versus public safety. Railroad executives portrayed the steam engine, with its unparalleled power, its smooth movement, and even its elegant design, as a modernizing force; giving free rein to locomotive travel within the city would, they argued, facilitate exchange and stimulate industry. They envisioned an urban world remade by steam: skylines studded with smokestacks, and streets populated by powerful engines. Urbanites, for their part, never spoke with one voice on the locomotive question, but most viewed the prospect of steam power on public roads with trepidation. Even places like Chicago that grew up around rail transportation saw fierce opposition to the presence of these literally combustible forces in urban neighborhoods.[4] Citizens called on city governments to regulate railroad traffic, and in doing so, they made urban space a uniquely troublesome site for railroad operations.

Like other railroad companies, the B&O found that its repeated attempts to run locomotives through Baltimore's city center yielded only partly successful results. Perhaps mindful of what John Frisby termed "the notorious hostility of our community" to urban steam engines, the B&O's managers did not, like their Kentucky counterparts, try their luck in court. Instead, the company's managers sought a spatial solution to their dilemma, creating new types of urban infrastructure and even new neighborhoods to accommodate the locomotive. First, the company laid tracks to a deepwater port in South

Baltimore known as Locust Point. Because this branch line ran through the lightly inhabited urban fringe, the municipal steam ban did not apply, and the B&O could send locomotives straight to the docks. Second, the company started work on a grand downtown depot called Camden Station. The new station promised to plug Baltimore seamlessly into the steam-powered circuits of long-distance travel, but doing so entailed first forcing the depot's densely populated environs to yield to the B&O's engines. Rather than accommodate steam power to the city, these initiatives accommodated the city to steam, reorienting urban space to facilitate the use of locomotives. Both of these innovations—the rail-to-water interface and the central city station—served as models for other rail companies looking to funnel traffic through American cities.

In the early 1850s, then, the B&O imprinted itself in Baltimore's built environment in novel ways, creating new neighborhoods or redeveloping old ones to serve the imperatives of mechanized movement (fig. 5.1). Yet the company could not simply transform the city as it pleased. Rather, the controversies over locomotive policy, the Locust Point Branch, and Camden Station reveal the negotiations and compromises attendant to the creation of a national rail network. They also highlight the role of urban space as a flash point in the increasingly contentious relationship between the city government and the railroad corporation.

The Urban Locomotive

Until 1848, all locomotives arriving in Baltimore from the West pulled first into Mount Clare Station. There, employees broke long trains into individual cars and attached them to teams of horses, which then dragged the cars via the Pratt Street tracks to local consignees or to other stations for through shipment. The 1831 ordinance that authorized the B&O to lay its tracks through city streets mandated this shift from steam to animal power in the hopes of mitigating the railroad's dangers and its disruption to urban life. Antebellum urbanites had compelling reasons to dread the prospect of locomotives in their midst; the same relentless force that hauled trains at hitherto unimaginable speeds was also susceptible to catastrophic failures. "Time was when the upsetting of a stage, which should cause the fracture of a limb . . . would shock the feelings of the community," wrote the *Sun* in 1840. "Since steam became a motive power on our roads and waters, destruction of life and injury to person have become so common, as to excite scarcely any special emotion." Running spark- and smoke-belching locomotives in dense urban environments magnified the inherent dangers of steam technology: in the city, an

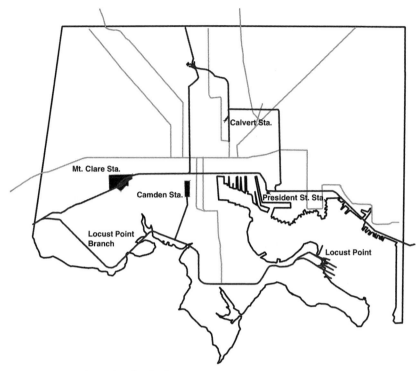

FIGURE 5.1. Baltimore's railroad infrastructure, ca. 1859. Dark-gray lines represent heavy rail track built by the railroad companies; black boxes indicate train stations and depots. Light-gray lines represent the early streetcar routes, first introduced in 1859. Map by author. Adapted from John F. Weishampel, *Map of Baltimore* (Baltimore: John F. Weishampel, 1859).

exploding engine could kill dozens of people in an instant and start fires that that might level whole neighborhoods. Even a properly functioning locomotive generated earthshaking rumbles and emitted shrill whistles that startled urban workhorses and rattled the nerves of city dwellers.[5]

Yet while the municipal government and much of the citizenry saw the locomotive as a threat to peace and safety, railroad companies saw the horse as a threat to the bottom line. Horses lacked the speed and power of locomotives and maintaining them required outlays for stables and food. B&O engineer Benjamin H. Latrobe estimated in 1847 that it cost 12.25 cents per ton per mile to haul goods by horse through the city streets, compared with 4.25 cents for locomotives.[6] To minimize these expenses, Baltimore's railroad companies built their main freight depots at the edges of urban settlement. The B&O's Mount Clare stood in the western fringe of the city, and the B&S's Calvert Station to the north of the city center. The Philadelphia, Wilmington & Baltimore Railroad (PWB) initially shared a downtown depot with the B&O on

Pratt Street but relocated to President Street Station in 1849 in order to, as the company's president put it, "dispense with the use of horse power in Baltimore."[7] These peripheral stations reshaped the city, drawing industrial and residential development away from the urban core. Yet all three companies continued to rely on horses for local deliveries and rail transfers. As of the mid-1840s, cross-city travel cost the B&O from $12,000 to $15,000 annually.[8]

B&O executives, resentful of this imposition, turned to the city council for relief in the early 1840s. In 1843, a sympathetic council committee advocated lifting the ban on urban locomotives. The committee argued that locomotives might actually improve safety in city streets; unlike horses, engines could maintain a constant speed and haul a greater number of cars at once, reducing the number of trains running daily through the city.[9] The council prepared an ordinance allowing B&O steam engines to enter the urban core, albeit subject to a number of safety regulations that later became standard limitations on urban steam power: engines were to burn coal (which produced fewer sparks than wood) and to move no faster than four miles per hour while passing through the city; a man was to walk in front of the engines to keep the track clear; and the locomotive was to be redesigned so as to reduce the chance of frightening horses.[10] The council narrowly passed the bill, but Mayor Solomon Hillen returned it unsigned. Railroad companies were already, he suggested, notorious for weakening and then bypassing public restrictions on their power. The B&O would doubtlessly acquiesce to these "manacles," knowing that, "the object once attained," the regulations would "fall harmless at its feet; leaving it free, to go in quest of new accessions to its power or convenience." As he saw it, corporate savings did not merit sacrifices to public safety.[11] Disappointed B&O executives warned stockholders to lower their expectations for the company's earnings in the face of this setback as the costs associated with urban transit continued to mount.[12]

Changes in the transportation landscape in western Maryland soon revived the urban locomotive question, however. In 1844, as the Chesapeake & Ohio Canal (C&O) approached the Cumberland coalfields, the B&O's president and board of directors warned that failure to permit locomotives in the city threatened Baltimore's competitive advantages: if the city did not make it easier for bulky commodities like iron and coal to pass through its streets, Baltimore might lose these trades to Washington.[13] In response, the council took two actions: first, it authorized the creation of a new branch of the B&O to tidewater at the south side of the Basin (Locust Point), and second, it permitted limited use of locomotives within city streets. A new ordinance empowered the B&O to run steam engines down Pratt Street between nine o'clock at night and sunrise, provided it followed the safety precautions that had been sketched out in earlier legislation.[14]

Within two years, leaders in the B&O began to push for further loosening of the city's locomotive policies. In March 1847, railroad officials lobbied the municipal government for permission to run steam engines through the city around the clock, anticipating that a crush of trade would greet the rail line once it reached the Ohio River. The company's chief engineer estimated that running engines at all hours as far as Howard Street, where the B&O's Pratt Street tracks intersected with the tracks of the B&S, would save $12,000 annually and facilitate the delivery of 225,000 tons of goods.[15] At least some in the city government agreed with this analysis. After the mayor and city council observed the operations of an experimental urban locomotive, some council members proposed granting the B&O the twenty-four-hour locomotive use it desired.[16] Their proposals never passed, however, and the use of horses within the urban core continued to slow cross-town traffic and inflate operating expenses for years to come.[17] Such restrictions drew condemnation from the *American Railroad Journal*, which in 1848 argued that Baltimore's "*councils*, and of course her citizens, are not liberal—nor even *just*—in their requirements of the railroad companies to use *horse* power to so great an extent as they do."[18]

As this suggests, railroad companies and their allies saw opposition to urban locomotives as a vain effort to slow the tide of progress. Thus, the attempts by John Frisby and others to stop the incursion of locomotives onto North Street in 1849 prompted the circulation of counterpetitions, signed primarily by merchants, arguing that local prosperity depended on accommodating the steam engine. They responded to the pastors' concerns about the disruption of funeral rites by shrugging their shoulders: the steam engine, they suggested, would inevitably change uses of the street by reorienting urban geography, and for the better. Locomotive traffic promised to transform North Street into a place "occupied by Depots, Warehouses, and Manufacturing establishments, which would render the street useless, as a thoroughfare for pleasure carriages," said one such petition.[19] Whereas city councilmen balked at permitting locomotives to run by day through Pratt Street, they evidently found this logic compelling for more peripheral North Street.[20] And indeed, as predicted, with the onset of locomotive travel the neighborhood began to change. After the B&S enlarged its depot and closed several streets, the heavy rail traffic drew forwarding and transportation companies to this once-bucolic thoroughfare. Such transformations gave the neighborhood an industrialized appearance that, for the *Sun*, "betoken[ed] the advancement of the age."[21]

At the same time, engineers worked to adapt locomotive technology to an urban setting, adjusting the engines' technical specifications and outward appearances so as to minimize disruptions to city life. After a few years of tinkering, the B&S unveiled what the *Sun* called a *"Street Locomotive"*—a large engine calibrated for heavy loads and low speed. The urban engine featured an ornate gothic covering of ironwork that disguised its function so as not to frighten horses and could carry twenty-five cars up North Street's steep grades with ease.[22] Such innovations led some urbanites, in Baltimore and elsewhere, to believe that the locomotive might represent a safer alternative to horse-drawn cars.[23] As the B&O neared the Ohio River in 1852, the *Wheeling Daily Intelligencer* chalked up opposition to urban locomotives to the "universal dread of innovation" and reminded its readers that unlike horses, engines never misunderstood a command, demanded rest, or startled from fright: "We shall live in the hope of seeing it a useful and familiar personage in our city thoroughfares."[24]

During the 1850s, the city council continually modified the provisions governing the use of steam engines within the city, increasing the speed limit from four miles per hour to five, mandating the use of specially adapted street locomotives, and forbidding the use of steam whistles within the central city.[25] Yet these changes did not reflect a growing embrace or even tolerance of the urban locomotive among Baltimoreans. Rather, the citizens of Baltimore responded to the presence of this technology in their neighborhoods unevenly. To its proponents, steam power enabled urban expansion, allowing the city to enlarge its borders. Some even called for the use of steam power in the streetcar system that developed in Baltimore after 1859. But to opponents of steam, dangers to life and limb remained primary concerns, unallayed by the continuing development of the technology.[26] Persistent public unease with the locomotive spelled uncertainty for railroad corporations: even if they gained the right to run engines in the street, they faced the threat of political reversal. In light of such pressures, the B&O turned to a spatial solution for its locomotive dilemma.[27]

Locust Point

As early as 1852, the civil engineer Charles Ellet Jr. decided that rail travel was incompatible with urban life. Ellet did not believe that the railroad would corrode the urban fabric—in fact, he optimistically imagined that railroads could be "properly designed for the accommodation of the cities." Rather, the problem lay in passing trains through the city, as urban traffic and regulations hindered efficient operations. "At an early day," he opined, "the *through trade and travel* of this country must be accommodated by lines which pass around the great cities, and avoid the obstructions which a dense population offers."[28]

These obstructions were as much political as physical. As the B&O's legal team freely conceded, heavy concentrations of people and buildings distinguished urban environments from other kinds of space and legitimated government oversight of movement through the city, subjecting railroads to regulations not found in the countryside.[29] In practice, the city government's ad hoc and inconsistent enforcement mechanisms softened this burden. Typically, it fell to citizens to lodge complaints about railroad practices with the city council. Petitions concerning poorly laid tracks or speeding trains went to council committees, which then launched investigations. If the committee found that the grievance was legitimate, it either recommended passing a new ordinance that addressed the problem or called for enforcement of existing laws. This process yielded slow and uneven results, and the council returned to the same problems repeatedly.[30] In 1855, for example, when property owners complained that B&O tracks on Pratt Street blocked the gutters, causing their basements to flood during heavy rains, the council asked the city commissioner to look into the matter. A year later, the offending track remained in place and the basements remained as flood-prone as ever. Again, the council instructed the city commissioner to return to the scene and demand action from the B&O. That the spring rains the following year did not bring a new round of petitions suggests that this time, the intervention may have had the desired effect.[31]

As this episode suggests, the city government had the power to legislate and investigate, but few means to enforce compliance. Baltimore's railroads, for their part, promised to police themselves so as to ward off penalties and regulation, but their interest in speeding up traffic and minimizing expenditures often clashed with the municipality's interest in the safety and openness of the public streets.[32] When they would not cooperate, the city government found it had limited tools at its disposal. The legislation authorizing the B&O to lay tracks in 1831 had vested in the mayor and city council power to remove the rails entirely should they obstruct ordinary use of the street, a provision that Mayor Jacob Davies argued in 1845 had provided "a wholesome check" to the B&O's actions.[33] Yet this all-or-nothing provision left municipal authorities with a machete when they needed a scalpel. Baltimore's elected officials soon conceded that minor infringements required a more subtle municipal response.[34] In 1850, the council tasked the city commissioners with examining railway tracks and reporting obstructions or impediments to the mayor, endowing them with the power to impose penalties on railroad companies for violating municipal regulations.[35] Commissioners began to walk the streets armed with forms on which they documented irregularities in the tracks.[36] City police also took a more active role in monitoring railway practices, fining or even arresting railroad authorities for speeding and parking violations.[37]

Municipal regulations, however inefficient, coupled with the ban on steam engines, played a major role in the B&O's decision in 1845 to remove at least some of its operations from the urban fabric. The same act that sanctioned the use of locomotives on Pratt Street at night also authorized the B&O to build a branch road to a largely undeveloped section of waterfront on the South Baltimore peninsula between Federal Hill and Fort McHenry, known as Locust Point. The new Locust Point Branch skirted the densely inhabited urban core and thus bypassed the urban ban on steam power, which applied only within the built-up parts of town. Initially, the B&O, hoping to remove the new branch and its traffic from municipal oversight entirely, sought permission to alter street grades and run locomotives at will. Mayor Davies refused to grant unchecked control of this part of the city to the railroad company, however, stating that the people's representatives should not abandon their regulatory prerogatives within the city limits. As such, the Locust Point bill as passed mandated a speed limit of four miles per hour; rendered the B&O liable for any damages to life, limb, and property incurred by its steam engines within city limits; and kept jurisdiction over street grades in the public's hands.[38]

As one group of workers extended B&O tracks over the mountains, another laid new tracks through the city. After three years of surveys and construction, the branch and its waterfront facilities opened in 1848.[39] The arrival of the railroad spurred permanent settlement in a part of the city that had heretofore seen little development. A recalcitrant landowner had left the territory largely untouched for decades, and only a handful of industrial concerns stood on the ground when the B&O moved in. The prospect of commodity-laden trains pulling into the waterfront territory primed the area for investment.[40] The B&O itself purchased much of the land in and around Locust Point, scooping up large lots for use as wharves, depots, and water stations. When extant acreage could not serve the company's needs, it reclaimed land on the waterfront to make room for shipping infrastructure. Developers added slim row houses to accommodate the area's growing workforce.[41] As early as 1850, the B&O could boast in its annual report that "Locust Point . . . which two years ago existed only in name, has, since its opening, assumed the appearance of an active and growing settlement."[42]

Locust Point was a new kind of railroad terminal and a new kind of neighborhood. Because its residential population grew only after the B&O laid its tracks, locals found themselves grandfathered out of municipal restrictions on

FIGURE 5.2. Rail-to-ship transfers at Locust Point, ca. 1869. Courtesy of the Library of Congress. Detail from E. Sachse, & Co., *Bird's Eye View of the City of Baltimore, 1869* (Baltimore, 1870).

motive power and thus had to live with locomotives running past their houses at all hours. The perils and inconveniences borne by residents—mostly B&O workers and their families—constituted an unparalleled boon for the railroad and shipping merchants. Although all traffic bound for Baltimore or connecting rail lines continued to rely on horses, steam engines could haul freight trains directly to the water's edge for transshipment. Stevedores, working on special railed docks, transferred cargoes from railcars directly onto waiting ships (fig. 5.2). These new facilities promised both to speed the transfer of through trade and alleviate the pressure this traffic had formerly placed on the city streets.[43]

One commodity in particular came to dominate the landscape of Locust Point: coal. When the B&O reached Cumberland in 1843, it gained access to the rich coalfields of the Allegheny Mountains. Thomas Swann, during his stint as president, anticipated that this fossil fuel would play an important role in the company's future business and kept rates on coal low in order to cultivate this trade. His efforts paid off: by the 1850s, coal accounted for more than half of the B&O's tonnage and fully a third of its freight revenues.[44] The B&O purchased a number of Allegheny coal mines outright, as did high-ranking officials like John W. Garrett, guaranteeing the company favorable rates on this commodity and giving it a monopoly on its transportation. Taking advantage of the seemingly limitless supplies at its doorstep, the B&O became one of the first railroads to switch from firewood to coal in its engines.[45]

Depositing western Maryland's rich coal reserves in Baltimore also provided a ready source of power for nearby factories. As of 1859, approximately a third of the B&O's annual coal shipments—some fifty-eight thousand tons—

remained in Baltimore for local use.[46] The city council considered cheap access to coal essential for the comfort and prosperity of Baltimore's citizenry (or at least its manufacturers) and fought, with occasional success, against the B&O's repeated efforts to hike coal rates.[47] Between 1833 and 1860 the number of steam-powered factories in Baltimore increased from thirty-two to eighty, a two-and-a-half-fold rise that roughly mirrored the city's demographic growth in that period. Steam engines allowed industrial production to spread out to the urban fringe, particularly in the western and southwestern parts of the city, where machine shops churned out components for the Baltimore's railroads and steamships. More remarkable than their number was their scale. Steam-powered factories typically employed more than twenty workers, and the largest of them—the B&O's machine shops—employed nearly a thousand. Of the nonmechanized industries, only garment shops had comparable figures.[48]

By the Civil War it had become a local trope that western coal, borne by the B&O, catalyzed Baltimore's industrial development. William Prescott Smith's *Book of the Great Railway Celebration of 1857* credited the western railroad for much of Baltimore's manufacturing business. The cheap and constant supply of coal furnished by the railroad transformed the city's landscape. If observers were to float above Baltimore in a hot-air balloon, they would see a city "surrounded on almost every side by lines of factories, mills, and manufacturing establishments, whose columns of dark smoke and jets of steam, demonstrate the constant activity and innumerability of her productive interests."[49] When the sun went down, gas generated from coal mined in western Virginia and shipped by rail to South Baltimore illuminated the city's streets, commercial establishments, and posh homes.[50]

Locust Point became the epicenter of Baltimore's coal trade. Swann had ordered the construction of this branch in no small part to handle the B&O's valuable and growing coal shipments.[51] Coal wholesalers and mining companies snatched up land at Locust Point at ever-rising prices. The *American* declared of one Locust Point coal yard that it "might itself almost be termed a succession of mines, so largely and well is it stocked with every variety of coal."[52] Locust Point served as a distribution hub for coal used throughout the world and a regular refueling site for coastal steamers that linked Baltimore with ports up and down the eastern seaboard.[53]

In building Locust Point, the B&O summoned into existence a new form of urban rail infrastructure. Other trunk rail lines eventually created their own rail-to-water facilities, but only many years later. More than a decade after Locust Point opened, for example, the Pennsylvania Railroad still used horses to haul freight to the Delaware River docks in eastern Philadelphia. The Erie Railroad built waterfront facilities at Jersey City in 1861, and the New York Central started work on its Hudson River freight terminal in Manhattan in 1867.[54] The B&O moved first in this field because of the fortuitous availability of desirable yet undeveloped waterfront land within the city limits. At Locust Point, the company created a new terminus and a new kind of city neighborhood to suit its needs without abandoning its founding city.[55]

Yet some Baltimoreans saw little difference between building a terminus at Locust Point and establishing a new city beyond the city limits. As a shipping center, Locust Point posed a particular threat to Fells Point, which had long handled much of Baltimore's maritime trade. The new district's rapid development struck a bitter chord with the property owners of Fells Point, who looked on with dismay as the B&O, supported in part by their own tax payments, turned a wasteland into a bustling port. Aggrieved Fells Pointers reported that property values in Locust Point now rivaled their own, while they remained disconnected from the B&O's channels of trade.[56] To remedy this imbalance, the city government authorized the B&O to extend its tracks from Mount Clare to Fells Point while continuing work on its Locust Point Branch. Over the following several decades the company failed to act on this privilege, however, despite Fells Point residents' repeated requests, for the simple reason that Locust Point had satisfied the company's need for a waterfront outlet. Where once the company had proposed to vault over the city to reach Fells Point, it could now safely ignore that neighborhood in favor of its own bespoke alternative.[57]

Fells Pointers' grievances reflected the threat Locust Point posed to their property values and the economic future of their neighborhood, but there was more at stake than simple neighborhood rivalries. Where and by what means railroads funneled trade through cities became more important as rail companies expanded through the American countryside, and the prospect of smooth, mechanized passage through urban space could as easily diminish a city's fortunes as raise them up. In 1849, the editors of the *Sun* weighed in against a plan, briefly entertained, to unite all of Baltimore's railroads in a single depot. Such a "suicidal policy," said the *Sun*, would "tempt travelers to pass through our city as they do over the Alleghanies [*sic*], without stop[p]ing or spending a dollar, or even knowing whether there are any houses in Baltimore."[58] The mechanized through travel found at Locust Point did not as yet pose this sort of threat, because most passengers still transferred via the Pratt Street tracks. Nonetheless, the B&O initiated its other principal mid-century intervention in the urban landscape, Camden Station, in part to allay such anxieties. This new depot placed the B&O in the heart of Baltimore, which presented a different set of problems for company officials and their new neighbors.

Camden Station

The *Proceedings of the Sundry Citizens*, the B&O's founding document, said much about Baltimore as a whole but nothing about the city's free black population. As William Watkins discovered, though, the railroad's expansion had immediate implications for himself and his neighbors. In the antebellum period, Watkins enjoyed renown as a teacher and minister, not only within Baltimore's African American community but also nationwide. Born free circa 1800, Watkins first rose to prominence by rejecting the colonization movement, rebutting arguments made by John H. B. Latrobe and others concerning racial hierarchies and African Americans' prospects in Liberia. He drew death threats for his advocacy but caught the eye of David Walker in Boston, who praised Watkins's skill at dismantling colonizationist canards. Watkins also met William Lloyd Garrison in 1829–1830 when the latter lived in Baltimore, and he wrote regularly for the *Liberator* while helping to launch the National Negro Convention Movement in the 1830s. But although he held a national profile, Watkins remained deeply rooted in Baltimore. His family home on Camden Street sat in the midst of a densely populated neighborhood located near the center of the city, just to the west of the Basin, which since the early nineteenth century had served as the heart of Baltimore's free black community. This area, today known as Otterbein, held the Sharp Street Methodist Church, a hub of black education, organization, and activism where Watkins taught and preached. Many of Baltimore's antebellum civil rights leaders lived nearby. The wooden houses in this district also accommodated working-class African Americans employed in the maritime trades, draymen and carters, and day laborers. All that the editors of the *Sun* saw when they looked at this area, though, were "rude and dilapidated tenements." In 1852, Watkins's neighborhood, with its central location and its disenfranchised population, came within the sights of the Baltimore & Ohio Railroad.[59]

As workers neared the Ohio River, the B&O's board of directors assessed the capacities of its stations within Baltimore. Mount Clare Station, which handled freight and passengers and housed the company's machine shops, stood far from downtown. Pratt Street Depot enjoyed a central location, but reaching it required the use of horses. And Locust Point, then only recently opened, lacked the facilities to handle Baltimore-bound shipments or passengers.[60] A select committee determined that none of these stations could accommodate the trade expected to arrive in Baltimore once the line opened to the Ohio River. As it stood, the committee reported, even a modest increase in traffic would flood the city's already congested thoroughfares with drays. The expense and difficulty of street travel threatened to undermine Baltimore's competitive advantages as well. Shipping a barrel of flour eighty miles from Martinsburg to the Mount Clare depot cost around twenty cents, but it cost six cents to ship the same barrel one mile from Mount Clare to a merchant's warehouse. Without a downtown depot, all heavy trade would leave the built portions of Baltimore behind—and go instead to Locust Point. It would be a cruel irony, read the committee's report, for the "Citizens of Baltimore who have patiently, and courageously, struggled through nearly 25 years of onerous taxation" in support of the railroad, "to see the grass growing before their doors, whilst a new city arises," adding, "The Capital of our City has been expended to advance the prosperity of *Baltimore*, and not to build up new cities around us to sap her prosperity."[61]

The committee recommended creating a new depot that could handle the B&O's Baltimore-bound freight and passenger trades at one centrally located site. They selected a block between Howard and Eutaw Streets fronting Camden Street, just south of Pratt, which would give passengers easy access to the city's hotels while depositing freight close to merchants' warehouses and the harbor, reducing the need for drayage. Crucially, the company could use steam locomotives for all travel to and from this location. Camden Station would connect not with the Pratt Street tracks but with the Locust Point Branch, and the lobbying efforts of company president Thomas Swann secured municipal legislation that empowered the B&O to run locomotives to its new depot, provided it followed the usual safety precautions. Swann estimated that avoiding horsepower in this way would save the company nearly $25,000.[62]

Building Camden Station required unprecedented interventions in Baltimore's landscape. The B&O had placed both Mount Clare and Locust Point on greenfield sites at the fringes of urban settlement, and the Pratt Street Depot was a modest structure that did not interfere with the buildings around it. The proposed site for Camden Station, by contrast, sat in the heart of the city. For the board of directors, and indeed for white Baltimore as a whole, the dense settlement of this area posed no obstacle. The B&O pledged to pay nearly $375,000 to clear five blocks of land, and demolition began in December 1852. The *Sun* celebrated the new Camden Station as a form of "slum clearance." As landlords pocketed the money, a displaced free black community searched for new housing within and around Baltimore. Some moved a few blocks away to Federal Hill, others headed west to the residential districts south of Mount Clare, and still more into the northern parts of the city. But the advent of Camden Station coincided with a period of intensifying discrimination for African Americans in Baltimore, and wherever they turned, they faced narrowed prospects. In the 1850s, rural legislators in Annapolis wrote new laws that threatened free black citizens with enslavement for petty crimes while European immigrants waged violent campaigns to take jobs formerly held by African Americans in the manufacturing and maritime trades. These worsening political and economic conditions prompted some residents to look further afield in the wake of the destruction of their neighborhood. William Watkins would continue his fight for civil rights, but not from Baltimore. As the B&O claimed his neighborhood for its station, he joined seventy-two fellow members of the Sharp Street Church in relocating to Canada, where he remained until his death in 1858.[63]

Not for the last time, the city's African American community faced eviction to make way for the infrastructure of modernity. As the area's poverty made the land affordable, so its residents' marginality within Baltimore's white power structure rendered their dislocation uncontroversial; the B&O's annual report for 1852 declared, "No act of this Board, it is believed, has been received with more favor by the entire community, than the location of this noble station—holding out the advantages that it does to the whole city."[64] The B&O's executives envisioned their new station as a transformative improvement, a monument to the efficiencies of steam travel that would plug Baltimore into an expanding network of rail communications. Two decades after the track debates fragmented the city into rival factions seeking to capture railroad traffic for themselves, the new station promised, at last, to act as a unifying force within Baltimore. But this construction of unity built on and ultimately contributed to the hardening racial lines of antebellum Baltimore. Conferring the advantages of mechanized travel on "the whole city" meant demolishing one part of it.

Locomotives and Local Mobility

The B&O turned to in-house architect John F. Kemp to design the building, later adding the Baltimore firm Niernsee & Neilson to the project. The designers looked to London for structural and artistic precedents. Camden Station, like most new urban depots built in the 1840s and 1850s, adopted an architectural mode inspired by Italian villas—low-lying, horizontal structures punctuated by dramatic bell and clock towers, a form that architects in the 1850s referred to as "railroad style." Baltimore already had two stations—Calvert and President Street—designed in this Italianate manner, but Camden Station eclipsed both in scale and ambition. Where Calvert Station, itself the largest railroad terminus in the United States when it opened in 1850, had two short towers, Camden's design called for three, including a central campanile that stretched 180 feet in the air, surpassing in height, if not in elevation, Baltimore's 178-foot Washington Monument. (The central tower proved dangerously unstable, and in the 1880s the company took it down). A full city block wide, Camden Station's design reflected its function as a liminal space between the realm of steam-powered long-distance travel and the horse-powered urban environment. Writers in the nineteenth century commonly analogized the modern railroad station to the city gate of ancient times, and perhaps in a nod to this conceit the plans originally called for arched tunnels on the flanks of the depot in order to accommodate drays and wagons (fig. 5.3). The central approach to the station served passenger trains; the other two handled freight traffic. The station's interior contained ticket offices, baggage facilities, and waiting rooms (including a separate space for women), and, innovatively, an expansive concourse for entry and exit (fig. 5.4). The upper floors of the new station served as executive headquarters for the B&O, giving the company a central location within the city to match its central importance.[65]

As with its marine terminal at Locust Point, the B&O's grand central-city station set a precedent that other eastern railroad companies eventually followed. In Boston, as in Baltimore, the 1840s and 1850s saw a flurry of depot construction, but railroads there largely relied on landfill rather than demolition to create their downtown stations. The most famous urban station in

THE PROPOSED CAMDEN STREET STATION.

FIGURE 5.3. Illustration of Camden Station as proposed, with arched gateways. Bowen, *Rambles in the Path of the Steam-Horse*, 129.

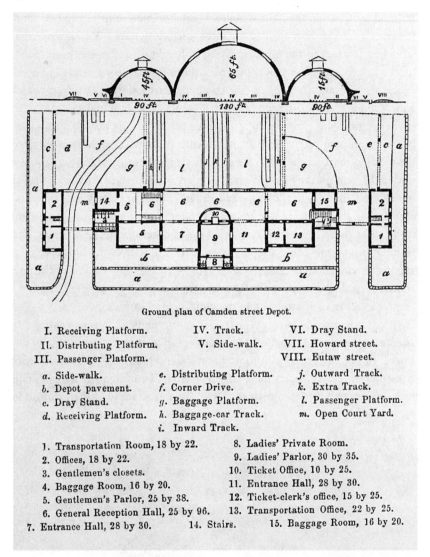

Ground plan of Camden street Depot.

I. Receiving Platform.   IV. Track.   VI. Dray Stand.
II. Distributing Platform.   V. Side-walk.   VII. Howard street.
III. Passenger Platform.   VIII. Eutaw street.

a. Side-walk.   *e.* Distributing Platform.   *j.* Outward Track.
b. Depot pavement.   *f.* Corner Drive.   *k.* Extra Track.
c. Dray Stand.   *g.* Baggage Platform.   *l.* Passenger Platform.
d. Receiving Platform.   *h.* Baggage-car Track.   *m.* Open Court Yard.
    i. Inward Track.

1. Transportation Room, 18 by 22.   8. Ladies' Private Room.
2. Offices, 18 by 22.   9. Ladies' Parlor, 30 by 35.
3. Gentlemen's closets.   10. Ticket Office, 10 by 25.
4. Baggage Room, 16 by 20.   11. Entrance Hall, 28 by 30.
5. Gentlemen's Parlor, 25 by 38.   12. Ticket-clerk's office, 15 by 25.
6. General Reception Hall, 25 by 96.   13. Transportation Office, 22 by 25.
7. Entrance Hall, 28 by 30.   14. Stairs.   15. Baggage Room, 16 by 20.

FIGURE 5.4. Ground plans for Camden Station. Bowen, *Rambles in the Path of the Steam-Horse*, 131.

America, the New York Central Railroad's Grand Central Depot, opened in 1871, and it too allowed long-distance trains to use steam power when pulling into or out of the terminus. But while this station was grand from the start, it became central only later, as New York real estate continued the march up Manhattan. Whereas the B&O planted its station in the urban core, the New York Central's edifice stood at Forty-Second Street, the southernmost limit for steam power as allowed by New York's common council and well north of dense settlement until the 1880s. The Pennsylvania Railroad's Broad Street

Station, opened in 1881, offers a closer parallel to Camden Station. After decades of avoiding Philadelphia's urban core, the Pennsylvania decided in 1879 to extend its service into the city center with a new terminus opposite the City Hall. The elevated tracks that conveyed steam-powered trains into this station soon became an obstacle for urbanites and a bottleneck for railroad managers.[66]

Given the difficulties they encountered, it is perhaps no surprise that the Pennsylvania's managers waited so long to bring their services into the urban core. A busy station saw dozens of trains come and go daily, shaking the earth and exhaling smoke on the way. Eventually, at the end of the century, the B&O conducted pioneering experiments that resolved this problem by running electric engines underground through long, unventilated tunnels, but in the age of steam, bringing mechanized power into the heart of city meant going through people's backyards.[67] As it turned out, the 1852 demolition of Watkins's neighborhood was just the start of a larger project: the reorientation of much of South Baltimore around the prerogatives of rapid transportation. Turning Camden Station into an efficient transit hub proved more challenging than clearing the land. In public fights in the 1850s over the use of two streets, Cecil Alley and Conway Street, property owners and white residents joined with some of their African American neighbors to oppose measures that sacrificed street space to steam engines. In the process they raised questions of property and politics that challenged the B&O's assurances that mechanizing long-distance travel served the public good (fig. 5.5).

In 1853, when the line finally opened to the Ohio River, the B&O asked the city council to widen Cecil Alley, a small lane between Howard and Eutaw Streets that linked the Locust Point Branch to the under-construction Camden Station. An interracial contingent of property owners and residents on Cecil Alley objected to what they called an unfair imposition on their property rights. They did not critique eminent domain per se. Were the city to desire "ground for the defence of the City, for the introduction of public works, or for any public purpose or use," wrote the petitioners, "the rights of the individual must yield to the sovereign power." But they took issue with the seizure of private property for "mere corporate advantage." They rejected, in other words, the company's contention that facilitating rail travel served a public function, or at least the notion that long-haul travelers' interests in mobility outweighed their own right to move freely within their neighborhood. As another set of petitions pointed out, once widened the alley would be "entirely monopolized by said company," as "the running of locomotives through the same . . . excludes all use and enjoyment of it by the public."[68]

The B&O's representatives, frustrated by this opposition, insisted that

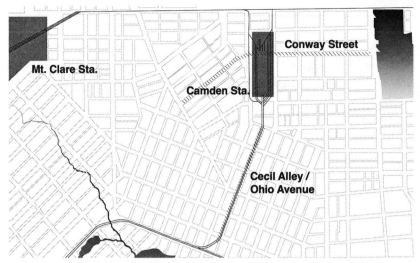

FIGURE 5.5. Camden Station, Cecil Alley, and Conway Street. Map by Lai Tin Wai. Adapted from Simon J. Martenet, *Scott's Map of the City of Baltimore* (Baltimore: s.n., 1856).

making room for long-distance transit met an abiding public need. President Thomas Swann grumbled, "The track in Cecil Alley has been a source of vexatious expenditure, owing to the impracticable spirit evinced by persons binding on said alley." Local property owners—alley dwellers, no less—held up an improvement that promised to transform the experience of transportation by improving Baltimore's connections to distant places. Their claims to the alley were dwarfed, as Swann saw it, by the magnitude of the system this alley would join.[69] The B&O's position won out, and by May 1855, the *Sun* reported that workmen were removing structures on Cecil Alley to make way for an additional track to Camden Station. The *Sun* declared the measure necessary in order to ease delays and improve operations.[70] Ultimately, the B&O made Cecil Alley into a full street and gave it what the *Sun* called "the more appropriate and euphonious name of 'Ohio Avenue.'"[71] As an alley became an avenue, the property relations of Cecil gave way to the imperatives of a national railroad network.

The debate over Conway Street in 1859 similarly involved the B&O's efforts to increase the efficiency of Camden Station. The company sought to close Conway Street, which intersected the depot, so as to accommodate passenger trains waiting for departure. The *Sun* noted that the B&O's inability to assert permanent control over this street had left Camden Station with a "ragged and unfinished appearance."[72] The B&O sought permission from the city council to close Conway Street.[73] Property owners in the area objected strenuously to the proposal. The construction and operation of the station had already disrupted their community, as cars passed through the streets at all hours, encumbering traffic and endangering children. When the council approved the request, residents and property owners on Conway Street did not give up; they instead called an outdoor meeting to denounce the decision. Nearly five hundred persons gathered at the corner of Conway and Paca, bearing transparencies saying "Conway Street must not be Closed" and "Hold Up for Your Rights." Speakers objected to sacrificing their property for the B&O's benefit and asked the mayor to veto the measure.[74]

Despite his complaints about the Cecil Alley protests during his tenure as B&O president six years earlier, Thomas Swann, as mayor of the city, opposed the closure of Conway. In his annual report for 1859, B&O president John W. Garrett groused about this decision but expressed confidence that the company would get its way in the end. The greater good demanded street closure, he said, as it would beautify the neighborhood, promote the interest of nearby property owners, and allow the company to better serve the traveling public.[75] His prediction proved correct, if premature: after several abortive attempts and considerable lobbying from B&O executives, the municipal government finally approved the closure of Conway Street in 1875. By this time, though, the constant flow of cars into and out of Camden Station monopolized the nearby streets, to the consternation of the station's neighbors. As a petition pointed out, "If one of us obstructs the highways of the city for 15 minutes we are taken in charge by a Policeman." Yet railroad cars stopped in the streets in front of their houses for hours on end. The petitioners asked that "the same law that rules the *beggars* to control the *Millionaire*," but to no avail. Railroad traffic effectively closed Conway Street well before the city council made it official.[76]

Yet if Camden Station threw the neighborhood into disarray, it also worked to construct a sense of the city as a whole. Presented in the press as an icon of modernity, efficiency, and organization, it helped define the city by assuming a prominent and central place within the built environment. The new station took well over a decade to build; in 1864, the *Sun* reported that the "commodious and handsome depot" was nearly complete. "The building altogether is pronounced one of the best of its kind in the country," the paper boasted (fig. 5.6). The Italianate structure, clad in high-quality Baltimore brick, became a local landmark, known particularly for its prominent central clock tower, which displayed Baltimore's "railroad time"—ten minutes behind New York and two minutes ahead of Washington. This tower, standing far above its surroundings, "serve[d] as a guide post to enquiring travellers, as it may be seen from various points on Baltimore and other distant streets of the city."[77] The tower in return offered those who climbed up a panoramic vista

FIGURE 5.6. Camden Station as completed, ca. 1869. Courtesy of the Library of Congress. Detail from Sachse, *Bird's Eye.*

FIGURE 5.7. Camden Station and its environs, ca. 1869. Courtesy of the Library of Congress. Detail from Sachse, *Bird's Eye.*

from which to take in the city as a whole, "a delightful view . . . of the city and suburbs" (fig. 5.7).[78] It reflected as well Baltimore's integration into an expanding system of steam-powered transit, even as it obscured the disruptions that made the system possible. The ability to view the city as a whole came at the cost of fragmentation and dislocation.

Conclusion

Locust Point and Camden Station represented two complementary strategies for adapting urban form to the demands of steam power and integrating the city into rapidly expanding railroad networks. The former looked to the periphery, creating a new kind of neighborhood devoted to transit that developed outside of municipal locomotive restrictions. By building a neighborhood from scratch, the B&O extended the efficiencies of steam transportation across its entire route and saved money in the process. But as the property owners of Fells Point observed, it also reflected a troubling emphasis on through travel that pulled trade away from Baltimore's historic core. Camden Station marked a very different imposition on the built environment and raised a different set of concerns. The B&O's new downtown depot took advantage of Baltimore's racialized political economy to bring steam engines into the heart of the city. In effect, the station privileged long-distance movement over the customary traffic and residential patterns of South Baltimore, sacrificing the mobility and housing of one neighborhood to provide mechanized travel for the city as a whole. Long-distance mobility hinged on short-distance disruption, and the company successfully branded opposition to its interventions as local obstructionism, overridden by the higher public goal of rapid transit. This reflected the uneven development intrinsic to industrialization as a whole, as the B&O capitalized on and deepened existing inequalities in Baltimore's social structure.

Yet the story of Camden Station does not only reveal the power of the railroad to bend urban space to suit its needs. As the five-hundred-person protest against the closure of Conway Street suggests, questions of locomotive power and control over the streets served as vectors for the growing conflict between municipal and corporate authorities. Charles Ellet's conception of a railway network belting the city and the B&O's proposals for specially designed steam engines that would tirelessly haul goods through city streets were visions of modernity, but visions that discounted the concerns of people most directly affected by this technology. When those people had access to the channels of urban politics, they had the potential, however unlikely, to disrupt the progress narratives that railroad companies advanced and put forward alternative visions of the city. The public good looked different from Cecil Alley than it did from the second floor of Camden Station.

Privatizing the B&O

In July 1858, city director Joseph B. Brinkley's frustrations with his fellow B&O board members reached a boiling point. Brinkley, a wholesale grocer and commission merchant by trade, had represented the city on the board since 1856. As a city director, he fought to offer free delivery for Baltimore merchants, to secure a discount on coal for Baltimore consumers, to block a new dividend that threatened to undermine the company's fragile growth, and to preserve local journalists' access to board meetings. On each of these fronts, he found himself voted down by the private directors and a handful of defecting city and state representatives.[1]

Brinkley's problems on the board went beyond policy disputes. Corruption, intrigue, and infighting beset the B&O's governance in the mid-1850s, rancor that manifested in company minutes and in press reports. The *Sun* accused B&O directors of directing contracts to their cronies; board members leveled personal attacks on one another; two city directors claimed to have been offered bribes for their votes in selecting the company's president. The company's adoption of formal rules of order for board meetings in 1857 did little to allay this acrimony.[2] In the face of this dysfunction, Brinkley and three other city directors submitted their resignations to Mayor Thomas Swann in 1858, declaring that disunion among the city directors and differences of opinion with other board members made it impossible to advance the city's interests. Brinkley subsequently withdrew his resignation at the request of the city council, but after finishing his term he left the board and stayed away for the next two decades.[3]

The heated contests that drove Brinkley from the company's upper management concerned matters that sound mundane: procurement practices, dividend policies, and elections to the board of directors. In another era of the B&O's history, these subjects may not have generated hard feelings, but in the 1850s they reflected deeper disputes about the railroad's direction and objectives. Starting in 1854, the private stockholders, acting as a unified bloc, launched a coordinated campaign to place the reins of the company in the hands of its "real" owners: themselves. They sought, in short, to turn the B&O into a private enterprise. The time had come, the stockholders argued, for the company to set policies that maximized traffic and rewarded investors rather than fostered urban growth. But the government support that had, until that point, sustained the corporation made these objectives controversial and tricky to achieve. Millions of dollars in public aid had given the city and state a majority of the seats on the board of directors and left the company's policies subject to scrutiny in city hall and in the press. To privatize the B&O, then, the stockholders had to reconfigure the railroad's relationship with its terminal city. The process by which they did so was public, political, and deliberate.

The campaign to remake the B&O did not unfold in isolation; the stockholder revolt came at a pivotal moment in the history of the American railroad. In the 1850s, as questions about the future of slavery fractured the Union, railroad corporations moved in the opposite direction, consolidating their affairs and expanding their influence. In these years, the trunk lines—the New York Central, New York & Erie, Pennsylvania, and B&O—extended their reach into the interior and accumulated economic and political power. They did so in part by professionalizing and bureaucratizing their operations. From the late 1840s until the Civil War, salaried managers tightened their control over day-to-day affairs while channeling the railroad's multifarious activities into geographical and functional divisions governed by a complex hierarchy. The directors and managers who orchestrated these changes framed them as essential accommodations to a new economic order. Only by maximizing profit and expanding their operations, they suggested, could the trunk lines compete with one another for trade.[4] Railroad corporations instead of cities would vie for control of hinterlands.

In Baltimore as in other cities, efficiency and corruption were the watchwords of the day, but vested stockholders—not salaried managers—led the way. Private stockholders maintained that they alone could guide the company to a prosperous future. Partisan political crises close to home aided their efforts to seize the company; as riotous elections placed Know-Nothings in charge of the city and state governments in the late 1850s, private stockholders characterized public involvement in railroad operations as corrupt and counterproductive. Yet private control did not translate reliably into improved operations. Instead, it inaugurated a new era of instability, as railroad companies fought bitter rate wars, partook in speculative schemes, and provoked labor strife. Conflicts over these practices, which pitted investors and company officials against merchants, mechanics, and politicians, represented more than a disagreement over corporate strategies—they reflected diverging views about what constituted, in their words, the "true policies" of railroad enterprise. The decade from 1853 to 1863 witnessed campaigns on the board, at the state legislature, and in the courts over whether the company would pursue dividends and expansion or serve the urban public and local traffic. These struggles over the identity and purpose of the railroad doubled as debates about the nature of private corporations and their power within public life.

The Stockholder Revolt

In 1854, even as the city council agreed to lend $5 million to the B&O to improve the Main Stem, another conflict simmered within the company. As with controversies over rate discrimination, this one concerned control—who should run the company? To what ends should it operate? Now more than ever, the board of directors split into clearly defined public and private factions. While the city government and its representatives on the board remained divided, stockholders after 1854 acted as a united bloc, mounting a coordinated campaign to seize control of the company and minimize the public directors' influence. In mid-1854 private stockholders began meeting on their own to diagnose the company's problems and propose solutions. Deliberating in private allowed them to present a unified front in public. In October, two hundred stockholders representing 23,745 shares gathered at the Merchants' Exchange, where they composed and published a platform to guide their representatives on the board of directors. It called for rigid economy in all aspects of management—dismissal of unessential employees, elimination of free passes, minimization of the use of horsepower, and increased rates on local traffic, particularly for coal. Significantly, the platform also declared that the time had come for the railroad to begin *"payment of regular Dividends."*[5]

   In making these demands, the stockholders characterized themselves as the legitimate owners of the line. The company owed its limited successes to date, they said, to the policies of private stockholders, and its shortcomings reflected the influence of the city and state directors' pernicious public agenda. Private stockholders had drafted the charter, private stockholders' capital had funded initial construction, private stockholders' efforts had carried the project forward, and "it owes to them whatever of vitality it now possesses." Yet they had received little return on their investment. They argued that the railroad had, as promised, filled Baltimore's streets with trade, but the company's finances were in a state of disorder, its credit and reputation sullied. Public directors had rejected private investors' efforts to remedy these problems by restructuring fares and improving finances, instead subjecting stockholders to "denunciation and calumny." As the private investors saw it, they claimed "no undue exercise of power. They are endeavoring to do their duty, not only as Stockholders, but as citizens of Baltimore."[6]

To effect these changes, the stockholders first installed a new slate of directors on the B&O's board. Earlier, in the 1840s, and later, in the 1860s, investors largely returned the same directors to the board year after year, but in the 1850s, they cleaned house. In 1854, private stockholders replaced half of their representatives with new men; by the end of the decade, only two private directors from the pre-1853 era—the merchant and financier Johns Hopkins and self-styled "gentleman" Samuel W. Smith—remained on the board. The directors elected after 1854 were, like their predecessors, some of the wealthiest men in Baltimore, but they differed in generation and in outlook. Virtually all of them had come of age in the nineteenth century, and the youngest had grown up with the railroad itself. And, the gentleman Smith notwithstanding, they oriented themselves overwhelmingly toward business. In the 1840s, politicians and attorneys not infrequently found positions as private directors on the B&O, but the private directors after 1854 were almost entirely men with a hand in commerce or industry—iron manufacturers, grocers, tobacco merchants, leather dealers. They secured positions on the board by promising their fellow stockholders they would seize control of the railroad and make it pay.[7]

Although the stockholders' grievances dated back decades, recent dysfunctions catalyzed their activism. At an investors' meeting in 1855, private stockholder Cornelius McLean traced the company's difficulties to the completion of the line two years prior. "No sooner was the whistle of our locomotives heard on the banks of the Ohio river, than new elements were attempted to be incorporated into the working of the machine," he declared. Certainly there was a lot of new blood; the crop of stockholder representatives who joined the board after 1853 represented less than one-fifth of the eighty-one new directors who joined the board in the 1850s. Whereas between 1845 and 1851 the city had filled vacancies by appointing a new director to the board on nineteen occasions, and the state eight times, the next six years saw the number of first-time city and state directors climb to thirty-two and thirty-three, respectively. The majority of these new public directors served only one or two years before departing, leaving the city and state without experienced representatives on the board. McLean, a Washington-born, Harvard-educated attorney with an address in Baltimore's fashionable Franklin Square,

did not disguise his contempt for these newcomers. Public directors, he alleged, shirked their responsibilities while stockholder directors handled the
company's day-to-day management. He blamed Maryland's Board of Public
Works in particular for selecting unqualified men as state directors, but he
added that city directors often voted with them. In 1853, the public faction had
combined to advance one of their number—state director William G. Harrison, a Baltimore auctioneer and commission merchant—to the presidency
after Thomas Swann stepped down. The results of this public control, McLean
asserted, were "ruinous . . . and, I am sorry to say, derogatory to our character
as a commercial and intelligent community."[8]

McLean argued that the time had come for the B&O to adopt rigorous,
economical, and, above all, private management. By 1855, as McLean pointed
out, state governments were increasingly relinquishing their stakes in internal improvements. New York State had already abandoned its interest in the
New York & Erie Railroad, and the Commonwealth of Pennsylvania would
soon sell the Main Line of Public Works to the Pennsylvania Railroad as well.
"In all these instances," McLean said, "it has been deemed most useful to the
public to have the works well managed by the real owners, instead of being
badly managed by political, temporary and frequently unfit public agents."
This did not mean the end of public *investment*—in fact, city and county governments filled the financial vacuum left by the states, ultimately contributing
some $125 million to internal improvement projects before the Civil War. Yet
for the most part, municipalities did not play a substantial role in railroad
management. In this sense, the B&O, with its public majority on the board
of directors, was an outlier. To bring the company in line with these trends,
McLean encouraged the City of Baltimore to divest itself from its western
railroad by selling its shares in the B&O to private stockholders. Private managers would, McLean promised, work assiduously, of their own volition, to
"bring trade to the city."[9]

Not everyone accepted the stockholders' contention that they constituted
the "legitimate owners" of the company, however, or that public directors deserved the blame for its malaise. After all, city and state investments had sustained the B&O during its first quarter century. By 1855, the city had invested
more than $10 million in the B&O in the form of loans, bond endorsements,
and stock subscription. The city directors argued that the sum warranted
continued municipal participation in the railroad's management.[10] Others
warned that placing the B&O in private hands risked converting the railroad
into a vehicle for stock speculation. Since the Swann administration, critics
had contended that private directors manipulated financial records to create
an illusion of prosperity; without public oversight, such abuses might con-

tinue unchecked.[11] But the most pressing reason to maintain a municipal stake in the company was to safeguard its developmental mission. State director George R. Vickers, a miller and commission merchant who later represented Maryland in the U.S. Senate, spoke in defense of his fellow public directors at a stockholders' meeting. He dismissed McLean's assertion that privatizing the company would contribute to the city's economic growth. Private stockholders had already tipped their hands, he argued, in the disputes over rate discrimination. If the city sold them its shares, they would reduce Baltimore to "but a way station."[12]

In the end, the proposed buyout—which promised an annuity of only $143,528 and did nothing to ease the city's debt burden—failed to entice the mayor and city council.[13] The city retained a substantial stake in the B&O until the 1890s. Nonetheless, the conversation in 1854–1855 about the nature of private investment and the legitimacy of public management set the stage for a decade of conflict about the company's policies and goals. As the public-private fault line widened, corporate profits and urban prosperity began to look like incompatible goals. Where once public and private directors fought over the best means to accomplish common ends, they now grappled over the function of the railroad itself.

The Extra Dividend

Nothing more clearly illustrated the private stockholders' vision for the railroad than the emphasis they placed on dividends. Wanting a return on their investment was not radical per se. In addition to increased trade, investment, and industry, Baltimoreans had long included regular cash dividends in their visions of the prosperous future that awaited their city once the railroad reached Wheeling.[14] Private stockholders, though, fixated on these payments. Dividends became both their principal demand and a symbol of their grievances. They grew restless even before the line reached Wheeling, concerned that the company had dismissed their claims on its revenues.[15] Private stockholders chalked up the want of dividends to the influence of public interests in the road. One investor noted with concern in 1853 the "growing disposition in this community to treat the interests of the stockholders as altogether subordinate to those of the public."[16]

The stockholder may have had a point; while the city government's substantial holdings of B&O stock meant that it too stood to profit from a dividend, city officials argued consistently that the public's stake in the line transcended its monetary return on investment. As Mayor Samuel Hinks put it in 1856: "Baltimore has an interest in the Baltimore and Ohio Railroad in value, compared with which a dividend of six per cent dwindles into the merest insignificance. It is to her a main artery of commercial vitality, and she has contributed to build it, in consideration of the augmentation of her commerce, trade and general prosperity."[17] Dividends threatened to destabilize the railroad's developmental function by distributing revenue to stockholders that could instead go towards reducing rates, raising wages, or improving infrastructure.

In 1856–1857, this impasse came to a head in an extended controversy over a financial initiative called the extra dividend. Its origins lay in decisions B&O executives had made a decade earlier. Corporations typically financed their expansion by issuing stock or floating bonds; profits from their operations then returned to the shareholders as dividends. But in the 1840s, the urgency of completion led the B&O to instead channel surplus revenues into construction. B&O president Louis McLane argued in 1848 that it would be foolish to distribute present receipts to stockholders when income on reaching the Ohio River would be much greater. Although investors suffered the "temporary inconvenience" of suspended dividends, they would later reap the "profits of a complete road," he reasoned; his successor, Thomas Swann, concurred.[18] Because applying surplus revenue to construction increased the capitalization of the company, stockholders received new shares (called "dividend stock") proportional to their investments.[19]

The troubles that followed the company's opening to Wheeling left little room for a dividend; only in May 1856, after Chauncy Brooks, a private director, replaced William Harrison as company president, did the company offer a cash return to its investors.[20] The private stockholders pocketed that dividend, but they kept their eyes on the revenues that had funded the line's completion during the McLane and Swann administrations. In December 1856, the B&O's board of directors discussed the propriety of issuing an "extra dividend," a post hoc recompense to the stockholders for the profits earlier consumed in construction. To its advocates, the extra dividend represented a "moral obligation." As the special committee that first floated this possibility put it, "The profits of the Road belong to the Stockholders—you have used their money." Its report called for a thirty percent dividend on these funds. To finance this substantial outlay, the committee recommended that the company issue a bond, thus incurring new debts to pay a dividend on decade-old profits.[21]

The man who proposed the extra dividend was John Work Garrett, who joined the board in July 1855 and quickly became one of the company's most influential and active private directors. Garrett, born in Baltimore in 1820, likely attended the parade that marked the start of construction on the B&O in 1828. He had monitored the company's affairs ever since. His father, Robert

Garrett, an immigrant from Ireland who settled in Baltimore in 1819, ran a dry goods business that dealt extensively with customers in the trans-Appalachian West, an interest that led him to purchase eleven shares in the B&O at its inception. Robert brought his sons, Henry and John, into the family enterprise after the Panic of 1837, and starting in the 1840s, the firm, now called Robert Garrett & Sons, focused increasingly on international trade and securities exchange, including the purchase and marketing of B&O bonds. As the company's horizons broadened, the family sunk its earnings into Baltimore enterprises and real estate. By the 1850s, the Garretts' fortune topped $1 million, making them one of the wealthiest families in the United States. Around 1854, shortly before John took up his position on the board, he moved with his family to a three-story townhouse on Franklin Square, not far from Cornelius McLean's residence, where they lived with one enslaved and four hired servants.[22]

The Garrett family had watched with frustration as the B&O stumbled its way toward the Ohio River. Robert Garrett & Sons had deep business ties in Pittsburgh, and the family patriarch played a leading role in the doomed campaign to terminate the railroad in that city rather than Wheeling. "Our R.R. is a hopeless concern," John lamented in 1848. Yet the Garretts responded to these disappointments not by divesting themselves of the company but by doubling down, increasing their stockholdings in the 1850s and thereby garnering more influence over the B&O's affairs.[23] John took a leading role in the stockholder revolt, convening meetings and preparing reports to bolster the investors' case about the mismanagement of the road.[24] Upon joining the board, he teamed up with Johns Hopkins to advance the stockholders' interests. When Garrett proposed the extra dividend in late 1856, it represented his latest salvo in the ongoing public-private conflict over the direction of the company. Speaking at a contentious board meeting, he observed that "in the present measure, like all the other important steps taken for and in conformity with the development of this great work, the stockholder interest" had faced "adverse influences" and "prejudices" from the state and city directors.[25]

The board of directors postponed voting on the extra dividend bonds for one week, and debate over the proposal raged in the columns of Baltimore's newspapers in the interim. Proponents of the extra dividend framed it as a matter of honest accounting. Attorney William H. Norris argued that only by issuing dividends on all appropriated revenue could the company keep track of its capital stock and expenditure. More to the point, the extra dividend affirmed the primacy of profit maximization as an operating principle. If the B&O did not issue this dividend, Norris warned, "From time to time the *public interest* composition of the board of directors . . . [and] the freight interests of the community, would be found crying out for a reduction of tolls under the deceptive assertion that the shareholder ought to be satisfied with six per cent., as the road was, in a measure, a public institution, which is not meant for *money making*."[26]

To opponents, though, the proposed dividend represented the triumph of stockholders' personal interests over the wellbeing of the company, to say nothing of the community. Arguments for the extra dividend, they said, presented a convoluted understanding of accounting and corporate responsibility. After all, the company could not have distributed profits to the stockholders in the 1840s and 1850s without hobbling its operations at a critical juncture in its history. "By no possible ingenuity," opined the *Sun*, "can any impartial man be made to believe that a stockholder has a right to earnings already expended in the road."[27] To some, the bond-backed dividend represented the flip side of the enterprising "spirit of the age"—financial sleight of hand that rested on manipulation of company reports rather than sound corporate practices.[28] The city council, speaking as a major stockholder, condemned the measure as a threat to the B&O's "stability and future credit." After all, to pay interest on these bonds, the B&O would have to shell out $180,000 per annum, destabilizing its finances while doing nothing to improve its operations or aid the city's growth. Garrett's proposal might bolster the company's stock price in the short term but would in the long run endanger Baltimoreans' heavy investments in the railroad. The council voted, eighteen to two, to reject the extra dividend.[29]

Critics of the extra dividend contended that most Baltimoreans opposed the measure. The *Sun* deemed the proposal "entirely at conflict with plain business principles." The "mere monetary or personal power and influence of a bare majority of the directorship" advanced this measure with disregard for the B&O's responsibilities to the public. The paper declared that popular opinion both inside and outside Baltimore denounced the dividend as a swindle and a blemish on the company's reputation.[30] Mayor Swann, taking stock of public sentiment, entreated his former colleagues to withdraw their proposal, citing the "universal condemnation of the community."[31] Nonetheless, when the board reconvened, the measure passed by a vote of seventeen to twelve. The private directors voted unanimously in favor; the public representatives showed no such unity. Two city directors disregarded the council's directive and voted to issue the dividend, as did two state directors.[32] As the B&O prepared to move forward, the city government readied an injunction.[33]

Each side made its case in court. The city's legal counsel maintained that the company had every right to use its revenues to pay for essential infrastructure and equipment. The profits never belonged to the stockholders in the first place, obviating the need for a compensatory dividend. Companies could only declare dividends after providing for both current and contingent expenses, the city argued, meaning that revenues put to productive use in construction were no longer subject to redistribution. Furthermore, the debt incurred to pay the dividend would hurt the city as both a mortgage holder and a stockholder in the company. The B&O's attorneys, Reverdy Johnson and John H. B. Latrobe, countered that the company held a legal right to declare dividends on previously used profits and insisted that this had been the plan all along. The net earnings of the company were not so absolutely vested in the B&O as to "deprive the Stockholders of all right to them."[34]

Behind this lawyerly debate on the fine points of revenues and responsibilities was an argument about control. Since the completion of the line, private stockholders had insisted that the road had to become more profitable; with the extra dividend, they showed to whose benefit the profit would accrue. Surplus earnings would not be funneled back into the company—they belonged to the "real owners" of the B&O, its stockholders. Together, the City of Baltimore and State of Maryland held a majority of the B&O's stock, but as long as the private directors acted in unison and could convince enough state and city directors (many of whom owned stock themselves) to vote with their bloc, the mayor and city council's vision for the line would go unfulfilled. Perhaps the extra dividend was a deliberate provocation—a display of power, as a plurality of stockholders commandeered a massive corporation and, in the face of opposition from the press, from the government, and from the public at large attempted to pay a (supposed) debt from the past by incurring a debt to the future. The dividend engineered by Garrett and his cohort complicated (if it did not outright contradict) the claim that stockholder control would enhance the company's ability to compete or render its operations more efficient. By the same token, though, the extra dividend represented more than just plunder. Garrett evidently had long-term objectives in mind. In addition to showcasing the stockholders' power within the company, Garrett articulated a theory of railroad operations that made regular dividends a shareholder's right and rendered shareholder interest the company's first priority. The case for the extra dividend was also a case for private enterprise unfettered by the demands of a local public.[35]

The stockholders had to wait; the injunction lingered in court for years. The courts finally settled the matter in the B&O's favor in the summer of 1860, and the extra dividend went into effect in October of that year.[36] The company's annual report for 1860 reveled in this success. "The extraordinary opposition made to the legitimate discharge of the plain duty of this Company" had finally lifted.[37] As the court case finally neared settlement, John W.

Garrett and his brother Henry advised several anxious confidants to hold on to their shares.[38] Even after years of debate, not everyone accepted their sanguine assessments. As one investor put it, the planned dividend was "a movement . . . of John Garrett's to put up the stock. . . . I do not believe the stock is worth intrinsically one half of what it is selling for."[39]

Labor in a Privatizing Railroad

If eight-year-old John Garrett did in fact attend the B&O's inaugural parade in 1828, he witnessed a vision for the company's future that he would do much to unravel. The workers' procession reflected a commonly held conviction that the railroad's service to the local public would go beyond the goods and people the line would bring to Baltimore—the company would also, directly or indirectly, provide work to thousands of citizens. Baltimoreans held on to this conceit through the railroad's tumultuous first quarter century. As work crews neared Wheeling, the *Sun* anticipated that "Baltimore may easily become the great workshop of supply" for its new hinterland.[40] The completion of the line belied this prediction, as the B&O laid off workers in Baltimore and opened shops further west along the Main Stem. Nonetheless, many citizens continued to believe that the company had an obligation to support local industries.

Unsurprisingly, then, when word got out at the end of 1856 that the B&O had purchased locomotives outside Baltimore, it sparked public uproar. On New Year's Eve, with controversy over the extra dividend still in full swing, an article in the *Sun* (subtitled "Baltimore Enterprise Repudiated") revealed that Henry Tyson, the B&O's master of machinery, had looked into procuring engines from shops in Massachusetts and Delaware. Such arrangements would throw thousands out of work, and the city council vowed to investigate.[41] A memorial from the "industrial classes of Baltimore" to the council called the decision to acquire engines built in other cities an insult to local mechanics and a violation of the company's mandate to foster Baltimore's industrial development. The mechanics pointed out that they had paid taxes to support the very corporation that was now endangering their livelihoods. "The city has not yet received a benefit commensurate with the noble sacrifices she has made," the memorialists declared.[42]

At the center of this dispute stood eccentric engine manufacturer Ross Winans. Winans had arrived in Baltimore from New Jersey at the dawn of the railroad age, and his innovations helped the B&O surmount many of its early technical problems. Winans opened railcar and locomotive manufacturing shops south of Pratt Street near Mount Clare Depot, an area called Pigtown for the swine that passed through its streets on their way from livestock cars to the slaughterhouse. Winans's signature contribution to the B&O was an oddly shaped but powerful coal-burning engine of his design, known as the "camel" for its vertical, humplike boiler. The engine, though ungainly, could handle steep grades that bedeviled other machines; Baltimore-made camels thus became common sights along the B&O's tracks in mountainous western Virginia. But the camel's prodigious power came at the cost of slow speed, heavy fuel consumption, and frequent accidents, which prompted Tyson to look for new engines elsewhere. Winans characterized the B&O's moves as part of a larger sinister design to monopolize the machine trade in Baltimore and depress workmen's wages.[43]

Henry Tyson implicated Winans in return: the company had gone north because it wanted to use a ten-wheel engine that the obdurate Winans simply refused to make. Tyson claimed that he went to Baltimore industrialists for the B&O's supplies whenever possible—but he reserved the right to look outside the city should he consider it necessary.[44] A correspondent to the *American* signed "Nary Share" took the matter further, lambasting the notion advanced in the mechanics' memorial that local loyalties should constrain managers' choices. The writer likened calls to support Baltimore industry to charity. Trying to govern the B&O's purchases in the public interest would make the "railroad company . . . a soup house on a gigantic scale, every body to have gratis the tickets he calls for, with a right to order any changes in the bill of fare."[45] Yet this argument misrepresented the claims the mechanics had made on the company: their memorial, by invoking the local taxes that supported the B&O, had characterized citizenship as a form of investment comparable to shareholding. The mechanics' return on investment took the form of jobs rather than dividends. By dismissing industrial workers' demands as charity rather than earned benefits, Nary Share reinforced the doctrine that stockholders constituted the real owners of the railroad. The author's pseudonym lampooned the notion that those who did not own B&O stock might influence its decisions.

Tyson won his case; Winans never produced an engine for the B&O again. Nonetheless, corporate procurement practices remained objects of public inquiry over the next decade. The city council took the protection of Baltimore industry as its prerogative and used its representatives on the board of directors to influence business decisions. As one proposed resolution in 1858 put it, city directors were to "watch over and protect the interest of the Mechanicks of this City" by preventing the B&O from awarding contracts to firms outside of Baltimore.[46] Such actions did not deny the legitimacy of the company's pursuit of profit but rather sought to limit the extent to which that pursuit undermined the urban development that had been the railroad's raison d'être.

For workers employed by the company, stockholder control had less ambiguous results. By 1857, nearly 6,500 people worked for the B&O, including close to 1,000 in Baltimore, making the railroad the largest private employer in the city. In addition to the conductors, engineers, and brakemen who ran the trains, the company employed machinists, bricklayers, stablemen, clerks, and sundry other varieties of laborer, each classed into distinct departments within the multiple-tiered bureaucracy that the McLane administration pioneered in the 1840s. Despite Baltimore's large free black population, this workforce consisted almost exclusively of white men, including large numbers of Irish immigrants.[47] City directors on the B&O's board traditionally looked out for the interests of this sizable and politically enfranchised workforce, mediating disputes and intervening periodically on workers' behalf in strikes.

The leaders of the stockholder revolt had a very different set of ideas about how to approach labor relations. Shortly after the procurement controversy died down, and with the extra-dividend dispute still in the headlines, John W. Garrett put forward another initiative that demonstrated the new order on the railroad. Complaining of "serious losses" from theft on freight trains, Garrett proposed to make freight conductors personally responsible for sealing the merchandise cars and preventing the loss of their contents. The board, accepting this proposal, declared that, starting in late April 1857, freight conductors would be dismissed if the seal on any such car broke in transit, and they would have to pay out of pocket to make up for any losses resulting therefrom.[48] Freight conductors reacted sharply to this new burden. They pointed out that the company's locks were so flimsy they could be broken "with the blow of a fist." Moreover, frequent errors in the freight manifests made it hard for conductors to get an accurate count of the cargo of any given merchandise car and thus determine what might be missing. They characterized the new arrangements as "onerous and unjust." As the start date for this new policy approached, the conductors planned a strike.[49]

On April 29, conductors in Baltimore and in the railroad town of Martinsburg, Virginia, blocked the passage of freight trains in protest of this policy. William Prescott Smith and a posse of Baltimore police officers tried to run a train out of Mount Clare, but as they crossed the city limits, the policemen's jurisdiction became unclear, and a crowd of more than a hundred people mounted the train and applied the brakes.[50] Over the following several days, protestors, many of whom were not in the employ of the company (the *Sun*

referred specifically to a "large number of females" on the scene), continued
to gather at key railroad junctions to prevent freight trains from leaving Baltimore. As crowds numbering by some estimates in the thousands blocked rail
traffic, B&O president Chauncy Brooks asked Governor Thomas W. Ligon
to apply military force. With the governor's assent, the company attached a
passenger car to a freight train and placed state militiamen on board; when
strikers and their sympathizers threw stones at the passing train, the soldiers
responded with bullets, killing one man—Henry Houser, an unarmed Pratt
Street resident with no connection to the company.[51] Several militiamen sustained injuries in the attack, and the company awarded them compensation
as a show of gratitude.[52]

The deadly affray and the fate of the striking conductors led to tense con-
frontations on the board. When city director J. Irwin Smith asked to read the
strikers' memorial of protest aloud at a meeting, private director Wesley Starr
objected, declaring that the rebellious conductors had "handed the memorial
in one hand and held the sword in the other." Smith pointed out that as not
all of the conductors had participated in the freight blockade, they deserved
an audience. He added, "There were those who held eight hundred shares of
stock of the road who had no sympathy with the poor, but would crush them
down." Starr took this as a personal affront (as was probably intended) and
accused Smith of sympathizing with and even encouraging the strikers' riotous behavior. President Brooks felt compelled to call for order in the face of
these ad hominem attacks.[53]

As for the conductors, the strike marked the start of a new labor regime.
Evidently cowed by the demonstration, the head of the company's transportation department announced that he would relax and modify the policy,
reducing the penalties and purchasing better locks for the cars. But the company moved firmly against all men who had taken action, working with the
state's attorney to prosecute the offenders. Garrett personally ordered the
blacklisting of all strikers. The presidents of other rail lines looked on approvingly. Samuel Felton, president of the Philadelphia, Wilmington & Baltimore,
commented that Garrett's "firm stand . . . will save a great deal of trouble for
the future." Soon, Garrett would join the ranks of the presidents himself.[54]

John W. Garrett and the Balance of Power

As the 1857 strike came to its deadly conclusion, the editors of the *Sun* bemoaned the intrusion of "politics and politicians" into the management of
Maryland's largest railroad enterprise.[55] In the mid-1850s, though, politics did
not just influence the railroad; railroad managers shaped urban politics. In

1856, Baltimore voters got to choose between two former railroad presidents in their mayoral election: the Democrat Robert Clinton Wright, who had formerly helmed the Baltimore & Susquehanna, and the Know-Nothing Thomas Swann. Swann, like many Baltimore industrialists, had found a home in the anti-Catholic and anti-immigrant American (or Know-Nothing) Party after the Whig Party collapsed earlier in the decade. Two years earlier, in 1854, the Know-Nothings had swept to power in the city in a wave of nativist sentiment. That year, as secret shareholder meetings set the stage for the stockholder revolt, clandestine nominating conventions put forth political neophyte Samuel Hicks as the Know-Nothing candidate for mayor. Hicks had won the office after a two-week campaign. Now, in 1856, the party looked to cement its gains while the Democrats sought to reverse them. Swann and Wright traded barbs over whose railroad company had treated its workers—potential voters—the least callously during their tenures.[56]

The Know-Nothings did not let Swann's reputation speak for itself. Although the party's leadership came from the city's erstwhile Whig elite, it drew its rank and file from the nativist street gangs who made Baltimore notorious for rioting even in an unusually riotous moment in American history. In 1856, rival gangs faced off in the streets and at the polls. Know-Nothing toughs used easily concealed shoemakers' awls to stab rival voters. Sometimes they intimidated Democrats more openly, brandishing firearms and even artillery pieces. Violence in the municipal election in October, which brought Swann to power, and the national election in November, which gave Maryland's electoral votes to Know-Nothing candidate Millard Fillmore, took the lives of between twenty and thirty people, many of them bystanders. Once in office, the party expanded the municipal bureaucracy and public services—between 1854 and 1860, the city professionalized its police force, augmented its waterworks, acquired horse-drawn streetcar lines, and purchased a large park outside the city limits. Understandably, though, the violence of the party's rise to power dominated public discourse about the Know-Nothing administration in Baltimore.[57]

Pundits had warned of the dangers of partisan control of the B&O since the 1830s, but the election violence of the Know-Nothing years cast those concerns into particularly stark relief by bringing the legitimacy of the municipal government itself into question. The *American*, bemoaning the "demoralization which marks municipal affairs throughout the Union," pinned this urban malaise on the "brutality, depravity and ignorance" of voters in large cities, and called on elite nominating committees to ensure that only "good men" entered public office.[58] Public railroad directorships were positions of par-

ticular concern, especially as reports circulated in the late 1850s indicating
that public directors sought to turn the company into an instrument of patronage. As one correspondent to the *American* put it, railroad boards needed
"men of business habits," not *"mere politicians."*[59]

It was in this environment that B&O president Chauncy Brooks announced his resignation in November 1858. Johns Hopkins nominated John
Work Garrett to take his place. The nomination surely surprised no one; in his
three-year tenure as stockholder director, Garrett's influence had only grown.
In addition to taking a leading role among his fellow private investors, he
represented the company in negotiations with other rail lines and acted as
president pro tem in Brooks's absence.[60] He proved to have a canny hand
with the media, planting items in the press and seeking alternately to permit
or prevent reporters' access to the increasingly contentious board meetings as
it served his purposes.[61] But he also engendered fierce opposition from some
of the state and city directors, both because of his initiative in policies like the
extra dividend and for what one writer called his "dictatorial" personal manner.[62] In light of this entrenched opposition, Johns Hopkins spent the weeks
leading up to the election treating board members to dinners of champagne
and frog legs while lobbying on his young friend's behalf. His efforts paid off,
narrowly. After learning of Garrett's nomination, the city council instructed
its representatives to vote instead for Brooks, despite his resignation and the
fact that he was himself a friend and ally of Garrett. With a united front the
public directors could have stopped Garrett's ascendance, but two public de-
fectors tipped the election in his favor, and he assumed the presidency by a
vote of sixteen to fourteen.[63] Garrett remained there until his death in 1884.

Garrett took control of a corporation worth $31 million, with more than
five hundred miles of track and gross revenues of $4.6 million. He grasped the
company's reins tightly, opting for micromanagement instead of delegation.
Garrett personally reviewed invoices for even minor purchases and chastised
subordinates for delays in executing his requests. He kept up with the company's affairs on a minute-by-minute basis thanks to a small squadron of teleg-
raphers who sat near his office and accompanied him on trips. Whereas in the
1840s the B&O had led the way in diffusing authority over operational matters
to professional managers, in the late 1850s and 1860s Garrett concentrated
power in himself even as other rail lines expanded their bureaucracies. He
sought input from family members like his brother Henry and a few trusted
advisors, such as William Prescott Smith, but did not follow the lead of the
Pennsylvania and other trunk lines in appointing vice presidents to alleviate
his burdens or offer advice. When he finally succumbed to the pressures of

the job and created vice presidential positions in the B&O's upper management (first in 1866, then 1871), he tempered this apparent decentralization by choosing family members John King Jr. and William Keyser for the posts.[64]

Garrett moved quickly to eliminate the public majority on the board of directors. In 1860, an act came before the state legislature that proposed to nearly double the number of stockholder directors from twelve to twenty-three (approximately one director for every 2,500 shares of privately held stock), while holding public representation steady at ten state and eight city directors, each representing 4,000 and 4,375 shares, respectively.[65] A memorial signed by Baltimore's "largest tax payers and most influential citizens" praised the measure as a way to insulate railroad management from "the violent and exciting movements of political parties."[66] The city council, outraged by the measure, resolved that should it pass, the city would make a quick cash sale of its entire interest in the railroad, divesting itself of the company rather than retaining only a nominal role in the enterprise.[67]

George Vickers, though no longer a board member, anonymously authored a pamphlet condemning the proposed changes to the board. The imbalance between private and the public representation would be of little consequence, he wrote, if the railroad were "a mere *private* corporation," but the B&O was "in its very nature, a *public work*" and required public representatives to safeguard the people's interests in the line.[68] Should the railroad fall into exclusively private hands, Garrett would become the most powerful man in Maryland, easily eclipsing the clout of the governor. Garrett, at least, was a Baltimorean born and bred; Vickers predicted that the real danger of turning the railroad into "*a mere money making concern*" lay in the prospect of speculation. As stockholders placed B&O shares on the market, Philadelphians would buy them up and put their own slate of directors in charge, rendering the company a Baltimore enterprise in name only.[69]

This time, Vickers won; the bill did not pass in 1860, and similar attempts to alter the composition of the board in 1864 and 1867 failed as well.[70] But in a sense, Vickers and his allies had already lost. By the late 1850s, the notion that state and local governments should not intervene in the day-to-day management of railroad corporations had become predominant, if not hegemonic, in the northern states. The decade's tumultuous, centrifugal politics, coupled with railroad advocates' active efforts to promote their independence, helped cement the conviction that, as the Philadelphia *Public Ledger* put it in 1857, the "*only legitimate objects* of a government are much fewer and simpler than are commonly supposed. . . . It is not for a government to make itself into a bank, or canal, or railroad company."[71] In Maryland, the violent rise of the Know-

Nothing Party offered a particular spin on this liberal conviction by placing the validity of the state and municipal governments in doubt. The murderous elections that secured the Know-Nothings' perch in state and local politics abetted Garrett's efforts to rebrand public oversight of his company as partisan interference. Under his administration, with the private stockholders united in their efforts and public directors fractured in theirs, the railroad operated largely unbound by the supervision of the city and the state representatives. Attempts by the municipal government to counter the company's policies subsequently came from legislation, suit, and injunction rather than from within the board of directors.

Rate Wars

By the middle of the century, as William Prescott Smith discovered in his tour of the West, railroad managers could no longer assume that merchants would default to the shortest route to market. This left the four trunk lines scrambling to figure out how to apportion traffic now that natural laws of trade would not do the work for them. All four monopolized travel within a local hinterland, where they could set rates as they pleased, but traffic at competitive points became the object of strenuous and destabilizing competition. This situation, exacerbated by the depression that followed the Panic of 1857, spurred the trunk lines to internecine rate wars in the second half of the 1850s. During these conflicts, company agents deployed deception, subterfuge, and manipulation to bid against other rail lines "for every pound of freight," as the *New York Times* put it.[72] The result was the railroad equivalent of Hobbes's state of nature: executives exchanged nasty words in their correspondence, agents deployed brutish tactics to recruit traffic, and the rate agreements designed to ameliorate these conditions were invariably short lived. Each company blamed the others for breaking compacts and for slashing rates to unsustainable levels.[73] Still, some favored this state of affairs. The B&O's Boston agent, echoing Thomas Jefferson, advised Garrett that the company should "cut herself loose from entangling alliances with the northern roads, whose good faith remains good just so long as it will serve their interest."[74]

Cutting ties with other rail lines would have been the free market solution, but it was not the direction that Garrett and other trunk line officials took. The backstabbing and personal affronts of the rate wars reflected the economic and even existential crisis that confronted the rail industry: what constituted legitimate trade practices in a new era of competition? Railroad officials met frequently at urban hotels and resort towns in the late 1850s to resolve this question. They agreed that freewheeling, unregulated competition had led not to higher returns, but to feuds in which companies prioritized damaging their competitors over seeking profits for themselves. As executives hashed out their differences over oysters and cigars, they formed cartels in the hopes of helping their companies' bottom lines and improving a public image that had been tarnished by their reckless and erratic behavior.[75]

A rate agreement reached in September 1857, though quickly violated, demonstrates their vision for the railroad industry. The compact aimed to standardize corporate practices so that "business" could "be left to take its own course and its most convenient channel." To accomplish this end, the railroads vowed to cease employing runners and agents to recruit passengers or freight, to ban the use of free passes to bribe shippers, and to set standard rates at competitive points. The agreement insisted as well that companies confine their advertisements to bulletins that displayed timetables, connections, and rates—they could print nothing that disparaged other routes. The agreement aimed, its signatories said, "to place all on a fair and equal footing in their competition for the passenger and freight traffic over their respective Lines," but with advertisement, solicitation, and rates all taken out of the equation, competition returned to the field of geography.[76] Rather than scramble and scrape for traffic, the railroads' managers envisioned a struggle over territory.

Distance thus emerged again as the prime determinant of rate structures, but the nature of distance itself had changed. In the 1820s and 1830s, B&O promoters had assumed that the railroad would transmute geographical space, with its physical and seasonal variances, into a number—distance—and that that fixed number would then entrench Baltimore's standing as the principal entrepôt of the West. The railroad, however, did not annihilate space as fully as they expected, since topographical hazards made some routes slower, more expensive, and more dangerous than others. The railroad managers who tried to establish rates in the late 1850s responded to this new reality by abstracting distance still further. Rather than a measurement of space between two points, distances would serve as standards by which to set rates. Distance, in other words, did not automatically regulate rates—it had to be deployed as a benchmark through the agency of the railroad men. Consider for example this letter from the B&O's western freight agent to John W. Garrett in 1858 concerning a rate dispute: "The Marietta & Cincti R. R. Co. by its Tariff proposed to convey Live Stock from Cincti to Parkersburg for $40.00 per car load. The rate via Columbus to the river is $47.00. This rate is based upon that to Cleveland. . . . [T]he Baltimore & Ohio RR being obligated to charge the

same rate from Wheeling as via Parkersburg produces an unjust discrimination against the Central Ohio R.R."[77] The Marietta & Cincinnati, which linked
the Queen City with Parkersburg and hence to the Northwestern Virginia line
of the B&O, had proposed a rate structure that was deemed unfair because it
was lower than that charged by the Central Ohio Railroad from Columbus to
Wheeling, which in turn set its charges according to the rates from Cleveland.
As this shows, the results of new geographic rate structures were far from
straightforward. The rate agreements, though quickly violated, showcased
the changing nature of competition as railroad managers saw it: routes of
different distances, modes of travel, and different companies were supposed
to be rendered comparable and interchangeable; violations of these agreements constituted an unfair advantage. The centrality of fairness to this equation suggests that using geographic reference points to set rates represented
a form of moral economy, a way of distributing trade to the companies that
"deserved" it based on their location.

Distance standards sought to preempt competition for through trade, but
they also delegitimized efforts by railroad companies to set rates that benefited their home markets. Even in the late 1850s, the notion that railroads
would, in their own fashion, bolster the interests of their terminal cities remained commonplace, but under this system, this goal could not take priority. Pennsylvania Railroad president J. Edgar Thomson rebuked Garrett for an
apparent effort by the B&O to adjust its fares to favor Baltimore over Philadelphia in 1858. Like Garrett, Thomson had risen to power amid conflicts over
his railroad's relationship to its terminal city—whether its rates and policies
would serve the corporate bottom line or Philadelphia's development. Thomson favored the former. Because state law in Pennsylvania limited city directors to a minority role on the company's board, his principal antagonists in
the struggle had been private directors who represented the interests of Philadelphia's mercantile community; when Thomson ascended to the presidency
in 1852, it marked the triumph of his vision for the Pennsylvania Railroad.
In 1858, his counterpart in Baltimore appeared to be playing by a different
set of rules: although the distance between their two cities prescribed a fare
to Philadelphia only fifty cents greater than to Baltimore, the B&O charged a
full dollar more.[78] Thomson argued that this discrimination in favor of Baltimore threw shipping arrangements off balance and if uncorrected would in-
validate the B&O's agreements with the Pennsylvania. Garrett's rates, Thomson chided, "seem to have been adopted for the purpose of meeting popular
sentiment, and in violation of the true principles that should govern in the
adjustment of Rail-road rates."[79] The true principle was of course not urban

development but profit maximization. Thomson expressed surprise as well as outrage: "This does not look as though you were desirous of making money for your Stockholders?"[80]

Discrimination Redux

Railroad compacts offered only temporary respites from the recurrent rate wars of the late 1850s. As trunk lines jousted over through trade, they laid the groundwork for renewed antidiscrimination campaigns at the cusp of the Civil War. Railroad executives framed discrimination as a matter of survival— and of pride. "Was the object of the road to carry a little freight to Frederick and to Martinsburg?" asked a director on the B&O in 1858. "It was said the through business would kill the road; but take it away, and it would be killed."[81] In practice, variable traffic patterns made it difficult to assess through trade even in terms of raw numbers. The *American* reported in 1860 that 90 percent of the B&O's freight traffic came to or from Baltimore, whereas company records indicated that through travel constituted roughly half of the B&O's passenger miles and a third of its freight tonnage by the end of the decade (tables 6.1 and 6.2). Sometimes the proportion was not clear even to the employees reading the freight manifests.[82] Furthermore, fluctuating rate structures made the profitability of this traffic hard to ascertain. Garrett insisted in 1858 that through trade accounted for $900,000 of the previous year's revenue—nearly a fifth of the company's gross intake.[83] George R. Vickers painted a different picture, claiming that the railroad, by abandoning its "true policy" of fostering growth in the city and state, had actually undercut its revenues. The company's profit structure had changed since reaching the Ohio, Vickers said: before reaching the river, 40 percent of gross receipts had been profit, but from 1852 to 1856, profits had represented only 26 percent of gross, even as local rates increased. Thus "the further West the Road went, the less it made," he said, while the burden of maintaining the line fell ever more heavily on local constituents. Dependable local traffic supported the company's operations and generated the revenue that went into dividends while fickle through traffic served as little more than an ornament.[84]

Amid this confusion, debates over rate discrimination intensified in the early years of Garrett's administration, reflecting concerns within Baltimore's mercantile community that the B&O's emphasis on through trade undermined the city's market position. In February 1860, at the behest of the Corn and Flour Exchange (CFE), a Baltimore merchant collective, a special committee of the Maryland state legislature held hearings in Annapolis to investigate the B&O's discriminatory rate practices. Whereas the debates over discrimination

TABLE 6.1. Passenger through and way travel on the Main Stem, 1855–1860

	Local passengers	Through passengers	Local passenger miles	Through passenger miles	Through passengers as % of travelers	Through passengers as % of miles
1855	285,781	6,712	17,330,817	2,544,226	2.29	12.80
1856	278,309	28,405	17,976,743	10,207,398	9.26	36.22
1857	317,171	38,236	17,577,618	13,659,205	10.76	43.73
1858	261,383	35,051	12,516,013	12,679,295	11.82	50.32
1859	302,429	32,523	13,577,930	12,288,242	9.71	47.51
1860	288,499	34,645	12,869,308	13,030,320	10.72	50.31

Source: Data are from Transportation Report Tables, table A, in AR 29; table D in AR 30; and table E in ARs 31–34, respectively.

Note: Some tables, without explanation, list half passengers; I have truncated those figures here.

TABLE 6.2. Through and way tonnage on the Main Stem and NWV, 1859–1860

	Way tonnage	Through tonnage	Through tonnage as % of total freight
1859	428,197	201,596	32.01
1860	614,693	222,538	26.58

Source: Data are from AR 33, tables U, N, I–K, Q–T; AR 34, tables U, V, Y, AA, BB.

Notes: Figures do not include the Washington Branch; I have not included data from 1857 and 1858 because those reports appear not to record through and local trade on the NWV.

in 1853 concerned the propriety of municipal regulation, the hearings in 1860 focused on the growing power that railroad corporations wielded in public life. The Baltimoreans who lodged complaints about discrimination registered the stakes in vivid language: the B&O was now "a cruel step-mother" to Baltimore and "a handmaid" to the city's northern rivals, thanks to its "parricidal policy" of discrimination. These metaphors framed the company's practices in the wake of the stockholder revolt as oedipal inversions. The railroad company, created to serve the urban public, now threatened to subordinate it.[85]

The immediate context for the hearings was a rate war between the trunk lines in the first half of 1859. The B&O had undercut the rates of the New York Central while John W. Garrett attempted to negotiate a rate floor that would preserve, in his words, "the commercial and geographic rights of Baltimore and [the B&O's] dividend earning capacity for its stockholders."[86] As Garrett saw it, achieving this long-term strategic goal justified short-term tactical sacrifices, and thus the B&O had offered fares to New York below the per-mile rates it charged to Baltimore. The CFE rejected this explanation, however, and blamed the city's recent slump in trade, particularly in flour, on this policy of discrimination.[87] The president of the CFE, John S. Williams, alleged that the company had, in secret, not only cut the per mile rates but actually offered

fares to New York identical to the company's fares to Baltimore. He argued
that the B&O should match any rate cuts to eastern cities with abatements
for Baltimore-bound freight. "The difference would not be material to the
railroad company, but it is all important to Baltimore—it is these constant
homeopathic doses of discrimination that kill."[88]

Anxieties about the long-term consequences of the railroad's policies for
Baltimore's economy ran through the hearings in Annapolis on rate discrimination. A variety of Baltimore businessmen testified before the special committee, examined by James Tyson, a mill owner and member of the CFE, and
by John W. Garrett. Tyson himself took the stand first, with Garrett cross-
examining. When questioned, Tyson defined discriminatory rates as those
that failed to reflect Baltimore's geographic position. Garrett protested that
abandoning discrimination would effectively drive the B&O out of Cincinnati
and many other western markets, and he reminded Tyson that the company
fought its rate wars to advance Baltimore's interests. Tyson took no comfort
in Garrett's arguments, though. Given the short life span of the railroad compacts, the B&O would shortly again resume its discrimination, to the detriment of his mill and the Baltimore flour industry more generally.[89]

The committee found in favor of the B&O, ruling that the competitive
market for transportation rendered discrimination unavoidable. To compete for western trade, particularly during fierce rate wars, the company had
to have flexibility as it determined its fares. And although some committee
members expressed "regret" that circumstances had called for unfavorable
rates to Baltimore, others dismissed such sentiments entirely, pointing out
that all railroads charged more for short than for long hauls. Whereas Vickers
characterized the company's "true policy" as economic development, these
committee members declared, "The true object for which the Baltimore and
Ohio Rail Road was built was that it might be at once a source of profit as a
work, and a means of commerce, as an avenue of trade." The company could
not fulfill the latter role unless it made money, and it could make money only
through discrimination.[90]

Such defenses of discrimination added up to an understanding of trade
quite different from the one that had prompted Baltimoreans to create a railroad in 1827. No one on the committee—nor John W. Garrett, for that matter—
denied that the B&O should (and did) work ultimately to the city's benefit. At
the same time, though, the state legislature granted Garrett the discretion to
determine how and when to pursue policies favorable to economic development of the city and state. The flexibility allowed to him in the event of a rate
war undermined the certainty with which Baltimore's natural advantages had
been touted as the permanent basis for the city's prosperity. The railroads had

created a national market, in which the cheapest route to New York City (or any other desired market) would get the traffic.

After 1860, protests about discrimination in Baltimore dissipated but did not disappear. Even the *American*, which supported the B&O's right to set its rates without political interference and described railroad management as a "science," blanched at the notion of absolute discrimination of the sort John Williams had alleged, in which the railroad charged the same or less overall for shipments to Philadelphia and New York than to Baltimore. It remained important, according to the paper, that the B&O "not operate injuriously to those interests for the benefit of which the road was primarily built."[91] Furthermore, not everyone accepted that competitive exigency required even the proportional rate discrimination that the *American* deemed unavoidable. Mayor John Lee Chapman, who in his tenure at City Hall became a vocal adversary of the B&O's management, condemned the railroad's practice of discriminating in favor of through trade while charging exorbitant local rates on key freights like coal.[92]

These issues resonated well beyond Maryland. In the 1850s and 1860s, antidiscrimination measures came before state legislatures from New England to Virginia. Outside of Baltimore, these were not, by and large, urban political movements. Mercantile interests in New York City largely benefited from discriminatory rates, and thus saw efforts at rate control as threats to their commercial supremacy. Although Philadelphians lost traffic to New York and Boston in the trunk lines' rate wars, they, too, opposed such legislation, fearing they would slip further behind if the reforms were enacted. The closest parallel to Baltimore's political movement arose in Pittsburgh. There, as in Baltimore, merchants fumed as the taxpayer-funded Pennsylvania Railroad whisked freight past their doorsteps to cities west of the Ohio River. They called on the state legislature to protect their status as a terminus.[93]

For the most part, though, anger over railroad rate policies was the province of farmers and small-town merchants, who considered the high local rates they paid an exploitative outcome of monopolistic practices, and who hoped to stem the concentration of power and capital in major cities. Where the CFE had called for rebates on shipments to Baltimore to foster urban development, rural reformers called for fares that levied the same charge per mile regardless of destination—pro rata rates—so that all places received equal treatment at the hands of the railroads. Bills mandating pro rata rate structures came before state legislatures repeatedly in these years, but they invariably failed in the face of organized opposition from railroad officials, who argued that such regulations would push their companies into bankruptcy and drive capital out of state. The Boston-based *American Railway Times* argued that the laws reflected an antediluvian understanding of railroad enterprise. In 1860, commenting on recently defeated pro rata bills in New York, the *Railway Times* explained that the expenses incurred in laying track and financing debt saddled railroads with high fixed costs, which meant that the per-mile cost of shipping one item decreased the further that good traveled by rail. Reducing charges for long-distance freight would attract more traffic and subsidize long trips, thus allowing distant shippers to communicate with one another more efficiently and enabling railroads to serve larger hinterlands than they could otherwise. This logic did not remove fairness from the equation but rather turned the moral logic for pro rata rates on its head. "To be fair with long distances," wrote the *Railway Times*, "we should not extract therefrom a greater *profit* per ton per mile than upon short ones."[94] Even rural reformers came to concede that rate structures demanded a measure of flexibility. In the late 1860s, as the center of gravity for antidiscrimination politics shifted from the eastern states to the Midwest, its proponents abandoned calls for strict fare equality. When the postbellum Granger Laws set maximum rates without demanding pro rata consistency along rail routes, they laid the groundwork for future regulatory practices.[95]

Historians, attentive to the railroads' high fixed costs, have largely echoed the *American Railway Times'* analysis, concluding that the financial structure of the rail industry made the pro-rata proposals of the 1850s and 1860s impracticable. Yet the railroaders' account of the fixed-cost problem had a normative as well as a technical dimension: it represented a vision for the railroad industry that centered on large, long-distance railroad systems.[96] This in turn pointed toward an unchecked expansion of railroad enterprise that troubled the opponents of discrimination. Baltimore grain merchants, small-town and rural easterners, and the Midwestern Grangers differed in their objectives and their preferred remedies but shared a discomfort with the fact that railroad companies, operating largely outside of public oversight, set policies that determined winners and losers, not just among particular firms but also among cities and even states. They posited that a system of local roads developing mineral and agricultural resources would benefit society more than a system comprising enormous corporations vying for distant trade.[97] To this end, they sought both to regulate railroad companies' rate structures and to curb their expansion. In Pittsburgh, for example, advocates of pro rata transportation also called for the Pennsylvania Railroad to "abandon its protectorate over Western roads" beyond the Ohio River, curtailing its expansion and leaving western lines to compete among themselves.[98] A similar idea animated the fight over the B&O's acquisition of the Central Ohio Railroad in the early 1860s.

"Rail-Road Napoleons"

Soon after the debates over rate discrimination ended, the B&O became embroiled in another lengthy conflict, this time over its power to operate beyond the Ohio River. The railroad had of course been founded on the premise that a city's interests extend far beyond its borders. It took only small leaps in reasoning for Baltimore's municipal government to fund improvements that began and ended nowhere near the city limits, or even the state of Maryland. By the late 1850s, though, as the B&O escalated its competition with the northern trunk lines for through trade, some in the municipal government began to argue that the company's continued expansion undermined rather than served the city's objectives. This manifested most clearly in a conflict in the first half of the 1860s over the B&O's investments in the Central Ohio Railroad.

At first the Central Ohio, which ran from Columbus to Wheeling (fig. 6.1), connected only with the B&O, but by the late 1850s the ever-expanding Pennsylvania Railroad began to vie for its through traffic as well. Central Ohio president H. J. Jewett used the Pennsylvania's attentions as leverage against the B&O. In 1858, he complained that the B&O's management sent too much of its westbound traffic to Cincinnati via the Northwestern Virginia instead of to Columbus via the Main Stem, and he threatened to look to the Pennsylvania for support if the B&O did not funnel traffic via his line.[99] By setting himself in opposition to the NWV, Jewett provided yet another channel for the ongoing conflict between the public and private directors on the B&O.

FIGURE 6.1. The B&O and its trans-Ohio connections, ca. 1860. The B&O's Main Stem ran from Baltimore to Wheeling, and the NWV branched from the Main Stem and ran to Parkersburg. At Wheeling, the B&O connected to the Central Ohio, which ran to Columbus; at Parkersburg, it connected with the Marietta & Cincinnati. Map by Yiu Sze Ki. Adapted from *A Map of the Baltimore & Ohio Railroad and its principal connecting lines uniting all parts of the East & West.* (Baltimore: A. Hoen & Co., 1860).

The city had, at the B&O's request, invested heavily in the NWV, and thus the city directors objected to plans to deprive it of traffic. The private directors, led by John W. Garrett (shortly before his election as president), declared the Central Ohio the more promising of the two connections.[100] This was not a disinterested assessment. Many private directors, including Garrett and Johns Hopkins, had significant personal stakes in Central Ohio Railroad bonds, and thus a vested interest in sustaining this line.[101]

Propping up the Central Ohio was no easy task. In the mid-1850s, B&O managers issued glowing reports on the line, predicting that "the Central Ohio Road is on the eve of pouring into the lap of our Company such a magnificent dowry."[102] Nearly every outside observer contradicted these sanguine accounts. One railroad official sent west to investigate the line described it as poorly built, poorly managed, and poorly run. Some Ohioans refused to ride on or even ship freight via the Central Ohio.[103] Unsurprisingly, by 1860 the line was in perilous financial condition, and Garrett and the board of directors began to contemplate assuming control of the corporation in order to turn it around.[104]

This was an increasingly common maneuver for the trunk railroads, which after 1853 tended to make "alliances" with western lines instead of laying new tracks. Escalating competition encouraged empire building; by offering financial aid, arranging for through transportation, and ultimately gaining control of rail lines in the Ohio River valley, the trunk railroads hoped to secure a robust share of western traffic while minimizing capital expenditure.[105] J. Edgar Thomson, of the Pennsylvania, characterized such maneuvers as defensive efforts to prevent western railroads "from being used as clubs in the hands of others."[106] Garrett used the same logic to justify his proposed bailout of the Central Ohio Railroad: if the B&O rescued the Central Ohio from bankruptcy by acquiring its first mortgage bonds, it could keep that company from falling under the Philadelphians' sway.[107] When the matter came before the city government, some in the council accepted this logic immediately. The majority of the Joint Standing Committee on Internal Improvements found that although the NWV was the "natural channel" through which trade from Cincinnati and points further West would flow, they could not afford to lose the Columbus route to "rival roads and interests." The majority dismissed the notion that Garrett's and others' personal investments in the Central Ohio had influenced the B&O's decision.[108]

Yet in light of the board's recent shift toward private management, the minority on the committee—and ultimately the municipal government as a whole—deemed the B&O's proposed investment in Central Ohio bonds contrary to the public interest. In part, like the extra-dividend controversy six years earlier, this dispute reflected concerns that private managers had sacrificed the wellbeing of the corporation for personal gain. Rather than pursue complicated financial arrangements west of the Ohio, the minority suggested, the company should concentrate on improvements to the Main Stem. The most pressing factor cited in the minority report, though, was the rapidly expanding power of the railroad, which the authors hoped to curtail. The "true policy of rail-road management," wrote the minority, lay in "a consistent regard to the great laws of supply and demand; not in efforts to underbid or outreach or overcome, by buying up line after line of tributary road." If railroads extended their operations without geographic restrictions, soon nothing would check their ambition: "Our rail-road Napoleons, or rather Alexanders will cross the Ohio, like another Indus, and their ambition will not be satisfied, till, having mastered successive lines from the Ohio to the Mississippi and the Mississippi to the Pacific, they finally pause on the ocean's edge, and weep that there are no more rival companies to conquer!"[109] The council agreed, and issued an injunction to prevent the B&O's acquisition of the first mortgage bonds of the Central Ohio.

In the court hearings that followed, John H. B. Latrobe defended the company's actions by invoking the familiar specter of interurban competition. If the B&O ceased expanding, he contended, railroads based in Philadelphia and New York would seize control of western lines and thus subvert Baltimore's natural advantage of proximity to the West.[110] But to William Price, who represented the city, the conceit that the B&O could, acting against the expressed wishes of the city government, undertake policies intended to benefit Baltimore's trade prospects was precisely the problem. Price, the U.S. district attorney for Maryland and a prominent figure in the state's legal circles, had three years earlier issued a brief affirming the legitimacy of the extra dividend. Now, though, he sought to circumscribe the B&O's powers. Latrobe's logic of interurban competition, he pointed out, dated to an era before the rise of boundary-crossing, influence-peddling corporate behemoths. When Maryland and Virginia had chartered the B&O, they had specified the Ohio River as "the length of [its] tether." By initiating this westward expansion, the railroad arrogated to itself a power that the state had never granted. If the court did not curb the B&O's expansionist impulses, Price argued, railroad companies would soon eclipse the clout of the states that had incorporated them. "The Governor of your State is a mere circumstance in comparison with the President of a Rail Road," Price said. Men like Garrett, "with the immense wealth they wield, with their immense number of employees, servants and agents, have it in their power to exert an influence which they were never intended to possess."[111]

The court sided with the B&O. The railroad corporation was "in its very nature extraterritorial." Its historical origins, the judge ruled, implied a power to cross state lines in order to bring western trade to Baltimore. Already, the B&O had negotiated with state governments and exerted its influence far beyond Maryland to accomplish the goals specified in its charter. Extending its operations into Ohio furthered rather than contradicted this mission, he determined.[112] With this judicial sanction, the B&O acquired the Central Ohio mortgage bonds.[113] In 1865, John W. Garrett and other trustees purchased the company outright for $1 million.[114]

For Mayor John Lee Chapman, the B&O's decision to invest in a failing railroad represented the latest in a string of affronts to the urban public. "The question arises," he said in his annual address for 1864, "was this road built to impose enormous freights upon its customers, thereby amassing large sums of money to be used as private caprice may desire? or was it built to furnish cheap transportation for the farmer, the manufacturer, the coal miner."[115] Ten years of policies that prioritized paying dividends over improving facilities, vying for through trade at the expense of local traffic, and expanding into Ohio while stretches of the Main Stem remained single tracked, left Chapman thinking about what might have been were the B&O not "controled entirely by the President and private stockholders for their individual interests." Had the B&O completed its double track, lowered rates on coal, and dedicated itself to serving its terminal city, Chapman speculated, Baltimore "would have been the greatest manufacturing city on the Atlantic coast, and would now have had a population numbering 500,000 persons." Instead of an instrument of revival, the railroad had become an agent of decay.[116]

Chapman's grim assessment may have been a minority view. Most commentators who weighed in on the company's effects in the press pronounced the increasingly profitable and expansionist B&O under Garrett's command a credit to the city. Maryland politician and longtime B&O ally Reverdy Johnson, for example, credited the railroad with pouring trade into Baltimore and spoke of its promise "to make Baltimore one of the first cities of the American continent, if not of the world."[117] Baltimore's elected officials would have little say in how the B&O fulfilled that promise.

Conclusion

The B&O opened its tracks to the Ohio River in 1853, completing its founding mission; in 1863, when it crossed that river, it commenced a new era of expansion and competition. In the decade between those events, private stockholders transformed the B&O from an urban improvement into a private enterprise. Stockholders' representatives on the board of directors defined company policies concerning rate structures and labor practices as private matters, beyond the scope of public oversight, and proclaimed themselves the legitimate owners of the company.

These were not entirely novel ideas. Voices within the company and in the press had called for private, self-interested stockholders to take the lead in managing the B&O since the 1830s, and with intermittent success. After 1853, though, changes in the market for transportation and political tumult at all levels of government helped these ideas become hegemonic. As the American railroad network grew denser and trunk lines spanned the Appalachians, railroad companies introduced new organizational structures, professionalized their operations, and instituted policies that favored long-haul traffic. Simultaneously, state governments, burdened by mounting internal improvement debts and reeling from party realignment, withdrew from the fields of railroad promotion and regulation, leaving railroad management in private hands. This process took on a distinctive character in Baltimore, where the tumult that accompanied a half decade of Know-Nothing rule at the city and state levels played into the private investors' narrative. The economic, political, and institutional currents of the 1850s, both local and national, set the stage for the railroad's privatization and allowed stockholders to characterize such changes as essential, even inevitable, adaptations to a changing competitive landscape.

But the stockholders who transformed the B&O were making history, not following it. After all, the company they sought to control was among the largest and most powerful of its kind, the prime mover in the railroad industry; the B&O had the capacity to set trends as well as conform to them. And while the stockholders framed their maneuvers as necessary steps for the survival of the company, the effects of their changes were more ambiguous. The stockholder revolt was hardly a move toward more efficient operations. Initiatives like the extra dividend sacrificed the company's stability in order to line the pockets of its investors, for example; here the city government, not the stockholders, sought to safeguard the railroad's viability. And although stockholder control may well have positioned the B&O to compete with the other trunk lines for through traffic, the relationship between that competition and the company's bottom line was not self-evident. The chaotic rate wars revealed that no one, including the men in charge, truly knew how to control these expansive enterprises or to what ends they should operate. Even rate discrimination, a bedrock principle of railroad operations by the postbellum period, reflected assumptions about the function of the railroad corporation that developed amidst political clashes waged in Baltimore and elsewhere in this period. For a railroad company to justify rates that discriminated against particular places—including, in the B&O's case, its terminal city—it first had to define itself as a private corporation acting independent of urban public interest. Stockholders never ceased to argue that their actions served the interests of their home city, but they made sure to establish that they would advance these interests through their agency and at their discretion.

By the 1860s, the railroad represented a new actor in American political economy. As privately run corporations that crossed state lines, commanded millions of dollars in capital, and employed thousands of workers, railroads set policies that favored some communities over others, influenced (or even controlled) local and state governments, and determined the direction of trade. The spoils of this new corporate regime went to stockholders in the form of dividends. Efforts to check the growth of private power within the board, through strikes, in city hall, in the state legislature, and in the courts, largely came to naught. Yet the critics who tried to introduce rate abatements for Baltimore, secure wage increases for mechanics, and limit the B&O's expansion represented the first wave of a long-term effort to regulate the American railroad industry. Conflicts in Baltimore over the direction of the B&O contained the germ of broader questions that would have a profound influence over late nineteenth-century American politics: How should a capitalist economy function? And who should be in charge?

7

The Railroad Unbound and the City Contained

Fort Sumter heard the first shots of the Civil War, but Pratt Street saw the first bloodshed. Late in the morning of April 19, 1861, newly recruited soldiers from Massachusetts and Pennsylvania arrived in Baltimore on the Philadelphia, Wilmington & Baltimore Railroad, en route to Washington, DC. After pulling into President Street Station, they boarded horse-drawn cars for the mile-long crosstown trip to Camden Station, where trains waited to carry them on the last leg of their journey. Crowds had feted the federal troops as they passed through the streets of New York and Philadelphia, but in Baltimore, a city roiled with secessionist fervor, the slow transfer posed a grave danger. Several cars made the journey safely despite verbal abuse from Confederate-flag-waving onlookers, but local merchants and clerks dumped sand and anchors on the tracks to obstruct the passage of the remainder. Unable to continue by rail, the soldiers, swarmed by an enraged mob armed with brickbats and pistols, proceeded to march double-quick toward Camden Station. Finally, finding themselves cornered, with stones and bullets flying at their heads, the soldiers fired back. The resulting melee left four soldiers and twelve civilians dead and many more injured.

In the aftermath of the riot, Mayor George William Brown and Governor Thomas Hicks ordered the railroad bridges to the city's north and east burned to prevent additional soldiers from entering the city. Both the riots and the officials' destructive response demonstrated to federal officials that problems traversing urban space held the potential to disrupt national communications. The crowds, sharp turns, and mandatory horsepower that slowed the passage of trains in cities were now more than nuisances to rail companies—they were impediments to the war effort. As federal troops instituted martial law in Baltimore, the city street became military infrastructure.[1]

The Civil War accelerated shifts in the legal status and popular understandings of both railroad corporations and municipalities. During the war
and its aftermath, railroad corporations became national enterprises in both
scope and conception as their tracks spanned the continent and their rates
structured the economy. At the same time, cities became local polities—sites
for investment, their political agency circumscribed by their borders. Neither
of these changes arrived suddenly. The B&O's supporters had characterized
the company as a project of national importance since the 1830s, and they
used this framing to delegitimize municipal (or "local") policies intended to
safeguard the public or encourage urban growth. During the war, though, the
strategic utility of northern railroads underscored their national identity. The
heads of the trunk lines cooperated with federal officials to handle the challenges of mobilization, forging close ties with Washington and reaping handsome profits in the process. After Appomattox, the railroads' ability to move
troops quickly across the continent helped the federal government extend its
sovereignty and consolidate its authority. Such practices affirmed the national
scale of railroad operations and helped entrench the business corporation in
the postbellum American economy.[2]

The corollary to the national scale of railroad enterprise was the localization of urban space and government, a change that unfolded in realms of law
and politics. New legal doctrines that took hold in the 1870s narrowed the
scope of municipal agency. In his influential 1872 treatise, *Commentaries on
the Law of Municipal Corporations*, the jurist John F. Dillon rejected common law arguments for urban home rule, instead casting cities as subordinate
instruments of state governments, their powers confined to those expressly
limned by their parent legislatures. The notion of state supremacy over municipalities and other public corporations was not in and of itself new; Dillon's
innovation was to apply this principle in such a rigid manner as to render all
municipal law subject to challenge and the right of urban self-government
itself provisional. "Dillon's Rule," which quickly became—and remains—a
cornerstone of municipal jurisprudence, implied an understanding of urbanism far more restrictive than that which had underwritten projects like the
B&O. "Strictly, a municipal corporation is an institution designed to regulate
and administer the mere local or internal concerns of the incorporated place,"
Dillon wrote. It followed from this that "the *geographical limits* or boundaries
of the corporation *ought to be defined and certain*."[3] This circumscribed vision
of city politics resonated with bourgeois northern urbanites, who, wary of
the "machine" politicians put in office by working-class and immigrant electorates, called for statutory and constitutional reforms that would limit the
ability of municipal governments to tax and spend. As the scope of municipal

authority contracted, the nature of municipal politics changed; the second half of the nineteenth century witnessed the remaking of the urban landscape with the construction of parks, boulevards, and charitable institutions, amenities that extended the forms and values of bourgeois private life into the public realm. A sense of interurban competition never disappeared, but urban policy became increasingly inward looking.[4]

These processes—the nationalization of rail enterprise and the localization of urban governance—took material form in new urban infrastructure, built at great expense in the 1860s and 1870s, that was dedicated to the unencumbered circulation of goods and people. The control of movement within the city had been for years a key arena in which railroad companies asserted their power and city governments defended their prerogatives—it is no coincidence that Dillon first formulated his position when he ruled in favor of a railroad that sought unfettered access to city streets in Iowa.[5] In the decade after the Civil War, though, railroad companies' efforts to smooth and standardize their passage through cities dovetailed with bourgeois urbanites' desire to remake the city in their image, manifesting in systems of tunnels, deep cuts, ferries, and bypasses intended to funnel rail traffic through the urban core. In Baltimore, removing through traffic from city streets revived track removal campaigns, which sought to cast the street as a site of localized movement.

Physical changes in the built environment at once reflected and enabled conceptual changes in the geographies of railroad operations and urban life. Corporate executives, municipal officials, and citizens embedded new ideas about the railroad and the city in the postbellum urban landscape. Railroad tunnels, urban bypasses, and steam-powered port facilities provided critical infrastructure for both the consolidation of corporate power and the rise of bourgeois urbanism in these years. The infrastructural projects of the 1860s and 1870s advanced a vision of the city that privileged the movement of goods, people, and capital. As municipal government retrenched and railroad networks expanded, politicians and capitalists worked together to make the city a site of circulation.

The B&O in the Civil War

In the aftermath of the Pratt Street Riots, the Lincoln administration had good reason to doubt the loyalties of the B&O Railroad and its president. Although the railroad's tracks ran to the west and it competed with lines to the north, in publicity materials the company self-identified as a "southern improvement, identified with southern interests, and built by southern capital,"

and it informed enslavers that only by taking the B&O could they travel with
their human property from east to west "without setting foot on a single inch
of inhospitable ground."[6] After his company played a critical role in suppressing John Brown's rebellion at Harpers Ferry, Garrett brashly declared that his
"*Southern* line" would serve as "a sure agency for home defense" in the event
of Maryland's secession. As a Southern Democrat and an enslaver himself,
Garrett's personal sympathies lay with the Confederacy, as did those of his
immediate family. Garrett's brother Henry openly championed the Confederacy throughout the war, and his son Robert served briefly in Robert E. Lee's
army.[7] Pro-Confederate groups thus saw Garrett as a powerful potential ally.
During the Pratt Street Riots, one hundred anonymous "firm Respectable,
Resolute men" beseeched him to serve his "Southern Fellow Citizens" by refusing to assist Lincoln's war effort. They paired appeals to a common cause
with threats to the line, pledging to tear up the tracks if the B&O transported
Union troops.[8]

Nonetheless, political and geographical realities inexorably pushed the
B&O into the service of the Union cause. Few doubted that Lincoln would
use his war powers to assume control of rail lines if necessary. In 1862, federal legislation affirmed that the B&O and other railroads could continue to
operate as private lines, but only so long as they met the government's needs.
Garrett had little interest in testing the government on this point.[9] Furthermore, he faced pro-Union threats as credible as those of the "firm Respectable, Resolute men." As of 1861, the B&O's tracks traversed 514 miles of border
territory from Baltimore to Wheeling and Parkersburg, mostly in Virginia.
Yet while Virginia seceded, the territory through which the B&O ran did not.
The relative absence of slavery and staunch Unionist sentiment in the western
part of the state spurred a number of Appalachian counties to form their own
government, the new state of West Virginia. Company agents warned Garrett that angry civilians in these regions would burn bridges and depots if the
B&O supported the Confederacy. After it became clear that the B&O would
aid the federal cause, its tracks shaped the geography of the new state: the
three counties that comprise West Virginia's eastern panhandle participated
in the state constitutional convention, despite a large enslaved population,
because they lay on the B&O's path.[10]

Once Garrett recognized that his company's survival and his own tenure
as president required him to align with the federal government, he did not
equivocate. Although his loyalties did not go unquestioned in Washington or
in the press in the North, he quickly earned the trust and even admiration of
prominent government officials. His relationship with the Lincoln administration improved markedly once Simon Cameron, a close ally of the Pennsyl-

vania Railroad, was replaced by Edwin Stanton as secretary of war. Stanton knew Garrett personally through his legal work in peacetime on behalf of Robert Garrett & Sons and the Central Ohio Railroad. They enjoyed a cordial working relationship throughout the war. Stanton wrote glowingly that Garrett held the administration's "entire confidence in his loyalty and disposition to aid the government."[11]

This disposition proved essential during the Civil War as, for the first time in American history, railroad executives and military officers cooperated closely to coordinate supply chains and troop movements. Railroads enabled armies to shift from one theater to another in days instead of months, altering the geography of war. Command of transportation routes assumed paramount importance—William Tecumseh Sherman, for example, centered his strategy on the destruction of southern rail lines. In these conditions, railroad junctions that barely warranted a dot on the map in peacetime, like Grafton, West Virginia, where the B&O's Main Stem and Northwestern Virginia tracks diverged, now became significant strategic locales.[12]

At the start of the war, though, most commanders did not yet grasp the military significance of the railroad, and fewer still knew how to orchestrate rail transport on their own. For that, they turned to the presidents and transportation officers of the northern rail lines, who set aside their rivalries in order to figure out how to move entire corps over thousands of miles of track owned by dozens of rail lines. The B&O's strategic position made it a particularly important participant in these maneuvers. In addition to the Washington Branch, which, as the capital's only rail link north and west, was perhaps the busiest stretch of track in the nation during the war years, the company's Main Stem offered the shortest route between the eastern and western theaters. This provided flexibility for the federal military at critical junctures. In 1863, for example, after Major General William Rosencrans's defeat at the Battle of Chickamauga, Stanton ordered the transfer from Virginia of more than twenty thousand men—along with their weapons, equipment, and horses— to reinforce the Army of the Cumberland, a journey of more than 1,200 miles. Officials from the B&O coordinated with their counterparts in the Pennsylvania and other rail lines to make the necessary arrangements. In less than two weeks, the troops and their supplies crossed the Appalachians and the Ohio River to arrive at Chattanooga. The scope and speed of this troop movement was unprecedented, and it remained unmatched until the twentieth century.[13] For the railroad companies involved, heroic efforts met with heroic compensation from the federal government, which received a modest discount on shipping rates but more than made up for it with the heavy volume of traffic.[14]

The B&O's role in the federal government's mobilization made its destruction an objective for the Confederates, and from 1861 to 1864 the line was severed and reopened no fewer than twenty times. These assaults reflected more than the strategic value of the railroad. Secessionists fumed that the B&O had betrayed the Confederate cause; one Virginia newspaper charged that company "more or less Yankeeized the entire region between the tracks and the Pennsylvania border." Confederate commanders such as Stonewall Jackson and Jubal Early targeted the B&O's Main Stem repeatedly; Jackson particularly delighted in disabling the road and stole several locomotives at Martinsburg. To ward off such attacks, the U.S. military placed the entire Washington Branch under guard, and employees at Mount Clare worked overtime forging track and building engines to replace what the Confederates had destroyed.[15] As traffic congestion increased on the trunk lines, reopening the B&O became, in the *Sun*'s words, "a national necessity."[16] Garrett lamented that his line was "constantly subject to the vicissitudes and embarrassments connected with vast military operations."[17]

The federal government became at once the patron, protector, and client of the B&O. The company relied heavily on income from military transportation at a time when freight movement was irregular. Garrett became an intermediary between civilian and military operations and passed intelligence picked up by his employees to the government.[18] Eventually he started anticipating maneuvers and coordinating transportation. He apprised Edwin Stanton of Jubal Early's actions near Martinsburg, West Virginia, in 1864, and volunteered that he had already arranged for the transportation of troops to the scene.[19] Such communiqués established Garrett as a man who could speak to highly placed government officials on behalf of military officers and civilians alike.[20] He used these powers both to advance the war effort and to advocate on behalf of friends and family who sympathized with the Confederacy. During the war, he secured releases for men imprisoned for treason at Fort McHenry, including erstwhile B&O contractor and ardent secessionist Ross Winans. After the war, he persuaded Stanton to let former Confederate vice president Alexander Stephens out of jail in Georgia and worked behind the scenes for Jefferson Davis's release as well.[21]

Garrett's arrangements with the federal government also provided a new disciplinary tool to wield against his employees. Major General Lew Wallace wrote to Garrett in 1864 that the "importance of your road as a line of Military Communication is fully appreciated. Interruption of it by your employees would be as serious and reprehensible as if done by the enemy." If such disruptions occurred within a sphere of combat, Wallace promised that military commanders would arrest the company's employees and hold them in custody, awaiting Garrett's orders.[22] Military authority could even be brought to bear on Baltimore's notorious gang rivalries. Riots started by a nativist gang at the Mount Clare workshops in 1862 led to investigations not just by the Baltimore police but also by General John Adams Dix.[23]

The exigencies of wartime likewise introduced a new lens through which to view urban space. The imperatives of military shipment through Baltimore led military, civilian, and railroad officials to think of the city in strategic terms, particularly because troubles moving through urban streets precipitated the war's first casualties. After the military stabilized the city, Baltimore served as an important staging ground for Union military operations. Locust Point became in essence a military installation as freight trains took on supplies from steamships and ran straight to the capital. The B&O refitted old warehouses to store materiel and laid new tracks through the neighborhood to accommodate the traffic.[24] But parts of the city not tailor-made for rail travel remained an obstacle to rapid transit. Baltimore was not alone in this. Railroad officials and military commanders alike characterized cities as choke points in an otherwise efficient system. For travel between New York and Washington, city streets in Philadelphia and Baltimore proved particularly troublesome, as heavy traffic and limited track capacity hindered the free flow of military traffic. Most vexing of all were the municipal restrictions on steam power. Samuel Felton, president of the PWB, characterized these regulations as impediments to rail travel, and by extension to the war effort. Felton recommended that Congress pass legislation mandating the use of steam power along the entire route from New York to Washington.[25]

Ultimately a different threat persuaded Baltimore politicians to relax long-standing policies concerning locomotive traffic in the street—plans for a federally funded "airline." In nineteenth-century parlance, an airline was a straight, direct rail route between two points. Simon Cameron, Lincoln's first secretary of war, proposed that Congress fund such a line between Washington and New York, bypassing Baltimore and Philadelphia, in part because of complaints about delays in urban transfers attributable to the use of horsepower. Given Cameron's ties to the Pennsylvania Railroad, Garrett saw this as a sinister move. Advocates of an airline, he stated, merely used war as a pretext to deploy federal authority and public money in the construction of a railroad that would in peacetime advance commercial rivalries and leave Baltimore outside the main paths of travel.[26]

The federal government never built the airline, but the threat to do so had significant effects on municipal policy and the built environment. The airline threat persuaded the city government to sign off on proposals designed to facilitate the movement of government freight, such as laying new heavy rails on Howard Street and widening the radii of curves in the track to enable faster transfers.[27] Most importantly, the city government agreed to relax its locomotive laws, allowing steam engines to move government freight through the streets despite the objections of abutting property holders. A council committee stated that fears of "placing Baltimore out of the great highway of travel between the capitol of the Nation and its great commercial emporium" compelled the municipality to adopt such measures.[28] Garrett promised the House of Representatives' Committee on Military Affairs that the new infrastructure and policies would eliminate all annoyances stemming from urban transfers.[29]

The Civil War prompted new understandings of the B&O and of Baltimore. The B&O's critical role in moving supplies to Washington and the West framed the railroad's actions as matters of national importance. Similarly, the military's need for rapid transportation turned Baltimore's streets into strategic infrastructure, overriding the power of Baltimore's government to regulate movement within its borders. Of course, the strategic lens on urban space lasted only as long as the war itself. The city government reasserted its regulatory authority after the Confederate Army surrendered, reinstating the ban on locomotives in major thoroughfares in September 1865.[30] But the railroad's new stature proved more enduring. Long-standing demands for local control of the line to ensure that it served Baltimore's interests appeared parochial in the midst of the war. One pamphleteer wrote in 1864 that attempts to ensure continued public representation on the board aimed to drag the B&O "down to the level of a county road," whereas the "people of this country, the Government, all the States of the Union, know that it is *a national highway*."[31] No longer an urban improvement or a southern line, the B&O was operating at a national scale.

Railroad Traffic in the City

Widely publicized partisan violence in Baltimore during the waning days of the Johnson administration ensured that the notion of urban space as an obstacle to national communications persisted after the war. In October 1868, weeks before the first post–Civil War presidential election, a contingent of Republicans traveling from Washington to Philadelphia were assaulted by gangs of Democrats as they transferred through Pratt Street in horse-drawn cars. The victims reported that men brandishing pistols and knives had entered the cars, cheering for Democratic candidate Horatio Seymour. Hearing this, the *Washington Star* revived the wartime idea of a federally funded airline from the capital to New York, citing the threat to the public of "having their brains blown out . . . by a gang of desperadoes [in Baltimore] who take possession of the through cars whenever they choose."[32]

Media accounts of partisan violence highlighted the disorderly potential of the street. The pro-Republican *American* argued that flagrant attacks such as those on Pratt Street occurred frequently and with the tacit consent of the city police. The Democratic-leaning *Sun* dismissed the charges, deeming it an "infamous libel that passage through Baltimore is unsafe. Railroad trains are passing at all times of every day through our city, and who hears of their passengers being troubled?"[33] This rhetorical question had an obvious answer, but not the one the *Sun* implied: thanks to widespread press coverage, *everyone* had heard such accounts. Urbanites had long complained that overlaying the infrastructure of national communications on the spaces of daily life interfered with localized patterns of movement, but the partisan assaults underscored the converse: the potential of the city street to disrupt national politics.

The assaults on Pratt Street offered a dramatic illustration of a much broader problem: the difficulties railroad companies encountered as they tried to run rail traffic through the urban streetscape. Many issues remained consistent from the railroad's earliest days. Railroad officials complained that sharing right of way with drays, wagons, and carts on uneven city streets led to accidents and wear-and-tear that damaged cars, equipment, and track on a daily basis.[34] Passing through urban space also exposed trains to a range of nuisances, including rocks thrown at moving cars and the theft of goods from cars or depot platforms.[35] In hard times, families in need of fuel incorporated the railroad into their survival strategies, sending children and young women to lift coal from unattended freight cars.[36] And neither the railroad company nor the city government ever devised a means to prevent children from jumping on and off the cars. The council repeatedly passed ordinances that condemned the practice and prescribed a one-dollar fine for violators, but to little effect.[37]

But if the problems associated with urban rail operations remained constant, the public's attitude toward them did not. By the 1860s, railroad companies in Baltimore found themselves held liable for the types of accidents that in the 1830s had been blamed on the victim. Citizens increasingly insisted on greater precautions from railroads within the city limits.[38] Even on the Locust Point Branch, created expressly to bypass municipal regulations, the B&O faced heightened scrutiny, as the case of the Banen brothers shows. In October 1860, a number of local boys, including eleven-year-old Peter Banen and his eight-year-old brother Patrick, jumped on the tail end of a seventy-car-long coal train as it pulled out of the station in Locust Point. These boys habitually "amused themselves by playing about the brakes of the rear cars, and climbing upon them," reported the *Sun*. On this occasion, though, Peter Banen was thrown from the car and it ran over his head, killing him. His brother lost a hand in the same accident.[39] As John H. B. Latrobe explained to Garrett, courts of law and public opinion would likely both find the company at fault. The accident did not reflect willful negligence on the company's part, but the urban setting complicated matters. Even though this was hardly the boys' first joyride, none of the train's crewmen had taken the precaution of standing on the hindmost cars to shoo them away. Because these children could get on this particular car unobserved as it backed around a curve, because the train tracks ran through a public street, and because the boys were so young, Latrobe concluded that the courts would find the company liable.[40]

Latrobe reached this conclusion in part because of changing legal precedents concerning railroads' urban operations, but he also knew that the B&O confronted increasingly unsympathetic juries in Baltimore. In a case from 1866, B&O officials found themselves placed in an awkward position by both the jury's prejudices and the unsympathetic behavior of their operatives. The plaintiff, an elderly man severely injured by a B&O train, asked for $2,000 in damages. The plaintiff's witnesses alleged that the B&O's driver had not blown his horn and was driving swiftly. The B&O's witnesses denied these claims, but John Toole, a company manager who witnessed the scene in the courtroom, wrote to William Prescott Smith, "I could see from the countenances of the jury that they did not believe this." The driver in question, Reuben Smith, had been arrested once before for speeding, and one of the company's key witnesses arrived at court in a "beastly state of intoxication." The jury awarded the plaintiff $1,000 more than he had originally sought. A number of factors contributed to the verdict, Toole wrote, including that the plaintiff "was and is poor, and the railroad rich."[41] John W. Garrett, frustrated by what he called "the heavy and extraordinary verdict," rebuked his subordinates for their poor handling of the case, but by 1866, personal experience had predisposed Baltimore juries to believe accounts of railroad recklessness.[42]

Baltimore's traffic troubles were not unique. Cities up and down the seaboard confronted difficulties integrating rail traffic with the urban streetscape. After the Civil War, as the railroad system expanded and traffic increased, one New York newspaper deemed the question of how to move rail cars through dense cities "the problem of the age."[43] The accidents, delays, noise, and smoke that accompanied steam transit in the city bedeviled railroad corporations and urban publics alike. Journalists fishing for solutions looked enviously at England, where underground tracks allowed trains to move smoothly through urban centers like London and Liverpool. Solving the urban transit dead-lock would require the belated introduction of just such a "system" or "net-work" to the city.[44] In Philadelphia, where by 1871 it cost more to transport cargo through the city than to ship it to Harrisburg, proposals circulated to "belt" the city with tracks or tunnel under the streets to a central depot.[45] The situation was even more dire in Manhattan, where proposals circulated every couple of years offering new solutions—a "two-story street" to run rail traffic below street grade at the cost of $10 million per mile, a "depressed railway" that would place steam cars on tracks running in deep cuts through the city, or an elaborate system of tunnels linking Lower Manhattan to New Jersey, Long Island, and Harlem.[46]

Supporters of these projects characterized them as at once restorative and progressive, undertakings that would return streets to their original condi-tion while pointing the way toward a new status quo. In the 1870s, a growing movement to remake the street as a space of local movement took shape in popular discourse, urban regulation, and legal theory. In his *Commentar-ies*, John Dillon argued that maintaining streets "for all purposes of free and unobstructed passage" constituted one of city governments' most important responsibilities. He singled out railroad traffic as a violation of this principle. Deploying logic that would have resonated with Philip Uhler forty years ear-lier, Dillon wrote that travel on railroads "bears no analogy to our notions of travel on an ordinary street or highway, where every one travels at plea-sure. . . . The uses are totally different, and even inconsistent. The one is ex-clusive, in favor of private interest, and the other is open and free to all."[47] The *Sun*, which had once dismissed the notion that locomotives interfered with urban life, came by the 1870s to a similar conclusion and began to look for-ward to a day when cities ejected steam railroads from their busiest streets.[48] Removing rail traffic from the street enabled railroads to extend the efficien-cies of steam travel to their urban operations; getting rid of railcars offered urbanites the prospect of standardizing movement within the city, returning the streets to the urban public.

Baltimore's railroad corporations developed a bifurcated approach to urban through travel. The Northern Central (formerly the Baltimore & Sus-quehanna) and two new lines, the Western Maryland and the Baltimore & Potomac, worked together to form what a city guidebook called "a system of underground communication" that let out at the waterfront at Canton.[49] The B&O, for its part, adapted its Locust Point facilities to send through traf-fic across the harbor. Reports on these developments often used the passive voice: a "need" for better through travel "was met" by tunnels, bridges, cuts, and bypasses. This syntax gave these changes a sense of inevitability but obscured the negotiations, the technical accommodations, and the financial outlay that tunneling the city required.[50]

Systems for Through Trade

The tunnel system's origins lay in the rivalry between the B&O and the Pennsylvania Railroad. In 1858, Maryland's legislature chartered a line called the Baltimore & Potomac (B&P) to link southern Maryland with Baltimore. The B&P charter contained a provision allowing the construction of branch lines, including one to the District of Columbia. This drew the attention of the Pennsylvania Railroad, which purchased the B&P in 1867 with an eye to breaking the B&O's monopoly on travel to and from the capital. As the Pennsylvania had already acquired the Northern Central, the B&P would complete its through route from New York City to Washington.[51]

When the city council authorized this new construction in 1869, it sought to make the new line as inconspicuous as possible. The B&P branched off from the tracks of the Northern Central in North Baltimore and passed through well-heeled residential districts in the northwestern part of the city before turning south to the capital. The ordinance authorizing the B&P to lay its tracks specified that all rails within the city limits would run below street grade in tunnels or deep cuts. The council charged the company with keeping its trains "entirely concealed from the view of persons using the streets," ordered that steam ventilation take place "without annoyance to persons or property in proximity thereto," and demanded that conductors use bells, not whistles, for signaling purposes, so as not to disturb the railroad's neighbors. The ordinance also insisted that the B&P tunnel under or bridge over all the principal thoroughfares into town once it left the city limits. The company agreed to these strictures and the plans went forward despite opposition from residents of North Baltimore, who worried that the new rail infrastructure would harm their property and hamper movement uptown.[52]

The B&P's tunnels and deep cuts represented one half of a new subterranean crosstown rail route. The other half was the Union Railroad, a short line financed in part by the city government, which ran partially belowground through northeast Baltimore before turning south outside the city limits to terminate at the wharves of the Canton industrial complex.[53] Together, the B&P and Union Railroad system, completed by 1873 at the cost of around $5 million, allowed western freight to reach tidewater without breaking bulk. Transfers that took a day by surface rail in horse-drawn cars could move through town in as little as ninety minutes via the tunnels. More broadly, though, the new through route's sponsors, including both the rail corporations and the municipality, contended that this underground system advanced a new vision for the city. The costly work of digging ventilated tunnels and building bridges represented a step toward, in the words of the Union Railroad's president (and former B&O president) William G. Harrison, "remov[ing] from the now crowded streets the passage of trains."[54]

For the railroads, going below the city avoided the troubles attendant with urban space and regulation. For urbanites, too, putting the tracks out of sight opened up the possibility of a new urbanism marked by expansion and free movement. Indeed, by the 1870s surface rail was so anathema that even plans by the B&P to build tracks at street grade outside the city limits elicited controversy. On learning that the new rail line, in violation of its authorizing ordinance, intended to cross major thoroughfares leading into the city at street level, the city council protested that this would create an "iron blockade" constricting movement and hindering future urban expansion.[55] The *Sun* warned that with these tracks in place, "the city itself [is] to be dwarfed and contained," made subservient to "the great Pennsylvania corporation." The B&P, for its part, responded that the tracks in question lay beyond Baltimore's borders and thus beyond the council's jurisdiction, its ordinance notwithstanding. When the city moved to issue an injunction, the company paid a team of workers overtime to lay the tracks in one night, making its street-level route a fait accompli.[56]

Shortly after the B&P and Union Railroad route opened for through traffic, the Western Maryland, the B&P, and the Northern Central began work on infrastructure projects that reoriented the city's transportation geography. The Northern Central built new piers and grain elevators at Canton to counter the B&O's improvements at Locust Point, and the Western Maryland and B&P erected new stations or renovated old ones in West Baltimore.[57] Passengers wishing to travel far afield could go to the B&P's new "Union Station" on North Charles Street, today the site of Amtrak's Penn Station. From this depot, forty-seven passenger trains ran in all directions around the clock. "Persons traveling out Charles street after dark are struck with the brilliant and animated appearance of the Union depot, illuminated by numerous gas burners, and kept noisy by passing trains," wrote the *Sun*.[58] The station's location, far north of the city center, made it an island of rail activity in a sea of darkness. For all the station's conveniences for through travelers, Baltimore-bound passengers stepped off the train only to find themselves stranded (fig. 7.1).[59]

The B&O declined to participate in the tunnel system, finding a solution to the through traffic dilemma in its Locust Point facilities instead. In 1869, Garrett announced that to reduce the use of horse-drawn cars in Baltimore's

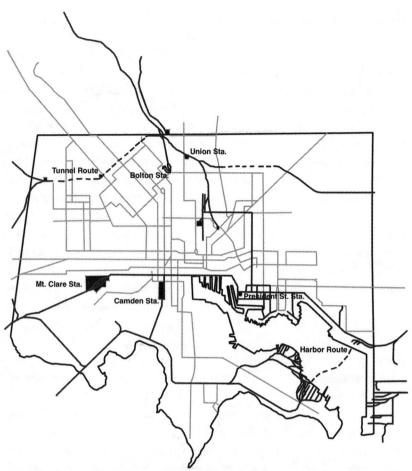

FIGURE 7.1. Baltimore's railroad infrastructure, ca. 1887. Dark-gray lines and black boxes indicate railroad tracks and depots; dotted lines represent the harbor crossing and underground tracks, controlled by the B&O and Pennsylvania Railroads, respectively. Light-gray lines represent streetcar routes. Map by author. Adapted from Frank A. Gray, "Gray's New Map of Baltimore" in *Gray's Atlas of the United States* (Philadelphia: O. W. Gray & Son, 1887), 61.

streets, the company would start running through traffic from Locust Point directly to the tracks of the PWB in Canton. The company built floating docks to connect the tracks on either side with purpose-built railed barges capable of accommodating up to ten cars at a time, effectively extending the tracks over the water so that trains could run without breaking bulk to Philadelphia and beyond.[60] The new route opened in 1870, and by 1876, 250 cars crossed the harbor daily during the busy season. Whereas it took freight as long to cross Pratt Street by horse as it did to move from Baltimore to Cumberland, travelers and tonnage alike could transfer from the PWB to the B&O in as little as thirty minutes by water.[61]

The urban bypasses built by the B&O and the Pennsylvania Railroad's proxies (the B&P and Northern Central) may seem like logical solutions to ever-increasing traffic, but these multimillion-dollar projects represented new visions of urban life and new understandings of the place of the city in an expanding capitalist system. When the tunnel and harbor systems were under construction, the *American* published a front-page editorial titled "RAILROADS THROUGH AND UNDER BALTIMORE." The editors argued that routing all railroad through traffic below street grade would allow Baltimore to capitalize on its favorable location and become a great center of commerce and exchange. Even the B&O's new ferry system represented only a temporary expedient: "The true policy of that road will finally be found in the construction of a tunnel, into which the trains will enter on the south side of the harbor, pass under the river, and come out on the north side, beyond the populous part of the city."[62] The railroad metropolis of the future would be a city of tunnels, situated both within and above a web of rail that linked it to the outside world.

In practice, though, even tunnels could not entirely insulate rail traffic from the urban fabric. Agents for the B&O warned travelers that taking the tunnel route meant trading the delays and danger of the street track for the muck and effluvia of the city's underbelly: "The road 'passed under Baltimore . . . through a mile or two of sewer, which carries off the filth and offal of that city, and is consequently, at all times, the hot-bed of miasma and pernicious and unwholesome exhalations.'" By taking the aboveground B&O route, by contrast, one could "breath[e] the pure air of heaven."[63] In fact, periodic flooding did at times close the tunnels and force travelers to switch to the B&O lines instead. Meanwhile, North Baltimore residents found that gaining facilities for through travel meant sacrificing quiet nights, as they now confronted whistles blowing and bells ringing around the clock.[64] Even an editor of the *American* had to face up to the nuisances of underground rail traffic—a resident of northwestern Baltimore, he penned a complaint in 1873 about the "demoniacal sounds" of the locomotive whistle which seemed to be "instigated in large degree by sheer wantonness, as if those who had charge of the engines were just trying [to see] how much noise they could make." Still, this complaint pointed only to the ultimate telos of railroad construction in the city: "It ought to be that the tracks of all railroads were enclosed. . . . Then with a thorough system of telegraphic communications . . . the abominable, unearthly scream of the steam whistle might be forever abolished."[65] When the editor of the *American* imagined railroad traffic as an invisible, demate-rialized phenomenon, conducted out of sight and out of mind using tunnels and telegraphs, he pointed toward a future in which an urbane lifestyle could proceed without notice of the systems that enabled it.

The Frog Pond

As the sleep-deprived newspaper editor fantasized about silent trains hurtling unseen through tunnels, a very different experiment in railroad urbanism un-folded four miles to his southeast. After the Civil War, the B&O devoted more attention and resources to its waterfront facilities at Locust Point. There, in a space removed from the urban core and largely free from the municipal gov-ernment's regulatory hand, railroad executives sought to realize their vision of the city as a node in a transnational system of movement and exchange. In this compact district, the infrastructures of long-distance rail, city streets, in-ternational steamships, and commodity processing overlapped, bringing to-gether coal from the Allegheny Mountains, wheat from the Ohio River valley, and immigrants from Europe.[66] The result was a strikingly new type of urban space, a place where, as the *American* put it in 1874, "commerce has supreme control." The defining infrastructure for this neighborhood was not the street, the park, the market, or even the tunnel—it was the frog pond, so called be-cause of the dense concentration of crossing tracks ("frogs" in railroad lingo) in one location. The perils of the frog pond meant that Locust Point was no place for "sentimental promenading," the *American* warned. "The railroad tracks that radiate from the wharves form such inexplicable combinations with each other, that nobody but the switch-tenders know where to run to keep out of the way of the shifting trains." As North Baltimoreans complained about steam whistles disrupting their sleep, the residents of Locust Point encountered snorting, hissing steam engines on their streets day and night (fig. 7.2).[67] The frog pond represented the apotheosis of the locomotivized city—an urban neighborhood given over to rail travel. Railroad executives, citizens, travelers, and politicians projected onto this space ideas about the future of the city and the future of capitalism itself.

That future was one of seamless, steam-powered travel, in which ship-ments moved over land and water without distinction. Garrett's ambition—and therefore that of the B&O as an institution—was to transform Locust Point into a central hub for global commodity exchange. Doing so entailed investing in oceangoing steamships. The steamer represented a vision of the future for nineteenth-century pundits as the railroad had before it, a way to

The Marine Terminus of the Baltimore & Ohio Rail Road—Locust Point, Baltimore, Md.

FIGURE 7.2. Illustration of Locust Point, ca. 1878. Courtesy of the Library of Congress. Detail from Walter F. Elmer, *Map of the Baltimore and Ohio Rail Road with its Branches and Connections* (Baltimore, 1878).

eliminate barriers to mobility. Steam technology had leveled mountains, and so it could bridge the ocean: "Steam Ships are the Railways of the sea," wrote one of Garrett's European correspondents in 1860.[68] Like railroads, steamships could depart on demand, without waiting for prevailing winds, and could traverse open water at a steady, rapid clip. Still, this writer's imagination slightly outpaced the technology, which did not become commercially viable until after the Civil War. Although steamers started crossing the Atlantic in the 1840s, the coal stores required for ocean crossings took up valuable space in the cargo hold, and the engines remained prone to catastrophic failures. Subsidies from the United States and other national governments kept steamships on the high seas until the invention of the screw propeller and the compound engine in the 1860s reduced the risk of mechanical problems and enabled the conveyance of larger freights, enticing private capital.[69]

"Steam as the sole power," wrote a correspondent to the *Sun* in 1859, "is making a total change . . . in the trade of the world." The writer conjured a future in which ships departed the Chesapeake for Havana, Rio de Janeiro, and Antwerp, fueled by the Allegheny coal piled high at Locust Point.[70] But while Locust Point's mountains of coal, given enough time, might have produced a diamond, making Baltimore into an international steam port required considerable initiative from the B&O. By 1860, Baltimore's well-stocked collieries had made the city a hub of coastwise steam travel, but its transatlantic connections remained paltry. John W. Garrett argued that unless his company established direct links to Europe, neither Baltimore nor the B&O could compete effectively for western trade, much of which was grain destined for Liverpool or Le Havre.[71] Oceangoing steamships already crowded the harbors of New York and Boston, and by the Civil War, the Pennsylvania Railroad had started its own experiments with Philadelphia-based transatlantic lines. Garrett believed that an independent steam-powered route to Europe would make Locust Point a critical junction in the global economy.[72]

In 1865 the company purchased four steamships sold as war surplus by the federal government for $75,000 and used them to inaugurate regular runs between Baltimore and Liverpool.[73] The venture flopped: by 1874, the company had taken losses ten times greater than its initial investment. Garrett argued that this failure nonetheless set the stage for subsequent international steam lines.[74] Shortly after launching its steam service to Britain, the B&O forged a partnership with the North German Lloyd steamship company, agreeing in 1866 to sail two first-class steamships between Baltimore and the Hanseatic port of Bremen.[75] When the first Bremen-line ship, the *Baltimore*, docked at Locust Point in 1868, the city council declared a general holiday. The *Sun* deemed the festivities that accompanied the steamer's arrival the city's greatest public event since the B&O's cornerstone-laying ceremony forty years prior.[76]

Establishing the B&O as a major player in international shipping entailed reconfiguring land, water, and infrastructure at Locust Point. The company bought up ever-larger swathes of waterfront and industrial buildings. By 1868, the B&O owned approximately fifty acres of land on the peninsula, including more than a half mile of wharf fronts.[77] Increasingly large ships demanded deeper berths, and the company stretched its piers ever farther into the harbor.[78] The B&O announced new piers in 1868 and 1875, a new wharf in 1869, new grain elevators in 1870 and 1873, and a coffee warehouse in 1875.[79] With every addition, the frog pond grew denser, as tracks and sidings proliferated to link the mushrooming structures, leaving the whole area "gridironed."[80] By 1877, the B&O's property in South Baltimore, independent of its facilities at Camden Station and Mount Clare, was valued at $1,423,089.17, including machine shops, roundhouses, and nearly twenty miles of track.[81] All of this private investment was meaningless, though, without constant dredging of the channel from Fort McHenry to the Chesapeake Bay. The municipal government funded this vital work, a task that one engineer likened to "sweep[ing] our streets and clean[ing] our roadways"—that is, a public responsibility. As the costs of this maritime "sweeping" escalated, both John W. Garrett and city officials lobbied Congress for support, arguing, successfully, that Baltimore's rail links to the West made the state of its harbor a matter of national import.[82]

This accumulated investment, public and private, turned Locust Point into an emblem of industrial modernity. Reporters marveled as cars laden with freight from Chicago or St. Louis delivered cargo directly onto steamers, obviating transshipment and allowing freight to move at hitherto-unimaginable speeds.[83] Immigrants traveled in the opposite direction, walking off the ship and straight into cars that waited on the pier to carry them westward.[84] In light of these expeditious arrangements, the *New York Times* in 1874 dubbed Locust Point "a model terminal station," an emblem of "the American ideal of speed, economy, and convenience."[85] In Manhattan, by contrast, horses still handled much of the in-town rail traffic, and it often cost as much to move freight across town as it did to convey it from the interior of the country.[86] Locust Point caught the eye of Bostonians as well. In 1875, a committee from the Massachusetts legislature paid the port a visit and came away impressed with the transfer arrangements they found there. Animated by Baltimore's example, the legislature prepared to spend $10 million on a comparable modernization of Boston's waterfront.[87]

To some observers, the smooth transfers made possible at Locust Point pointed to a future marked by commercial growth and prosperity. An 1876 guidebook praised Locust Point for its one-step transfers and predicted that the neighborhood's rapid growth would soon "root out Fort McHenry as a military depot, and replace its barracks and arsenals with the warehouses and granaries of commerce."[88] This swords-to-plowshares transition never materialized, but it reflected a vision of a city transformed by steam and given over to corporate control. From the street level, though, Locust Point took on another aspect. In *Electro Pete, the Man of Fire*, a dime novel published in 1884 and set in the neighborhood, one character vividly warns another of the dangers of walking through Locust Point's frog pond at night: "There's a lot o' cars an' engines busy there this night, an' if ye're heel takes a twist in the rails, ye'l be a goner yet, d'ye mind."[89] The same frog pond that annihilated space for train companies also threatened to annihilate the residents and laborers who traversed it.

Track Removal in the 1870s

Outside of Locust Point, as railroad infrastructure began to circumvent the urban core, citizen opposition to urban tracks intensified. Increasingly, urbanites and their elected representatives asserted that tracks had no place in their streets and worked to eliminate grade crossings.[90] Long-standing track removal campaigns on Howard and Pratt Streets picked up steam in the 1870s while new ones percolated in East Baltimore. As with the original track removal campaigns in the 1830s, the citizens' grievances centered on the obstructions, nuisances, and dangers posed by rail infrastructure, but with two key differences. First, all sides, including the railroad companies and the merchants who used their street tracks, had come to agree that train travel meshed uneasily with the urban streetscape.[91] Second, rather than hoping to redirect commerce to draymen and carters, track removal advocates in the 1870s took for granted that most rail traffic would pass straight through Baltimore; they simply did not want it to do so at street level. Anti-track campaigns contributed to a broader conversation in the 1870s about the nature and function of city streets. Debate over track removal coincided with efforts to remove cattle and swine from city streets, for example. Collectively, these measures underscored new principles of mobility—a privileging of circulation and local transit.[92] But they also highlighted the limits of these ideas. The successful track removal efforts on Howard Street suggest the power of upper-class retailers and residents to remake their street; the unsuccessful campaigns in East Baltimore and the city center highlight the class-based contingency of access to the new urban landscape (fig. 7.3).

On May 1, 1871, a track removal campaign twenty years in the making came to fruition as workers pulled up the rails on Howard Street and replaced them with cobblestones. The Howard Street tracks had long served as the most direct link between the Northern Central and the B&O. In the 1830s, the flour merchants who lined the street had used the tracks to connect their warehouses to the B&O's Main Stem. By the 1850s, though, these wholesalers gave way to retailers and residents who felt that the busy track hindered their use of the street.[93] For two decades, railroad officials and the street's

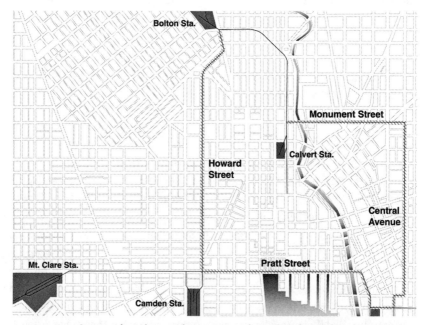

FIGURE 7.3. Streets with track removal campaigns in the 1860s and 1870s. Map by Li Lok Him. Adapted from *Gray's Atlas City of Baltimore, Maryland* (Philadelphia: Stedman, Brown & Lyon, 1873).

remaining merchants resisted campaigns to remove the track by arguing that the long-distance freight transit constituted a public good. Track supporters pointed out that marble from Baltimore County made its way to the Capitol in Washington, then under renovation, via Howard Street, which made preserving the tracks quite literally a matter of national importance. By this logic, Howard Street's place within a broader railroad network transcended citizens' concerns about traffic congestion and public safety.[94] As the years went on, though, the challengers gained in strength while the number of railroad supporters declined.[95] Finally, in 1869, the council responded favorably to Howard Street residents' request and ordered the track removed within two years.[96]

The difference this time reflected shifts in the landscape of through travel—the B&O had just instituted the harbor transfer and construction on the B&P and Union Railroad tunnels was under way.[97] In some ways, the removal of track on Howard Street accomplished the fundamental demand of track removal campaigns since the 1830s—the restoration of the street to its "original condition." But the use of the street and understandings of the city had changed significantly in the previous four decades. At the most basic level, the residents were not so much eliminating trains as swapping one type for another: soon, the City Passenger Railway would lay streetcar tracks through Howard Street, replacing the infrastructure of interurban freight with that of intraurban transit. More significant was the way the tunnels and ferries altered the relationship between public and private space. Where track supporters in 1859 had been able to cast Howard Street as a critical link in a national system, a decade later the urban bypass projects made the street "local" again, a bounded space subject to property owners' will.

This was not the antimonopolistic, democratic streetscape championed by the draymen in the 1830s. Howard was a retailer's street and a fashionable promenade; removing the freight tracks served a distinctly bourgeois urban vision. The process of track removal itself betrayed the residents' fears of the unruly street. Howard Street residents, leery of disruptions, summoned a police force ahead of time to monitor the process.[98] They also eyed the workers tasked with removing the track with suspicion—the *American* reported that residents provided them with lager for refreshment but dissuaded one of their number from offering whisky. Although the neighbors had booked a brass band to celebrate the successful conclusion of this decades-long campaign, they ultimately decided to dispense with that as well, worried that boisterous music might draw "irresponsible persons" to the scene. The carefully managed celebration was part and parcel with the change in the character of the street. Where once produce houses had dominated, wrote the *American*, "Dry goods stores, notion houses, furniture warerooms, clothiers and retail dealers generally occupy the street, to the exclusion of other businesses."[99]

Working-class districts had a harder time exercising this new urban prerogative. No sooner had workers laid cobblestone on Howard Street than residents of central and eastern Baltimore demanded track removal in their own neighborhoods. They posited the same arguments as their Howard Street counterparts, noting that increasingly lengthy trains passed through their streets an average of sixty times a day. All too often this traffic presented a mortal danger.[100] Dr. Milton N. Taylor, an East Baltimore physician, played a leading role in this campaign. Years of medical practice had convinced him that the tracks posed a threat to public health. He had personally attended to twenty-three street railroad accidents, several of which resulted in death or permanent injury.[101] Taylor and the other protestors argued that with tunnels and ferries capable of whisking trains through the city, there was no longer any reason for the residents of East Baltimore and downtown to make these deadly sacrifices in the name of railroad commerce.[102]

Wholesalers in these districts felt otherwise. They had built their businesses around the tracks, which allowed them to connect directly with the B&O and thus to national markets. As one mercantile house put it, the Pratt Street tracks represented a "system of delivery" that had served Baltimore firms for "nearly half a century"—a once-radical imposition on public space now had the patina of tradition. Hundreds of signatories joined this and other petitions calling for the retention of tracks on Pratt and other streets.[103] They conceded that "railroad tracks through cities . . . are objectionable in some degree," but they argued that the tracks remained essential for the city's economy.[104]

But as the tunnel and ferry infrastructure expanded, anti-track sentiment grew. Campaigns in Pratt Street in 1873 spread in 1874 to Monument Street and Central Avenue. Track removal advocates from different districts coordinated their efforts, sharing information and forming alliances across ethnic lines to achieve their ends. Religious groups, both Catholic and Protestant, joined the fight, while German speakers and Anglophones established committees to devise tactics.[105] Milton Taylor traveled to different streets and neighborhoods to rally support for track removal. In public addresses, he appealed to the council to place the community's interests ahead of the railroad companies."[106]

Yet they made no headway. An East Baltimore anti-track group expressed bewilderment that the council would remove the tracks from Howard Street while permitting those in their neighborhood to remain.[107] Taylor, when told that "Howard street was a different place from the streets east of the Falls,"

FIGURE 7.4. "A Train Passing through an American City," 1885. From "Railways, English and American," *Harper's New Monthly Magazine* 71 (June/November 1885): 387.

asked "if the comforts of East Baltimore people were not as worthy of consideration as were those of the residents of Howard Street."[108] The trains passing through his neighborhood answered his question. Howard Street had become a fashionable retail site, and removing the freight tracks enabled a genteel vision of urban space. East Baltimore, by contrast, retained an industrial character. Even with alternative paths available to funnel through traffic, the residents of Fells Point and central Baltimore watched freight trains rumble past their stoops for years to come (fig. 7.4).

Baltimore in the Competitive Landscape

The Pennsylvania Railroad's tunnel system and the B&O's harbor route meant that by 1873, Baltimore had two competing channels for through traffic. Both passages avoided Baltimore's urban core to move goods and travelers between Washington and New York City. They supplied, in effect, the long-contemplated airline between the political and financial capitals of the nation.[109] As competition grew fiercer, the Pennsylvania denied B&O cars access to its route from Philadelphia to New York; in retaliation, the B&O cut its rates dramatically and looked into building an independent line through New Jersey in collaboration with Jay Gould.[110] This competition for East Coast travelers produced a windfall for western merchants; both companies slashed rates on their main lines as the feud escalated.[111]

The completion of the B&O's long-planned extension to Chicago in 1874 likewise prompted rate wars by placing the company in direct competition with the other trunk lines for traffic to and from the railroad hub of the West. The intuitive appeal of the B&O's straight-line route to St. Louis had not accounted for the rise of Chicago as the lynchpin of nineteenth-century American rail systems. Garrett hoped to flank his northern rivals by building a competing line to Chicago that could challenge rates set in New York, and he deliberately withheld his signature from a rate-setting compact devised by the other trunk lines at Saratoga Springs in 1874 to test the proposition.[112] When the Chicago Extension finally opened, the *Sun* crowed that the "time when Baltimore was expected to dance attendance upon the railroad kings in New York has long since passed."[113] The *Chicago Tribune* even suggested that this new line might upset New York's dominance in foreign trade (fig. 7.5).[114]

The B&O's managers and their allies in the press did not hesitate to link Baltimore's prosperity with the railroad's fortitude in the face of this competition. "Is it not known to all that the chief point in the policy of the Baltimore and Ohio Company has been to build up the trade of Baltimore?" Garrett asked, rhetorically.[115] Observing that the Chicago Extension had led to destructive rate wars, the B&O's annual report for 1876 stated that the company would continue to resist combinations with other trunk lines that ignored Baltimore's "immense geographical advantages" when setting rates, instead

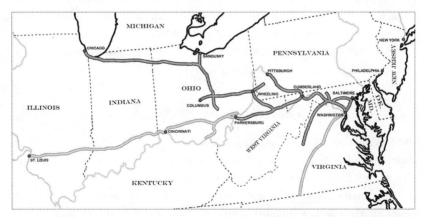

FIGURE 7.5. The B&O and its major connecting lines, ca. 1876. Map by Yiu Sze Ki. Adapted from *General Map of the Baltimore and Ohio Rail Road & its Connections; the Great Route between the East and West* (Chicago: Rand McNally & Co., 1876).

allowing trade to accrue to the most convenient route.[116] Yet there was something anachronistic about insisting that geography dictated rate policy in the wake of decades of complaints about discrimination. As the rate wars suggested, the B&O engaged in competition primarily to secure traffic bound for points beyond Baltimore. One of the B&O's coups, for example, was its announcement in 1874 of a partnership with the Union Pacific Railroad. The Union Pacific connected with the B&O at St. Louis, but its shipments then passed through Baltimore via Locust Point or the Pratt Street tracks to their destination in New York.[117]

Few questioned the B&O's relationship to Baltimore even as the company slashed rates to New York dramatically. This is not to say that none noticed the shift in the company's orientation. A New York paper reported in 1874 that the B&O had looked into buying land in Jersey City and remarked drolly that it would be "curious . . . if, after all, the railway company which was to have made Baltimore the great commercial city of the continent decides to make New York its terminus." B&O officials vehemently denied these charges, insisting that the company's overriding goal was to develop Baltimore's trade. Even a Philadelphia paper defended the B&O, noting that the company had done much to improve Baltimore by building "vast grain elevators, storehouses, docks, and railroad tracks running directly to the water's edge." Yet this was the infrastructure of through trade, built to funnel goods onward as quickly as possible.[118] In any event, the B&O's remonstrations notwithstanding, the New York paper's report proved not so much incorrect as premature. Garrett sought an independent route to New York as early as 1871, although the company secured a terminus there, on Staten Island, only in 1887, several years after his death.[119]

Changes south of Baltimore unfolded more quickly. Before the Pennsylvania Railroad launched the B&P, the B&O's monopoly on traffic to and from Washington left the capital with weak rail connections, a fact dramatically underscored during the Civil War. Western congressmen complained bitterly about the B&O's rates and practices, bemoaning the fact that they had to travel east to Baltimore before heading west to their home states.[120] In 1865, to answer such complaints, the B&O announced plans to build a route from Washington to the Main Stem that would shorten the distance for travelers between the capital and the West by up to sixty miles. Called the Metropolitan Branch, the company built this new line expressly to forestall the creation of rival airlines direct to the West.[121] By eliminating the transfer at Baltimore, it cut one to two hours off westbound travel from Washington, but it also reoriented travel patterns for Baltimoreans. Once the branch opened in 1873, the B&O routed all nonlocal passenger trains to and from the West via Washington, meaning that passengers in Baltimore had to first go to the capital before heading west.[122] Unseating Baltimore as the terminus for western travel reflected a broader shift in the B&O's identity. Embracing the Washington terminus emphasized the line's central place in the American nation. Eventually the B&O incorporated the Capitol dome into its logo and boasted of its national scale of operations with a new slogan: "Linking 13 Great States with the Nation."[123] As the B&O became a national enterprise, the city became a node in a railroad system. This process manifested not only in infrastructure but in municipal politics as well.

Municipal Retrenchment

Many mayors of Baltimore grappled with the B&O in the nineteenth century, but only John Lee Chapman made it his vocation. Chapman, a glass manufacturer by trade, won a seat in the city council as a Know-Nothing in 1859. In 1861, as the question of secession roiled Maryland politics, he became a die-hard Unionist and later joined the Republican Party. He assumed the office of mayor ex officio after Mayor George William Brown went to jail for sedition and then won the mayoralty outright in two subsequent elections.[124] While in office, Chapman waged a war of words with John W. Garrett over the railroad's responsibilities to the urban public. He accused the B&O of engaging in monopolistic practices that enriched private shareholders but stunted Baltimore's development. The railroad, he charged, levied exorbitant rates on local traffic, bought votes in the state legislature, and bullied its critics into submission.[125] B&O representatives returned fire, calling the mayor an ignoramus, even a madman: Garrett likened Chapman's critiques to the "ravings of an inhabitant of the Mount Hope Asylum."[126] Hearing this, the council nearly passed a resolution censuring Garrett, declaring such "epithets and abuse" unfitting from a man "animated by selfish motives and interests."[127]

The city government had clashed repeatedly with the railroad's upper management in the decade since the stockholder revolt, but the disputes in the mid-1860s differed from the earlier conflicts not only in intensity but also in kind. Chapman did not propose to wrest the company from the private stockholders or use municipal regulation to temper Garrett's policies. Instead, he sought to tame the B&O through competition, courting the Pennsylvania Railroad and channeling municipal funds to a new railroad line that paralleled the Main Stem.[128] These initiatives provoked Garrett to ad hominem invective, but they conceded that the B&O had moved beyond municipal control. Chapman sought instead to position Baltimore within a postwar economy shaped by private capital.

The competing line, the Western Maryland Railroad (WMd), had incorporated in the 1850s to link Baltimore to the agricultural and mineral resources of Hagerstown, located at the foot of the Allegheny Mountains.[129] The new railroad sought to break the B&O's monopoly on transportation in the western part of the state. During his mayoralty, Chapman became a vocal supporter of the WMd, believing that it could force the B&O to lower shipping rates on essential items like coal.[130] In 1866 the city government decided to give the perpetually struggling line a shot in the arm in the form of a $200,000 investment. An unusually large volume of petitions came before the council concerning this measure. The opponents objected to any further municipal investment in railroad enterprise in light of the city's already-burdensome debt.[131] Supporters countered that such arguments reflected nothing more than the B&O's jealous grip on the coal trade and pointed out that public funds had long sustained that line.[132] The ordinance authorizing the subscription passed overwhelmingly in the council; the city paid the $200,000 in part with income from the extra dividend, thus using revenues derived from an earlier conflict with the B&O to fund its competitor.[133] Shortly after, John Lee Chapman, still serving as mayor, became the president of the Western Maryland.

The WMd investment did not end well for the city government. Chapman and many of his supporters lost their seats in the election of 1867, and the new council launched an investigation into the Western Maryland. The councilmen decried the WMd's management as incompetent and their predecessors as corrupt. The council fired Chapman from the presidency of the WMd and expelled three sitting councilmen for soliciting bribes from a contractor on that line. Chapman's dual service as the mayor of Baltimore and president of the Western Maryland, though not formally regarded as corruption, earned him censure from the *Sun*.[134] Still, however questionable the investment may have been, it could not be revoked. The council continued for decades to infuse the struggling company with cash to keep it afloat.[135] The president of the city council complained in 1871 that Baltimore's municipal government had "nurs[ed] the road like a baby." But, as another councilor noted, "the 'baby' was of their own creation," and the city's credit would suffer if the WMd could not pay its bills. The line did bring coal and other commodities into Baltimore, but at a heavy cost—by 1902, municipal outlays for the WMd topped $9 million.[136]

Questions of municipal investment and responsibility were at the heart of shifting conceptions of city government in the 1860s and 1870s. John Dillon considered outlays for railroad corporations prime examples of municipal overreach. It has, he wrote in 1872, "unfortunately become quite too common with us to confer upon our [municipal] corporations extraordinary powers, such as the authority to aid in the construction of railways . . . which are better left exclusively to private capital and enterprise." Dillon's argument here built on decades of legal challenges in places like Pennsylvania and New York State. Opponents of municipal investment there had argued since the 1840s that the powers of urban governments ended at the city limits, making expenditure on long-distance railroads inherently illegitimate. When, in Pennsylvania, the courts upheld Philadelphia's right to invest in railroad stock, the opponents moved to amend the state constitution, and, with little popular opposition, implemented a statewide ban on such investments in 1857. In New York, a state constitutional amendment accomplished the same goal in 1875. But as Dillon had to concede, there was no judicial consensus on this point. Even as he wrote, the Supreme Court upheld municipal railway investments in *Olcott v. The Supervisors* (1872) and other cases. Nonetheless, he opined, "compulsory taxation in favor of railways . . . is an exercise of power going quite to the verge of legislative authority."[137]

Dillon's concerns about taxation reflected the core grievance of a broader movement to restrict the powers and limit the expenditure of city governments after the Civil War. As white southerners used violence and terror to sabotage interracial democracy, their elite northern counterparts waged their own political campaigns against representative government in the cities. In the postbellum years, propertied urbanites wary of the growing power of working-class electorates condemned municipal expenditures as lavish and wasteful. Mobilizing not as citizens but as taxpayers, they sought to curtail urban democracy by securing state-level oversight of city finances, reinstituting property requirements for suffrage, filing lawsuits to halt spending projects, and escaping with their property to suburban tax havens.[138]

In Baltimore, John Lee Chapman's ouster was the result of one such municipal austerity campaign. Chapman and the Union Party had governed the city since 1861, and in his administrations the city ran a deficit that by 1868 exceeded half a million dollars. The *Sun* blamed this "general extravagance" on government officials who "held their places without the sanction of the people."[139] This claim rested on the *Sun*'s particular definition of "the people." Even during the military occupation of the city, the elections that placed the Unionists in power were contested, and the party won an election after the war as well. But the short-lived state constitution of 1864 contained provisions that barred Confederate soldiers and their sympathizers from voting, significantly shrinking the electorate and outraging Democrats. The constitution meanwhile did nothing to enfranchise African Americans, who did not attain the right to vote in Maryland until the ratification of the Fifteenth Amendment in 1870.[140]

In 1867, Thomas Swann—who had become the governor of the state in 1866 and had recently converted to the Democratic Party—called a new constitutional convention that effectively restored white Democrats to power at the state level and created an opening for them in Baltimore as well. In the municipal election that year, the Democratic candidate, Virginia-born merchant and novice politician Robert T. Banks, defeated Chapman in the mayoral race. Banks wasted no time placing his mark on city government. He pledged economy in municipal expenditure, launched investigations into corruption, and signed resolutions that lavished obsequious praise on President Andrew Johnson.[141] Yet the mayor himself soon came under suspicion for channeling construction contracts for the new City Hall to his cronies. Banks's promises of frugality notwithstanding, elite taxpayers continued to consider themselves an oppressed political faction, "groaning under the oppressive load placed upon us by inefficient and corrupt *masters*" in city government. By 1869, some businessmen, acting in their capacities as individual taxpayers, went so far as to file injunctions to halt municipal spending.[142]

In Baltimore, efforts to rein in the municipal government focused particularly on its railroad expenditures. The new state constitution in 1867 mandated special elections to approve such investments. The editors of the *Sun*, aggrieved by the growing municipal tax burden, argued in 1870 that Baltimore had at last reached a "stage" in its development in which it would no longer need to give aid to railways.[143] But even as taxpayers (or a vocal segment of them) became more penurious, the logic underwriting municipal rail investments had not changed. The *American*, although it claimed to oppose further municipal investment in railroads, nonetheless supported initiatives to underwrite half-finished lines like the Pittsburgh & Connellsville, arguing that it would in time contribute to the city's industrial development. "Railroads always do pay," wrote the editors. Whether they paid or not, the city government surely did. The municipality continued extending credit and loaning money to the P&C even after it reached Pittsburgh in 1871.[144] John P. Kennedy's 1836 exhortation to his fellow citizens to "imitate the spider" echoed through the 1870s; even the *Sun* endorsed public investment in a new line to North Carolina in 1870 that was to connect with the B&O, insisting, "It is only by reaching forth our iron hands to distant productive regions that we can grasp the prize of commercial greatness."[145] In any event, the special election requirement did little to halt municipal spending. The off-year elections attracted little interest from voters, and small fractions of the electorate consistently rubber-stamped new railroad investments; from 1864 to 1886, the city devoted $6 million to rail companies near and far.[146]

The B&O, in any case, had no cause to complain about municipal expenditures. Per its 1827 charter, the company's property and profits remained exempt from taxation at both the local and state levels. John W. Garrett worked assiduously to keep it that way. Longtime B&O vice president William Keyser later recollected, "There was nothing the President of the Company was so averse to as the payment of taxes; it really hurt him." Garrett installed his associates in political offices in West Virginia and thus ensured that the B&O paid no taxes in that state.[147] In 1870, Oden Bowie, who served simultaneously as governor of Maryland and president of the B&P, tried to tax fares on the B&O's Washington Branch; the next year, railroad money helped one of Garrett's close friends, William Pinkney White, take Bowie's seat in the governor's mansion.[148] Sometimes, when confronted with a tax bill, Garrett simply ignored it. Under his leadership, the B&O refused to pay federal taxes owed on interest for the city's $5 million loan from 1853, sticking the municipal government with a tab that by the late 1860s ran to $80,000 per annum. John Lee Chapman complained bitterly about this imposition: "If you loaned your friend a thousand dollars, what would you think of him if he refused to pay for the postage stamp on the check[?]"[149]

The railroad's representatives and political allies defended these policies by arguing that the B&O contributed to the common weal through the trade it brought to Maryland, the tracks and equipment it built, and the dividends it paid to its public benefactors. By this logic, the railroad's commercial activities constituted a tax payment in kind.[150] This reasoning was as old as the railroad itself. Yet decades of conflict over rate structures, stockholder dividends, and labor practices made the railroad's contributions less straightforward than its advocates suggested, particularly because these ostensibly public contributions came at the behest of an avowedly private company. More to the point, such claims pointed ultimately towards tax breaks for all productive corporations. "The argument," said one delegate in the Maryland legislature in 1876, "that the Railroad Company has been of such value to the State in developing its resources . . . and therefore all its stockholders should hold their interests free of taxation," implied that only the "poor and unenterprising, the thriftless, and idle, then, should pay all the taxes."[151]

The Railroad at Fifty

As the B&O approached its golden anniversary in 1877, it enjoyed a string of positive press. The B&O bankrolled some of this praise itself; the company supplied politicians, literary figures, journalists, and other notables with year-long free passes for travel on the line. (Among the many thank-you letters Garrett received every January for these favors between the late 1850s and

1877 were notes from Chief Justice Roger B. Taney, orator Edward Everett, and president-elect Rutherford B. Hayes).[152] The company also kept close tabs on Baltimore's news media. Although he never had complete control over the B&O's publicity in the *American* and the *Sun*, Garrett and his subordinates periodically planted articles in the papers and chastised editors for "errors . . . made by indiscreet reporters." Garrett's secretary in 1877 "quietly and kindly cautioned" a writer for the *American* "regarding his RRd articles in the future . . . and suggested that in future cases it would be better to submit such matters to a proper official of the road for endorsement as to accuracy, &c."[153]

Much of the praise for the B&O in the late 1860s and 1870s invoked its service to Baltimore's interests. Some paeans looked backward at the company's founding and marveled at a half century of railroad progress. Others, such as an 1873 guidebook, looked to the present, crediting the line with "making Baltimore a great manufacturing and commercial centre" and pronouncing Garrett's administration "a series of uninterrupted successes."[154] These celebratory accounts foregrounded the public reach of private power. The railroad had so transfigured American society that some began to comment optimistically about political possibilities for railroad men. At a banquet for President Andrew Johnson in 1869, with Garrett in attendance, a toast to "Internal Improvement" proclaimed, "Politically no man can be greater than President but Railways and Canals have their Kings who rule for the people."[155] In fact, many suggested that Garrett himself would do well at the top of the Democratic ticket in the 1872 election.[156]

Garrett chose not to run for president of the United States. Instead, he remained identified with the city of his birth—or rather, he identified the city with himself. Garrett told the Maryland state legislature that his role on the B&O made him effectively "a representative of the city," adding: "I cannot see the difference between the City of Baltimore and the Balto & Ohio. They are necessarily identical."[157] Likewise the committee from the Massachusetts legislature that investigated Locust Point attributed the efficacy of the port to the "belief, on the part of the citizens of Baltimore and of the State, that there is a unity of interest between them and the railroads, which belief leads them to impose no unnecessary municipal or legislative restrictions upon the corporations, but to give them all the aid which lies in their power." The secret of success lay in a light regulatory hand and low taxation.[158] In such accounts, the B&O had accomplished its founding goals, but the development of the city came at the initiative—and presumably at the discretion—of private enterprise. The city government could assist the railroad, but it could not influence it.

Two new institutions in Baltimore epitomized this privatization of urban development—the Johns Hopkins University and Hospital. At his death in 1873, only the City of Baltimore and the State of Maryland owned more B&O stock than Johns Hopkins. In 1876, the stock he bequeathed to found these institutes left each with a starting capital valued at approximately $3 million, a sum that made his eponymous university the best-endowed school in the country.[159] The B&O used this donation as another example of its contributions to the public weal and another reason to avoid paying taxes. The success or failure of the new institutions, a matter of considerable importance to the city as a whole, depended on the price of B&O stock, thus tethering Baltimore's fortunes ever more closely to the railroad.[160] Befitting the legacy of Johns Hopkins' tenure on the B&O's board of directors, these institutions, though dedicated to the public good, would be entrusted to private management. Many of Baltimore's prominent industrialists and financiers served as trustees in the Johns Hopkins institutes, including John W. Garrett, who tried unsuccessfully to brand the university as a vocational school instead of an internationally oriented research institution. The municipal government enjoyed no such voice in its affairs. The trustees of the Johns Hopkins University pledged in their first annual report to keep the institution "forever free from . . . partisanship." In practice, this meant excluding the city's elected officials from the university's governance.[161]

By the 1870s, Maryland's premier railroad had inverted the political order that prevailed at its founding; rather than a semiprivate line serving public ends through urban development, it had become a private line serving semipublic ends through competition with other rail lines. Although it could be hard to tell from the pages of the Baltimore press, not everyone saluted the new order, least of all the thousands of people who worked under Garrett's cost-cutting management. Moving out from Baltimore, a broader picture of discontent emerged. Farmers and small-town merchants fumed at the seemingly arbitrary ways in which railroad rate structures decided their fortunes. In the Midwest, the Grange movement picked up where East Coast reformers left off, seeking to impose government oversight on these massive, state-spanning private corporations.[162]

The Grangers also shared a common target with their Baltimore predecessors: the stockholder. Stockholders held a special place in the antimonopolist imagination because their interests did not coincide with those of the public, whether considered in terms of rate structure, safety, or service. Stockholders cared only about dividends, and the best way to maximize dividends was to maximize profit, regardless of the social costs. Perversely, as reformers saw it, stockholders' narrow interests took precedence over the broader needs of the public in setting railroad policy.[163] The *Sun* opined that railroad corporations in the West "are managed exclusively in the interest and for the benefits of the individuals who own or control them, and not to a sufficient degree for the good of the people at large, from whom they derive their corporate existence."[164] That this critique could plausibly apply to the B&O the editors did not—or perhaps could not—point out.

Charles Francis Adams Jr., grandson of former president John Quincy Adams, warned the readers of the *North American Review* in 1869 that the railroad corporation represented a novel configuration of power that demanded new political approaches. Like the railroad advocates of the 1820s and 1830s, he invoked natural laws: "Gravitation is the rule, and centralization the natural consequence, in society no less than in physics," he wrote in "A Chapter of Erie." But gravitational principles now worked towards corporate consolidation, concentrating power in particular institutions, or even individuals. "Our great corporations," he wrote, "are fast emancipating themselves from the State, or rather subjecting the State to their own control."[165] Adams, at the behest of the Massachusetts legislature, would go on to play a part in devising state-level regulatory measures to rein in these artificial beings, as would his counterparts in the Midwest.[166] Yet he felt that even state legislatures could not meet the urgency of the situation. "It seems almost inevitable," Adams opined in another essay, "that the national government must . . . assume a jurisdiction."[167] He was not alone; others conceived of the railroad as a national instrument, demanding national management. The city, by contrast, would be a mere place of transit.

Conclusion

An array of political, corporate, individual, and even military interests converged in efforts to route rail traffic around Baltimore's urban core. Creating new infrastructure offered railroad companies and segments of the urban public a chance to realize distinct but complementary visions of the city. Railroad travel maps had long depicted cities as dots within a ribbonlike system of rail lines; railroad executives hoped that smoothing traffic through the city would turn this cartographic representation into an operational reality. By 1877, a steam-powered system of piers, tunnels, and barges enabled locomotives from Cincinnati to swap cargos with steamships from Bremen as passengers moved through Baltimore without interruption. Westbound travelers in Baltimore might have to walk a mile from the urban core to Union Station or go thirty miles south to Washington before departing for Ohio, but these inconveniences also fostered a bourgeois urbanism that opened streets to the free flow of pedestrians, hacks, and streetcars, recasting urban space as a site of local mobility. Railroad officials and elite urbanites both privileged the idea of circulation, conceiving of the city as a site for unrestricted movement of goods, capital, and people. The expensive work of digging tunnels enabled bourgeois taxpayers to reinvent their streets as fashionable promenades and allowed railroad executives to boast of having annihilated space.

The construction of Baltimore's system of tunnels and bypasses thus reflected an urban vision that cast the city as a node within the circuitry of corporate-controlled communications networks, a site for investment and the unfettered movement of goods and capital. This mode of thinking strayed far from the conceptions of hinterland and entrepôt that had sparked the earliest railroad investments. The costly construction of urban rail infrastructure coincided with efforts to curtail the agency of the city government. Such movements characterized the city as a local place, defined by its borders, rather than an entrepreneurial agent. The railroad, meanwhile, moved to the center of the corporate capitalist system rapidly taking shape in postbellum America.

The Great Strike

The armory of Baltimore's Sixth Regiment, located across from the shot tower at Front and Fayette Streets, was the scene of the trouble. There, on the evening of July 20, 1877, the men of the Sixth, having been summoned to put down a strike among Baltimore & Ohio Railroad workers in Cumberland, found themselves instead staring down an angry crowd just outside the armory's gates. Earlier that day, the governor had sounded the city's military alarm in order to amass the militiamen at the regimental building, from whence they were to march to Camden Station for transportation to the scene of the strike. The alarm also alerted the citizenry at large to their plans, however, and several thousand people, varied in age and sex, gathered outside the armory, incensed at the prospect of state forces suppressing strikers on behalf of the B&O. By 7:00 p.m., the crowd had turned violent. Laborers had recently torn up the street to lay new gas pipes, and people began to pick up detritus from the worksite—rocks, bricks—to throw at the building. The troops huddled inside, pushed back to the far corner of the room to avoid the stone missiles as they shattered the windowpanes. As darkness fell, with no prospect of relief, the soldiers fixed their bayonets, marched to the armory door, and fired into the crowd.[1]

As the Sixth Regiment proceeded to Camden Station, it traced the path of the grand parade that had inaugurated the B&O half a century earlier. The troops ran down Baltimore Street, encountering more protest and firing more rounds. The pursuing crowd weaponized the street, hurling paving stones as soon as they could be found. Initial reports indicated that the militiamen killed nine citizens and wounded fourteen more—according to the *Sun*, mostly "innocent people on the sidewalks"—as they made their way to the station. The dead ranged in age from a fourteen-year-old newsboy to a forty-year-old

FIGURE 8.1. The Maryland Sixth fires on the crowd. *Harper's Weekly*, 11 August 1877.

fresco painter. More would join the list of fatalities as new bodies were found and as wounds turned fatal (fig. 8.1).[2]

The uprising in Baltimore inaugurated a new phase in the Great Strike of 1877, and in American industrial-labor relations more broadly. The strike had started days earlier when B&O workers in the railroad town of Martinsburg blocked freight traffic to protest the latest in a string of wage cuts; it had spread from there to other rail systems, great and small. Now, as news of the bloodshed in Baltimore traveled via railroad tracks and telegraph wires, cities across the nation exploded with anger and violence. In Pittsburgh, on July 21, long-simmering frustrations with the Pennsylvania Railroad sparked affrays that left upward of twenty people dead and reduced acres of railroad property to rubble. Several days later, the strike reached Chicago, where local police led attacks against working-class immigrants, killing thirty people. When the members of the Workingmen's Party in St. Louis learned of the events unfolding in the east, they coordinated a general strike that briefly brought the city to a standstill.

Conditions and consequences varied locally, but the cascading demonstrations and their bloody suppression reflected Americans' shared experiences with an emergent system of corporate capitalism. By the late 1870s, American railroad corporations employed vast labor forces: thousands of employees sorted into complex bureaucratic hierarchies, governed by a bewildering profusion of internal rules. This system, coupled with the expanding influence of railroad corporations in the American economy and widespread unemployment during the economically depressed 1870s, enabled railroad bosses to consolidate control over the wage-earning men who built the equipment, maintained the track, and ran the trains. When strikers and citizens in these and other cities took to the streets, they used blockades, brickbats, and bullets to register their opposition to an economic order that was decades in the making.[3]

The B&O had helped pioneer this labor system. The company faced employee protests, strikes, and riots from its inception, and on more than one occasion, management, typically prodded by city directors, had acceded to the workers' demands. The rise of stockholder control in the late 1850s signaled the beginnings of a new approach to labor, however, one that accelerated during Reconstruction as market-oriented wage work became the centerpiece of the liberal economic imagination. By 1877 the idea of a market wage governed the B&O's policy toward its workers. Workers could accept or refuse the wages proffered, but they could not organize, protest, or obstruct travel. The workingmen themselves had other ideas, and during the Great Strike of 1877 they challenged the stockholders' authority by staking a claim to the company's profits. The company's response to the uprising demonstrated the central place that railroads now occupied in the economic and political order of the United States: Garrett confidently called on the federal government to repress the riots and run the trains.[4]

Working Conditions

Railroad workers embodied the spatial transformations of the nineteenth century. Shopmen, such as the employees at Mount Clare in Baltimore, built the infrastructure for the emerging industrial economy, assembling cars, forging locomotives, and molding tracks. Trackmen, responsible for maintaining the line and switching the cars, witnessed both the power and the fragility of this new system of communications, where a slight bend in a rail could cause an accident that killed dozens and interrupted the flow of goods over a vast territory. And trainmen, who played a central role in the strike, lived lives dispersed over hundreds of miles. Many B&O trainmen made their homes in Baltimore, in neighborhoods just north of Mount Clare or in row houses erected in South Baltimore for the Locust Point workforce. Trainmen, including engineers, conductors, and firemen, operated the instruments of modernity.[5]

Situated at the forefront of the railroad revolution, the workers were also its least heralded victims. Accidents involving children playing in rail yards caught the disapproving attention of the newspapers; accidents involving pedestrians launched lawsuits. But by far the most common victims of railroad accidents were the employees themselves. Between October 1854 and September 1855, the B&O reported sixty-one accidents, of which thirty-seven were fatal. More than three-quarters of the accidents and well more than half of the fatalities fell on railroad employees, particularly trainmen. Twenty trainmen died that year, some run over by trains, some scalded to death by burst engines, some crushed between cars.[6] The board of directors initially dealt with accidents on an ad hoc basis through its Special Committee of Grievances. The committee provided workers' families with six months' pay for fatal accidents, and purchased artificial limbs for workers who lost a leg or an arm on the job.[7] In 1853 the board began to standardize its responses, creating a standing committee and specifying that injuries "received in the discharge of their duty and not under the influence of liquor" would receive no more than three months of compensatory pay; six months if the worker was crippled for life or killed.[8] Loss of limb was common enough that in 1865 an artificial leg manufacturer tried to strike a deal with Garrett: a $25 discount on artificial limbs for the company in exchange for season passes.[9]

The B&O was the largest private employer in Baltimore by the Civil War. As of 1873, some 1,600 people worked at the Mount Clare shops alone.[10] The company also employed laborers and stevedores at Locust Point, and many of the trainmen and trackmen had permanent residences in Baltimore. The B&O's management was not known for its friendliness to labor. In 1858 the board of directors came under fire when one of its members allegedly declared that day laborers should be satisfied with wages of only fifty cents a day. The board denied that any of its members had voiced such sentiments, but the story spread in the press.[11] Baltimore's *Clipper*, reporting on the controversy, attributed the remarks to a state director and argued that public directors had fallen under the influence of the stockholders' representatives. With private investors holding sway in the company's management, the *Clipper* characterized the board as "despisers of labor and of the *laboring* and *mechanical interests of the community*."[12]

Public directors, especially those representing the city, had earlier served as a counterweight to the private directors when dealing with workers' complaints. City directors, for example, intervened on workers' behalf in strikes in 1853 and 1857. But as stockholders solidified their control of the company, the city government's influence over labor matters waned. A major test of the new order came in 1866, when around three hundred machinists at Mount Clare walked off the job, complaining that their overtime rates did not meet the standard set in other Baltimore shops. In early January, the strikers gathered at Hollins Market, a locale just north of the shops that had long served as a meeting ground for B&O workers when they planned collective action, to demand time and a half instead of time and a quarter for night work and overwork.[13] One hundred fifty strikers signed a memorial to the mayor and city council explaining their grievances. The company often required them to work until ten in the evening without allowing them to return home for dinner, and complaints to the foremen prompted summary dismissal. The workers contested "the right of any employer to discharge a man as punishment for not overtaxing his health," especially when that employer paid substandard wages. The strikers recognized that their efforts represented an important test for organized labor. The machinists reported that their department head had resolved to "test the strength of our union" and that Garrett had declared his opposition to such societies. As such, they asked the city to use its substantial stake in the B&O to intervene on their behalf.[14] The council responded favorably, adjudging the machinists' demands reasonable and calling on the board to grant them.[15] But this time, the council's intervention did not achieve the desired ends; the board left its established system for overtime intact.[16]

The unsuccessful strike of 1866 marked the start of a decade of retrenchment, cutbacks, and clampdowns for the B&O's workforce. As the national economy slid into depression in the 1870s—caused by overextension of the railroad lines, particularly in the West—workers bore the brunt of the hard times.[17] Workers in Baltimore suffered particularly in these contractions, because the B&O's expansion drew jobs away from its terminal city. As the Chicago Extension neared completion in 1873, the company announced it would cut five hundred men from its Baltimore shops, building instead a new facility in Ohio projected to employ around 1,200 mechanics.[18] But employees up and down the line felt the pinch. News of layoffs and pay reductions tended to come at once. The B&O kicked off a plan to dismiss "surplus" employees with fifty layoffs in December 1874, and at the same time reduced hours and wages.[19] October 1875 saw 550 employees discharged at Mt. Clare and another reduction in hours. Across the line, approximately 1,000 of the company's 12,000 employees lost their jobs in one swoop.[20] A month later, the company reduced the standard workday from ten to eight hours while again slashing wages.[21] In May 1876, the company announced 10 percent wage cuts for a number of positions, reducing the income of laborers on the Locust Point steamship piers to $1.15 per day, and continued its efforts to shrink the workforce whenever possible.[22]

The *Sun* said next to nothing critical of the B&O's practices, but when other companies laid off workers, the editors took the opportunity to criticize railroad management. When one company reduced laborers' wages to ninety cents per day, the paper observed, "Economy may be necessary in these times, but have any of the large salaries of the railroad magnates been reduced accordingly?"[23] The paper levied blame in part on railroad managers' favorite pastime: rate wars. For all the crowing about the cheap travel available to manufacturers and western travelers, the rate wars for through trade had reduced fares to drastically low levels. But with vast numbers of workers unemployed, these low rates could not be called "unsustainable"—it would simply be the workforce that bore the brunt of ever-thinner profit margins.[24] The *Sun* cast railroad companies as "middle age barons" who used their employees as "serfs . . . bound to render military service to these parvenu railroad lords."[25] Although the paper refrained from targeting John W. Garrett in particular, he certainly fit the bill. His investments, including thousands of shares of B&O stock that regularly, at his own initiative, paid handsome dividends, enabled Garrett to maintain a mansion valued at over half a million dollars in Baltimore's posh Mount Vernon neighborhood, which he equipped with gas lighting, running water, and marble stairs. He also owned a country estate northeast of the city called Montebello, where he kept stables of thoroughbred horses and flocks of prize-winning livestock that he liked to bestow as party favors to his houseguests. The industrialist Andrew Carnegie later described Garrett as "one of the few Americans who lived in the grand style of country gentlemen."[26]

While Garrett entertained a transatlantic elite, B&O trainmen experienced increasingly severe constrictions. As they traveled up and down the line, they found themselves forced to remit much of their ever-shrinking income to the company to pay for room and board on overnight trips. Garrett took a personal interest in the workers who sought meals and beds gratis. "I am surprised to hear," he wrote in early July 1877, that company-owned hotels were "allowing sleeping car and other employees to get meals without paying for them." He directed the master of transportation to "Order absolutely—and do not fail to see that the order is obeyed—that all parties must pay for meals and use of our hotels, in every form." The "costly properties" had not been making good "net results." "Dismiss at once any employee in the hotel who does not collect proper charges in all cases from all parties," he instructed. In a postscript he inquired, "Are the full regular charges made for the use of billiard table, ten-pin alleys, etc.?"[27]

The company also took a hard line on employee efforts to resist the cutbacks. Those who attempted to unionize faced prompt dismissal. When workers on one division started a branch of the Train Men's Union in late June 1877, a company superintendent ordered the discharge of everyone involved. In this case, that meant firing eleven engineers, fifteen firemen, four conductors, thirty brakemen, a switchman, and two engine wipers. The depressed economy gave the company the power to treat its workforce this way seemingly without consequence. The B&O received hundreds of applications for the vacant positions and consequently experienced no interruption to work on the line.[28]

The Strike

On July 11, 1877, the board of directors of the B&O made an announcement:

> Whereas, the Depression in the General business interests of the country continues, thus seriously affecting the usual earnings of railway Companies, and rendering a further reduction of expenses necessary; therefore, be it Resolved, that a reduction of ten per cent. be made in the present compensation of all officers and employees, of every grade, in the service of the Company, where the amount received exceeds one dollar per day, to take effect on and after July 16th, instant.
>
> It is hoped and believed that all persons in the service of the Company will appreciate the necessity of, and concur cordially in this action.[29]

The 10 percent reduction in wages came even as the board renewed its 10 percent dividend on stock. The trunk lines had reached an agreement four months earlier to end the rate war and distribute the westbound freight from New York among themselves; Garrett summed the "great principle upon which we all joined to act" as "to earn more and to spend less." Yet although banker Junius Morgan in London advised Garrett to reduce the company's dividends in order to pay down its floating debt, Garrett and the other rail executives knew precisely where they would find the room to "spend less"—workers' wages.[30] Garrett attempted to defuse criticism of this wage reduction by noting that other trunk lines had already implemented similar cuts.[31] Even with this explanation, the workers did not "concur cordially," as he hoped they would.

The strike began on July 16, the day the pay reduction went into effect. Firemen and engineers who walked off the job in South Baltimore and other B&O centers were quickly replaced, but in Martinsburg, a West Virginia town ten miles west of the Potomac River and home to B&O maintenance shops and switching yards, the situation unfolded differently. There, some twenty-five to thirty-five employees coordinated to prevent freight trains from passing through. While the papers criticized the strikers for attempting to "persuade and intimidate" scabs, they conceded that their efforts were nonviolent. Firemen stood at the forefront of this strike. First-class firemen had seen their pay reduced from $1.75 to $1.58 per day; second-class firemen saw their pay cut from $1.50 to $1.25. Even though the company reported confidently that ten eager applicants waited to replace every employee who left, the Martinsburg strikers' blockade stifled freight traffic. Passenger trains went through uninterrupted—these expresses typically carried mail as well as travelers, and strikers knew that interruption of mail service was a federal offense.[32]

By July 17, seventy-five trains totaling 1,200 cars had been detained in Martinsburg with their freight, including six hundred head of cattle trapped in sweltering stock cars, dehydrated and delirious from the summer heat. The strikers' numbers had swelled to two hundred, concentrated at Martinsburg but increasingly dispersed across the line. In Baltimore, strikers argued that the proposed wage reduction "would be almost equivalent to starvation." Firemen already brought home only $20 to $27 per month, which after expenses left almost nothing for their families.[33] Their wages had been as high as $3 per day as recently as 1873, but the company had chipped away gradually at their income over the previous four years. One way of doing so was introducing "classes" for the trainmen. An engineer on the first division of the B&O (which ran from Baltimore to Martinsburg) explained in the *American* that the company had divided its train crews into different classes as a way to cut pay without announcing wholesale wage reductions. When the system began, the managers dubbed all the conductors and engineers "first-class men," but new hires came in at the lowest class and the company consequently preferred to recruit fresh workers instead of giving more work to existing employees. Meanwhile, experienced trainmen accused of violating the hundreds of rules and bylaws laid out in the company's handbook faced "a poor man's trial (all law and no justice)" that knocked them down to the fourth class. Promotions to first class were rare.[34]

Strikers objected just as vigorously to the deteriorating conditions of work as to the reductions of pay. Employees protested that the company treated them "just as the rolling stock or locomotives," interchangeable factors of production. Even as the B&O kept more men in its employ, management reduced the number of workers on any given train. The job had become more dangerous and arduous thanks to understaffing. The company had added eight additional cars to eastbound freight trains in the previous year alone, but it kept in place a skeleton crew consisting of a conductor, brakeman, engineer, and fireman. Longer cars meant more work and greater risk of accidents, and brakemen were dying at the rate of one a month. The strikers attributed at least two of these recent deaths not to accident but to "melancholy," when "brakemen after loss of rest and under the depression of reduced wages, &c., have purposely thrown themselves under the wheels." Firemen, too, held dangerous jobs, and their responsibilities had come to include cleaning the engines at the end of a trip, a task formerly assigned to specialized workers.[35]

The company had a number of policies designed to increase workers' responsibilities and lower their take-home pay. Trainmen were paid not by the hour but by the trip. If a trip was supposed to take a day but, because of delays and accidents, took forty hours, the crew still received only one day's wages. And when, as often happened, there were no available trains to make the return journey, a worker had to wait at Martinsburg, paying for board and spending thirty cents on company meals on top of paying rent at home, leaving them with little remaining from the proceeds of their work. A recent directive that allowed the discharge of any man whose "wages are attached for debt" compounded their troubles; staying out of debt was difficult when the company could be up to two weeks behind in paying its wages. One B&O worker described the conditions wrought by these policies: "We eat our hard bread and tainted meat two days old on the sooty cars up the road, and when we come home, find our children gnawing bones and our wives complaining that they cannot even buy hominy and molasses for food."[36] "Many of them," the *Sun* reported, "declare they might as well starve without work as starve and work. They now say that, having once acted, they are determined to have the worth of their labor"—two dollars a day—"or nothing."[37]

Although the *Sun* sympathized with the workers' plight in the abstract, its editors and those of other major media outlets did not endorse their actions. Newspapers created a thin margin of legitimacy for strikers. The *Sun* admitted that the reduction of wages curtailed the "scanty comforts" of poor railroad workers. But it declared that with the Martinsburg blockade in place the question was no longer one "between employers and employed" but rather of "public order and of the supremacy of the law." Employees could refuse to work for the wages offered, but they overstepped their bounds in trying to prevent the movement of freight traffic. Only passive, individual resistance was morally or legally acceptable in this framework.[38] The *American* gave the workers more space in its columns to state their case than the *Sun*. Ultimately, though, that paper cautioned readers not to "take a purely sentimental view of the struggle" and to remember that railroad managers "are only agents or trustees for the shareholders"—a group that the editors repeatedly (and somewhat implausibly) insisted contained a number of "widows and orphans." The *American*, like the *Sun*, chastised the workers for interfering with the labor market.[39] Newspapers in other major cities agreed. The *Philadelphia Ledger* counseled workers to consider themselves lucky to have jobs at all in a period of unemployment. The *New York Times* stripped this position of its niceties, arguing that the workers' suffering was immaterial to the matter at hand: "the proposed reduction did not bring wages below the market rate." It fell, then, to the B&O to resist efforts at "intimidation."[40]

The strikers responded to these arguments by advancing a very different understanding of political economy. Rather than seeing their labor as a commodity, its price determined by the market, they framed themselves as partners in the railroad enterprise. As one striker put it at a meeting in Hollins Hall in Baltimore, the "employe contributes his labor to the railroad just as the stockholder does his capital."[41] Yet although the stockholder's contributions to the B&O paid dividends at rates above the industry average—10 percent in cash, compared with 6 percent to 8 percent for the Pennsylvania Railroad—workers' contributions generated ever-narrowing returns.[42] Strikers in Martinsburg told reporters that they could not understand why they alone should feel the effects of the depression. They felt that if they did not act right then, the company would make its workforce "the only victim of the retrenchment policy . . . while the stockholders will [not] be affected at all."[43] The equivalence between employees and investors at the heart of the strikers' arguments reflected an alternative vision for corporate governance, one that would give workers a stake in the company's profits and a voice in its operations. Newspaper editors reacted to this prospect with alarm; the *American* cautioned that to yield to the strikers "would establish a precedent that would blot capital out of existence by making it wholly subject to labor."[44]

The strikers' perspective was not far removed from the public vision of the railroad that stockholders had worked so hard to eliminate in the 1850s. Indeed, one writer from Grafton, West Virginia, made this point explicitly, tying together the questions of rates, dividends, and wages that had aroused public animus as the railroad privatized: "The policy it [the B&O] has pursued in laying extortionate rates on local freight, oppressing shippers on its line as well as reducing the pay for increased labor that ten per cent dividends might be paid its stockholders, has made it the enemy of the people as well as the employes. The people and men ask, why not reduce the dividend on its stock held by the capitalists as well as the pay of the employes, who toil honestly for their bread? Why not reduce the rate on local freights as well as on through traffic?" The company had long answered such questions by invoking the need to vie with other rail lines for traffic, but the writer refused to accept that competitive exigencies outweighed questions of distributive justice. "The people as well as the employes have complaints," the West Virginian concluded.[45]

Federal Force

In Martinsburg, the second day of the strike saw the first violence. William Vandergriff, a striker, diverted a freight train onto a sidetrack and took a shot at a freight conductor, John Poisal, who tried to stop him. Poisal sustained a flesh wound and returned fire, Vandergriff losing his left arm, his right thumb, and twelve days later his life. The sound of gunfire drew a large assemblage of angry railroad employees and citizens to the scene. As the crowd grew in numbers, the militia, which had been summoned to Martinsburg by Governor Henry M. Mathews of West Virginia, withdrew. Colonel J. C. Faulkner, the captain of the nearby Berkeley Light Infantry, tried to get a freight train moving but could not find sufficient men to do so. Considering his duties fulfilled in the attempt, he disbanded his company. Having been "largely composed of railroad men," the Berkeley Light Infantry had been "unwilling to act," the *Sun*'s Martinsburg correspondent reported.[46]

The violence in Martinsburg, however isolated, and the workers' successful embargo on freight traffic convinced John W. Garrett that the situation called for troops of a higher authority. On July 16, even before the Vandergriff shooting, Garrett told Governor Mathews that he had heard of threats of violence on the line and feared the "disaffection" would spread. With state forces thin on the ground, he advised the governor to request military aid from Washington.[47] Two days later, Garrett took the case to the president himself. Telegraphing Rutherford B. Hayes, Garrett declared that the West Virginia militia had proved unable to execute state laws in the face of coercion and violence at Martinsburg. "Unless this difficulty is immediately stopped," he warned, "I apprehend the greatest consequences, not only upon our line, but

upon all lines in the country which, like ourselves, have been obliged to introduce measures of economy." As he had during the Civil War, he took it upon
himself to offer advice to the president: "If I may be permitted to suggest, Fort
McHenry and Washington are points nearest to the scenes of disturbance,
and from which the movement can be made with the greatest promptness
and rapidity."[48] Hayes agreed, ordering troops from these locations to board
trains for Martinsburg. He issued a presidential proclamation commanding
the "insurgents" to go home. "It is unfortunate," Garrett lamented, "that so
many of our men have been so misguided as to their real interests." He trusted
that "the Supreme Power of our country" would set them straight.[49]

This marked the first use of federal troops to put down labor unrest since
the administration of Andrew Jackson. Hayes justified the move as a means to
preserve the peace, but there was no question whose interests he served. An
account of the strikes published a few months after the fact claimed that dispatches from Garrett and from Pennsylvania Railroad president Thomas A.
Scott "left on the minds of one or two of the Cabinet Ministers the impression that the 'railroads wanted to run the Government,'" an impression compounded by the fact that they called on the troops not only to ensure order
but also to run the trains.[50] Moreover, the federal government paid the B&O
for the privilege of doing so: the *Martinsburg Independent* reported that the
railroad charged the military for the transportation of soldiers to the seat of
the conflict. "Verily," the paper editorialized, "our American railroad managers have not lost in the recent struggle any of their grasping proclivities."[51]

As federal troops made their way to Martinsburg, the *Sun* stated confidently that the matter was finished. Now that they had to contend with the
power of the whole United States, it was inconceivable that the strikers would
continue "their unlawful and riotous demonstrations."[52] The troops themselves welcomed the opportunity to escape the boredom of a listless Washington summer.[53] At the same time, however, the strike continued to move
westward along the B&O tracks. Soon reports surfaced of a likely strike on the
Ohio & Mississippi Railroad, the B&O's connecting route to St. Louis. Talk of
strikes also spread from the B&O to the Pennsylvania Railroad at Pittsburgh.
Coal and petroleum shipments ground to a halt, and released cattle roamed
freely in the grasslands near Martinsburg.[54]

Most portentously, trouble brewed in western Maryland. As Garrett cor-
responded with the governor of West Virginia and the president of the United
States, other B&O officials spoke behind closed doors with the governor of
Maryland and the mayor and police chief of Baltimore about putting down
riots in Cumberland.[55] John King Jr., B&O vice president, urged Garrett to
call on Governor John Lee Carroll for state troops. The city's police chief had

volunteered to send officers to guard the train from Baltimore to Harpers Ferry, but police had no authority outside the city limits and would need special authorization. Besides, the "formidable" appearance of the militia would enable the company to "make a great display of military force all the way from Baltimore to the Ohio River."[56]

On July 20, Governor Carroll set up headquarters at Barnum's Hotel in Baltimore and conferred with B&O officials about conditions on the line. By then, dispatches from Cumberland had indicated that strikers had blockaded freight traffic, and Carroll decided to use state authority to put them down. He would deploy the Fifth and Sixth Baltimore Regiments for the task; the question was how to summon them. Word went out to the militiamen and by 6:00 p.m., the captain of the Fifth Regiment reported that one hundred men had reported for duty, with one hundred more expected. General James R. Herbert, a Confederate veteran commanding the First Brigade of the state militia, suggested sounding the military alarm, a measure reserved for grave emergencies, to get the last hundred into place. The alarm had never rung in Baltimore before, and Carroll feared that using it would "produce exaggerated alarm among the citizens." But at 6:35 p.m., Carroll ordered the alarm sounded anyway, signaling troops to gather at their armories and march to Camden Station for transport to Cumberland.[57] When the alarm went off, the epicenter of the conflict shifted from Martinsburg to Baltimore.

The Riots

The Sixth Regiment's violent path down Baltimore Street pockmarked the city's buildings with bullet holes and left blood on the streets. The men of the Fifth Regiment, by contrast, encountered far less resistance as they made their way to the station. The only trouble came near the depot gates, where they were pelted with stones and bricks but refrained from using their weapons. By the time the two regiments reached Camden Station, however, there were no trains to ride. Arsonists set the depot ablaze, and rioters fought the fire department as it tried to extinguish the flames. Others tore up track and burned railcars (fig. 8.2). The passenger trainmen refused to go out under these conditions, and B&O vice president John King determined that attempting to run the trains would only enrage the crowd further.[58] He informed his boss that Eutaw and Howard Streets were "lined with people," and that the rioters were "gathering strength." The police had been "unable to control the mob." Garrett had left Baltimore earlier to attend his mother's funeral; King suggested he had best stay away.[59] "It is said to be the fiercest mob ever known in Baltimore," he said.[60] Historian David Stowell's study of the Great Railroad Strike

FIGURE 8.2. Burning Camden Station. Pinkerton, *Strikers, Communists, Tramps and Detectives*, 190.

in upstate New York argues that anger at the railroad's disruption of urban life motivated the rioters, but in Baltimore, the crowd's grievances centered on labor practices: the Northern Central Railroad was no less disruptive a presence in city streets than the Baltimore & Ohio, but it paid higher wages, and its operations continued almost without interruption throughout the strike.[61]

One of Garrett's correspondents informed him that as arrests were being made, "in hardly a single instance have any Railroad men been participants in the trouble—the crowd being mainly composed of the worst elements of the city."[62] A correspondent from Boston declared that "Irish Roman Catholics" were responsible for the riots, and although it is unlikely that this writer could assess the composition of the crowd with any accuracy from such a distance, the riots do appear to have been an all-white affair: Baltimore's African American community remained indoors and out of the press.[63] Garrett received advice from all corners. Some, including the *American*, suggested that a committee of "*disinterested* citizens" broker a compromise.[64] Others responded in a less conciliatory fashion. One man suggested that Garrett use his influence to disband the unreliable militia and replace them with a volunteer force of "men of property."[65] An industrialist wrote to the press to reject the notion of compromise and averred that "the solution in my opinion is by force of arms, let the consequences be what they may."[66]

As armchair railroad presidents mused about the proper course of action, city police struggled to deal with the riot, and the state militia remained cooped up in Camden Station. Governor Carroll took the next logical, albeit controversial, course of action: he called on the federal government. The Maryland soldiers on hand objected to Carroll's decision, and the governor, having sent a dispatch for federal troops, reconsidered and tried to withdraw his request. But it was too late.[67] Secretary of War George W. McCrary agreed at once to redeploy troops stationed in Norfolk and Hampton, Virginia to Baltimore. Closer to home, soldiers from Fort McHenry moved out immediately to protect bonded warehouses at Locust Point.[68]

As of 5:00 a.m. on Sunday, July 22, federal troops had taken control of parts of Baltimore, and more were on the way. Artillerymen stood with their weapons on Howard Street, and fifty marines protected B&O property at Mount Clare Junction.[69] The Fifth and Sixth Maryland regiments had remained holed up in Camden Station overnight, and military guards replaced the police on Eutaw Street. The *Sun* compared the city's appearance to the federal occupation early in the Civil War.[70] Some one thousand U.S. regulars were expected in Baltimore by 4:00 p.m. People took to the streets in the spirit of curiosity rather than anger, retracing the route of the Sixth and looking for remnants of the previous night's affray.[71]

This show of federal force had its intended effect. The U.S. troops successfully suppressed the riot and turned their attention to the movement of the trains. The strike continued, and the workers met with B&O executives at Cross Street Hall in South Baltimore to air their grievances and attempt a settlement. Strikers repudiated the violence and demanded a rollback of the wage cuts and the reinstatement of all men on the line. Vice presidents King and Keyser held firm, offering more hours but no wage increase. Keyser argued that the riots grew directly out of the employees' actions, even if they had not participated: "You have aroused a spirit, which unless curbed and quelled, strikes at the very fundamental root of the liberty and life of this country." It was "out of the question" to restore the prestrike wages; doing so would set a bad precedent.[72] An aggrieved B&O engineer, for his part, responded that anyone "who would get [on] another man's engine under the circumstances was no better than a Chinaman."[73]

By July 28, Garrett determined that the time had come to resume railroad traffic. "The tide has turned," he wrote to Vice President Keyser, "the power is with us and not a *moment* must be lost . . . in opening the Road."[74] The company called on civilian and military authorities, along with a few "loyal men," to move the trains.[75] Military commanders positioned artillery so that they could respond quickly to any disruption, and they placed a detachment of troops on each train. A supporting column of 250 soldiers guarded the train as it pulled out of Locust Point. The strikers encamped at Riverside Park in South Baltimore watched the trains pass by and expressed confidence—unfounded,

as it happened—that the company would not be able to find enough com-
petent workers to run their trains.[76] When it became clear that the company
would not budge on wage questions, the *Sun* reported that the majority of
the strikers quit rather than return to work under the B&O's terms.[77] Even
though the company faced continuing wildcat strikes and guerrilla attacks on
the trains as they passed through striker strongholds in West Virginia, Keyser
reported to Garrett on July 29 that the "Road is opened from the Chesapeake
to the Ohio River."[78]

Aftermath

As federal troops put down the disorder in Baltimore (and raced to suppress
it in cities like Pittsburgh, Chicago, and St. Louis), railroad officials and their
friends in the press mused about the proper response to strikes and riots.
The same corporate executives whose rate wars drove wages below subsistence levels now met to discuss their shared predicament. They announced
a combination against trainmen's unions, hiring detectives to uncover the
ringleaders.[79] Pennsylvania Railroad president Thomas A. Scott and John W.
Garrett concurred that the "General Government" would have to "take some
action . . . in a way that cannot be misunderstood."[80] Garrett assumed the
public was on their side; he had his assistant inform the *Sun* that the July pay
cut had reduced wages only to the levels of 1861. Garrett evidently thought
that this information would work in the company's favor—that readers would
agree that trainmen deserved no more in 1877 than they had earned sixteen
years prior.[81]

The B&O offered some concessions in the wake of the strike. The company
agreed to pay partial wages to trainmen for cancelled runs and to provide
boardinghouse accommodations between shifts. The B&O Employees Relief
Fund, launched by Garrett in 1880, also reflected the influence of the strike.
Financed by a company endowment and by employees' contributions, the
fund furnished money for workers suffering from sickness and injury. Yet
Garrett did not lose sight of his main goals, either. He issued another dividend on company stock in October 1877.[82]

The newspapers, for their part, took the riots as an opportunity to pro-
claim the importance of law and order and to reassert the importance of the
market in setting wages. Even as the *Sun* blamed low wages on the overexpansion of rail lines and acknowledged that workers had little to do with
the riots, it tied its condemnation of the strike to an admonishment of mob
action.[83] The paper saw that there were "two sides" to the wages question—
"the employer's ability to pay" and "the employee's ability to live upon the

wages actually offered"—but it advised workers that they could do no more than choose whether to accept those wages.[84] Labor and capital did not form a partnership, the *Sun's* editors argued, because in a partnership both sides expected to benefit as a business prospered. The relationship between employers and employees was more that of "buyer and seller." Strikes would only reduce capitalists' willingness to invest and thus reduce the number of jobs available.[85] Instead of striking, workers ought to relocate in order to meet the labor market's demands; the paper informed out-of-work trainmen in Baltimore that, in light of labor shortages on western farms, they should simply move west.[86] By this program, the railroad, rather than foster growth within Baltimore, would act as a safety valve, distributing the city's underemployed masses. The *American* agreed; bemoaning the concentration of labor in the cities, it called for the creation of programs to diffuse the "surplus" workforce. The paper suggested that "colonies could be formed" to create "more channels for [American] productions, and more markets for them."[87]

Striking railroad workers also came under scrutiny for interfering with the infrastructure of modern life. "We hardly realize our dependence upon modern and artificial modes of transportation until we are suddenly in danger of being temporarily deprived of them," the *Sun* wrote.[88] The strike presented an opportunity to witness the interconnectedness of the modern industrial economy, which linked businesses to one another in a web of mutual dependency. For the city's press, the lesson of this suddenly manifest economic system was that society could not allow workers' grievances to gum up the works.[89] Indeed, railroad executives looked upon the strike with something resembling pride, marveling to themselves at the ways in which the fissure had revealed their essential role in modern society. Garrett declared that the "complete lock up of business in Baltimore showed more clearly than could have been done in a year of writing . . . the vast business interests sustained and kept alive by the facilities afforded by the railroads."[90] To Pennsylvania Railroad president Tom Scott, this underscored the need for "absolute and uninterrupted freedom of movement," a principle that railroad advocates had first articulated as long ago as the track debates of the 1830s.[91]

The lessons of the strike went beyond the dependence of labor on capital and the integration of the U.S. economy by rail, however. Reformers had denounced the power held by railroad corporations for more than a decade; now they saw it in full force. It was, significantly, a national power. Railroad executives who could agree on little else concurred that workers' efforts to prevent the passage of freight trains warranted federal military intervention. Local police, in Baltimore as in Martinsburg, could not put down threats to their power. State forces proved scarcely better able to serve their interests.

Only the "majesty" of the federal government could resolve these crises—crises understood as national in scope even as they unfolded in urban space. The cooperation and coordination of northern railroad companies with federal authorities during the Civil War had created some of the channels of power and expectations of reciprocity that Garrett and other railroad executives used to resolve their labor troubles.

This was not the last time in the nineteenth century that the federal government intervened in a labor dispute on behalf of a railroad corporation. But Garrett's correspondence suggested yet another path the company might take. A month after the Great Strike, with trains once again running smoothly, he received a letter from Edgar T. Welles, the treasurer of the Gatling Gun Company of Hartford, Connecticut. Even before he scanned Welles's neat handwriting, Garrett would have noticed the graphic at the top this communiqué. The Gatling Gun Co.'s letterhead printed the corporation's name in ornate gothic font, with the words flanking a large gun mounted on wheels (fig. 8.3). The gun faces away from the reader—or perhaps the reader is positioned behind the gun, adopting the perspective of the shooter. This was certainly the perspective Welles intended his reader to take. "The recent riotous disturbances throughout the country," he wrote, "have shown the necessity of preparation by such corporations as the one over which you preside, to meet violence by superior force and skill." The Gatling Gun Co. received more orders from railroad companies than it could fulfill during the late-July conflagrations, but Welles suggested that Garrett could guard against future emergencies by stocking up on Gatlings now. He emphasized the utility of this instrument for railroad operations. "One Gatling, with a full supply of ammunition, can clear a street or track, and keep it clear. Hence, a few tried employees supplied with Gatlings, afford a Railroad Company a perfect means of defence within itself."[92]

No response or invoice suggests that Garrett followed this advice. But the turn of phrase—"a perfect means of defence within itself"—still seems apt. It reflects the ways in which railroad power had changed over the previous fifty years. Railroad corporations came to exercise power exceeding that of the state governments that created them, and neither local police nor state militia could reliably sustain their interests. Welles wrote with the knowledge that railroad corporations had access to the full military authority of the United States, yet his letter suggested that ultimately even this might prove inadequate. Railroad companies needed to provide the firepower themselves. The suppression of the Great Strike provided an epitaph for the early history of the B&O, burying, at least for the moment, the notion that the railroad

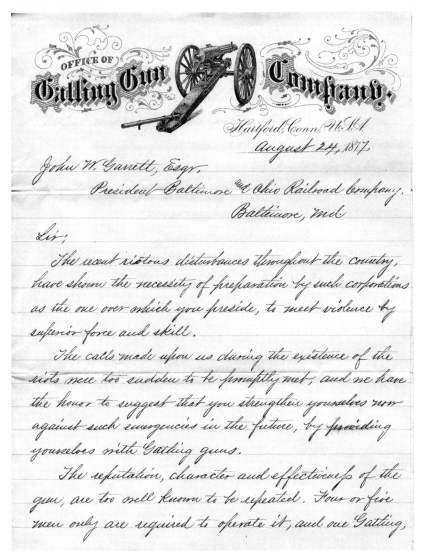

OFFICE OF
Gatling Gun Company.

Hartford, Conn. U.S.A.
August 24, 1877.

John W. Garrett, Esqr,
President Baltimore and Ohio Railroad Company,
Baltimore, Md.

Sir;

The recent riotous disturbances throughout the country, have shown the necessity of preparation by such corporations as the one over which you preside, to meet violence by superior force and skill.

The calls made upon us during the existence of the riots were too sudden to be promptly met, and we have the honor to suggest that you strengthen yourselves now against such emergencies in the future, by providing yourselves with Gatling guns.

The reputation, character and effectiveness of the gun, are too well known to be repeated. Four or five men only are required to operate it, and one Gatling,

FIGURE 8.3. First page of Welles's letter to Garrett. Courtesy of the B&O Railroad Museum.

served the needs of a local public. Welles's letter signaled in turn the rise of a new order, one in which corporations backed their authority with machine guns. Soon, Pinkerton detectives would provide paramilitary force as railroads assumed political, economic, and even military power unimaginable a generation earlier.[93]

And for the companies themselves, building empires, moving goods, and paying dividends became the principal objects of concern. The B&O's 1877 report to the stockholders, its fifty-first, noted that coal shipments were down, petroleum shipments up; it offered details about new tracks at Locust Point that would allow trains to reach steamship piers more smoothly. If readers received their news solely from annual reports, they would never know that the strike even happened.[94]

Conclusion

The B&O kept growing after the Great Strike. At his death in 1884, Garrett helmed a rail system that spanned 1,700 miles, with lines to the Shenandoah Valley, Chicago, Columbus, and Pittsburgh. The company continued to modify Baltimore's landscape as its network expanded. In the late 1880s, the B&O launched an initiative dubbed the "Baltimore Belt Railroad" to link Camden Station with the company's new route to Philadelphia. This multiyear construction project cost $5 million in total, roughly half of which went to digging an electrified tunnel under Howard Street, the last in a long line of B&O innovations in urban rail infrastructure.[1] Connecting to Philadelphia in turn helped the company finally reach New York. In 1887, the B&O completed a line to Staten Island, where it built two piers into New York Harbor; in the early 1890s, it added a terminus at Jersey City as well. These outlets gave the B&O an independent route along the eastern seaboard from Washington to New York, and made Locust Point only one of its three paths to the ocean.[2]

Garrett and his successors financed this expansion with debt rather than equity. During Garrett's presidency, share capital increased by only 50 percent, and bonded debt increased more than threefold. Garrett floated bonds both to extend and maintain the line. If the escalating costs associated with this financial strategy troubled him, he did not air his concerns in the annual reports, which trumpeted new initiatives while sweeping debts and doubts under the rug. The investors, sated by the B&O's regular cash dividends, seem not to have scrutinized the company's accounts and happily returned Garrett to the presidency year in and year out. Even had they wanted to examine the company's books, they may have had trouble getting hold of them—Garrett kept tight control over the company's finances until near the end of his life. In fact, control emerged as something of a motif in the railroad president's later days; his power over his domains tightened after 1877. At his death, Garrett held almost unchecked authority within the B&O, leverage over Johns Hopkins University and Hospital, a close relationship with the Maryland Democratic Party, and a powerful hand in West Virginia politics.[3]

The heavy indebtedness that funded the B&O's expansion and allowed Garrett to consolidate his power also ensured the company's downfall. As his biographer observes, Garrett's practices did not necessarily amount to fraud when judged against the financial norms of his day. Garrett likely convinced himself that his maneuverings worked ultimately to the company's benefit. In any event, he did not live long enough to deal with the consequences of his obfuscations. At his death, the presidency passed into the hands of his son, Robert, who lacked the temperament and acumen to run a railroad. (John Garrett's daughter, Mary, would likely have proved a more capable choice, had the gender norms of the day afforded her the chance). Robert stepped down in 1887. His successor, Samuel Spencer, was compelled to wade through the Garretts' decades of opaque accounting records. In 1888, for the first time in thirty years, the B&O did not pay a dividend on its stock.[4]

Once again, the B&O turned to the city government for relief. As he suspended dividend payments, President Spencer asked Mayor Ferdinand C. Latrobe for more time to repay the $5 million loan from 1853, proposing to return the principal with 4 percent interest over the following fifty years. Mayor Latrobe, son of longtime B&O counsel John H. B. Latrobe, entertained the offer, but many local officials saw it as an affront. "Why should Baltimore be burdened with the debts of the Baltimore and Ohio for the next half century?" asked city finance commissioner Enoch Pratt. He continued, "I do not see why the city should be run in the interest of the Baltimore and Ohio Railroad." The city government rejected Spencer's proposal, and in 1889 the B&O finally repaid the money it had borrowed from the city thirty-six years earlier. One year later, the City of Baltimore made a clean break, selling its holdings of B&O stock and thus relinquishing its stake in the management of the company.[5]

The city picked an opportune moment to jump ship. As the public gleaned the scope of the company's debt obligations—which by the mid-1890s reached upward of $90 million—the B&O's stock price declined. The State of Maryland sold most of its stock in the railroad at the same time as the city, retaining only two directors on the board until 1906, when it eliminated this token representation as well. Buckling under the weight of its debt, the B&O went into receivership in 1896. When the company was purchased in 1899, it was not by Baltimoreans but by a consortium of Chicago businessmen. Baltimore, as a municipality, and Baltimoreans, as individuals, no longer managed the

B&O Railroad. In 1901, only one of the company's twelve directors came from Baltimore, compared with seven from New York. That year, the Pennsylvania Railroad purchased the B&O and integrated the line into its system.[6]

A similar trajectory played out in other Baltimore industries. The B&O had helped to locate Baltimore within the tangible networks of steam and rail and the less tangible relations of credit and exchange that together fueled industrial growth in the late nineteenth century. The city's robust shipping facilities and immigrant workforce, both cultivated by the B&O, encouraged the development of manufacturing in the 1880s and 1890s. So did the city government, which exempted manufacturing equipment from taxation after 1877. The number of industrial corporations in Baltimore increased from less than forty in 1881 to more than two hundred in 1895. But neither the number of firms in Baltimore nor the volume of their output matched other eastern cities at this time. During the Great Merger Movement of the 1890s, those Baltimore companies that competed in a national market quickly came under the dominion of New York–based pools and trusts. American Tobacco, American Sugar Refining, and Standard Oil all purchased Baltimore-based companies, and the House of Morgan acquired the city's steamship lines. Baltimore entered the railroad age as an entrepreneurial agent, projecting iron bands far beyond the city limits; it entered the twentieth century as a branch-plant town.[7]

In the last quarter of the nineteenth century, the economic, political, and cultural currents of American capitalism took forms that are recognizable today. Indeed, many features of the postbellum economic order, formerly tempered by Progressive or New Deal reforms, have resurfaced since the 1980s, prompting some scholars to dub the present era a "Second Gilded Age." Rampant income inequality, exploitative labor practices, and ideologies of individual freedom characterize both the late-nineteenth-century world and our own. The two eras share as well the experience—or at least the discourse—of spatial annihilation. Writers have drawn parallels between the transportation revolution of the nineteenth century, which forged new bonds between once-distant places, and the rise of social media and e-commerce, which have reorganized the landscapes of consumption, sociability, and politics.[8] A common actor binds the electronic circuitry of the digital present with the coal-fueled engines of the steam-powered past: the private corporation. Historians have traced the origins of the modern business corporation to the postbellum period, when, amid a set of intertwined legal, political, organizational, and cultural shifts, these artificial persons began crossing state and national boundaries and acquired a set of rights that have expanded since the nineteenth century to include speech and conscience.[9] Unlike the B&O, which owes whatever notoriety it retains to Monopoly (the game, not the practice), companies formed in the late nineteenth century like Coca-Cola, DuPont, and General Electric form a line of continuity from the First to the Second Gilded Age.

To understand the material underpinnings of the modern corporation, though, we must look back further. This book has suggested that corporate power, as we understand it today, rests on a spatial order that took shape in city streets during the first half century of the railroad age. The assumptions and practices of corporate capitalism—the mobility of capital, the scale of corporate competition, the resistance to regulation, the commodification of labor—gained traction through the transformation of the physical spaces of the city, as Baltimore morphed from a compact, walking-oriented market center to a diffuse, steam-powered place of transit. The tracks in Pratt Street; the tunnels and deep cuts in North Baltimore; the frog pond and wharves of Locust Point; the streetcars moving passengers through fashionable retail districts and the freight trains running through their working-class counterparts; the central station with its teetering clock tower, and the multiracial neighborhood disturbed by its traffic—all gave form to and enabled the rise of an economic system centered on private corporations.

The railroad's origins as a municipal project gave these transformations a double meaning. The rail infrastructure that crisscrossed Baltimore by the 1870s helped realize the spatial order of corporate capitalism both by facilitating mechanized movement and by insulating the B&O from political currents that had, since the 1820s, sought to work the corporation to other ends. From the vantage point of the twenty-first century, many of the goals espoused by the railroad's founders and, later, advocates of public control seem like obvious pipe dreams. When Baltimoreans kick-started the American railroad industry in the 1820s, they premised their efforts on ideas about interurban competition and laws of trade that proved chimerical, undone by the railroads themselves. Although the language of natural advantage never disappeared—to this day the Port of Baltimore touts the city's position close to the Midwest as a "tremendous asset"—companies like the B&O changed the relationship between geographic proximity and economic productivity.[10] Baltimore had little prospect of upsetting New York's commercial dominance; analogies that cast railroads as waterways were equally flawed. But the tracks and tunnels also served to counteract other, less whimsical visions for the railroad corporation and the city. Efforts to ensure that the public had a voice in the railroad it had funded, to channel surplus revenues into urban development instead of dividends, and to safeguard citizens as they crossed the streets did not represent the cockamamie schemes of rearguard traditionalists but rather a viable path for railroad enterprise. If the trajectory plotted by John W. Garrett and the private stockholders now appears inevitable, it is because the infrastructure they implemented made it so, locking in patterns of movement that rendered the city a mere place of transit. The infrastructure of through trade served as an iron counterpoint to visions of municipal control, a statement, no less symbolic for its practicality, of the role the city would play within corporate capitalism.

Examining the urban history of the railroad thus underscores the political nature of the railroad's transformation from an urban improvement to a private corporation. Narratives that frame the privatization of the railroad as a matter of institutional maturation or competitive exigency gloss over the alternative visions for the B&O articulated in midcentury Baltimore and miss the sometimes-flimsy premises on which the stockholders advanced their claims. The railroad did not evolve into the private, managerial corporation — stockholders made it so by pursuing initiatives within a political arena. They characterized this as an inexorable process, but their ability to shake public authority depended not only on the development of a national market for transportation but also on matters as contingent as partisan realignments in late-antebellum Maryland. Reconstructing the manner in which the stockholders wrested control of the railroad from the urban public reminds us that economic systems develop not because of technological teleologies or invisible hands, but through decisions about how, and in whose interests, to order society.

Many of the institutions, practices, and ideas forged in the nineteenth century have endured across more than a century of social and technological change. We can still see the legacies of the struggles recounted in this book in Baltimore's landscape. Passengers who board trains at Camden and Penn Stations in Baltimore travel along routes first opened between 1830 and 1875, including the outdated Baltimore & Potomac Railroad tunnels that have become perpetual headaches for Amtrak administrators.[11] Asphalt has long since covered the freight tracks that drew the wrath of Pratt Street residents, but iron rails still jut through the cobblestones at Fells Point. Dense threads of track continue to wrap around Locust Point, although on inspection one will find that many of them now are overgrown with weeds — the prophecy of "grass growing in the streets" at last fulfilled. Other legacies are less immediately obvious. Today, as in the nineteenth century, a map of transportation infrastructure is a map of power, race, and class. In part, this is because, despite efforts by the B&O's founders to distance themselves from slavery, income derived from forced labor and human commodification helped underwrite the city's principal railroad, both directly in the form of individual investments and, in a more attenuated fashion, through the municipal tax base and initiatives like the B&O note. Even in the absence of enslaved labor on the line, slavery helped shape the landscape of industrial capitalism. Moreover, the railroad, by carving up space, allotting facilities, and distributing burdens, built from and reinforced an understanding of who mattered within Baltimore's political economy. The blithe destruction of African American housing to make way for Camden Station in the 1850s reflected a racialized spatial politics that persisted into the highway age and beyond.[12]

As railroad companies defined the prerogatives of private enterprise, they forged a spatial order in which mobile, border-crossing corporations exercised economic agency while cities served as sites for investment and circulation. Much has changed in the politics, technology, and economics of city building since the nineteenth century, yet these assumptions remain largely intact. To understand the rise of the railroad, we must look to urban history, but the converse may be true as well: the history of the nineteenth-century railroad has implications for twenty-first century urbanism.

Acknowledgments

If not for the support of many people and benefactors, I would have run out of steam long ago. Now, as I approach the end of the line, it is my pleasure to thank those who kept me on track.

I am fortunate to have found communities, both in Baltimore and in Hong Kong, that have offered inspiration, criticism, and company. I owe a particular debt of gratitude to Mary Ryan, who supported this project from the start, and whose adroit spatial analysis and engaged citizenship offer models of scholarship I can only try to follow. This book is an imperfect tribute to her guidance and friendship; I cannot thank her enough. I benefited, too, from lively discussions with urban historians whom Mary recruited to Johns Hopkins University—Rob Gamble, Paige Glotzer, Katie Hemphill, and Mo Speller—whose interventions and insights helped me understand Baltimore's past and present in new ways. I owe all of you a crab cake.

Conversations, support, and feedback from Ron Walters, Michael Johnson, Angus Burgin, Nathan Connolly, Toby Ditz, Louis Galambos, Philip Morgan, Seth Rockman, Daniel Walkowitz, and Judith Walkowitz have shaped my analysis in material ways. Likewise, discussions in and out of workshops with Ian Beamish, Julia Bowes, Will Brown, Claire Cage, Jessica Clark, Chris Consolino, Sara Damiano, James Fichter, Staci Ford, Stephanie Gamble, Jonathan Gienapp, Amanda Herbert, Jason Hoppe, Kendall Johnson, Gabriel Klehr, Edward Kolla, Khalid Kurji, Pat McGrath, Ren Pepitone, James Roberts, Justin Roberts, Monica Steinberg, and many others have provided welcome criticism while maintaining a sense of community. Xia Shi's perceptive readings have sharpened a number of the chapters in this book. Lauren MacDonald offered words of encouragement at a crucial juncture. Nan Zhang has been a valued interlocutor for many years. Joseph Adelman and Sarah

Adelman have been exceedingly generous with their time and advice from the very start. Stimulating conversations with Claire Gherini, Katie Hindmarch-Watson, and Natalie Elder have pushed me to frame this study in new ways. Helen Ma has given me new modes of expression. David Hershinow, Stephanie Hershinow, and Maggie Vinter have held me accountable.

The history department at Hong Kong Baptist University has been a welcoming, supportive academic home. Much of the credit for this goes to Clara Wing-Chung Ho, who, as department head, has cultivated a productive, collegial, and rigorous environment. Renee Chan, Joan Chan, Crystal Poon, and Michelle Chan have been more than patient as I learned the ropes of a new educational system. An Early Career Scheme (ECS) grant from the Research Grants Council of Hong Kong provided essential support for this book: it funded research trips and two semesters of leave that enabled me to complete this work in a (somewhat) timely fashion. I am grateful to Chan Ka Lai, Chow Kai Wing, and Lam Kai Yin for taking up my teaching responsibilities. The ECS also allowed me to hire a number of research assistants whose work has made this book more comprehensive and easier to read than it would be otherwise: my thanks to Chen Tianpei, Simone Lee, and Tracy Leung for tracking down obscure research materials, and to Lai Tin Wai, Li Lok Him, Tracy Leung (again), and Yiu Sze Ki for designing many of the beautiful maps that adorn this volume.

My research would not have been possible without help from a number of librarians and archivists. At Johns Hopkins University, John Buchtel, Jim Gillispie, Chella Vaidyanathan, Amy Kimball, and Lynne Stuart kindly guided my research. Chris Baer at the Hagley Library, Kevin Fredette at West Virginia University, Pat Anderson and David Angerhoffer at the Maryland Historical Society, and Becky Gunby, Tony Roberts, and Saul B. Gibusiwa at the Baltimore City Archives all helped me navigate their records. John Maranto, Allison Seyler, Travis Harry, and Daniel Zink of the B&O Museum worked to accommodate my unusual research schedule and pointed me to gems in their collections. James Garrett kindly expedited my access to the Robert Garrett Family Papers at the Library of Congress and has offered unflagging support. Earlier versions of chapter 2 and parts of chapters 1 and 4 were published in the *Journal of Urban History* and *Early American Studies*, respectively, and I thank the editors and reviewers of both journals for helpful suggestions and permission to republish this material.

At the University of Chicago Press, I am grateful to Timothy Mennel for bringing this book from proposal to print. Careful readings and probing questions from Sean Patrick Adams and Tamara Plakins Thornton prompted me to go at once deeper into the urban setting and wider in analytical scope.

Susannah Engstrom provided indispensable guidance in placing the manuscript in production. Katherine Faydash's attentive and astute edits brought clarity and precision to the manuscript. Timothy Gilfoyle's comments, questions, and editorial suggestions have played an especially large role in shaping this book. His interventions have made it both more rigorous and more readable, and I am grateful for his time and attention.

Finally, I would like to thank my family. My parents, Bill Schley and Joan Fisher, have offered steadfast support and encouragement from the very beginning. I was inspired to study history by the example of my grandparents, Harriet Schley and David Fisher. The hospitality of my Baltimore-based grandparents, David and Margaret Fisher, made my move to that city a pleasant one. It is hard to imagine what life would look like without Jessica Valdez. As a partner, she broadens my horizons; as a scholar, she sets an example I aspire to emulate. Certainly, this book would not exist without her critical eye and encouragement. As such, I dedicate it to her.

Appendix

The Board of Directors during the Stockholder Revolt

To prepare a general portrait of the people who joined the B&O's board of directors during the stockholder revolt of the 1850s, I triangulated a number of sources. Foremost among them was G. F. May's *Chronological and Alphabetical List of President and Directors . . . of the Baltimore and Ohio Railroad Company*, published in 1929 and kindly furnished by Daniel Zink of the B&O Railroad Museum. This pamphlet lists every person who sat on the board or held a position in the B&O's upper management; from these data, I was able to determine who served, when, and in what capacity. The results show that the 1850s saw a rapid increase in the number of first-time public directors, most of whom left or were replaced within two years, as table A.1 indicates.

But it also reveals considerable changes among the stockholders' representatives. From 1846 to 1852, an average of two and a half new private directors joined the board each year. The tumult within the company's upper management first registers in 1853, the year the B&O reached the Ohio River, when, suddenly, five new private directors appeared on the board, all of whom served for only one year. Then, in 1854, the private stockholders replaced fully half of their slate of directors with six newcomers (one of whom had served in this capacity a few years earlier). From 1854 to 1860, turnover continued, with new private directors replacing old, until only two holdovers from the pre-1853 days remained.

To get a sense of who these directors were and what, if anything, set them apart from their predecessors on the board, I compiled basic biographical information on two sets of directors, ten years apart—the private directors from 1844 to 1846, and those from 1854 to 1856. The former group comprised fourteen people, the latter fifteen, and three individuals fit into both columns. To

TABLE A.1. Turnover on the board of directors, 1845–1858

Years	New private directors	New private directors serving less than 2 yrs.	New city directors	New city directors serving less than 2 yrs.	New state directors	New state directors serving less than 2 yrs.
1845–1851	12	3	19	10	8	0
1852–1858	16	4	32	23	33	22

track them down, I started with the city directories: *Matchett's Baltimore Directory* for 1837, 1842, 1849–1850, 1851, 1853–1854, and 1855–1856; *Woods' Baltimore Directory* for 1856–1857 and 1860; and *E. M. Cross & Co.'s Baltimore City Business Directory* for 1863–1864. From these I learned where these men lived and what they did for a living. To find out when they were born, I turned to the manuscript U.S. Federal Censuses for 1850 and 1860, which also indicated the size of their households and, sometimes, the value of their real and personal property holdings. In two cases I relied on the genealogy website Find a Grave. When these sources did not turn up results, I consulted J. Thomas Scharf's *History of Baltimore City and County* (Philadelphia: Louis H. Everts, 1881), particularly the "Necrology" in chapter 45, which lists the deaths of prominent citizens, often with reference to their age and occupation. Finally, to confirm particular information or determine which of several people with the same name actually served on the board, I turned to the *Sun*, particularly the death notices. I am reasonably confident that this method yielded accurate results, although in some cases I did have to make an educated guess, and the year of birth for one director from the 1840s, the judge James Harwood, remained elusive. I have summarized the most important findings in tables A.2 and A.3.

Some things did not change from the 1840s to the 1850s. The stockholders did elect a few younger representatives in the 1850s—John W. Garrett and C. Oliver O'Donnell were both in their thirties when they joined the board, whereas the youngest directors a decade earlier had been in their forties. But the directors' average and median ages actually went slightly up during the stockholder revolt; clearly this was not a youth movement. Still, there is a palpable generational shift at work here. The directors elected in the mid-1850s overwhelmingly came of age in the nineteenth century—a third of the directors were born in the new century and the oldest were barely into their teens in 1801. The directors of the 1840s, by contrast, were all well into adulthood when the B&O launched in 1828. This is in one sense to be expected—of course younger people would join the board as the century progressed. Yet it is not as inevitable as it appears, because after the stockholder revolt, turnover

TABLE A.2. Private directors, 1844–1846

Name	Year of birth	Occupation
Jacob Albert	1787	Merchant (hardware)
John I. Donaldson	1791	Lawyer, insurance company president
James Harwood	Unknown	Judge
Samuel Hoffman	1782	Merchant
Samuel Jones Jr.	1804	Merchant, financier (bank president)
John P. Kennedy	1795	Lawyer, politician
Fielding Lucas Jr.	1780	Printer, publisher, bookseller
William H. Marriott	1795	Lawyer, port collector
William F. Murdock	1799	Merchant (dry goods)
Columbus O'Donnell	1790	Gas company president
Edward Patterson	1788	Merchant (iron), manufacturer (nails)
Samuel W. Smith	1801	Gentleman
James Swan	1792	Financier (bank president)
Joseph Wilkins	1782	Physician

TABLE A.3. Private directors, 1854–1856

Name	Year of birth	Occupation
Francis Burns	1791	Brickmaker
Benjamin DeFord	1800	Hide and leather dealer
Marcus Denison	1800	Grocer, merchant (tea)
John W. Garrett	1820	Financier, merchant
Andrew Gregg	1789	Grocer, merchant (produce)
William A. Hack	1813	Provision dealer
Johns Hopkins	1795	Financier (bank president), merchant
William Lamping	1815	Merchant (tobacco)
William H. Norris[a]	1811	Lawyer
Columbus O'Donnell	1790	Gas co. president
C. Oliver O'Donnell	1822	Insurance agent, coal company president
Edward Patterson	1788	Merchant (iron), manufacturer (nails)
Samuel W. Smith	1801	Gentleman
Wesley Starr	1790	Merchant (tobacco/general commission)
Nathan Tyson	1788	Miller, merchant

[a]The occupation for William Henry Norris relies on a bit of guesswork: there were three people with that name in Baltimore in the mid-1850s who were of an appropriate age to serve on the B&O's board, including a lawyer, a banker, and a physician. I have surmised that the Norris on the board—and the Norris who defended the extra dividend in public—was the attorney, since he later represented the B&O; see *Sun*, "The Railroad 'Extra Dividend' Case," 30 July 1859.

became rare: from 1864 to 1875, only four new faces joined the board. By and large, they aged as a cohort together.

The second notable shift concerns the directors' occupational profile. In the 1840s as in the 1850s, men of commerce predominated on the board. Yet the stockholders in the 1840s also saw fit to elect a physician, a "gentleman," and, especially, attorneys, including people who played an active role in government, like Harwood, the statesman John Pendleton Kennedy, and William H. Marriott. By contrast, the private board members of the 1850s almost all had a hand in industry or trade. This may account for the more single-minded focus on dividends and seems as well reflect the divide, increasingly asserted in the 1850s, between the worlds of politics and business. It is also possible that the directors selected in the 1850s were wealthier than their counterparts a decade earlier: insofar as the censuses contained information on the value of their estates, the 1840s directors had an average household wealth of less than $72,000, whereas the directors of the 1850s averaged more than $87,000. That said, the data on property and estate value are too incomplete to render any firm conclusions.

Abbreviations in the Notes

AR *Annual Report of the President and Directors to the Stockholders of the Baltimore and Ohio Railroad Company* (Baltimore: Various publishers, various years); these citations include the annual report number and year; when two years are listed, the year in parentheses indicates that for the report, and the year in brackets indicates that for publication

BCA Baltimore City Archives, Baltimore

B&O Business Letters Baltimore & Ohio Railroad Co. Business Letters, 1854–1881, MS 1925, Maryland Historical Society, Baltimore

B&O Museum Baltimore & Ohio Railroad Museum Archives, Hays T. Watkins Research Library, Baltimore

B&O Papers Papers of the Baltimore & Ohio Railroad Co., 1827–1866, MS 1135, Maryland Historical Society, Baltimore

CCR City Council Records, Record Group 16, Series 1, Baltimore City Archives

CComR City Commissioners Records, Record Group 3, Series 1, Baltimore City Archives

GPC Garrett Papers Collection, Baltimore & Ohio Railroad Museum Archives, Hays T. Watkins Research Library, Baltimore

JWG Letterbooks John W. Garrett Letterbooks, 1867–1887, MS 2719, Maryland Historical Society, Baltimore

Laws and Ordinances *Laws and Ordinances, Relating to the Baltimore and Ohio Rail Road Company* (Baltimore: John Murphy & Co., 1850)

MC Mayor's Correspondence, Record Group 9, Series 2, Baltimore City Archives

MdHS Maryland Historical Society, Baltimore

Minute Book Minute Book [with letter], Baltimore & Ohio Railroad Museum Archives, Hays T. Watkins Research Library, B&O Railroad Museum, Baltimore

NWR *Niles' Weekly Register*

Ordinances *The Ordinances of the Mayor and City Council of Baltimore* . . . (Baltimore: Various publishers, year)

PWB Minute Book Minute Book of the Philadelphia, Wilmington & Baltimore, Accession No. 1807, V-236, Hagley Museum and Library, Wilmington, Delaware

PWB Board Papers Philadelphia, Wilmington & Baltimore Papers, Accession No. 1807, B-1347, Hagley Museum and Library, Wilmington, Delaware

RGFP   Robert Garrett Family Papers, Library of Congress, Washington, DC

Swann Collection   Thomas Swann Collection, 1815–1853, MS 1826, Maryland Historical Society, Baltimore

WPA   Works Progress Administration and item number for documents in the Baltimore City Archives

Notes

Introduction

1. *Detailed and Correct Account of the Grand Civic Procession in the City of Baltimore, on the Fourth of July, 1828; in Honor of the Day and in Commemoration of the Commencement of the Baltimore and Ohio Rail-Road, as published in the "American"* (Baltimore: Thomas Murphy, 1828).

2. The classic analysis of railroad technology and its relationship to travel is Wolfgang Schivelbusch, *The Railway Journey: Trains and Travel in the 19th Century*, trans. Anselm Hollo (New York: Urizen Books, 1979). On spatial annihilation: Karl Marx referred to spatial annihilation as "the annihilation of space by time," in *Grundrisse: Foundations of a Critique of Political Economy*, trans. Martin Nicolaus (1857–1858; London: Penguin Books, 1973), 524. The notion of spatial annihilation emerged at the same time as the railroad: Michael Freeman, *Railways and the Victorian Imagination* (New Haven, CT: Yale University Press, 1999), 78. On the railroad and the development of corporate form: Alfred Chandler, *The Visible Hand: The Managerial Revolution in American Business* (Cambridge, MA: Belknap Press of Harvard University Press, 1977), ch. 3; William G. Roy, *Socializing Capital: The Rise of the Large Industrial Corporation in America* (Princeton, NJ: Princeton University Press, 1997); L. Ray Gunn, *The Decline of Authority: Public Economic Policy and Political Development in New York, 1800–1860* (Ithaca, NY: Cornell University Press, 1988); Harry N. Scheiber, *Ohio Canal Era: A Case Study of Government and the Economy, 1820–1861* (Athens: Ohio University Press, 1969); Sean Patrick Adams, "Soulless Monsters and Iron Horses: The Civil War, Institutional Change, and American Capitalism," in *Capitalism Takes Command: The Social Transformation of Nineteenth-Century America*, ed. Michael Zakim and Gary J. Kornblith (Chicago: University of Chicago Press), 249–276. On the railroad and economic development: Richard White, *Railroaded: The Transcontinentals and the Making of Modern America* (New York: W. W. Norton, 2012); William Cronon, *Nature's Metropolis: Chicago and the Great West* (New York: W. W. Norton, 1991); Gerald Berk, *Alternative Tracks: The Constitution of American Industrial Order, 1865–1917* (Baltimore: Johns Hopkins University Press, 1994); Allan R. Pred, *Urban Growth and the Circulation of Information: The United States System of Cities, 1790–1840* (Cambridge, MA: Harvard University Press, 1973); George Rogers Taylor, *The Transportation Revolution, 1815–1860* (New York: Holt, Rinehart, and Winston, 1951); Albert Fishlow, *American Railroads and the Transformation of the Antebellum Economy* (Cam-

bridge, MA: Harvard University Press, 1965); James A. Ward, *Railroads and the Character of America, 1820–1887* (Knoxville: University of Tennessee Press, 1986); William G. Thomas III, *The Iron Way: Railroads, the Civil War, and the Making of Modern America* (New Haven, CT: Yale University Press, 2011).

3. *Detailed and Correct Account of the Grand Civic Procession*, 6; David Nye, *American Technological Sublime* (Cambridge, MA: MIT Press, 1994), 49; Neil Harris, *Building Lives: Constructing Rites and Passages* (New Haven, CT: Yale University Press, 1999), 20–27. On the substance and dimensions of the stone: James D. Dilts, *The Great Road: The Building of the Baltimore & Ohio, the Nation's First Railroad, 1828–1853* (Stanford, CA: Stanford University Press, 1993), 9.

4. On private corporations and the public good in the early republic: John Lauritz Larson, *The Market Revolution in America: Liberty, Ambition, and the Eclipse of the Common Good* (Cambridge: Cambridge University Press, 2010); Larson, *Internal Improvement: National Public Works and the Promise of Popular Government in the Early United States* (Chapel Hill: University of North Carolina Press, 1998); Pauline Maier, "The Revolutionary Origins of the American Corporation," *William & Mary Quarterly*, 3rd ser., 50, no. 1 (January 1993): 51–84; Andrew Shankman, *The Crucible of American Democracy: The Struggle to Fuse Egalitarianism & Capitalism in Jeffersonian Pennsylvania* (Lawrence: University Press of Kansas, 2004); Andrew M. Schocket, *Founding Corporate Power in Early National Philadelphia* (DeKalb: Northern Illinois University Press, 2007); Jason M. Opal, "Enterprise and Emulation: The Moral Economy of Turnpikes in Early National New England," *Early American Studies* 8, no. 3 (Fall 2010): 623–645. Many of these projects—notably the Erie Canal, the New York & Erie Railroad, and the Western Railroad of Massachusetts—received state but not municipal aid; nonetheless, in public discourse they were characterized as essential to the development of their respective termini; see, e.g., Craig Miner, *A Most Magnificent Machine: America Adopts the Railroad, 1825–1862* (Lawrence: University Press of Kansas, 2010), 33–40. The Panic of 1837 helped cool public support for financing railroads: L. Ray Gunn, "The Crisis of Distributive Politics: State Debts and Development Policy in New York, 1837–1842," in *New York and the Rise of American Capitalism: Economic Development and the Social and Political History of an American State, 1780–1870*, ed. William Pencak and Conrad Edick Wright (New York: New York Historical Society, 1989), 168–201; Alberta M. Sbragia, *Debt Wish: Entrepreneurial Cities, U.S. Federalism, and Economic Development* (Pittsburgh, PA: University of Pittsburgh Press, 1996); Michael J. Connolly, *Capitalism, Politics, and Railroads in Jacksonian New England* (Columbia: University of Missouri Press, 2003).

5. Carter Goodrich and Harvey H. Segal, "Baltimore's Aid to Railroads: A Study in the Municipal Planning of Internal Improvements," *Journal of Economic History* 13, no. 1 (Winter 1953): table 1, 6–7. The state of Maryland invested millions in the B&O as well. Only New York City incurred more debt than Baltimore in the 1830s: Leonard P. Curry, *The Corporate City: The American City as a Political Entity, 1800–1850* (Westport, CT: Greenwood Press, 1997), 60, 223–240. On municipal parsimony in this period: Robin L. Einhorn, *Property Rules: Political Economy in Chicago, 1833–1872* (Chicago: University of Chicago Press, 1991); Terrence J. McDonald, *The Parameters of Urban Fiscal Policy: Socioeconomic Change and Political Culture in San Francisco, 1860–1906* (Berkeley: University of California Press, 1986).

6. See Chandler, *Visible Hand*; Taylor, *Transportation Revolution*; Miner, *A Most Magnificent Machine*; Cronon, *Nature's Metropolis*; Schivelbusch, *Railway Journey*; Daniel Walker Howe, *What Hath God Wrought: The Transformation of America, 1815–1848* (New York: Oxford University Press, 2007), among others.

7. The notion of the walking city is from Sam Bass Warner Jr., *Streetcar Suburbs: The Process*

of Growth in Boston, 1870–1900 (Cambridge, MA: Harvard University Press, 1962); Warner, *The Private City: Philadelphia in Three Periods of its Growth*, 2nd ed. (Philadelphia: University of Pennsylvania Press, 1987 [1968]). Most works on changes in urban space in this period, like Warner, do not pay much attention to cities' changing modes of transportation and communications; instructive exceptions include Diane Shaw, *City Building on the Eastern Frontier: Sorting the New Nineteenth-Century City* (Baltimore: Johns Hopkins University Press, 2004); Noam Maggor, *Brahmin Capitalism: Frontiers of Wealth and Populism in America's First Gilded Age* (Cambridge, MA: Harvard University Press, 2017); Andrew Heath, *In Union There Is Strength: Philadelphia in the Age of Urban Consolidation* (Philadelphia: University of Pennsylvania Press, 2019). On the history of the railroad and the city in Europe: Schivelbusch, *The Railway Journey*; John R. Kellett, *The Impacts of Railways on Victorian Cities* (London: Routledge & Kegan Paul, 1969); Sigfried Giedion, *Space, Time, and Architecture: The Growth of a New Tradition*, 5th ed. (Cambridge, MA: Harvard University Press, 1967), pt. 7; Ralf Roth and Marie-Noelle Polino, eds., *The City and the Railway in Europe* (Burlington, VT: Ashgate, 2003). The literature on American cities is limited but growing, as scholars consider the ways in which railroads shaped uses and perceptions of public space: John R. Stilgoe, *The Metropolitan Corridor: Railroads and the American Scene, 1880–1935* (New Haven, CT: Yale University Press, 1983); Carl Condit, *The Railroad and the City: A Technological and Urbanistic History of Cincinnati* (Columbus: Ohio State University Press, 1977); Joel Schwartz, "'To Every Man's Door': Railroads and the Use of Streets in Jacksonian Philadelphia," *Pennsylvania Magazine of History and Biography* 128, no. 1 (January 2004): 36–61; Ari Kelman, *A River and Its City: The Nature of Landscape in New Orleans* (Berkeley: University of California Press, 2006), ch. 4; Ted Robert Mitchell, "Connecting a Nation, Dividing a City: How Railroads Shaped the Public Spaces and Social Understanding of Chicago" (PhD diss., Michigan State University, 2009).

8. On the boundaries between public and private in the long nineteenth century: John D. Fairfield, *The Public and Its Possibilities: Triumphs and Tragedies in the American City* (Philadelphia: Temple University Press, 2010); Barbara Young Welke, *Law and the Borders of Belonging in the Long Nineteenth Century United States* (Cambridge: Cambridge University Press, 2010); Mary P. Ryan, *Civic Wars: Democracy and Public Life in the American City during the Nineteenth Century* (Berkeley: University of California Press, 1997); William J. Novak, *The People's Welfare: Law and Regulation in Nineteenth Century America* (Chapel Hill: University of North Carolina Press, 1996).

9. Jeffrey Sklansky, *The Soul's Economy: Market Society and Selfhood in American Thought, 1820–1920* (Chapel Hill: University of North Carolina Press, 2002); Walter Johnson, *Soul by Soul: Life inside the Antebellum Slave Market* (Cambridge, MA: Harvard University Press, 1999); Amy Dru Stanley, *From Bondage to Contract: Wage Labor, Marriage, and the Market in the Age of Slave Emancipation* (New York: Cambridge University Press, 1998); Jonathan Levy, *Freaks of Fortune: The Emerging World of Capitalism and Risk in America* (Cambridge, MA: Harvard University Press, 2012); Stephen Mihm, *A Nation of Counterfeiters: Capitalists, Con Men, and the Making of the United States* (Cambridge, MA: Harvard University Press, 2007); Michael Zakim and Gary J. Kornblith, "Introduction: An American Revolutionary Tradition," in *Capitalism Takes Command*, 1–12; Brian P. Luskey and Wendy A. Woloson, eds., *Capitalism by Gaslight: Illuminating the Economy of Nineteenth-Century America* (Philadelphia: University of Pennsylvania Press, 2015); Joyce Appleby, *The Relentless Revolution: A History of Capitalism* (New York: W. W. Norton, 2010); Cronon, *Nature's Metropolis*.

10. Kenneth Lipartito, "Reassembling the Economic: New Departures in Historical Mate-

rialism," *American Historical Review* 121, no. 1 (February 2016): 101–139; Seth Rockman, "What Makes the History of Capitalism Newsworthy?" *Journal of the Early Republic* 34 (Fall 2014): 439–466; Roseanne Currarino, "Toward a History of Cultural Economy," *Journal of the Civil War Era* 2, no. 4 (December 2012): 564–585; Jeffrey Sklansky, "The Elusive Sovereign: New Intellectual and Social Histories of Capitalism," *Modern Intellectual History* 9, no. 1 (April 2012): 233–248; William H. Sewell Jr., "A Strange Career: The Historical Study of Economy Life," *History and Theory* 49 (December 2010): 146–166. This approach differs from the market revolution paradigm, which seeks to locate the contested origins of capitalism: Sean Wilentz, *Chants Democratic: New York City and the Rise of the American Working Class, 1788–1850* (New York: Oxford University Press, 1984); Charles Sellers, *The Market Revolution: Jacksonian America, 1815–1846* (New York: Oxford University Press, 1991); Tony A. Freyer, *Producers versus Capitalists: Constitutional Conflict in Antebellum America* (Charlottesville: University of Virginia Press, 1994); Joyce Appleby, "The Vexed Story of Capitalism Told by American Historians," in *A Restless Past: History and the American Public* (New York: Rowman & Littlefield, 2005), 163–182; Larson, *Market Revolution in America*; Howe, *What Hath God Wrought*; William R. Sutton, *Journeymen for Jesus: Evangelical Artisans Confront Capitalism in Jacksonian Baltimore* (University Park: Pennsylvania State University Press, 1998).

11. On capitalism and changing relationships to land: Elizabeth Blackmar, "Inheriting Property and Debt: From Family Security to Corporate Accumulation," in *Capitalism Takes Command*, 93–117. Environmental historians have been particularly effective at explaining the commodification of land: William Cronon, *Changes in the Land: Indians, Colonists, and the Ecology of New England* (New York: Hill & Wang, 1983); Cronon, *Nature's Metropolis*; Andrew C. Isenberg, *The Destruction of the Bison: An Environmental History, 1750–1920* (New York: Cambridge University Press, 2000). For a critique of the history of capitalism's emphasis on commodification, see Eli Cook, *The Pricing of Progress: Economic Indicators and the Capitalization of American Life* (Cambridge, MA: Harvard University Press, 2017), 5–7. Much excellent work has been done excavating the histories of particular sites of commodification, like the pawnshop in Wendy A. Woloson, *In Hock: Pawning in America from Independence through the Great Depression* (Chicago: University of Chicago Press, 2012); the commodities exchange in Jonathan Ira Levy, "Contemplating Delivery: Futures Trading and the Problem of Commodity Exchange in the United States, 1875–1905," *American Historical Review* 111, no. 2 (April 2006): 307–335; and the slave auction block in Johnson, *Soul by Soul*.

12. For example, Sven Beckert, *Empire of Cotton: A Global History* (New York: Alfred A. Knopf, 2014); Edward E. Baptist, *The Half Has Never Been Told: Slavery and American Capitalism* (New York: Basic Books, 2014); and Walter Johnson, *River of Dark Dreams: Slavery and Empire in the Cotton Kingdom* (Cambridge, MA: Harvard University Press, 2013), who lays out his debt to Harvey on p. 424n18. On Harvey's spatial fix: David Harvey, *The Urban Experience* (Baltimore: Johns Hopkins University Press, 1989).

13. This analysis is informed by Henri Lefebvre, *The Production of Space*, trans. Donald Nicholson-Smith (Malden, MA: Blackwell Publishing, 1991).

14. Doreen Massey, *World City* (Cambridge, UK: Polity Press, 2007), 23–24; Neil Brenner, "The Urban Question as a Scale Question: Reflections on Henri Lefebvre, Urban Theory and the Politics of Scale," *International Journal of Urban and Regional Research* 24, no. 2 (June 2000): 361–378; Brenner, "Between Fixity and Motion: Accumulation, Territorial Organization, and the Historical Geography of Spatial Scales," *Environment and Planning D: Society and Space* 16, no. 4 (1998): 459–481; Adam Moore, "Rethinking Scale as a Geographical Category: From Analysis to

Practice," *Progress in Human Geography* 32, no. 2 (2008): 203–225; Sallie A. Marston, John Paul Jones III, and Keith Woodward, "Human Geography without Scale," *Transactions of the Institute of British Geographers* 30, no. 4 (December 2005): 416–432; Eugene J. McCann, "The Urban as an Object of Study in Global Cities Literatures: Representational Practices and Conceptions of Place and Scale," in *Geographies of Power: Placing Scale*, ed. Andrew Herod and Melissa W. Wright (Oxford: Blackwell, 2002), 61–84. Some historians have started to examine scale as a category of practice: Cyrus Schayegh, "The Many Worlds of Abud Yasin; or, What Narcotics Trafficking in the Interwar Middle East Can Tell Us about Territorialization," *American Historical Review* 116, no. 2 (April 2011): 273–306; Beth Lew-Williams, *The Chinese Must Go: Violence, Exclusion, and the Making of the Alien in America* (Cambridge, MA: Harvard University Press, 2018).

15. Cronon, *Nature's Metropolis*, 81–92. On populist ire, see White, *Railroaded*. Much of the best recent work on railroads picks up shortly before or after the Civil War, as by then the nation's rail system was fairly well articulated: Amy G. Richter, *Home on the Rails: Women, the Railroad, and the Rise of Public Domesticity* (Chapel Hill: University of North Carolina Press, 2005); Barbara Young Welke, *Recasting American Liberty: Gender, Race, Law, and the Railroad Revolution, 1865–1920* (New York: Cambridge University Press, 2001); Eric J. Morser, *Hinterland Dreams: The Political Economy of a Midwestern City* (Philadelphia: University of Pennsylvania Press, 2011). Urban histories of the railroad also tend to focus on the post-1850 period and often look at Chicago, a city that, as Cronon shows, was decidedly shaped by railroad networks: Perry R. Duis, *Challenging Chicago: Coping with Everyday Life, 1837–1920* (Urbana: University of Illinois Press, 1998); David M. Young, *The Iron Horse and the Windy City: How Railroads Shaped Chicago* (DeKalb: Northern Illinois University Press, 2005); Ann Durkin Keating, *Chicagoland: City and Suburbs in the Railroad Age* (Chicago: University of Chicago Press, 2005).

16. This statement about Baltimore's population ranking works only if you include Brooklyn's population with that of New York City, and the pre-amalgamation Philadelphia suburbs with Philadelphia. For an overview of this period of the city's history: Sherry H. Olson, *Baltimore: The Building of an American City*, rev. ed. (Baltimore: Johns Hopkins University Press, 1997), 41–197; Matthew A. Crenson, *Baltimore: A Political History* (Baltimore: Johns Hopkins University Press, 2017), 101–306. See also Crenson's entries on Baltimore in Richardson Dilworth, ed., *Cities in American Political History* (Los Angeles: Sage Publications, 2011), 151–156, 243–249, 318–324.

17. On Baltimore and slavery: Christopher Phillips, *Freedom's Port: The African American Community in Baltimore, 1790–1860* (Urbana: University of Illinois Press, 1997); T. Stephen Whitman, *The Price of Freedom: Slavery and Manumission in Baltimore and Early National Maryland* (Lexington: University Press of Kentucky, 1997); Barbara Jeanne Fields, *Slavery and Freedom on the Middle Ground: Maryland during the Nineteenth Century* (New Haven, CT: Yale University Press, 1985); Frank Towers, *The Urban South and the Coming of the Civil War* (Charlottesville: University of Virginia Press, 2004). John Majewski argues that Baltimore's growth into a major metropolis is attributable to the city's large free labor hinterland: Majewski, *A House Dividing: Economic Development in Pennsylvania and Virginia before the Civil War* (New York: Cambridge University Press, 2000), 161.

18. Seth Rockman, *Scraping By: Wage Labor, Slavery, and Survival in Early Baltimore* (Baltimore: Johns Hopkins University Press, 2009); Mary P. Ryan, *Taking the Land to Make the City: A Bicoastal History of North America* (Austin: University of Texas Press, 2019); Martha S. Jones, *Birthright Citizens: A History of Race and Rights in Antebellum America* (New York: Cambridge University Press, 2018).

19. Most corporations are not global in this sense, and even many "global" corporations forge connections beyond the boundaries of their home countries that are attenuated at best. Sunk costs and infrastructural needs shape the conditions of corporate action, limiting their ability to uproot on a whim. But there is nonetheless a categorical spatial distinction between the city (formerly referred to as the "municipal corporation") and the business corporation, one that was worked out politically in the nineteenth century. The corporate form of the modern city means that its territoriality is conventional, but it nonetheless limits the legitimate sphere of municipal political action to territorial goals. On the global corporation: Peter Dicken, "'Placing' Firms: Grounding the Debate on the 'Global' Corporation," in *Remaking the Global Economy: Economic-Geographical Perspectives*, ed. Jamie Peck and Henry Wai-chung Yeung (London: Sage Publications, 2003), 27–44; Brian Roach, "A Primer on Multinational Corporations," in *Leviathans: Multinational Corporations and the New Global History*, ed. Alfred D. Chandler Jr. and Bruce Mazlish (New York: Cambridge University Press, 2005), 19–44. On sunk costs: Gordon L. Clark and Neil Wrigley, "Sunk Costs: A Framework for Economic Geography," *Transactions of the Institute of British Geographers*, n.s., 20, no. 2 (1995): 204–223. On corporations and place, see, for example, Jefferson Cowie, *Capital Moves: RCA's Seventy-Year Quest for Cheap Labor* (Ithaca, NY: Cornell University Press, 1999). On the possibilities and limitations of urban governance in the late twentieth century: David Harvey, "From Managerialism to Entrepreneurialism: The Transformation in Urban Governance in Late Capitalism," in *Spaces of Capital: Towards a Critical Geography* (New York: Routledge, 2001), 345–368. Conversely, on the legal development of the modern city: Hendrik Hartog, *Public Property and Private Power: The Corporation of the City of New York in American Law, 1730–1870* (Ithaca, NY: Cornell University Press, 1983); Curry, *Corporate City*; Eric H. Monkkonen, *America Becomes Urban: The Development of U.S. Cities & Towns, 1780–1980* (Berkeley: University of California Press, 1988), xi–xiv.

Chapter One

1. P. E. Thomas to B. C. Howard, 15 February 1832, Box 3, RGFP.

2. Quoted in James D. Dilts, *The Great Road: The Building of the Baltimore and Ohio, the Nation's First Railroad, 1828–1853* (Stanford, CA: Stanford University Press, 1993), 2; see also Gary John Previts and William D. Samson, "Exploring the Contents of the Baltimore and Ohio Railroad Annual Reports, 1827–1856," *Accounting Historians Journal* 27, no. 1 (June 2000): 1–42.

3. Michael J. Freeman, *Railways and the Victorian Imagination* (New Haven, CT: Yale, 1999), ch. 2; H. Roger Grant, *The Railroad: The Life Story of a Technology* (Westport, CT: Greenwood, 2005), 25; Wolfgang Schivelbusch, *The Railway Journey: Trains and Travel in the 19th Century*, trans. Anselm Hollo (New York: Urizen, 1979); David E. Nye, *American Technological Sublime* (Cambridge, MA: MIT Press, 1994), ch. 3; James A. Ward, *Railroads and the Character of America, 1820–1887* (Knoxville: University of Tennessee Press, 1986); H. Craig Miner, *A Most Magnificent Machine: America Adopts the Railroad, 1825–1862* (Lawrence: University Press of Kansas, 2010).

4. On interurban competition: George Rogers Taylor, *The Transportation Revolution, 1815–1860* (New York: Rinehart & Co., 1951), ch. 5; James Westin Livingood, *The Philadelphia-Baltimore Trade Rivalry, 1780–1860* (Harrisburg: Pennsylvania Historical and Museum Commission, 1947); Julius Rubin, "Canal or Railroad? Imitation and Innovation in the Response to the Erie Canal in Philadelphia, Baltimore, and Boston," *Transactions of the American Philosophical Society*, n.s., 51, no. 7 (1961): 1–106; Leonard P. Curry, *The Corporate City: The American City as a Political Entity,*

1800–1850 (Westport, CT: Greenwood Press, 1997), ch. 7. See also Carter Goodrich, *Government Promotion of Canals and Railroads, 1800–1890* (1960; Westport, CT: Greenwood Press, 1974).

5. *American,* 23 October 1838; see also *American,* 17 March 1827; Ward, *Railroads and the Character of America,* ch. 6; Schivelbusch, *Railway Journey,* ch. 6.

6. Francois Furstenberg, "The Significance of the Trans-Appalachian Frontier in Atlantic History," *American Historical Review* 113, no. 3 (June 2008): 647–677. See also Richard White, *The Middle Ground: Indians, Empires, and Republics in the Great Lakes Region, 1650–1815* (New York: Cambridge University Press, 1991); Christopher Clark, "The Ohio Country in the Political Economy of Nation Building," in *The Center of a Great Empire: The Ohio Country in the Early American Republic,* ed. Andrew R. L. Cayton and Stuart D. Hobbs (Athens: Ohio University Press, 2005), 148–149.

7. *American,* 23 October 1838. See also "Baltimore and Ohio Railroad," *North American Review,* July 1827, 62.

8. *Cincinnati Register* quoted in *American,* 26 March 1827. See also *American,* 23, 26 February 1827, 20 March 1827; *Report of the Engineers, on the Reconnoissance* [*sic*] *and Surveys, Made in Reference to the Baltimore and Ohio Rail Road* (Baltimore: William Wooddy, 1828). On urbanism, empire, and manifest destiny: William Cronon, *Nature's Metropolis: Chicago and the Great West* (New York: W. W. Norton, 1991), 41–45.

9. Stephen J. Hornsby, *British Atlantic, American Frontier: Spaces of Power in Early Modern British America* (Lebanon, NH: University Press of New England, 2005), ch. 5; D. W. Meinig, *The Shaping of America, A Geographical Perspective on 500 Years of History,* vol. 2, *Continental America, 1800–1867* (New Haven, CT: Yale University Press, 1993), 256–257, 363–369; Robert Greenhalgh Albion, with Jennie Barnes Pope, *The Rise of New York Port, 1815–1860* (1939; Boston: Northeastern University Press, 1984).

10. The overview in this paragraph is drawn from Gary Lawson Browne, *Baltimore in the Nation, 1789–1861* (Chapel Hill: University of North Carolina Press, 1980), 3–4, 82–83; Seth Rockman, *Scraping By: Wage Labor, Slavery, and Survival in Early Baltimore* (Baltimore: Johns Hopkins University Press, 2009), 18–22; Brooke Hunter, "Wheat, War, and the American Economy during the Age of Revolution," *William & Mary Quarterly,* 3rd ser., 62, no. 3 (July 2005): 522–526; Sherry H. Olson, *Baltimore: The Building of an American City,* rev. ed. (Baltimore: Johns Hopkins University Press, 1997), 47–48; Christopher Phillips, *Freedom's Port: The African American Community of Baltimore, 1790–1860* (Urbana: University of Illinois Press, 1997), 8–14. Mayors Montgomery and Johnson both spent funds dredging the harbor even in the fiscally lean early 1820s: [John Montgomery,] Mayor's Message, 1 January 1821, 367–376, *Proceedings of the First Branch of the City Council,* RG16 S2, Reel 346, BCA; Edward Johnson, Mayor's Message, 6 January 1823, 274, *Proceedings of the First Branch,* RG16 S2 Reel 346, BCA. On Baltimore's "mud machine": Rockman, *Scraping By,* ch. 3. On the National Road: Theodore Sky, *The National Road and the Difficult Path to Sustainable National Investment* (Newark: University of Delaware Press, 2011). On the limitations of "natural advantages": Cronon, *Nature's Metropolis,* esp. 34–35, 57–62.

11. Browne, *Baltimore in the Nation,* 77–83; Carol Sheriff, *The Artificial River: The Erie Canal and the Paradox of Progress, 1817–1862* (New York: Hill and Wang, 1996), ch. 3.

12. [William Hollins], *Remarks on the Intercourse of Baltimore with the Western Country, with a view of the Communications Proposed between the Atlantic and the Western States* (Baltimore: Joseph Robinson, 1818), iii–iv, 3, 5. Hollins is referred to as a civil engineer in *Gazette,* 5 March 1830.

13. J. Montgomery, Mayor's Annual Message, 3 January 1825, 121, 122, *Proceedings of the First*

Branch, RG16 S2 Reel 346, BCA. Also see 19 March 1824, 89, *Proceedings of the First Branch*, RG16 S2 Reel 346, BCA.

14. [Robert Harper], *Gen. Harper's Speech, to the Citizens of Baltimore, on the Expediency of Promoting a Connexion between the Ohio, at Pittsburgh, and the Waters of the Chesapeake, at Baltimore, by a Canal through the District of Columbia. With his reply to some of the Objections of Mr. Winchester. Delivered at a meeting, held at the Exchange, on the 20th day of December, 1823* (Baltimore: Edward J. Coale, 1824), 19. See also *Report of the Commissioners Appointed to Examine into the Practicability of a Canal from Baltimore to the Potomac, together with the Engineer's Report* (Baltimore: Fielding Lucas, Jun., 1823), 21.

15. Mayor's Communication, 2 January 1826, Box 5, MC; *NWR*, 14 January 1826, 308–309 (quote) and 315.

16. Rubin, "Canal or Railroad?" 67.

17. John H. B. Latrobe, *The Baltimore & Ohio Railroad. Personal Recollections. A Lecture, Delivered before the Maryland Institute, by John H. B. Latrobe, March 23d, 1868* (Baltimore: Sun Book and Job Printing, 1868), 5–6; Lawrence Buckley Thomas, *Genealogical Notes: Containing the Pedigree of the Thomas Family of Maryland* (Baltimore: Lawrence B. Thomas, 1877), 33. On the Thomases, see also Dilts, *The Great Road*, 32–33, 36–37; Rockman, *Scraping By*, 224–228; Leroy Graham, *Baltimore: The Nineteenth Century Black Capital* (Washington, DC: University Press of America, 1982), 18. Philip Thomas took an active role as early as 1810 in seeking a "*permanent* plan for the support of the poor, which will hereafter obviate the necessity of further applications to the citizens for that purpose": Baltimore *Federal Republican*, 31 January 1810. On early precursors to the American railroad: Grant, *Railroad*, 2–3. On potential rail projects in Pennsylvania, New York State, and Maryland: *NWR*, 17 September 1825, 35; *American*, 18 January 1826; *Patriot*, 22 February 1826; Matthew A. Crenson, *Baltimore: A Political History* (Baltimore: Johns Hopkins University Press, 2017), 115.

18. The Browns opened a branch office in New York in 1825. Edwin J. Perkins, *Financing Anglo-American Trade: The House of Brown, 1800–1880* (Cambridge, MA: Harvard University Press, 1975), 19–28, 33, 271n54; Dilts, *Great Road*, 37–38; *Matchett's Baltimore Directory for 1827* (Baltimore: R. J. Matchett, 1827), 41, 136, 204, 252.

19. *Proceedings of the Sundry Citizens of Baltimore, convened for the purpose of devising the Most Efficient Means of Improving the Intercourse between that City and the Western States* (Baltimore: William Wooddy, 1827), esp. 3, 5, 8, 20–30. See also Latrobe, *Personal Recollections*, 5.

20. *Proceedings of the Sundry Citizens of Baltimore*, quote on 4, references to publication on 32. Only one of the men present was an elected official: John V. L. McMahon, a Maryland House of Delegates representative; Crenson, *Baltimore*, 116.

21. *American*, 24 February (quote), 26 February 1827.

22. On the demographic decline of slavery in Maryland: Barbara Jeanne Fields, *Slavery and Freedom on the Middle Ground: Maryland during the Nineteenth Century* (New Haven, CT: Yale University Press, 1985), 6–18. The reference to the "white population" is in *Proceedings of the Sundry Citizens of Baltimore*, 30.

23. Ch. 123, "An Act to incorporate the Baltimore and Ohio Rail Road Company," passed 26 February 1827, in *Laws and Ordinances*, 15–26. Dilts, *Great Road*, 43–45. On special incorporation in the United States, see Eric Hilt, "Early American Corporations and the State," in *Corporations and American Democracy*, ed. Naomi R. Lamoreaux and William J. Novak (Cambridge, MA: Harvard University Press, 2017), 37–73.

24. Ch. 123, "An Act to Incorporate," in *Laws and Ordinances*, 15. Internal improvement pro-

moters across the United States assumed that governments would invest in these projects—see, e.g., John L. Sullivan, *Suggestion of a Plan of Uniting Roads with Railways to Facilitate and Extend the Internal Commerce of New-York* ([New York]: s.n., 1827), 9–10; Larson, *Internal Improvement*. This pattern holds for railroad development internationally, with the prominent exception of England: Goodrich, *Government Promotion*, 6–8.

25. The state also subscribed, though at a later date, purchasing its allotted stock in March 1828. Res. No. 41, "Resolution Relative to the Rail Road," in *Laws and Ordinances*, 123; [Maryland, House of Delegates] *A Supplement to the Act, Entitled, An Act for the Promotion of Internal Improvement* (Baltimore: William Wooddy, 1828).

26. Criticisms turned on fears of speculation and opposition to taxation for a project with unevenly distributed benefits: *Continuation of Essays of "A Baltimorean," Published in the National Intelligencer, and Re-Published in some of the Counties in Maryland, in Pamphlet Form. No. 8* (Baltimore: s.n., 1831), 17; Resolution relative to Rail Road Stock, 12 February 1828, Box 37 [WPA 1126] CCR; *Gazette*, 29 February 1828, 4 March 1828.

27. *American*, 27 March 1827; Dilts, *Great Road*, 45–46; Crenson, *Baltimore*, 116–117.

28. *Gazette*, 13 August 1830; also *Gazette*, 14, 16 August 1830, 20 October 1832, 7 November 1835.

29. The Union Bank of Baltimore, for example, loaned the B&O $500,000 to repay a debt to the Bank of the United States: Minute Book B, 6 October 1832; *Gazette*, 13 August 1830.

30. Minute Book A, 2 May 1828.

31. Rockman's *Scraping By* details the operations of a "system that . . . blurred boundaries between categories of labor" (7) and also examines Thomas's Quakerism and relation to slavery (ch. 8, esp. 245). On the history of Mount Clare plantation: Teresa S. Moyer, *Ancestors of Worthy Life: Plantation Slavery and Black Heritage at Mount Clare* (Gainesville: University Press of Florida, 2015), esp. 147. Woolfolk is counted among the subscribers in Minute Book A, 7 April 1828. Woolfolk's business and role in Baltimore's mercantile community are treated extensively in Calvin Schermerhorn, *The Business of Slavery and the Rise of American Capitalism, 1815–1860* (New Haven, CT: Yale University Press, 2015), ch. 2. See also Steven Deyle, *Carry Me Back: The Domestic Slave Trade in American Life* (New York: Oxford University Press, 2005), 98–99.

32. *American*, 1 March 1827 ("new era"); Scioto (OH) *Gazette* reprinted in (Baltimore) *Gazette*, 28 July 1827 ("a single City"); *Gazette*, 19 February 1827 ("beyond the reach"). See also *American*, 23, 24, 26 February 1827, 14, 26 March 1827, 8 May 1827; *Gazette*, 2 March 1827.

33. Lt. Col. S. H. Long and Capt. Wm. Gibbs McNeill, *Narrative of the Proceedings of the Board of Engineers of the Baltimore and Ohio Rail Road Company, from its Organization to its Dissolution, together with an Exposition of Facts, illustrative of the Conduct of Sundry Individuals* (Baltimore: Bailey & Francis, 1830), 9 (quote); similarly, see *Report of the President and Directors of the Baltimore and Ohio Rail Road Company to the Executive of the State of Maryland* (s.l.: s.n., 1831), 3, 8–9; Minute Book A, 22 December 1831. On railroad origin stories: David E. Nye, *America as Second Creation: Technology and Narratives of New Beginnings* (Cambridge, MA: MIT Press, 2003).

34. Requests for aid and the definition of the railroad as a national project: Minute Book A, 20 December 1828; *To the Senate and House of Representatives of the United States, in Congress assembled, the Memorial of the President and Directors of the Baltimore and Ohio Rail Road Company* [s.l.: s.n., 1829]; *Patriot*, 7 June 1830; *NWR*, 19 June 1830, 293, 26 June 1830, 317–319; P. E. Thomas to Unknown, 9 January 1832, Box 3, RGFP; Minute Book B, 9 January 1832; *NWR*, 7 January 1832, 337. Lobbying: P. E. Thomas to B. C. Howard, 9 January 1832, Box 3, RGFP; P. E.

Thomas to Gen. S. Smith, 10 January 1832, Box 3, RGFP. On the use of military engineers: Colleen A. Dunlavy, *Politics and Industrialization: Early Railroads in the United States and Prussia* (Princeton, NJ: Princeton University Press, 1994), 57–60.

35. P. E. Thomas to Col. B. C. Howard, 10 January 1831, Box 2, RGFP.

36. *NWR*, 19 June 1830, 301; also *NWR*, 26 June 1830, 319.

37. Minute Book B, 9 January 1832 (quote). See also Minute Book A, 21 June 1830; Minute Book C, 7 November 1833, 19 December 1833, 2 February 1834.

38. [House of Delegates] *A Supplement to the Act, Entitled, An Act for the Promotion of Internal Improvement*, 2–3; ch. 46, "An Act further to provide for the payment of future instalments of the State's subscription for stock of the Baltimore and Ohio Rail Road or Chesapeake and Ohio Canal Companies," passed 17 February 1831, in *Laws and Ordinances*, 33; Ord. No. 3, "An Ordinance authorising a Loan for the purposes therein mentioned," passed 26 June 1828, in *Laws and Ordinances*, 126; Ord. No. 1, "An Ordinance to authorize a loan for the purposes therein mentioned," passed 28 August 1829, in *Laws and Ordinances*, 128–130.

39. *NWR*, 27 March 1830, 85–86; *NWR*, 17 January 1835, 332.

40. J. H. Hollander, *The Financial History of Baltimore* (Baltimore: Johns Hopkins University Press, 1899), 100, 137; Robin L. Einhorn, *Property Rules: Political Economy in Chicago, 1833–1872* (Chicago: University of Chicago Press, 1991); Crenson, *Baltimore*, 104–111. Local funding for railroads was often one of the few big-ticket items on municipal budgets: Terrence J. McDonald, *The Parameters of Urban Fiscal Policy: Socioeconomic Change and Political Culture in San Francisco, 1860–1906* (Berkeley: University of California Press, 1986), 48; Mary P. Ryan, *Civic Wars: Democracy and Public Life in the American City during the Nineteenth Century* (Berkeley: University of California Press, 1997), 17, 165; Philip Ethington, *The Public City: The Political Construction of Urban Life in San Francisco, 1850–1900* (New York: Cambridge University Press, 1994), 298–301.

41. *Gazette*, 10 February 1836; ch. 127, "An Act to authorize the City of Baltimore to subscribe to the Capital Stock of the Baltimore and Ohio Rail Road," passed 25 February 1836, in *Laws and Ordinances*, 70–71.

42. *Gazette*, 10 March 1836; *American* reprinted in *Gazette*, 11 March 1836.

43. *American*, reprinted in the *Gazette*, 11 March 1836; also *Gazette*, 10 March 1836; *NWR*, 12 March 1836, 17–18.

44. *Report of the Joint Committee of the City Council, on the Subject of Internal Improvements* (Baltimore: s.n., 1836): 8, 10; *AR* 10 (1836): 5, 8 (quote). For the council's actions: Res. No. 40, passed 17 March 1836, in *Laws and Ordinances*, 144; Ord. No. 37, "An Ordinance making provision for the City's Subscription of Three Millions of Dollars to the capital stock of the Baltimore and Ohio Rail Road Company," passed 26 April 1836, in *Laws and Ordinances*, 144–146; the ordinance provided for an additional director for each five thousand shares of stock.

45. Thomas Tredgold, *A Practical Treatise on Rail-Roads and Carriages: Showing the Principles of Estimating their Strength, Proportions, Exercise, and Annual Produce, and the Conditions which render them Effective, Economical, and Durable; with the Theory, Effect, and Expense of Steam Carriages, Stationary Engines, and Gas Machines* (New York: E. Bliss & E. White, 1825), 1, 2.

46. William Darby, *The United States Reader, or Juvenile Instructor, No. 2* (Baltimore: Plaskitt & Co., 1829), 131–132, 135. I am indebted to Linda Lapides for this source. On misconceptions about the railroad, see P. E. Thomas to B. C. Howard, 21 February 1832, Box 3, RGFP; "Rail Roads," *North American, or, Weekly Journal of Politics, Science & Literature*, 16 June 1827, 35.

47. Berkshire (MA) *Star*, reproduced in the *American*, 8 May 1827.

48. *Experiments on Rail Roads, in England, illustrative of the Safety, Economy and Speed, of*

Transportation, which this system, as now improved, is capable of affording (Baltimore: William Wooddy, 1829), 3.

49. Minute Book A, 29 January 1831—Knight estimated the per-mile cost of the railroad at $38,294, a considerable increase over the estimate by the B&O's founders in 1827. See also United States, House of Representatives, 22nd Cong., 1st Sess. Doc. No. 101, *Report on Steam Carriages, by a Select Committee of the House of Commons of Great Britain: With the Minutes of Evidence and Appendix. Reprinted by Order of the House of Representatives* (Washington, DC: Duff Green, 1832), 205; *American*, 26 February 1827; *NWR*, 3 January 1829, 299.

50. *Proceedings of Sundry Citizens of Baltimore*, 6–7. The Baltimore press was quick to note occasions when freezing disrupted waterborne commerce: *NWR*, 23 April 1831, 136; *Gazette*, 20 November 1827. On canals and disease, see *American*, 15 January 1829.

51. *Gazette*, 2 February 1830; *NWR*, 28 November 1829, 209; also *Patriot*, 22 February 1826; *NWR*, 5 December 1829, 228; *NWR*, 16 January 1830, 337–338; *NWR*, 23 April 1831, 132–138; *Report on Steam Carriages*, 205.

52. *NWR*, 17 March 1827, 33–34 (quote on 34); *American*, 20 December 1830.

53. *Report on Steam Carriages*, 237, 322; George Rogers Taylor suggested that opposition to railroads came from "vested interests, timid individuals, and conservative communities fearful of innovation." Taylor, *Transportation Revolution*, 75. More recently, a hoax letter purportedly from Martin Van Buren to Andrew Jackson dated 31 January 1829, says that the national government must defend canals against upstart railroads—a facile historical lesson in the nature of progress. See "Van Buren's Letter to President Jackson," Snopes, http://www.snopes.com/history /document/vanburen.asp.

54. *Report on Steam Carriages*, 237 (quote). Civil engineer Benjamin Wright also noted that the advanced technology of the railroad placed repairs beyond the ability of most users (240). On the commodification of travel, see Will Mackintosh, "'Ticketed Through': The Commodification of Travel in the Nineteenth Century," *Journal of the Early Republic* 32 (Spring 2012): 61–89.

55. [William Hollins], *Rail Roads in the United States of America: or, Protest and Argument against a Subscription on the Part of the State of Maryland to the Baltimore and Ohio Rail-Road Company. Addressed to the officers and representatives of the People in the several states of the Union, and the general government. By a Citizen of Baltimore* (Baltimore: Matchett, Printer, 1827), 14 (first quote), 31 (second quote). See also *American*, 13 February 1830. Shortly after the publication of this pamphlet, a correspondent to the *Gazette* dismissed Hollins as a "disappointed schemer," scorned by his fellow citizens. *Gazette*, 5 March 1830.

56. Minus Ward, *Remarks, Propositions and Calculations, relative to a Rail-Road and Locomotive Engines to be used upon the same, from Baltimore to the Ohio River* (Baltimore: John D. Toy, 1827); John E. Semmes, *John H. B. Latrobe and His Times, 1803–1891* (Baltimore: Norman, Remington Co., 1917), 324–328. On the use of free black labor, see *NWR*, 27 August 1831, 452–453. For a concise description of the often-deadly labor, see Mary Ellen Hayward, *Baltimore's Alley Houses: Homes for Working People since the 1780s* (Baltimore: Johns Hopkins University Press, 2008), 69–71.

57. [Charles Warfield, Protest against the Baltimore and Ohio Rail Road taking possession of part of his lands for their line of the road] (Baltimore, 1828), esp. 1–2, 4, 7–8; *Baltimore Patriot*, 16 June 1829. On lumber poaching: *Gazette*, 25 February 1830. Mayor Jacob Small comments on the "great influx of strangers engaged in the public works" in his annual message for 1829; see Small, Mayor's Message, *Proceedings of the First Branch*, 5 January 1829, p. 67, Reel 357, RG16 S2, BCA.

58. *NWR*, 9 July 1831, 327; see also *American*, 21 August 1829; *NWR*, 22 August 1829, 409; *Ga-*

zette, 24 August 1829; *NWR*, 29 August 1829, 1; *Gazette*, 25 February 1830; *NWR*, 27 August 1831, 452-453. On alcohol: "Baltimore and Ohio Rail-Road," *Journal of Humanity and the American Temperance Society*, 17 February 1831, 153. On labor: Matthew E. Mason, "'The Hands Here Are Disposed to Be Turbulent': Unrest among the Irish Trackmen of the Baltimore and Ohio Railroad, 1829-1851," *Labor History* 39, no. 3 (1998): 253-272.

59. *NWR*, 12 June 1830, 290; also *Frederick Citizen*, reprinted in the *American*, 8 February 1830; *Gazette*, 16 February 1828; *NWR*, 13 September 1828, 40; *Gazette*, 5, 8, 18 January 1830; *Patriot*, 11 January 1830; *Philadelphia National Gazette* reprinted in the *New York Spectator*, 15 June 1830; Samuel G. Smith to his Wife, 3 March 1831, Samuel G. Smith Papers, 1830-1833, MS 2308, MdHS. Former New York mayor Philip Hone recorded a ride in the sail car in his diary: entry for 18 March 1830, *The Diary of Philip Hone, 1828-1851*, ed. Allan Nevins (New York: Dodd, Mead & Co., 1936), 21. On the speed of the sail car: *New York Spectator*, 29 January 1830. On the B&O's early engagement with steam locomotion, see Dilts, *Great Road*, ch. 7.

60. *New York Journal of Commerce* reprinted in *Boston Weekly Messenger*, 24 June 1830. For other comments on the smoothness and prospects of railroad enterprise, see *New York Spectator*, 15 June 1830; Erskine Caldwell, *Dwelling Place: A Plantation Epic* (New Haven, CT: Yale University Press, 2005), 94.

61. *NWR*, 26 June 1830, 317-319 ("*space* and *gravity*"), 17 March 1827, 33-34 ("unconquered steam"); also, *NWR*, 20 May 1826, 201; *Boston Weekly Messenger*, "Rail Roads," 29 January 1829.

62. *American*, 14 March 1827 ("an empire to our doors"); see also, *American*, 23 February 1827, 27 June 1827. Continent-island rhetoric may be found in Minute Book B, 22 December 1831; the *American* asserted that the B&O would place Baltimore "in the neighbourhood of the most thriving agricultural region of the world." *American*, 1 January 1829. See also Schivelbusch, *Railway Journey*, 41-48.

63. *NWR*, 20 May 1826, 201; 16 June 1827, 260; 19 April 1828, 122; 27 September 1828, 67.

64. *Gazette*, 16 February 1828.

65. *Proceedings of Sundry Citizens of Baltimore*, 5; *Picture of Baltimore, containing a description of all objects of interest in the city; and Embellished with Views of the Principal Public Buildings* (Baltimore: F. Lucas Jr., 1832), 200; *American*, 23 March 1829; *Gazette*, 19 February 1827, 18 September 1829; *AR* 3 (1829): 8.

66. *Gazette*, 17 March 1835.

67. *Gazette*, 29 January 1829. See also *Gazette*, 19 February 1827, 6 April 1827, 10 February 1829; *American*, 1 March 1827, 23 July 1827, 20 December 1830; *Patriot*, 15 December 1828, 20 January 1829, 8 May 1830; Minute Book B, 22 January, 22 December 1831; *NWR*, 2 April 1836, 80-82; Memorial of P. E. Thomas & Others, 13 January 1835, Box 50 [WPA 637], CCR.

68. *Report of the Engineers, on the Reconnoissance [sic] and Surveys*, 7-8, 75-76.

69. Minute Book C, 17 December 1835.

70. Charles Ellet Jr., *An Essay on the Laws of Trade in Reference to the Works of Internal Improvement in the United States* (1839; New York: Augustus M. Kelley, 1966), 21; see also *American*, 21 January 1840.

71. On nature and teleology in classical economics: Jose R. Torre, "'An Inward Spring of Motion and Action': The Teleology of Political Economy and Moral Philosophy in the Age of Anglo-American Enlightenment," *Early American Studies* 8, no. 3 (Fall 2010): 646-671; Fredrik Albritton Jonsson, "Rival Ecologies of Global Commerce: Adam Smith and the Natural Historians," *American Historical Review* 115, no. 5 (December 2010): 1342-1363; Bernard E. Har-

court, *The Illusion of Free Markets: Punishment and the Myth of Natural Order* (Cambridge, MA: Harvard University Press, 2011); Donald Worster, *Nature's Economy: A History of Ecological Ideas*, 2nd ed. (New York: Cambridge University Press, 1994), chs. 1–2; Joyce Appleby, *Capitalism and a New Social Order: The Republican Vision of the 1790s* (New York: New York University Press, 1984), 26–34. Margaret Schabas argues that in the mid-nineteenth century a view of the economy grounded in human agency rather physical nature took hold: *The Natural Origins of Economics* (Chicago: University of Chicago Press, 2005); see also Philip Mirowski, *More Heat Than Light: Economics as Social Physics, Physics as Nature's Economics* (New York: Cambridge University Press, 1989).

72. *Gazette*, 8 February 1828; see also *Gazette*, 14 February 1828.

73. *Gazette*, 16 June 1827 (quote); see also *Patriot*, 16 February 1828; *NWR*, 3 January 1829, 297–299; *NWR*, 3 April 1830, 107; *Gazette*, 14 February 1828.

74. *NWR*, 26 March 1831, 60 (quote); *NWR*, 4 October 1828, 81; *NWR*, 8 January 1831, 330; *American*, 25 February 1828; *American*, 23 March 1829. Similar arguments about the transformative power of trade (and the railroad's role in facilitating that) may be found in *Gazette*, 15 January 1828; "Rail Roads," *North American*, 16 June 1827, 35.

75. That is, the "*capacity for acquiring the necessaries and comforts of life.*" Daniel Raymond, *The Elements of Political Economy: In Two Parts*, 2nd ed. (Baltimore: F. Lucas, Jun., and E. J. Coale, 1823), quote on 47.

76. *NWR*, 4 October 1828, 81; *NWR*, 14 April 1827, 113; *NWR*, 4 December 1830, 235.

77. *Gazette*, 19 February 1827.

78. *American*, 24 January, 23 July 1829.

79. *American*, 7 April 1828.

80. *NWR*, 4 December 1830, 234–240. On Niles's background: T. Stephen Whitman, *Challenging Slavery in the Chesapeake: Black and White Resistance to Human Bondage, 1775–1865* (Baltimore: Maryland Historical Society, 2007), 111.

81. *NWR*, 5 December 1829, 227 (quote); *NWR*, 23 January 1830, 357.

82. *NWR*, 23 January 1830, 357; on Latrobe, see Phillips, *Freedom's Port*, 186; Semmes, *John H. B. Latrobe*, 139–150; Crenson, *Baltimore*, 167–173. On Thomas's activities: *Patriot*, 1 October 1817, 27 June 1820, 19 December 1820. On antislavery and free blacks in postrevolutionary white political economy: T. Stephen Whitman, *The Price of Freedom: Slavery and Manumission in Baltimore and Early National Maryland* (Lexington: University Press of Kentucky, 1997), 140–157. On racism and white visions of transportation modernity: Elizabeth Stordeur Pryor, *Colored Travelers: Mobility and the Fight for Citizenship before the Civil War* (Chapel Hill: University of North Carolina Press, 2016), 44–45.

83. *American*, 27 June 1827.

84. Aaron Marrs, *Railroads in the Old South: Pursuing Progress in a Slave Society* (Baltimore: Johns Hopkins University Press, 2009), 57–66.

85. The company's *Ninth Annual Report* in 1835 introduced a new metaphor, suggesting that each of these roads leading out of Baltimore could be "considered as so many great arteries, whose prolonged extension and spreading ramifications tend to increase and secure the healthy and vigorous growth of the city which may be termed the heart of the system." *AR* 9 (1835): 19.

86. *Boston Weekly Messenger*, 3 July 1828, 29 January 1829. On the Western, see Miner, *A Most Magnificent Machine*, 143–144; John F. Stover, *Iron Road to the West: American Railroads in the 1850s* (New York: Columbia University Press, 1978), 30–31.

87. *Philadelphia Public Ledger*, 1 November 1837, 14 April 1838; Albert J. Churella, *The Pennsylvania Railroad*, vol. 1, *The Building of an Empire, 1846–1919* (Philadelphia: University of Pennsylvania Press, 2013), 77–79, 96–100.

88. *New York Spectator*, 14 March 1836, 1 August 1839 (quote); "Important to Baltimore *and* to New York," *American Railroad Journal and Advocate of Internal Improvement*, 14 March 1835, 77. These were requests for public investment in an already-languishing line; see Miner, *Most Magnificent Machine*, 60–64.

89. *Gazette*, 19 February 1827; also *Gazette*, 3 September 1834; *American*, 7 April 1828; *Proceedings of Sundry Citizens of Baltimore*, 4. On the South Carolina Railroad, see Goodrich, *Government Promotion*, 101–105.

90. [John Pendleton Kennedy], *Letters of a Man of the Times, to the Citizens of Baltimore. (Originally Published in the American.)* (Baltimore: Sands & Neilson, 1836), 3, 4, 5, 7; *Journal of the Proceedings of the Convention on Internal Improvements of Maryland, Held in Baltimore, May 2, 1836* (Baltimore: John D. Toy, 1836), 9–11.

91. On parades: Susan G. Davis, *Parades and Power: Street Theatre in Nineteenth-Century Philadelphia* (Berkeley: University of California Press, 1986), esp. 3–5; Simon P. Newman, *Parades and the Politics of the Street: Festive Culture in the Early American Republic* (Philadelphia: University of Pennsylvania Press, 1997), esp. 7–8; Mary P. Ryan, *Women in Public: Between Banners and Ballots, 1825–1880* (Baltimore: Johns Hopkins University Press, 1990), 20–26. On the decision to inaugurate the railroad on July 4: *Gazette*, 2 April 1828; *American*, 2 April 1828; *Patriot*, 24 May 1828. On Freemasons: Minute Book A, 23 May 1828. The municipal government pledged $400 in public funds to support the event, and city politicians participated in the ceremony: Resolution accepting the invitation of the Committee of the directors of the Baltimore & Ohio Rail Road Co. for the members of the corporation to unite in the celebration of the 4th July etc., 12 June 1828, Box 37 [WPA 1124], CCR; Res. No. 6, approved 26 June 1828, in *Laws and Ordinances*, 126.

92. H. H. Wood to P. E. Thomas, 1828, B&O Papers; *Patriot*, 4, 5 June 1828.

93. *NWR*, 12 April 1828, 105.

94. Committee of Blacksmiths to P.E. Thomas, 9 June 1828, B&O Papers; *NWR*, 14 June 1828, 250.

95. *Detailed and Correct Account of the Grand Civic Procession in the City of Baltimore, on the Fourth of July, 1828; in Honor of the Day and in Commemoration of the Commencement of the Baltimore and Ohio Rail-Road, as published in the "American"* (Baltimore: Thomas Murphy, 1828), 3.

96. *Detailed and Correct Account of the Grand Civic Procession*, 14; *Gazette*, 21 June 1828; Dilts, *Great Road*, 7.

97. *Detailed and Correct Account of the Grand Civic Procession*, 5, 6, 8.

98. Blacksmiths and printers have been discussed already; stonecutters donated the marble that was used for the cornerstone: Committee of Stone Cutters to President and Directors of the B&O, 25 June 1828, B&O Papers.

99. *Detailed and Correct Account of the Grand Civic Procession*, 28, 33.

Chapter Two

1. Uhler is named as a stockholder in Minute Book A, 7 April 1828. On his workplace and occupation: *Matchett's City Director for 1827* (Baltimore: R. J. Matchett, 1827), 259; *Matchett's City Director for 1829* (Baltimore: R. J. Matchett, 1829), 321; *Gazette*, 11 April 1827, 29 May 1828.

The number of people in his household is from the manuscript census: 1830 U.S. Federal Census, Baltimore, MD, Ward 9. On his political and civic engagement: *Patriot*, 28 December 1816, 3 October 1817, 30 September 1819, 12, 13, 17 September 1821, 27 July 1826. On his support for John Quincy Adams and the American System (and his opposition to Andrew Jackson): *Patriot*, 20 October 1824, 29 February 1828; *Gazette*, 10 October 1832. On his charitable activities: *Gazette*, 4 February 1829, 18 January 1831; *Sun*, 29 December 1837. The newspaper notice of his death in 1855 says he was sixty-seven years old, which would make him around forty in 1828: *Sun*, 12 December 1855. For his opposition to the road see *Patriot*, 13 March 1829, 14 April 1830; *American*, 7 October 1830; Memorial of Philip Uhler and Others to the Mayor and City Council of Baltimore, 26 March 1835, Box 50 [WPA 618-A], CCR. News of the accident can be seen in *Sun*, 26 September 1837. The resolution to Uhler's lawsuit is in *Sun*, 4 March 1839. None of these accounts provides Mrs. Uhler's given name.

2. John R. Kellett, *The Impacts of Railways on Victorian Cities* (London: Routledge & Kegan Paul, 1969); Wolfgang Schivelbusch, *The Railway Journey: Trains and Travel in the 19th Century*, trans. Anselm Hollo (New York: Urizen Books, 1979); Sigfried Giedion, *Space, Time, and Architecture: The Growth of a New Tradition*, 5th ed. (Cambridge, MA: Harvard University Press, 1967); Ralf Roth and Marie-Noelle Polino, eds., *The City and the Railway in Europe* (Burlington, Vt.: Ashgate, 2003).

3. John H. B. Latrobe, *The Baltimore and Ohio Railroad. Personal Recollections. A Lecture, Delivered before the Maryland Institute, by John H. B. Latrobe, March 23d, 1868* (Baltimore: Sun Book and Job Printing, 1868), 8.

4. Ch. 209, "A Supplement to the Act, entitled, an Act to incorporate the Baltimore and Ohio Rail Road Company," in *Laws and Ordinances*, 30.

5. Solomon Etting to Phil. E. Thomas, President of the Rail Road Co., 26 May 1828, Box 6 [WPA 1234], MC (quote); *Patriot*, 6 June 1828; see also *NWR*, 28 June 1828, 282.

6. *Gazette*, 15 February 1831.

7. Sherry H. Olson, *Baltimore: The Building of an American City*, rev. ed. (Baltimore: Johns Hopkins University Press, 1997), 56–58; Mary P. Ryan, *Taking the Land to Make the City: A Bicoastal History of North America* (Austin: University of Texas Press, 2019), 152–160.

8. *First Annual Report of the Board of Engineers to the Board of Directors of the Baltimore and Ohio Rail Road Company* in *AR* 2 (1828): 5–7; see also Minute Book A, 24 June 1828.

9. S. H. Long and Wm. Gibbs McNeill, *Narrative of the Proceedings of the Board of Engineers of the Baltimore and Ohio Rail Road Company, from its Organization to its Dissolution, together with an Exposition of Facts, illustrative of the Conduct of Sundry Individuals* (Baltimore: Bailey & Francis, 1830), 20; also *Patriot*, 12 February 1829.

10. Minute Book A, 2 February 1829.

11. *Gazette*, 27, 28 February 1829. See also *Patriot*, 13, 16 March 1829; *Gazette*, 13 February 1829(quote), 4, 10 March 1829. Philip Uhler led a Ninth Ward meeting to oppose tunneling Lexington Hill.

12. [James Carroll], *The Claim of the Western Navigation of the City of Baltimore to a Rail Road Deposit, Stated and Considered* (Baltimore: John D. Toy, 1828), 8, 11–13; *American*, 29, 30, 31 January 1829; *Patriot*, 12 February 1829. On Carroll: Teresa S. Moyer, *Ancestors of Worthy Life: Plantation Slavery and Black Heritage at Mount Clare* (Gainesville: University Press of Florida, 2015), 145–147.

13. *Gazette*, 18 February 1829; also *American*, 24 January 1829.

14. *Gazette*, 15 October 1830.

15. Carroll, *Claim of the Western Navigation*, v; *Gazette*, 16 February 1829; *Patriot*, 11, 24 February 1829; Olson, *Baltimore*, 76–79.

16. Delaying decision on how to enter the city: Minute Book A, 2, 9 March 1829; *NWR*, 21 March 1829, 53; *Gazette* 16, 21 March 1829; *Communication from the Baltimore and Ohio Rail Road Company to the Mayor and City Council of Baltimore. Presented February 7th, 1831* (Baltimore: Lucas & Deaver, 1831), 6, 12. On the city's real estate: Matthew A. Crenson, *Baltimore: A Political History* (Baltimore: Johns Hopkins University Press, 2017), 119.

17. Those meetings are announced or their reports given in *American*, 10, 14, 15, 17, 18, 19, 21, 22, 26, 28 February, 2 March 1831.

18. *American*, 24 February 1831; see also *American*, 4 March 1831, 17, 18 February 1831.

19. *American*, 21 February 1831 (first quote), 16 February 1831 (second quote); also 18 February, 2 March 1831.

20. *Address to the Citizens of Baltimore, Relative to the Contemplated Extension of the Rail Road, down Pratt-Street, to the City Block. Adopted at an adjourned meeting of citizens of the Western and Southwestern sections of the city, held at the Union Engine Committee Room, Thursday evening, September 30, 1830* (Baltimore: Printed at the Office of the Baltimore Republican, 1830). The participants in the meeting sought to get out their message before the B&O formally presented the Pratt Street plan for municipal approval.

21. *Address to the Citizens of Baltimore*, quotes on 4 and 6.

22. *Communication from the Baltimore and Ohio Rail Road Company*, 12–14. Even before workers finished laying the tracks through Pratt Street, the company's allies in the press reported that all concerns about disruptions to ordinary use of the street had been proven false: *Gazette*, 13 August 1831, 10 September 1831; *Patriot*, 4 October 1831; *NWR*, 8 October 1831, 98.

23. Minute Book B, 14 February 1831.

24. Ord. No. 18, "An Ordinance relating to the Baltimore and Ohio Rail Road Company," approved 4 April 1831, in *Laws and Ordinances*, 134–35.

25. Frederick Douglass, *Life and Times of Frederick Douglass, Written by Himself*, in *Autobiographies* (1893; New York: Penguin, 1994), 524, 526, 531.

26. *Address to the Citizens of Baltimore* lays out these patterns explicitly. Examples of conflicts and negotiations in the streets abound in the Baltimore City Archives. See Petition from Josiah Lee . . . and Others, subject of Hacks standing in South Calvert st [*sic*] to have them removed, 26 June 1828, Box 34 [WPA 423], CCR; Petition of John Skinner and others on the Subject of Removing Hacks from North Calvert Street, March 1828, Box 34 [WPA 422], CCR; Hugh Young et al., Petition to First Branch of City Council, 16 February 1827, Box 32 [WPA 466], CCR; Petition to First Branch of City Council from Thomas Williams and Others, 20 March 1827, Box 32 [WPA 424], CCR; John McAllister et al., Petition to the First Branch of City Council, 27 February 1827, Box 32 [WPA 507], CCR. On black and white hackmen, see Memorial [of] Alexander Brown & others—Counter to the Memorial of Sundry Citizens of Baltimore Praying that Persons of Color may be prohibited from driving Hacks, Carts, and Drays, 23 January 1828, Box 34 [no WPA], CCR; *American*, 2 and 11 April 1828; Report & Resolution on the Petition of Gerard T. Hopkins & Others, 27 April 1830, Box 40 [WPA 823], CCR; Letter from Nat. Wiliams to Mayor William Steuart, Subject of Boys &c., 14 September 1831, Box 7 [WPA 474], MC; Crenson, *Baltimore*, 134–135, 145 (Small quote); Ryan, *Taking the Land*, 163–171. On multiple uses of the street in the nineteenth century: Francois Bedarida and Anthony Sutcliffe, "The Street in the Structure and Life of the City: Reflections on Nineteenth-Century London and Paris," *Journal of Urban History* 6, no. 4 (August 1980): 379–396.

27. Minute Book B, 26 March 1832.

28. Ord. No. 40, "An Ordinance to regulate Rail Road Cars within the City of Baltimore," approved 16 April 1832, in *Laws and Ordinances*, 137, 138.

29. An Ordinance Relative to Certain Obstructions on the Footways of the Streets of the City, 23 April 1831, Box 43 [WPA 1251], CCR.

30. Ord. No. 25, "An Ordinance to regulate the loading and unloading of Rail Road Cars, within the limits of direct taxation," approved 30 March 1833, in *Laws and Ordinances*, 142.

31. *Communication from the Baltimore and Ohio Rail Road Company*, 11–12; Louis William Jenkins to P. E. Thomas, 22 March 1832, Box 44 [WPA 747], CCR; Minute Book B, 26 March 1832; Philip E. Thomas to J. H. Dorsey, Clerk of the City Commissioners, 12 May 1832, Box 42 [WPA 117], CComR; City Commissioners to the President & Directors of the B&O Rail Road Co., 11 & 12 May 1832, B&O Papers; Ch. 252. "An Act to vest certain powers in the Mayor and City Council of Baltimore," passed 9 March 1832, in *Laws and Ordinances*, 42–43.

32. Ord. No. 41, "An Ordinance to authorize the construction of certain Railways within the City," approved 6 April 1832, in *Laws and Ordinances*, 138–142, quote on 141; Ord. No. 42, approved 4 April 1832 and Ord. No. 26, approved 3 April 1833, both titled "A Supplement to an Ordinance entitled, an Ordinance to authorize the construction of certain Railways within this City," in *Laws and Ordinances*, 142, 143; Report of the Committee on Streets Relative to a Rail Way in Gay Street, 6 April 1835, Box 51 [WPA 803], CCR; Petition of Hopkins & Brothers for Tracks on Hollingsworth St., 1 February 1832, Box 43 [WPA 428], CCR. See also WPA nos. 464, 455, 465, and 89 for 1832.

33. Franz Anton Ritter von Gerstner, *Die innern Communicationen (Early American Railroads)*, ed. Frederick C. Gamst, trans. David J. Diephouse and John C. Decker (Stanford, CA: Stanford University Press, 1997 [1842–1843]), 597–599, 650. For the patent: *American Railroad Journal & Advocate of Internal Improvements*, 23 April 1836, 248.

34. Report and Resolution Entitled "A supplement to an Ordinance relating to the Baltimore and Ohio Rail road Company," 16 March 1835, Box 51 [WPA 887], CCR.

35. *American Railroad Journal*, 23 June 1832, 405 for these figures; on congestion, bustle, and the railroad: *Gazette*, 20 October 1832; see also *NWR*, 27 October 1832, 129–130; Report of the Select Committee on the Memorial of Philip Uhler, 4 (quote); see also *NWR*, 12 September 1835, 17.

36. *Patriot*, 13 February 1830, 5 October 1830 (quote); see also *American*, 9 April 1831.

37. *Gazette*, 26 April 1828 (quote); see also *Gazette*, 13 August 1831; *American*, 3 January 1832, 24 May, 6 June 1831.

38. Mary Ellen Hayward, *Baltimore's Alley Houses: Homes for Working People since the 1780s* (Baltimore: Johns Hopkins University Press, 2008), 74–76. These transactions are recorded in Minute Book A, 11 May 1829, 3 August 1829; Minute Book B, 5, 20 May 1831, 6 June 1831.

39. Katie M. Hemphill, "Selling Sex and Intimacy in the City: The Changing Business of Prostitution in Nineteenth-Century Baltimore," in *Capitalism by Gaslight: Illuminating the Economy of Nineteenth-Century America*, ed. Brian P. Luskey and Wendy A. Woloson (Philadelphia: University of Pennsylvania Press, 2015), 168–189, esp. 175–179. Some of these new buildings would have been clad in granite, as the B&O made quarries available for use in Baltimore's architecture: *Patriot*, 10 June 1831; *American*, 22 April 1831; *Gazette*, 28 March 1832; *NWR*, 6 September 1834, 6.

40. New York and Harlem Rail Road Company, *A statement of facts in relation to the origin, progress, and prospects of the New-York and Harlem Rail Road Company* (New York: George P. Scott & Co., 1833), 4 (quote), 12. See also Ely Moore, *Reply to the Pamphlet entitled "A statement*

of facts in relation to the origin progress and prospects of the New York and Harlem Rail Road Company" (New York: Peter Van Pelt, 1833), 21–22; *New York Spectator*, 1 May 1832. On the right of the common council to remove the rails: New York & Harlem Minutes for 18 May 1832, Vol. 1, Reel 26, Mss. Col 2372, Penn Central Transportation Company Records, 1796–1986, New York Public Library. Bostonians, too, had their eye on Baltimore—see *Boston Weekly Messenger*, 3 July 1828.

41. *Charleston Southern Patriot*, 4 December 1832.

42. Evan Thomas to Thomas P. Cope, 15 April 1835, Cope Family Papers, 1787–1908, Series III, Subseries a., Thomas P. Cope Personal Papers, Historical Society of Pennsylvania; Philip E. Thomas to Thomas P. Cope, 19 April 1835, Cope Personal Papers. See also Joel Schwartz, "'To Every Man's Door': Railroads and the Use of Streets in Jacksonian Philadelphia," *Pennsylvania Magazine of History and Biography* 128, no. 1 (January 2004): 35–61.

43. *Sun*, 5 April 1838.

44. Charlestown (VA) *Free Press* reprinted in *New York Spectator*, 7 May 1835.

45. Quoted in Eric Foner, *Gateway to Freedom: The Hidden History of the Underground Railroad* (New York: W. W. Norton, 2015), 17.

46. Douglass, *Life and Times*, 636, 641–647, quotes on 645, 647; on assistance from Anna Murray, see T. Stephen Whitman, *Challenging Slavery in the Chesapeake: Black and White Resistance to Human Bondage, 1775–1865* (Baltimore: Maryland Historical Society, 2007), 177, 257n29; David W. Blight, *Frederick Douglass: Prophet of Freedom* (New York: Simon & Schuster, 2018), 81–82, 84–85. See also Elizabeth Stordeur Pryor, *Colored Travelers: Mobility and the Fight for Citizenship before the Civil War* (Chapel Hill: University of North Carolina Press, 2016), 55–57.

47. *Sun*, 7 December 1840; *Philadelphia Public Ledger*, 10 December 1839.

48. Ch. 375, "An Act entitled an Act to prevent the transportation of People of Color, upon Rail Roads or in Steamboats," passed 4 April 1839, in *Laws and Ordinances*, 110–111. The title of the act says "People of Color," but the language in the body refers to "slaves."

49. Extra Session Ord. No. 6, "An Ordinance to direct the appointment of Special Police in favor of the Baltimore and Ohio Rail Road Company," approved 16 December 1853, in *Ordinances*, 12. They were outfitted with the accouterments of police power: Ord. No. 9, "An Ordinance in relation to Constables employed by the Baltimore and Ohio Rail-Road Company, Baltimore and Susquehanna Rail-Road Company, and Philadelphia, Wilmington, and Baltimore Rail-Road Company," approved 8 March 1853, in *Ordinances*, 16. Quote from "An Act to Amend the Act of 1826 ch. 123 and to give certain police powers to the Baltimore and Ohio Rail road Company," [1860?], Box 83, Folder 7559, GPC.

50. Minute Book D, 4 August 1841; John H. B. Latrobe to John W. Garrett, 1 April 1859, Box 89, Folder 13447, GPC. The PWB, because of its direct route to Philadelphia (and hence New York), had to pay such compensation more frequently than the B&O: PWB Minute Book, Vol. 1, 10 March 1840. The B&O did have to pay sometimes: Minute Book F, 9 January 1850. The last record of a foiled escape attempt I have is from *Sun*, 3 June 1861.

51. Report & Resolution on the Petition of Sundry Hackmen, Draymen and Carters for the Removal of the Rail Road out of the City, 19 March 1835, Box 51 [WPA 805], CCR. Track supporters claimed that "true" working-class Baltimoreans supported the railroad for "rais[ing]" our city from despondency to prosperity." *Gazette*, 11 and 19 October 1833; Report of the Select Committee on the Memorial of Philip Uhler and Others, 30 March 1835, Box 51 [WPA 804], CCR. On licensing, regulation, and rights: Robert J. Gamble, "The Promiscuous Economy: Cultural and Commercial Geographies of Secondhand in the Antebellum City," in *Capitalism by Gaslight*,

31–52, esp. 38–39; Martha S. Jones, *Birthright Citizens: A History of Race and Rights in Antebellum America* (New York: Cambridge University Press, 2018), 92–101.

52. Petition of William Drake and Others by George Gardiner, 4 February 1833, Box 45 [WPA 586], CCR. The petition suggested a tax on B&O cars to resolve this inequity. See also Petition of Carters & Draymen respecting obstructions in Pratt Street, & Rail Road Cars, 1833, Box 10 [WPA 1075], MC; and Petition of John McAlister, March 1835, Box 50 [WPA 618-A], CCR.

53. Carters & Draymen, "City Police," 1833, Box 10 [WPA 382], MC. See also Petition of William Drake and Others by George Gardiner, 4 February 1833, Box 45 [WPA 586], CCR; Petition of John McAlister and others Praying that the Rail Tracks may be Removed from the Streets, March 1835, Box 50 [WPA 618-A], CCR.

54. Report of the Joint Committee on Railroads, 19 March 1834, 1–2, Box 48 [WPA 635], CCR.

55. Minute Book B, 26 April 1831, 5, 20 May 1831, 6 June 1831, 5 September 1831; *NWR*, 14 January 1832, 375; Report & Resolution discharging the Committee on Streets from further considering a subject therein mentioned, 6 March 1832, Box 45 [WPA 804], CCR; Minute Book C, 27 May 1833; Petition of James Barroll and others relative to Franklin Street, 2 March 1832, Box 43 [WPA 462], CCR; Minute Book B, 24 June 1831, 1 August 1831, 14 December 1831.

56. Report of the Joint Committee on Rail Roads, on the Sewer in Pratt Street & the Rail Road in the Same Street, 6 March 1835, 1–4, Box 51 [WPA 800], CCR.

57. *New York Spectator*, 7 June, 13 August 1838.

58. *Sun*, 17 November 1837 (John Ball), 30 March 1840 (Lanchart Machey, quote); also Latrobe, *Personal Recollections*, 12; *Patriot*, 26 July 1834.

59. See, e.g., *Sun*, 26 September 1837, 8, 17 November 1837.

60. *Patriot*, 26 July 1834.

61. *Sun*, 18 June 1838.

62. Minute Book D, 9 January 1839; *Sun*, 4 March 1839. For examples of indemnities paid for street accidents, see Minute Book C, 18 January and 22 February 1836. On press coverage of the Uhler accident and lawsuit: Charleston (SC) *Southern Patriot*, 3 October 1837; Philadelphia *National Gazette*, 7 March 1839; *New York Spectator*, 11 March 1839 ("ordinary care"); Newark (NJ) *Centinel of Freedom*, 12 March 1839. On the law of railway accidents: Barbara Young Welke, *Recasting American Liberty: Gender, Race, Law, and the Railroad Revolution, 1865–1920* (New York: Cambridge University Press, 2001), pt. 1.

63. *American*, 12 October 1833; see also William R. Sutton, *Journeymen for Jesus: Evangelical Artisans Confront Capitalism in Jacksonian Baltimore* (University Park: Pennsylvania State University Press, 1998), 35–36.

64. Report of the Joint Committee on Railroads, on the Sewer in Pratt Street & the Rail Road in the Same Street, 6 March 1835, 6–9, Box 51 [WPA 800], CCR; Report & Resolution, relation to the Rail Way in Pratt Street, 19 March 1834, Box 48 [WPA 657], CCR.

65. *Patriot*, 24 and 26 (quote) March 1834.

66. Solomon Etting & Others, Petition for Removing Rail Road Track from Pratt Street, 4 March 1835, Box 50 [WPA 702], CCR.

67. Based on tallies of pro- and anti-track petitions collected at the BCA in the CCR for 1835, WPA nos. 618 and 618-A. I have included in these tallies WPA no. 702 for 1835, which is an anti-track petition by Solomon Etting that circulated simultaneously. I have also included WPA no. 803 for 1837, which is identical to printed copies of petition 1835:618-A and therefore, I think, misfiled with the 1837 records.

68. The pro-removal petitions: Solomon Etting & Others, Petition for Rail Road Track from

Pratt Street, 4 March 1835 [WPA 702]; Petition of John McAlister, March 1835, [WPA 618-A]; Memorial of Philip Uhler and Others to the Mayor and City Council of Baltimore, 26 March 1835, Box 50 [WPA 618-A], CCR. There are several signatories to the pro-permanency petitions, but they all take the form of the Memorial from James Jackson & Others, 25 March 1835, Box 50 [WPA 618], CCR.

69. Report and Resolution Entitled "A supplement to an Ordinance relating to the Baltimore and Ohio Rail road Company," 16 March 1835, p. 3, Box 51 [WPA 887], CCR. On the politics of the Joint Committee and Select Committee, see Crenson, *Baltimore*, 139-141.

70. Report of the Minority of the Select Committee Relative to the Rail Ways in the City, 19 March 1835, 1-3, Box 51 [WPA 799], CCR; also Memorial of Philip Uhler, 26 March 1835 [WPA 618-A].

71. *NWR*, 11 April 1835, 89; *NWR*, 25 April 1835, 129.

72. There was another round of petitions in 1840, for example: Petition from Benjamin C. Howard & Others, Praying for Removal of the Track, &c. 11 March 1840, Box 64 [WPA 337], CCR; *American*, 5, 10, 11 March 1840.

73. *Gazette*, 26 June 1834; also, Report and Resolution Entitled "A supplement to an Ordinance relating to the Baltimore and Ohio Rail road Company"; *American*, 24 March 1834.

74. *American*, 24 February 1831 (quote); see also *American*, 27 February, 4, 23 March 1829.

75. Report of the Joint Committee on Railroads (1835), 6-9. See also Report of the Minority of the Select Committee, 9-10.

76. *Communication from the Baltimore and Ohio Rail Road Company, to the Mayor and City Council of Baltimore*, 12; see also Minute Book B, 14 February 1831.

77. *American*, 19 February 1831; see also *American*, 14 February 1831; *American*, 26 March 1834; *Gazette*, 17 March 1835; Report and Resolution entitled "A supplement to an Ordinance relating to the Baltimore and Ohio Rail road Company," 4.

78. Minute Book C, 2 February 1836; Minute Book D, 11, 12, 18 October 1836.

79. *Reports of the Committees Respecting the Rail Road Depots in the City of Baltimore* (Baltimore: Joseph Robinson, [1837]), 3-5, 7-9; Minute Book D, 1 March 1837.

80. *Reports of the Committees Respecting the Rail Road Depots*, 16, 19.

81. Preamble & Resolution on the Subject of the Rail Road Depots, &c., 5 April 1837, Box 57 [WPA 1297], CCR.

82. Ibid.

83. Memorial to the Directors of the Baltimore & Ohio R. R. Co., 11 December 1838, PWB Board Papers. The PWB relocated its depot to the President Street Station in 1849: *Sun*, 9 April 1849.

84. Robert E. Shalhope, *The Baltimore Bank Riot: Political Upheaval in Antebellum Maryland* (Urbana: University of Illinois Press, 2009).

Chapter Three

1. *Sun*, 26 January 1842.

2. Estimates from John Kenneth Galbraith, *Money: Whence It Came, Where It Went* (Boston: Houghton Mifflin, 1975), 89. On shinplasters, see Joshua R. Greenberg, "The Era of Shinplasters: Making Sense of Unregulated Paper Money," in *Capitalism by Gaslight: Illuminating the Economy of Nineteenth-Century America*, ed. Brian P. Luskey and Wendy A. Woloson (Philadelphia: University of Pennsylvania Press, 2015), 53-75.

3. On the difficulties travelers had exchanging money on the road, see the story of William Lowndes, published in the *National Intelligencer* and reprinted in *American*, 23 October 1841; George T. Starnes, *Sixty Years of Branch Banking in Virginia* (New York: Macmillan, 1931), 96–97. Peter Temin explains this localized system in *The Jacksonian Economy* (New York: Norton, 1969), 31–36; see also Jessica M. Lepler, *The Many Panics of 1837: People, Politics, and the Creation of a Transatlantic Financial Crisis* (New York: Cambridge University Press, 2013), 16; Jane Kamensky, *The Exchange Artist: A Tale of High-Flying Speculation and America's First Banking Collapse* (New York: Viking, 2008), 51–54.

4. Stephen Mihm, *A Nation of Counterfeiters: Capitalists, Con Men, and the Making of the United States* (Cambridge, MA: Harvard University Press, 2007).

5. Moments of crisis provide opportunities to reflect on the social construction of the economy, though not always to change it: Lepler, *Many Panics of 1837*; Sean Patrick Adams, "How Choice Fueled Panic: Philadelphians, Consumption, and the Panic of 1837," *Enterprise & Society* 12, no. 4 (December 2011): 761–789; Ann Fabian, "Speculation on Distress: The Popular Discourse on the Panics of 1837 and 1857," *Yale Journal of Criticism* 3, no. 1 (Fall 1989): 127–142; Mary Poovey, *Genres of the Credit Economy: Mediating Value in Eighteenth- and Nineteenth-Century Britain* (Chicago: University of Chicago Press, 2008), 5–7.

6. Although a few have argued that states exercised monetary policy in the Jacksonian era, municipal monetary policy warrants further investigation. On states, see Jay C. Shambaugh, "An Experiment with Multiple Currencies: The American Monetary System from 1838–60," *Explorations in Economic History* 43 (2006): 609–645. Joshua Greenberg comments on the use of city scrip in times of financial hardship but characterizes the practice as illegal or extralegal, which was not the case for the B&O note: Greenberg, "Era of Shinplasters," 60–61.

7. Most recently, political scientist Matthew A. Crenson offers this positivist view on the notes' viability: "No amount of official recognition could save the stock orders from their fate. They were doomed to depreciate because they were backed by city bonds that traded at much less than face value." Crenson, *Baltimore: A Political History* (Baltimore: Johns Hopkins University Press, 2017), 181–183, quote on 182. The notes were doubtlessly an exploitative exercise, but to frame their history around fundamental laws of currency misses a far more interesting question of political economy. See also Gary Lawson Browne, *Baltimore in the Nation, 1789–1861* (Chapel Hill: University of North Carolina Press, 1980), 133–134; John A. Munroe, *Louis McLane: Federalist and Jacksonian* (New Brunswick, NJ: Rutgers University Press, 1973), 481–485, 493–496.

8. Jeffrey Sklansky points out that until the early twentieth century, the money question in America was intrinsically tied to class struggle: Sklansky, *Sovereign of the Market: The Money Question in Early America* (Chicago: University of Chicago Press, 2017).

9. *NWR*, 26 April 1834, 133. On currency, credit, and specie: *NWR*, 23 January 1830, 355–356; *NWR*, 19 July 1834, 345–346. On capitalism as confidence game: Mihm, *Nation of Counterfeiters*, esp. 6–11. On the tensions between interpretations of economic trends as market-driven and caused by individuals in this period: Jeffrey Sklansky, "William Leggett and the Melodrama of the Market," in *Capitalism Takes Command: The Social Transformation of Nineteenth-Century America*, ed. Michael Zakim and Gary J. Kornblith (Chicago: University of Chicago Press, 2012), 199–221.

10. For a detailed account of the historiography on the Panic of 1837, see Jessica M. Lepler, "1837: Anatomy of a Panic" (PhD diss., Brandeis University, 2008), 9–14. See also Edward E. Baptist, "Toxic Debt, Liar Loans, Collateralized and Securitized Human Beings, and the Panic of 1837," in *Capitalism Takes Command*, 69–92.

11. Mayor's Communication to City Council, 15 May 1837, Box 58 [WPA 663], CCR.

12. Sklansky, *Sovereign of the Market*, 93–98, 124–130; Eli Cook, *The Pricing of Progress: Economic Indicators and the Capitalization of American Life* (Cambridge, MA: Harvard University Press, 2017), 123–125; Sean Wilentz, *The Rise of American Democracy, Jefferson to Lincoln* (New York: W. W. Norton, 2005), 413–423, 438–441.

13. Browne, *Baltimore in the Nation*, 149–150; Crenson, *Baltimore*, 129–131; Robert E. Shalhope, *The Baltimore Bank Riot: Political Upheaval in Antebellum Maryland* (Urbana: University of Illinois Press, 2009), 21 (for reference to newspapers' party affiliations) and passim.

14. *American*, 23 October 1839.

15. *Sun*, 26 May 1837; also 31 May 1837, 7, 9 May 1838.

16. *American*, 8 October 1839; *Gazette*, 5 October 1836.

17. *Clipper*, 9 January 1841.

18. Resumption was planned, effected, and resuspended in the autumns of 1838 and 1839—*American*, 4 January 1838, 14 August 1838, 8 October 1839.

19. *American*, 11 October 1839.

20. Georg Simmel drew the connection directly, arguing that the intertwined ascendance of the money economy and the metropolis reflected the increasing pace and interconnectedness of modern life: *The Philosophy of Money*, ed. David Frisby, trans. Tom Bottomore and David Frisby, 2nd ed. (1907; London: Routledge, 1990), 300–301, 498–508. On the urban character of currency: David Henkin, *City Reading: Written Words and Public Spaces in Antebellum New York* (New York: Columbia University Press, 1998), ch. 6; Seth Rockman, *Scraping By: Wage Labor, Slavery, and Survival in Early Baltimore* (Baltimore: Johns Hopkins University Press, 2009), 174.

21. Mayor's Communication to City Council, 15 May 1837, [WPA 663]; *American*, 24 May 1838, 14 August 1838. On the nationwide ban on small notes: Susan Hoffman, *Politics and Banking: Ideas, Public Policy, and the Creation of Financial Institutions* (Baltimore: Johns Hopkins University Press, 2001), 66; Greenberg, "Era of Shinplasters," 58.

22. Mayor's Communication to City Council, 15 May 1837, [WPA 663]. The *Gazette* declared these small notes removed the earlier "difficulty of making change." *Gazette*, 18 July 1837; see also *Gazette*, 26 May 1837. On a public solution as a way to forestall shinplasters: *American*, 16 October 1839. Smith did not himself allude to other cities, but this was a not-uncommon approach to an all-too-common problem: Greenberg, "Era of Shinplasters," 60–61.

23. *Gazette*, 13 May 1837. See also: Mayor's Communication to City Council, 15 May 1837, [WPA 663].

24. *Gazette*, 24 July 1837.

25. *Sun*, 5 May 1838.

26. *Sun*, 13 July 1837, 30 December 1837, 7 November 1839.

27. *Sun*, 21 November 1839; see also *Sun*, 7 November 1839.

28. Efforts in 1839 to issue $400,000 more in notes ranging from $0.50 to $2 foundered when the mayor vetoed the bill on a technicality. Committee Report & Resolution of the Minority of the Joint Committee of Ways and Means, 14 October 1839, Box 62 [WPA 1067], CCR; *Sun*, 15 October 1839; *American*, 16, 19 October 1839.

29. *Gazette*, 13 August 1831; *NWR*, 15 November 1834, 161; *NWR*, 20 December 1834, 259.

30. Edward Hungerford, *The Story of the Baltimore & Ohio Railroad, 1827–1927*, 2 vols. (New York: G. P. Putnam's Sons, 1928), 1:135–141.

31. *American*, 15 October 1839.

32. *Baltimore Republican* reprinted in the *New York Spectator*, 18 May 1837; James D. Dilts,

The Great Road: The Building of the Baltimore & Ohio, the Nation's First Railroad, 1828–1853 (Stanford, CA: Stanford University Press, 1993), 223–227; John E. Semmes, *John H. B. Latrobe and His Times, 1803–1891* (Baltimore: Norman, Remington Co., 1917), 358–362.

33. Dilts, *Great Road*, 223–227; Munroe, *Louis McLane*, 232, 439, 448–449, 451, 457–459.

34. Joseph Patterson served as president pro tem in the months between Thomas's resignation and McLane's somewhat belated arrival: Dilts, *Great Road*, 224, 227 (quote).

35. Minute Book D, 13, 27 (quotes) November 1839.

36. An anonymous B&O insider explained the plan in a two-part series of editorials in the *American*, 6, 7 December 1839. The official unveiling of the program was in the company's *AR* 13 (1839 [1840]): 10–12, released on New Year's Day, 1840. On Leakin's endorsement: Mayor's Communication to City Council, 6 January 1840, in *Ordinances*, 9; on Democratic support: Browne, *Baltimore in the Nation*, 154.

37. *Sun*, 22 October 1838 (quote), 7 January 1840.

38. *American*, 4 January 1840.

39. Minute Book D, 4 December 1839; *American*, 22 January 1840.

40. *Baltimore Republican* printed in the *American*, 24 January 1840 (quotes); *AR* 14 (1840): 12–13.

41. On the assessment and taxation of real and personal property, including enslaved people: J. H. Hollander, *The Financial History of Baltimore* (Baltimore: Johns Hopkins University Press, 1899), 140–144; Rockman, *Scraping By*, 234–235; T. Stephen Whitman, *The Price of Freedom: Slavery and Manumission in Baltimore and Early National Maryland* (Lexington: University Press of Kentucky, 1997), 15–16; Robin L. Einhorn, *American Taxation, American Slavery* (Chicago: University of Chicago Press, 2006), 107–108, 208–209.

42. *Clipper*, 29 January 1841 (quote); *American*, 7 February 1840; *Sun*, 12 November 1841. The Committee of Finance made a similar argument: Minute Book D, 27 November 1839.

43. *Memorial of the Baltimore and Ohio Rail Road Company to the Legislature of Maryland* ([Baltimore], 1841), 4–5; *AR* 14 (1840): 12–13.

44. Minute Book D, 11 and 18 December 1839, 5 February 1840, 4 March 1840, 1 April 1840. On the amount in circulation: *AR* 14 (1840): 11.

45. On the illegality of the B&O's notes denominated less than $5: *Sun*, 1 February 1841.

46. See, for example, Petition of Henry D. Watson & others, 2 March 1840, Box 65, [WPA 339], CCR. The Baltimore Butchers' Association called on the City Council to authorize the issue of fractional notes and agreed that their members would accept only B&O notes, city scrip, and Frederick County Bank notes as tender: *American*, 20 February 1840.

47. Minute Book D, 10 February 1841; *Memorial of the Baltimore and Ohio Rail Road Company*, 4–5 (quote).

48. *Sun*, 11 February 1841.

49. *Clipper*, "The Common Good," 9 January 1841; see also *Clipper*, "RESUMPTION," 12 January 1841.

50. *American*, 19 May 1841; see also *Sun*, 18 March 1841, 10 May 1841, and *Clipper*, 20 May 1841.

51. *Sun*, 11 August 1840, 16 February 1841; *American*, 4 February 1842. The twelve-and-a-half-cent note modified to look like a fifty-cent note: *Sun*, 28 July 1841; also *Sun*, 15 March 1841. On the problems of "reading" money: Poovey, *Genres of the Credit Economy*; Joe Conway, "Making Beautiful Money: Currency Connoisseurship in the Nineteenth Century United States," *Nineteenth-Century Contexts* 34, no. 5 (December 2012): 427–443.

52. *Sun*, 27 October 1840.

53. Res. No. 29, passed 25 February 1841, in *Laws and Ordinances*, 155–156. On theft of shin-plasters: Greenberg, "Era of Shinplasters," 69. A case of pickpocketing: *Sun*, 20 July 1841.

54. *Sun*, 16 July 1841, see also *Sun*, 26 August 1841; *Sun*, 5 June 1841; *Clipper*, 3 June 1841.

55. PWB Minute Book, Vol. 1, 21 October 1841.

56. *Sun*, 23 July 1840, 11 August 1840, 5 November 1841. On small note circulation in Washington: *National Intelligencer* reprinted in the *American*, 18 November 1841. A Delaware paper warned its constituents against these notes as early as February—see *Clipper*, 3 February 1841.

57. *Sun*, 13 March 1841. Complaints came from Georgetown (*Sun*, 15 May 1841; *American*, 18 May 1841) and Alexandria (*Sun*, 20 July 1841).

58. *Sun*, 24 August 1841.

59. *Sun*, 7 February 1842. *Gouge's* referred to a long-standing monetary principle that later in the nineteenth century would be dubbed "Gresham's law." But as economists have noted, in addition to the many historical exceptions to this so-called law, "bad" money will only drive out "good" in the presence of legal strictures requiring people to accept both monies at face value; there were no such laws in Baltimore. See George Selgin, "Gresham's Law," *EH.Net Encyclopedia*, ed. Robert Wharples, 9 June 2003, http://eh.net/encyclopedia/article/selgin.gresham.law.

60. *Sun*, 24 August 1841.

61. *Memorial of the Baltimore and Ohio*, 6; *Clipper*, 4, 27 January 1841; *American*, 2, 28 January 1841.

62. Ch. 25, "An Act entitled an Act to authorize the Banks of the State of Maryland to receive and pay out the Orders drawn by the Baltimore and Ohio Rail Road Company, on the Stock of the City of Baltimore," passed 25 January 1841, in *Laws and Ordinances*, 112.

63. Minute Book D, 1 February 1841.

64. *Clipper*, 29 January 1841; *Sun*, 11 March 1841; *Patriot* reprinted in *Sun*, 1 October 1841; *American*, 1 October 1841; *AR* 15 (1841): 15.

65. *American*, 2 February 1841 (quote); *Clipper*, 15, 17 March 1841; *Sun*, 7 May 1841. On brokers and shavers: *Sun*, 15 October 1841. A respondent to this claim pointed to the "larger transgressions of the bankers": *Sun*, 26 October 1841.

66. "The people's circulation" is from a letter to the *American*, 25 November 1841; see also *American*, 2, 4, 8 February 1841.

67. *Clipper*, 31 March 1841, 1 April 1841.

68. *Clipper*, 3, 15 February 1841, 15, 17 March 1841, 2 April 1841 (quote); *American*, 3, 4 February 1841; *Sun*, 22 October 1841; Shalhope, *Baltimore Bank Riot*.

69. *Sun*, 26 February, 27 October 1841 (quote).

70. *Sun*, 5 October 1841; also *Sun*, 2 (quote), 28 December 1841.

71. *Sun*, 2 March 1842; see also *Sun*, 12 February 1842.

72. *Sun*, 4 February 1841. The council undertook these conversations at Mayor Sam Brady's suggestion: Mayor Sam Brady to City Council, 1 February 1841, Box 66 [WPA 412], CCR; Res. No. 9, passed 9 February 1841, in *Laws and Ordinances*, 154; *Clipper*, 6 February 1841. The council assigned guilt to the bankers, not the B&O: Preamble & Resolution Relating to the Stock Orders of the Balto & O RR Co, 24 December 1841, Box 69 [WPA 665], CCR.

73. *Sun*, 8 November 1841.

74. *Argus* cited in *Sun*, 10 November 1841.

75. *AR* 15 (1841): 18.

76. *American*, 16 October 1841.

77. *American*, 19, 20, 29 October 1841, 27, 29 November 1841, 3 December 1841, 20 January 1842, and "Measure of Common Sense" and "Equal Justice" from 27 January 1842.

78. *Sun*, 4 November 1841; on the ward meetings to elect representatives: *American*, 15 November 1841. On the Franklin Bank and its earlier failure: *Clipper*, 5, 7 January 1841.

79. Currency Committee to the Pres. and Directors of the Franklin Bank (Copy), 8 November 1841, Box 23 [WPA 878], MC (N.B., this item is filed with the papers for 1842); *American*, 13, 16 (quote) November 1841. The *Sun* (15 November 1841) anticipated the unusual spectacle of a "run" on the bank—"not to draw money out, but to put railroad orders in."

80. Mayor's Message, 17 January 1842, in *Sun*, 18 January 1842. See also *Sun*, 29 November 1841.

81. *Sun*, 27 October 1841.

82. *Sun*, 6 November 1841.

83. *American*, 10 December 1841.

84. Quoted in *American*, 2 November 1841. See also *American*, 6 February 1841.

85. "Creditor cities": American, "THE CURRENCY—*Fiscal Agencies*," 3 December 1841; "every rule of banking": American, 10 March 1842. Philadelphia and Baltimore experienced sharper currency contractions after the Panic of 1837 than New York and Boston: *New York Spectator*, 1 October 1839.

86. *American*, 3 December 1841; see also *American*, 15 February 1842.

87. *Sun*, 26 October 1841. The first meeting took place on September 30, and filled the Union Hall—*Sun*, 1 October 1841.

88. *Sun*, 13, 21 January 1842; see also *Clipper*, 15 February, 9 March 1841.

89. *Sun*, 28, 29, 30 October 1841, 4, 5 November 1841.

90. *Sun*, 21 January 1842. Van Ness's occupation from *Matchett's Baltimore Directory for 1842* (Baltimore, 1842), 382.

91. *Sun*, 2 December 1841; see also *American*, 29 October, 21 December 1841.

92. *New York Weekly Herald*, 13 November 1841, 5 March 1842 ("Ducklegs").

93. *American*, 6 December 1841; *American*, 13, 24 December 1841; *New York Spectator*, 1 October 1839.

94. Minute Book D, 8 October 1841.

95. Minute Book D, 30, 31 December 1841.

96. Minute Book D, 2 February 1842.

97. Sam Brady to City Council, 16 December 1841, Box 66 [WPA 411], CCR; Report of the Committee of Ways and Means on the Currency, 22 December 1841, Box 69 [WPA 574], CCR; "An Ordinance to Provide for the Redemption of the Stock Orders of the Balto & Ohio Rail Road Company," 21 December 1841, Box 67 [WPA 658], CCR; "An Ordinance Authorising the Register of the City to Pay Interest on the Stock Orders of the Baltimore & Ohio Rail Road Company, and to exchange the same for Notes of the Corporation of the City of Baltimore," 23 December 1841, Box 67 [WPA 657], CCR.

98. *Sun*, 5, 6, 7 (quote) January 1842.

99. Mayor's Message, 17 January 1842, in *Sun*, 18 January 1842.

100. *American*, 10 January 1842.

101. Carter Goodrich, *Government Promotion of American Canals and Railroads, 1800–1890* (1960; Westport, CT: Greenwood Press, 1974), 80, 162–164.

102. Preamble & Resolution Relating to the Stock Orders . . . , 24 December 1841. Some warned that government interference in and of itself depreciated the notes: Resolution relating to

the Stock orders of the Balto & Ohio RR Co., 29 December 1841, Box 69 [WPA 660], CCR (N.B.: this is filed with the papers for 1842). Rural legislators cast the problem as one of urban corruption: *Harford Republican* quoted in *American*, 28 February 1841; a counterpoint: *Hagerstown* (MD) *Torchlight*, quoted in *American*, 8 January 1842. See also *Sun*, 19 February 1842.

103. Ch. 219, "An Act entitled, an Act to repeal an act entitled, an act to authorize the banks of the state of Maryland, to receive and pay out the orders drawn by the Baltimore and Ohio Rail Road Company, on the stock of the city of Baltimore, and for other purposes," passed 5 March 1842, in *Laws and Ordinances*, 113–115, quote on 115.

104. *Sun*, 23, 24, 25, 26 February ("*Prophecy*") 1842; *American*, "RAIL ROAD ORDERS" (p. 2) and "MEETING OF THE DRY GOODS DEALERS" (p. 3), 23 February 1842; see also *Sun*, 22 February 1842.

105. *American*, "TO THE RETAIL DEALERS OF BALTIMORE," 28 February 1842.

106. *American*, "TO THE PUBLIC," 2 March 1842.

107. Petition from John McCormick & Others Relating to the Currency in which they are paid, 25 February 1842, Box 68 [WPA 396], CCR.

108. Minute Book D, 2, 16 March 1842; *Sun*, 2, 4 April 1842.

109. Minute Book D, 21 March 1842.

110. Early moves to retire the notes: *American*, 7, 9 February 1842; Ord. No. 4, "An Ordinance authorizing a temporary loan for the purpose of retiring $500,000 of the Stock Orders of the Baltimore and Ohio Rail Road from circulation" in *Laws and Ordinances*, 157–58; Ord. No. 11, "An Ordinance relative to the Stock Orders of the Baltimore and Ohio Rail Road" in *Laws and Ordinances*, 158–159. State authorization for these measures: ch. 304, "An Act relating to the City of Baltimore and for other purposes," passed 9 March 1842, in *Laws and Ordinances*, 115–116. Failed plans to raise taxes on behalf of the notes: *Sun*, 10, 13 March 1842; An Ordinance to Relieve the City of a Grievous Debt, 14 March 1842, Box 69 [WPA 781], CCR; Report and Resolution of the Select Committee of the Second Branch relative to Ordinance No. 26, 15 March 1842, Box 68 [WPA 484], CCR. On search for a private funder and city debt: Report & Resolution from the Joint Committee on Ways & Means Relative to redeem[ing] the Stock orders of the Baltimore & Ohio Rail Road Co. in payment of City Dues, 15 March 1842, Box 69 [WPA 573], CCR; Res. No. 52, passed 17 March 1842, in *Laws and Ordinances*, 161; Crenson, *Baltimore*, 183.

111. *American*, 14 March 1842.

112. The first to pronounce them dead was "Vindex," writing to the *Sun* in early March: *Sun*, 7 March 1842.

113. *Sun*, 14, 24 March 1842 (quote); *American*, 17 March 1842 (for depreciation), 19 March 1842.

114. *Sun*, 16 April 1842.

115. *Sun*, 12 January 1843; Crenson, *Baltimore*, 182–183.

116. Ch. 313, "An Act, Supplementary to an Act to Incorporate the Baltimore and Ohio Rail Road Company," passed 6 March 1846, in *Laws and Ordinances*, 119.

117. William Prescott Smith, *The Book of the Great Railway Celebrations of 1857, Embracing a Full Account of the Opening of the Ohio & Mississippi, and the Marietta & Cincinnati Railroads, and the Northwestern Virginia Branch of the Baltimore and Ohio Railroad, with Histories and Descriptions of the Same; and an Account of the Subsequent Excursion to Baltimore, Washington and Norfolk, and the Receptions and Entertainments there of the State Authorities of Ohio, and the Municipal Representatives of St. Louis, Cincinnati and Chillicothe* (New York: D. Appleton & Co, 1858), 38.

118. John M. Gordon, *An Account of the First Carnival in the City of Washington, with several Letters to Various Parties, by the Author, Jno. M. Gordon, of Louchdougan and Eagle's Nest, near Norfolk, Va., 22d February 1871* (s.l.: s.n., 1871), 8, 23–24.

119. On the greenback: Mihm, *A Nation of Counterfeiters*, ch. 7, esp. 307–318; Laura F. Edwards, *A Legal History of the Civil War and Reconstruction: A Nation of Rights* (New York: Cambridge University Press, 2015), 25–30. It is no coincidence that Gordon's discussion of currency was so heavily racialized: Michael O'Malley, "Specie and Species: Race and the Money Question in Nineteenth-Century America," *American Historical Review* 99, no. 2 (April 1994): 369–395.

120. Eric Helleiner, *The Making of National Money: Territorial Currencies in Historical Perspective* (Ithaca, NY: Cornell University Press, 2003).

Chapter Four

1. *AR* 19 (1845): 20. Also *AR* 16 (1842): 12–13; *AR* 17 (1843): 13. On public anxieties over the fate of the B&O (and the millions of dollars invested in it): Mayor's Communication, 6 January 1840, in *Ordinances*, 7; *American*, 6 December 1839, 24 October 1840; James D. Dilts, *The Great Road: The Building of the Baltimore and Ohio, the Nation's First Railroad, 1828–1853* (Stanford, CA: Stanford University Press, 1993), chs. 8 and 15.

2. On the expiration of natural advantages: *Sun*, 2 April 1839; *American*, 4 July 1838. On the need to counter New York and Philadelphia: *Sun*, 10, 12, 20 January, 27 February 1843, 13, 19 April 1849, 19 September 1850; *American*, 12 January 1838, 7 November 1839, 6 December 1839.

3. John F. Stover, *Iron Road to the West: American Railroads in the 1850s* (New York: Columbia University Press, 1978), 15–17, 45–52.

4. "Baltimore and Ohio Railroad Termination," *American Railroad Journal*, 28 August 1847, 545; *American*, 5 April 1845.

5. See Boston *Daily Advertiser* in *American*, 12 April 1845; *Pittsburgh Gazette* in *American*, 28 January 1845; *Sun*, 24 February 1845.

6. *The Law of Virginia, of February 19, 1845, Relating to the Baltimore and Ohio Rail Road Company. To the President, Directors and Stockholders of Said Company* [1845], 4–5. See also *Sun*, 1 February 1845; 3 February 1845. On the James River improvement: "Baltimore and Ohio Railroad," *American Railroad Journal*, 30 October 1845, 697. Another argument held that Baltimore owed Wheelingites for their continued support: James S. Wheat, *An Argument on Behalf of the City of Wheeling before the Committee on Roads and Internal Navigation upon the Memorial of the Baltimore and Ohio Railroad Company* (Richmond, VA: Shepherd & Colin, 1845), 59.

7. *Proceedings of a Meeting of the Stockholders of the Baltimore & Ohio Rail Road Company, held in the City of Baltimore, on the 12th July, 1845, — to consider the Act of the General Assembly of Virginia, passed February 19, 1845, to which is appended the Report made to the Meeting, by the Chief Engineer* [Richmond, VA, 1845], 6.

8. *Sun*, 29 January 1847; also 13 January 1847, 9 February 1847. For a map illustrating this straight-line principle, see Benjamin H. Latrobe, *Map, exhibiting the railway route between Baltimore & St. Louis, together with other principal lines in the eastern, middle & western states; prepared under the direction of Benj. H. Latrobe, Ch. Engr., B&O RR* (s.l.: s.n., 1843).

9. *Sun*, 5 February 1845; *The Law of Virginia, of February 19, 1845*, nos. 4–7; *Journal of the Proceedings of a Convention, of the Citizens of North-Western Virginia, Friendly to the Law of the Last Session of the Virginia Legislature. Relative to the Baltimore and Ohio Railroad; Held at Fairmont, Marion County, Va., Monday, July 7, 1845* (Wheeling, VA: James E. Wharton, 1845), 6.

10. *Sun*, 5 March 1846; see also *Railroad Journal*, quoted in *Sun*, 29 December 1845; "*Right of Way*," *American Railroad Journal*, 10 January 1846, 29.

11. Committee on Internal Improvements in the Pennsylvania House of Representatives in *Sun*, 4 April 1851; *Sun*, 17, 28 February, 4 March 1846.

12. Albert J. Churella, *The Pennsylvania Railroad*, vol. 1, *Building an Empire* (Philadelphia: University of Pennsylvania Press, 2013), 75–100; Andrew Heath, *In Union There Is Strength: Philadelphia in the Age of Urban Consolidation* (Philadelphia: University of Pennsylvania Press, 2019), 74–82.

13. *Sun*, 6 May 1846; *AR* 20 (1846); *Sun*, 18 December 1846, 31 March 1847, 2, 6, 7 April 1847, 1, 18, 21 May 1847. McLane's argument: *Sun*, 2 January 1847.

14. On P&C: *Sun*, 22, 29 January 1847; on Virginia: *Sun*, 2 March 1847.

15. "The Baltimore and Ohio Railroad," *American Railroad Journal*, 20 November 1845, 745; also see *Speech of Mr. Lee, of Hardy, in the Rail-Road Convention at Clarksburg, Harrison County, Virginia, on the 29th of May, 1845* [Richmond, VA, 1845], 12, 15; *Sun*, 28 January 1847. On the call for construction regardless of terminus: *Patriot* quoted in *American Railroad Journal*, 19 December 1846, 809.

16. *Report & Documents submitted by the committee appointed to confer with the authorities of the City of Wheeling, respecting the Late Law of Virginia, granting the Right of Way to the Baltimore & Ohio Rail-Road Co. through that state. Passed 6th March, 1847* (Baltimore: s.n., 1847), 6. See also *Sun*, 27 July 1847; *AR* 21 (1847).

17. On benefiting Philadelphia: Louis McLane, *Address of Mr. McLane, President, to the Stockholders of the Baltimore & Ohio R. Road Company, at their Meeting on the 5th of April, 1847, Respecting a Proposed Subscription to the Capital of the Pittsburg & Connellsville Rail Road Co* (Baltimore: James Lucas, 1847), 5, 11, 15; Jonathan Knight points out that Pittsburgh also would gain from this: Letter to T. Parkin Scott [s.l.: s.n., 1847], 4. *American*, 2 July 1847 (quote); *American*, 10 July 1847.

18. John F. Stover, *History of the Baltimore and Ohio Railroad* (West Lafayette, IN: Purdue University Press, 1987), 79–80.

19. *American*, 14, 31 May 1847, 3, 8 (quote) July 1847; *Sun*, 9 June 1847; *Baltimore and Pittsburgh: Report of the Committee of Citizens of Baltimore, who were appointed to visit Pittsburgh, with a view to confer with the Pittsburgh and Connellsville Railroad Company* [Baltimore?, 1847], 6, 17. See also the letter from J. P. Kennedy in *American*, 4 May 1847; "A Western Railroad," *American Railroad Journal*, 20 March 1847, 189.

20. McLane, *Address of Mr. McLane*, 17–19, quote on 18. Engineer Jonathan Knight argued that the Great Lakes trade was "too certainly within the attraction of northern enterprise." Knight to T. Parkin Scott, 6; also *Sun*, 27 July 1847. A similar case was made for Parkersburg: *Sun*, 14, 15 January 1847.

21. The company had turned its attention to through traffic in the 1840s, when it dubbed the series of connections between steamboats, stagecoaches, and railcars from Wheeling to Baltimore the "Great Central Route" and began fixing rates to Philadelphia: *Sun*, 19 December 1842, 10 January 1843, 17 March 1843; Minute Book E, 21 April 1843; Report of Committee relative to Through Ticket from Wheeling to Philadelphia, 26 June 1843, PWB Board Papers; J. H. Shriver to Mathew Newkirk, 20 April 1842, PWB Board Papers.

22. Knight to T. Parkin Scott, 2.

23. *Report & Documents submitted by the committee*, 16. A similar pattern could be seen in freight traffic: *AR* 16 (1842): 16.

24. *Sun*, 26 July 1847; Committee Report on Extension of B&O R.R. to the West, [1848], 28–29, Box 2, Swann Collection.

25. *Address and Report of a Select Committee of the Baltimore and Ohio Railroad Company: Also, a Letter from the President, Recommending Measures for the Immediate Prosecution of the Road to the Ohio River* (Baltimore: John D. Toy, 1848), 13; Thomas Swann, *Address of Thomas Swann, Esq. (President,) to the directors of the Baltimore and Ohio Rail-Road Company, on the importance of an early completion of their road to the Ohio River, and the report of B. H. Latrobe, Esq., Chief Engineer* (Baltimore: James Lucas, 1849), 15; *Patriot*, quoted in *Sun*, 14 December 1848.

26. Dilts, *Great Road*, 339–341; Stover, *History of the Baltimore and Ohio Railroad*, 65–69.

27. Dilts, *Great Road*, 345–347, 358–360, 368–373, 378–380; recruitment ad quoted in Mary Ellen Hayward, *Baltimore's Alley Houses: Homes for Working People since the 1780s* (Baltimore: Johns Hopkins University Press, 2008), 88.

28. *Sun*, 12 June 1850. Pittsburghers cried foul, as this would subvert their position: Philadelphia *Bulletin* in *Sun*, 3 September 1852; *Pittsburgh Chronicle* in *American*, 13 June 1850.

29. *American*, 8, 10 July 1851.

30. *Sun*, 21 August 1851; also 12, 26 July 1851, 6 February 1852; and *American*, 15 July 1851; also 14, 17 July 1851, 14 August 1851; *AR* 25 (1851): 14, 15. Similar views were echoed in the Cincinnati press, as reprinted by the *Sun*. See *Cincinnati Commercial* printed in *Sun*, 11 January 1851, and Cincinnati *Gazette* printed in *Sun*, 24 February 1851; Thomas Swann to W. B. Casilly, President of [Cincinnati] City Council (Draft), 15 May 1851, Box 1, Swann Collection; Alphonso Taft, *A Lecture on Cincinnati and her Rail-Roads. Delivered before the Young Men's Mercantile Library Association, January 22, 1850* (Cincinnati, OH: D. Anderson, 1850). See also Preamble and resolution for a Committee to apply to General Assembly for permission to subscribe an amount to further the object of the northwestern charter, 4 August 1851, 1–2, Box 91 [WPA 824], CCR.

31. *Sun*, 30 June 1852. This speech was published as *Address of Thomas Swann, Esq., on the Parkersburg Rail Road: delivered at the new assembly rooms, (Hanover Street,) June 28, 1852. Printed by Order of the Meeting* (Baltimore: J. Murphy & Co, 1852). See also Thomas Swann to Mayor J. Jerome (Draft), 3 January 1852, 4, Box 1, Swann Collection.

32. Ch. 146, "An Act giving certain Powers to the Mayor and City Council of Baltimore, in regard to the North Western Virginia Rail Road," passed 21 April 1852, in *Ordinances*, 163; *American*, 9 August 1853; Stover, *History of the Baltimore and Ohio*, 82.

33. *Patriot* reprinted in "Baltimore and Ohio Railroad," *American Railroad Journal*, 18 September 1852, 598. Similar predictions: *New York Post* in *Sun*, 11 April 1851; also *Sun*, 23, 29 September 1852. The *Sun* also anticipated transformation of the waterfront (23 September 1852). For predictions about the development of trade: *The Stranger's Guide to Baltimore, Showing the Easiest and Best Mode of Seeing all the Public Buildings and Places of Note, in and around the City, and in the Neighborhood: Together with some Brief Observations on its Trade, Resources, Prosperity, Commercial Advantages, and Future Prospects. By a Baltimorean* (Baltimore: Murphy & Co., 1852), 61, 66.

34. *AR* 26 (1852): 36; *Sun*, 31 December 1852, 10 January 1853.

35. *American*, 14 December 1852; Matthew A. Crenson, *Baltimore: A Political History* (Baltimore: Johns Hopkins University Press, 2017), 184–185, 189–191, 194, 201; Mary P. Ryan, *Taking the Land to Make the City: A Bicoastal History of North America* (Austin: University of Texas Press, 2019), 227–228. Only Cincinnati, which owned a railroad outright, matched Baltimore's investment in railroad enterprise in the nineteenth century. Baltimore's investments spanned a period of 1827 to 1886 and represented a commitment in aggregate of around $20 million:

Carter Goodrich and Harvey H. Segal, "Baltimore's Aid to Railroads: A Study in the Municipal Planning of Internal Improvements," *Journal of Economic History* 13, no. 1 (Winter 1953): 2–35.

36. *Sun*, 31 December 1852; *Wheeling Daily Intelligencer*, 12, 14 January 1853.

37. Thomas Swann, Speech Delivered at Opening Ceremony of the Wheeling Terminus, 18, Box 3, Swann Collection. See also *American*, 17 January 1853.

38. Statement dated 13 April 1853, in Thomas Swann, *Remarks of Thomas Swann, Esquire, upon his Resigning the Presidency of the Baltimore & Ohio R. Road Co. together with Statements of the Treasurer of said Company, and the Proceedings of the Board of Directors upon that Occasion. April 13th, 1853* (Baltimore: James Lucas, 1853), 16.

39. *Sun*, 9 April 1853.

40. *Sun*, 6 October 1853 (quote), 26 May 1853.

41. *AR* 27 (1853).

42. *American*, 28 July 1851, 6 August 1853; "Baltimore and Ohio Railroad," *American Railroad Journal*, 27 November 1852, p. 759; *Philadelphia Public Ledger*, 2 February 1853. A New Yorker pointed out that the Erie Canal still dwarfed the B&O's shipping capacity: "Baltimore and Philadelphia in Connection with Western Roads," *American Railroad Journal*, 9 October 1852, 650.

43. Ord. No. 22, "An Ordinance to close certain streets in the Depot of the Baltimore and Ohio Rail Road Company," passed 10 May 1850, in *Laws and Ordinances*, 171–172; on the anticipated "rapid extension of the City" driving the B&O to expand Mount Clare, see Minute Book F, 14 November 1849 and *AR* 24 (1850): 9. The company's request is in Application of the Balto & Ohio R R Co to close certain streets, 20 February 1850, Box 86 [WPA 276], CCR. Increases in production of cars and materials at Mount Clare: *Sun*, 5 January 1853; *Sun*, 21 September 1852. Ohio Street was intended to link Mount Clare to the Locust Point Branch: Ord. No. 17, "An Ordinance to Open a street to be called Ohio street, in the City of Baltimore," approved 19 April 1851 in *Ordinances*, 22. It is distinct from the Ohio Avenue discussed in chapter 5. On immigration, industrialization, and the building boom of this period, see Gary Lawson Browne, *Baltimore in the Nation, 1789–1861* (Chapel Hill: University of North Carolina Press, 1980), 190–191; Sherry H. Olson, *Baltimore: The Building of an American City*, rev. ed. (Baltimore: Johns Hopkins University Press, 1997), 102–107; Mary Ellen Hayward and Charles Belfoure, *The Baltimore Rowhouse* (New York: Princeton Architectural Press, 1999), 39–40, 49–50; Hayward, *Baltimore's Alley Houses*, 92.

44. *Sun*, 5 January, 11 February 1853.

45. Olson, *Baltimore*, 108; Crenson, *Baltimore*, 201.

46. *Sun*, 12, 14 February 1853; *New York Times*, 12 February, p. 1, 15 February, p. 4, 16 February 1853, p. 1; Browne, *Baltimore in the Nation*, 184–186.

47. *Sun*, 15 February 1853.

48. [William Prescott Smith], *Reports made to the General Superintendent of the Baltimore & Ohio Rail Road, by the Assistant Master of Transportation, of his Observations Concerning the Sources and Prospects of the Company's Trade with the West, Made by Authority, during a trip for that purpose, in May 1853, Shortly after the Road was opened to the Ohio River* (Baltimore: John Murphy & Co., 1853), 3–4, 22–25.

49. Smith, *Reports*, 5.

50. Ibid., 15. On the accident: [J. B. Ford Deposition, 1877], 5–12, J. B. Ford Legal Papers, A&M 1679, West Virginia and Regional History Collection, West Virginia University, Morgantown.

51. Ibid., 13. A different traveler found that western merchants were put off by the B&O's high rates—*American*, 3 December 1852.

52. Ibid., 5–18.

53. Ibid., 5, 6, 14. Other trunk rail lines had already started planting agencies in western towns (see *Sun*, 28 May 1853), and years later, in 1860, the *New York Times* would praise the B&O for its active agents, who established personal ties with merchants and bid with other rail lines for business—*Times* quoted in *American*, 9 January 1860.

54. Thomas Swann, *Remarks of Thomas Swann, Esq., President, to the Board of Directors of the Baltimore and Ohio Rail Road Company, on the Opening of the Bids for the Loan of $700,000, and the Application of the General Superintendent for a Large Increase in the Equipment of the Road on its completion. Published by Order of the Board* (Baltimore: John Murphy & Co., 1852); Thomas Swann, Address to the Board of Directors, [1852], Box 3, Swann Collection. The company echoed this call for a second track a year later: *AR* 27 (1853). The *American* would later characterize the line's condition in 1853 as unfinished: *American*, 29 March 1860, quoted in *Memoranda Concerning Baltimore City and its Surroundings. Dedicated to the Western Editors who visit Baltimore on the Editorial Excursion over the Baltimore and Ohio Railroad, and its Western Connecting Lines, May and June, 1860* (Baltimore: W. M. Innes, 1860), 34.

55. See, e.g., Benjamin H. Latrobe to Thomas Swann, 15 June 1850, Box 1, Swann Collection.

56. Churella, *Pennsylvania Railroad*, 139–144, 198–200.

57. William Parker, Genl. Superintendent of the B&O to Joshua Vansant, 13 and 21 June 1853, Box 97 [WPA 720], CCR. On Baltimore City's interventions in railroad management: Carter Goodrich, *Government Promotion of American Canals and Railroads, 1800–1890* (1960; Westport, CT: Greenwood Press, 1974), 85–86.

58. Communication from the Directors in B&O RR Co, 12 July 1853, Box 97 [WPA 721], CCR.

59. *American*, 24, 25 (quote) August 1853.

60. *Sun*, 1 September 1853, 15 November 1853; *AR* 27 (1853).

61. *Sun*, 22 November 1853.

62. *American*, 15 November 1853; civic institution: *American*, 23 November 1853.

63. Petition of James P. Kennedy, 22 November 1853, Box 96 [WPA 463], CCR. Kennedy's occupation: *Matchett's City Directory for 1853–54* (Baltimore: Richard J. Matchett, 1853), 170.

64. *Sun*, 18 and 26 (quote) November 1853.

65. *Sun*, 24 November 1853.

66. Memorial of Tiffany, Ward & Company & Miller, Mayhew & Company & Others, Merchants of the City of Baltimore, praying that such legislation may be had by the Mayor & City Council as will secure to the Citizens of Baltimore a fair and equal system of freight charges on the Baltimore & Ohio Rail Road Company, 28 November 1854 [1853?], Box 100 [WPA 410], CCR.

67. *American*, 5 August 1853.

68. *Sun*, "The Discrimination Question," 12 December 1853.

69. Extra Session 1853, Ord. No. 2, "An Ordinance to guaranty the Bonds of the Baltimore and Ohio Rail Road Company," approved 14 December 1853, in *Ordinances*, 6–8; *American*, 3 December 1853.

70. William G. Harrison, B&O Pres., to First & Second Branches of the City Council, 10 December 1853, Box 97 [WPA 718], CCR.

71. *Sun*, "To Johns Hopkins, Esq, a Director in the Baltimore and Ohio Railroad Company," 12 December 1853. See also, *American*, "SOMETHING FUNNY ABOUT THE BALTIMORE AND OHIO RAILROAD COMPANY" and "SOMETHING ABOUT RAILROADS," both 10 December 1853.

72. Petition of Duvall Keighton & 50 Others presented by J. N. Richardson, 5/6 wards, 14 De-

cember 1853, Box 96 [WPA 461], CCR. See also five other petitions from the same box, none of which have WPA numbers: Memorial of 166 Mercantile firms asking the Councils to give the B&O RR Co the aid asked for without onerous restricting clauses, 14 December 1853; Petition of Lintz & Flack & 50 others, presented Jno. Richarder, 5/6 wards, 14 December 1853; Memorial of 200 mercantile firms asking that available aid may be granted the B&O RR Co, 14 December 1853; Petition of S. R. Geary and others presented by J. M. Bill of 11 & 12 Wards, 14 December 1853; Petition of Kramer Stump & Others in relation to the five millions endorsement, 14 December 1853. See also George W. Porter, Secretary of the Board of Trade to J.B. Seidenstricker, President of Second Branch, 14 December 1853, Box 97 [WPA 719], CCR.

73. *American Railroad Journal* reprinted in *American*, 14 December 1853. The *Journal* referred specifically to Augusta, Georgia.

74. *American*, 12, 17 (quote) December 1853; see also *Sun*, 9 August 1853.

75. *American Railroad Journal* reprinted in *American*, 14 December 1853 (emphasis added); see also *Sun*, 13 January 1854.

76. "Local advantages" from *Sun*, 23 August 1853 (see also the Baltimore Board of Trade's statement in *Sun*, 7 September 1853); "restrictive system" from *Sun*, 26 August 1853; through ticket provisions from *Sun*, 7 September 1853. On merchants stopping in Baltimore while transiting: *AR* 30 (1856): 24. See also *Sun*, 24 December 1853 and an editorial in the *American*, "The Discrimination Question," 14 December 1853.

77. *Sun*, "Baltimore and Ohio Railroad," 12, 13 December 1853.

78. *American*, 23 December 1853; *Sun*, 23 August 1853, "Baltimore and Ohio Railroad," 12 December 1853; *AR* 30 (1856): 13.

79. Extra Session 1853, Ord. No. 5, "An Ordinance to aid the Baltimore and Ohio Rail-Road Company by a loan to the amount of Five Million of Dollars, to complete their Road to the city of Wheeling, to fund their debts, and especially to lay a second track as far as Piedmont, 218 miles distant from the city of Baltimore," approved 27 December 1853, in *Ordinances*, 9–12. The state legislature passed the bill, although a majority of the Baltimore City delegation voted to add an amendment prohibiting rate discrimination; see *Sun*, 7 February 1854.

80. *AR* 28 (1854): 10.

81. On the decision to redirect the money to the NWV: Minute Book H, 21 March 1856; Application of the Balt & O RR Co, 2 April 1856, Box 105 [WPA 460], CCR. The company had completed 91 miles of double track, but was far from finished. The city counselor explained that the reference to double tracking in the ordinance's title was not legally binding, but the council was not satisfied. Communication from City Counselor to Second Branch, 5 April 1856, Box 105 [WPA 459], CCR. Quotes from Preamble and Resolution relative [to] proposed loan to NWVa RR Co, 14 April 1856, Box 107 [WPA 837], CCR. The council then voted to rescind the injunction, but the mayor vetoed that decision: Minute Book H, 11 June 1856; *Sun*, 25 June 1856.

82. *Sun*, 30 June 1856.

83. Resolutions on the Resignation of Thomas Swann from the Northwestern Virginia Railroad Co., 28 April 1857, Thomas Swann/Baltimore & Ohio RR Papers Collection, 1851–1857, MS 1826.1, MdHS.

84. Thomas Swann, Mayor's Communication, 19 January 1857, in *Ordinances*, A3-A21.

85. *Sun*, 20 May 1857.

86. William Prescott Smith, *The Book of the Great Railway Celebrations of 1857, Embracing a Full Account of the Opening of the Ohio & Mississippi, and the Marietta & Cincinnati Rail-*

roads, and the Northwestern Virginia Branch of the Baltimore and Ohio Railroad . . . (New York: D. Appleton & Co., 1858), 1–3.

Chapter Five

1. Memorial of John J. Frisby and others remonstrating against the admission of locomotives on North Street, 14 March 1849, Box 83 [WPA 526], CCR (quoted). See also Memorial of Sundry Persons against Running Locomotives on North Street, 19 March 1849, Box 83 [WPA 525], CCR; and A Memorial . . . from Sam Harris & Son, George Jenkins & Others against the passage of an Ordinance authorizing the Balto & Susquho Rail Road Company to bring their Locomotives down North Street to their New Depot, 26 March 1849, Box 83 [WPA 527], CCR. On Frisby's occupation and neighborhood: *Matchett's Baltimore Director for 1851* (Baltimore: Richard J. Matchett, 1851), 98. On the B&S's request to use locomotives on North Street: Memorial of the Baltimore and Susquehanna Rail Road Company asking Permission to use Locomotives in the Street, 21 February 1849, Box 83 [WPA 522], CCR. On Greenmount: Mary Ellen Hayward and Charles Belfoure, *The Baltimore Rowhouse* (New York: Princeton Architectural Press, 1999), 57–58.

2. Petition of Thomas Atkinson & Others adverse to the introduction of Steam Engines on North Street, 15 March 1849, Box 83 [WPA 529], CCR.

3. Kentucky Court of Appeals, quoted in Charles Sellers, *The Market Revolution: Jacksonian America, 1815–1846* (New York: Oxford University Press, 1991), 52; New York State Supreme Court, quoted in Clay McShane, *Down the Asphalt Path: The Automobile and the American City* (New York: Columbia University Press, 1994), 12. Track mileage figures from John F. Stover, *American Railroads*, 2nd ed. (Chicago: University of Chicago Press, 1997), 205.

4. Ted Robert Mitchell, "Connecting a Nation, Dividing a City: How Railroads Shaped the Public Spaces and Social Understanding of Chicago" (PhD diss., Michigan State University, 2009).

5. On the scope and scale of steam engine disasters, see the account of a railroad accident in the entry for 28 March 1853, Mary Matthews Townsend Dobbin Diary, Vol. 1, Mary Mathews Townsend Dobbins Papers, 1856–1860, 1883–1884, MS 2385, MdHS; *Sun*, 10 August 1840 (quote); on the particular dangers in the city, see *Sun*, 28 December 1838. On mental stress associated with the locomotive, see *Sun*, 10 August 1841. On aversion to steam in American cities, see Clay McShane and Joel A. Tarr, *The Horse in the City: Living Machines in the Nineteenth Century* (Baltimore: Johns Hopkins University Press, 2007), 3–5. On fearful responses to the steam locomotive more generally, see David E. Nye, *American Technological Sublime* (Cambridge, MA: MIT Press, 1994), 52–56; Craig Miner, *A Most Magnificent Machine: America Adopts the Railroad, 1825–1862* (Lawrence: University Press of Kansas, 2010), ch. 7.

6. Communication of the Chief Engineer of the Baltimore and Ohio Rail Road relative to the economy of Steam Power, 10 June 1847, Box 79 [WPA 563-A], CCR.

7. The company started looking into alternative arrangements in the 1830s: Report of the Committee on a Site for a Depot East of Jones' Falls, 5 April 1836, Baltimore & Port Deposit Board Papers, Accession No. 1807, B-1324, Hagley Museum and Library, Wilmington, Delaware; *Sun*, 9 April 1849; *Twelfth Annual Report of the Philadelphia, Wilmington and Baltimore Rail-Road Company, with the Report of the Engineer and General Superintendent, made January 14, 1850* (Philadelphia: John C. Clark, 1850), 7–8 (quote).

8. *AR* 17 (1843): 7. See also *Sun*, 4 June 1847.

9. Report of the Joint Committee on Internal Improvements, 1843, Box 71 [no WPA, between 809 and 810], CCR.

10. Preamble and Resolution Allowing the Balto & Ohio Rail Road Co to Convey their Locomotives through the City, 11 April 1843, Box 71 [WPA 563], CCR; *Sun*, 10 March 1843.

11. Communication from the Mayor returning a bill to regulate the running of Locomotive engines . . . , 6 April 1843, Box 70 [WPA 436], CCR.

12. *AR* 17 (1843): 7. Shortly after the mayor's veto, Louis McLane made plans to redirect much of the passenger business from Pratt Street Depot to Mount Clare Station, which was accessible by steam engine: Minute Book E, 2 August 1843.

13. *AR* 18 (1844): 8; Report of the Joint Select Committee from *American*, 2 April 1845.

14. Ord. No. 21, "An Ordinance to provide for the Encouragement of Trade, in the City of Baltimore," passed 19 April 1845 in *Laws and Ordinances*, 164–166, quote on 166 (mislabeled as 168); *Sun*, 19 April 1845.

15. Memorial from the President of the Baltimore and Ohio Rail Road Company relating to the running of Locomotive Engines throught [*sic*] the Streets, 11 March 1847, Box 78 [WPA 359], CCR; Minute Book F, 10 March 1847; Communication of the Chief Engineer of the Baltimore and Ohio Rail Road relative to the economy of Steam Power, 10 June 1847, Box 79 [WPA 563-A], CCR. See also *Sun*, 4 June 1847.

16. Res. No. 43, "Resolution in favor of the Baltimore and Ohio Rail Road Company," approved 7 April 1847, in *Laws and Ordinances*, 169; A Supplement to an Ordinance entitled an ordinance to provide for the encouragement of trade in the City of Baltimore passed at the Sesion [*sic*] of 1845, 2 June 1847, Box 81 [WPA 1149], CCR; An Ordinance permitting the Baltimore and Ohio Rail Road Company to run their Locomotives as far into the City as Howard Street upon Certain Conditions, 19 March 1847, Box 81 [WPA 1147], CCR.

17. *AR* 21 (1847): 50.

18. "Baltimore and Its Railroads," *American Railroad Journal & Manufacturers' and Mining Gazette*, 22 April 1848, 258.

19. Petition for Jacob Green, Hugh Sisson and others, asking that the Baltimore & Susquehannah Rail Road may use Locomotive Power on North Street, 29 March 1849, Box 83 [WPA 524], CCR. For other pro-business, pro-locomotive petitions from merchants and the like: Memorial of Columbus O'Donnell and Others relative to Locomotives Running on North Street, 29 March 1849, Box 83 [WPA 531], CCR; Petition of Coleman Cox & Others praying that the B. & Susq. R.R. Company may be permitted to use Locomotive Power on North Street, 2 April 1849, Box 83 [WPA 532], CCR. See also Memorials in favor of the use of locomotive engines, 29 March 1849, Box 83 [WPA 530], CCR.

20. Report of the Joint Committee on Internal Improvement on the Memorial of the Baltimore and Susquehanna Rail Road Co. asking permission to run locomotives in North St., 3 April 1849, Box 86 [WPA 1250], CCR. The proposal cleared the First Branch of City Council by 16 to 4. *Sun*, 4 April 1849.

21. Memorial of the Balto & Susquehanna Rail Road Company, asking the closing of certain streets, 4 April 1849, Box 83 [WPA 521], CCR; *Sun*, 8 August 1849 (quote); *American* reprinted in *Sun*, 1 April 1851; see also *Sun*, 26 August 1853.

22. *Sun*, 14 July 1851; also, *American*, 12 July 1851. On efforts to design locomotives for urban use: Communication from Ross Winans on the Subject of Locomotive Engines, 29 March 1849,

Box 84 [WPA 789], CCR. Also: Letter from J. S. Murray on the subject of Locomotive Engines, 3 April 1849, Box 84 [WPA 788], CCR.

23. *Sun*, 12 December 1846; *Sun*, 19 May 1847; see also *Philadelphia Public Ledger*, 31 December 1853.

24. *Wheeling Daily Intelligencer*, 3 December 1852. For an example of pro-locomotive sentiment in Baltimore, see Communication of Sundry Persons, relative to the use of Locomotive Engines in Pratt Street, [1850], Box 87 [WPA 450], CCR.

25. *Sun*, 30 December 1853; Ord. No. 67, An ordinance regulating the Speed of Locomotive Engines and Cars within the limits of the city of Baltimore, approved 5 June 1858, in *Ordinances*, 225–226; Ord. No. 73, A Supplement to an Ordinance entitled "An Ordinance regulating the speed of Locomotive Engines and Cars within the limits of the city of Baltimore . . ." approved 12 July 1854, in *Ordinances*, 79. Back-and-forth in public opinion on urban locomotives was not limited to Baltimore; in New York City, too, locomotive regulations were always subject to change: see, e.g., Resolution re: Hudson River Rail Road, 22 June 1867, Box 14, Folder 4, New York Miscellaneous Collection, MSSCol 2156, New York Public Library.

26. In favor of steam power on city passenger railways: *Sun*, 14 December 1868, 12 February 1874; opposition to steam power in Howard and Pratt streets: Robt. Renwick, Son, & Others, Petition to Prohibit the use of Steam Engines on Howard St., 24 January 1870, Box 157 [WPA 2431], CCR; Petition signed by J. G. Hewes and twenty-eight others doing business on W. Pratt St., complaining of the annoyance and danger to life and property from the running of locomotives on said street, during business hours, between Mt. Clare and Howard St., 4 December 1872, Box 169 [WPA 972], CCR; *Sun*, 16 November 1876.

27. See for example a round of petitions opposing steam engines from 1860, which put the issue back on the local political docket: Report of the Joint Standing Committee on Highways with an Ordinance to Prohibit the Balto & Ohio R.R. Co. from using Locomotive Engines on Pratt St., 30 March 1860, Box 117 [WPA 639], CCR; First Branch to Second Branch, 5 April 1860, Box 119 [WPA 1574], CCR; An Ordinance to repeal so much of an ordinance entitled "An Ordinance to provide for the Encouragement of Trade in the City of Baltimore," approved April 19, 1845, as authorizes the Baltimore and Ohio Railroad Company to use Locomotive Engines on Pratt Street between Mount Clare Depot, Camden Station, and President Street Depot, [1860], Box 118 [WPA 1408], CCR.

28. Charles Ellet Jr., *Report on a Suspension Bridge across the Potomac, for Rail Road and Common Travel: Addressed to the Mayor and City Council of Georgetown, D.C.* (Philadelphia: John C. Clark, 1852), 8.

29. John H. B. Latrobe to John W. Garrett, 1 April 1859, Box 89, Folder 13447, GPC.

30. Poor condition of tracks, for example, remained a perennial concern. See Report of the Joint Committee on Police & Jail on the Petition of John R. Ridgely & Others, 12 March 1852, Box 95 [WPA 1053], CCR; Ord. No. 18, "A Supplement to an Ordinance entitled 'An Ordinance for the better regulation of Rail Road Cars,'—approved June 3d, 1850," approved 21 April 1852, in *Laws and Ordinances*, 16; Edward Spedden, City Commissioner to City Council, 21 February 1853, Box 98 [WPA 858], CCR; B. Clark & Bros. to John W. Garrett, 4 October 1860, Box 26, Folder 380, GPC.

31. For 1855: Res. No. 146, "Resolution directing the Baltimore and Ohio Railroad Company to alter their track on the corner of Pratt and Charles streets," approved 2 June 1855, in *Ordinances*, 127. See also Report of the Joint Committee of Highways in Reference to Petition

of T. Newton Kurtz and others, 18 May 1855, Box 104 [WPA 458], CCR. For 1856: Resolution, in Second Branch, 3 March 1856, Box 106 [WPA 739], CCR; Report and Resolution of the Joint Standing Committee on Highways, 15 April 1856, Box 106 [WPA 682], CCR. On water issues, see also Report of the Committee on Highway & Bridges on the Communication of the city Commission on obstructions in the streets caused by Railways and Bill No. 5, 26 February 1850, Box 88 [WPA 837], CCR; Minute Book G, 11 May 1853.

32. Benjamin Latrobe to City Commissioners, 5 April 1848, Box 66 [WPA 91-A], CComR. Even when promising to respect municipal rights, though, stockholders' interests came first. See, e.g., Communication from President Thomas A. Scott of the Northern Central Railway, 21 October 1876, Box 192 [WPA 1365], CCR.

33. Communication from the Mayor returning the bill entitled "An ordinance to provide for the encouragement of Trade in the City of Baltimore," 14 April 1845, Box 74A [WPA 383], CCR.

34. For example, see Report of the Committee on Highways & Bridges on the Communication of the City Commission on obstructions in streets caused by Railways and Bill No. 5, 26 February 1850, Box 88 [WPA 837], CCR; Report of the Joint Committee on Internal Improvements relative to grading rail road tracks, 31 March 1848, Box 83 [WPA 752], CCR.

35. Ord. No. 6, "A Supplement to an Ordinance, entitled, an Ordinance relating to the Baltimore and Ohio Rail Road Company, approved April 4th, 1831, and to an Ordinance, entitled, an Ordinance to authorize the construction of certain Railways within the city," approved 3 April 1850, in *Laws and Ordinances*, 169–171, quotes on 169, 170. A later example: Res. No. 331, "Resolution of notification to the Baltimore and Ohio Railroad Company," approved 16 October 1872, in *Ordinances*, 273–274. For one example of commissioners' many documented interactions with rail companies, see Notice to R. S. Hollins, 1 December 1871, Box 87 [WPA 363], CComR, instructing the Northern Central to attend to damaged infrastructure at Canal and Pratt Streets.

36. Copy of a Notice to the Baltimore & Ohio Rail Road Company, 3 October 1854, Box 75 [WPA 38], CComR.

37. For example: Resolution to the Joint Committee on Police and Jail, 23 February 1852, Box 95 [WPA 1267], CCR; Report of the Joint Committee on Police & Jail on the Resolution as to the Speed of Railroad cars, 8 March 1852, Box 95 [WPA 1049], CCR. A later example: Res. No. 250, "Resolution in relation to rail road cars standing on track on south Bond, Thames, and south Caroline street, in violation of Article 34 of Baltimore City Code," approved 2 July 1872, in *Ordinances*, 241–242. Arrest and fine of Northern Central "authorities": *Sun*, 17 September 1856.

38. *American*, 16 April 1845; Communication from the Mayor returning the bill entitled "An ordinance to provide for the encouragement of Trade in the City of Baltimore," 14 April 1845, 3–6, Box 74A [WPA 383], CCR; Ord. No. 21, "An Ordinance to provide for the Encouragement of Trade, in the City of Baltimore," passed 19 April 1845, in *Laws and Ordinances*, 164–166; *Sun*, 19 April 1845.

39. On negotiations and construction: Minute Book E, 10 September 1845; Minute Book E, 5 October 1846; Minute Book F, 9 June 1847; Minute Book F, 14 July 1847; Minute Book F, 13 October 1847. See also *Sun*, 12 June 1847.

40. R., "Baltimore," *American Railroad Journal*, 28 July 1849, 472; *Sun*, 1 October 1846.

41. On acquisition of land: Minute Book F, 17 July 1849; Minute Book F, 8 August 1849. On landfill: *Sun*, 1 July 1848. On row houses: Mary Ellen Hayward, *Baltimore's Alley Houses: Homes for Working People since the 1780s* (Baltimore: Johns Hopkins University Press, 2008), 102.

42. *AR* 24 (1850): 21. See also *Sun*, 18 August 1852, 1 December 1845, 12 December 1855, 23 June 1856.

43. R., "Baltimore," *American Railroad Journal*, 28 July 1849, p.472; *AR* 22 (1848): 5–6, 40–41, 43.

44. Thomas Swann, Statements Justifying his Administration, n.d., Box 3, Swann Collection; also: Thomas Swann, *Statement of Thomas Swann, Late President, to the President & Directors of the Baltimore & Ohio R. R. Company* (Baltimore: John Murphy, 1854), 27–28; John F. Stover, *History of the Baltimore and Ohio Railroad* (West Lafayette, IN: Purdue University Press, 1987), 89–90; Herbert H. Harwood Jr., *Impossible Challenge II: Baltimore to Washington and Harpers Ferry from 1828 to 1994* (Baltimore: Barnard, Roberts, 1994), ch. 7; John A. Munroe, *Louis McLane: Federalist and Jacksonian* (New Brunswick, NJ: Rutgers University Press, 1973), 499–500.

45. John F. Stover, *Iron Road to the West: American Railroads in the 1850s* (New York: Columbia University Press, 1978), 199–202; Sherry H. Olson, *Baltimore: The Building of an American City*, rev. ed. (Baltimore: Johns Hopkins University Press, 1997), 152.

46. Figures for 1859: Henry Varnum Poor, *History of the Railroads and Canals of the United States of America* (1860; New York: Augustus M. Kelley, 1970), 582. See also William S. Woodside, "Report of the Master of Transportation," in *AR* 31 (1857): 40.

47. See, for example, the uproar that surrounded the private directors' attempt to institute a $0.50 rate hike on coal in 1856: Minute Book H, 10 September 1856; *Sun*, 11, 21 August 1856; Preamble and Resolutions of Inquiry of Direction in B&O RR on the Transportation of Coal, 23 May 1856, Box 106 [WPA 742], CCR; Res. Relative to Coal Trade, 9 June 1856, Box 106 [WPA 743], CCR; Resolution relative to increasing freight on coal, 10 September 1856, Box 106 [WPA 741], CCR.

48. Edward K. Muller and Paul A. Groves, "The Emergence of Industrial Districts in Mid-Nineteenth Century Baltimore," *Geographical Review* 69, no. 2 (April 1979): 164–171, 176.

49. Smith, *Book of the Great Railway Celebration* quoted in *Memoranda Concerning Baltimore City and its Surroundings. Dedicated to the Western Editors who visit Baltimore on the Editorial Excursion over the Baltimore and Ohio Railroad, and its Western Connecting Lines, May and June, 1860* (Baltimore: W. M. Innes, 1860), 12–13. See also George W. Howard, *The Monumental City, Its Past History and Present Resources* (Baltimore: J. D. Ehlers & Co., 1873), 290. On the rhetorical alignment of coal smoke with progress, see David Stradling, *Smokestacks and Progressives: Environmentalists, Engineers, and Air Quality in America, 1881–1951* (Baltimore: Johns Hopkins University Press, 1999), ch. 1.

50. In 1854, the Gas Light Co. received a switch from the Locust Point Branch to receive gas coal: Minute Book G, 10 May 1854; also Columbus O'Donnell to John W. Garrett, 28 January 1860, Box 82, Folder 7153, GPC. On the origins of gas coal: *Sun*, 13 February 1872; Communication of the President of the B&O RR, 12 March 1872, Box 169 [WPA 1015], CCR. On gas production and lighting in Baltimore and elsewhere, see David E. Nye, *American Illuminations: Urban Lighting, 1800–1920* (Cambridge, MA: MIT Press, 2018), 35–37, 43.

51. On coal trade as justification for the branch: Thomas Swann, Materials for Annual Report: Canal Route, Coal Trade. n.d., Box 2, Swann Collection; *Railroad Journal* quoted in *Sun*, 3 May 1848; Minute Book E, 14 May 1845; Minute Book E, 5 October 1845; Minute Book F, 16 October 1847; Minute Book F, 11 November 1847.

52. *American* quoted in *Sun*, 15 August 1851; on rising prices: *Sun*, 11 February 1853. Baltimore's coal dealers anxiously awaited new infrastructure; see Petition from Edmund Murray and Others Praying that the Rail Road Track over Harford Run, at Canton Avenue, may be permitted to remain for a short time, 15 May 1848, Box 82 [WPA 551], CCR.

53. *Sun*, 28 June 1850, 23 January 1851, 23 March 1854. On steamers drawn by low prices for

fuel: George W. Howard, *The Monumental City its Past History and Present Resources.* (Baltimore: J. D. Ehlers & Co., 1873), 288–289; also, *Sun*, 17 May 1867.

54. Albert J. Churella, *The Pennsylvania Railroad*, vol. 1, *Building an Empire, 1846–1917* (Philadelphia: University of Pennsylvania Press, 2013), 214; David M. Scobey, *Empire City: The Making and Meaning of the New York City Landscape* (Philadelphia: Temple University Press, 2002), 74–78; Carl W. Condit, *The Port of New York: A History of the Rail and Terminal System from the Beginnings to Pennsylvania Station* (Chicago: University of Chicago Press, 1980), 39–40, 58–61.

55. R., "Baltimore," *American Railroad Journal*, 28 July 1849, 472; Ord. No. 37, "A Supplement to an Ordinance, entitled, an Ordinance to provide for the Encouragement of Trade, in the City of Baltimore, passed at the session of 1845," passed 2 May 1845, in *Laws and Ordinances*, 168.

56. *Copy of Petition Signed and Sent to B&O RR.* [1864] in B&O Railroad Pamphlet Book, 1836–1882, Evergreen Library. The petition cited here is from 1864, but the concerns it articulates dated to before the 1850s.

57. *American*, 8 April 1845; see also *American*, 7, 9, 11 April 1845, for the *American*'s assurances that the Locust Point Branch would benefit the entire city. The ordinance to lay tracks into Fells: Ord. No. 21, "An Ordinance to provide for the Encouragement of Trade, in the City of Baltimore," sec. 4, in *Laws and Ordinances*, 165. Petitions for track extension: Petition for Extension of Rail Road Track, 30 April 1856, Box 105 [WPA 302], CCR; see also Minute Book H, 12 March 1856. Other records on this point are in City Council Records for 1860 (WPAs 245, 640, 1033) and 1861 (WPA 885), and in *Ordinances*. On the company's satisfaction with arrangements at Locust Point: Draft of Answer to C. J. Baker, Esq., President 2d Branch City Council to Resolution, 10 January 1861, Box 35, Folder 541, GPC; Minute Book H, 10 October 1860.

58. *Sun*, 21 April 1849.

59. Quote from *Sun*, 3 July 1852. On the racial composition of the neighborhood, see "Map of black residence in 1860" from Christopher Phillips, *Freedom's Port: The African American Community of Baltimore, 1790–1860* (Urbana: University of Illinois Press, 1997), 56–57. On Otterbein and the black community, see Hayward, *Baltimore's Alley Houses*, 50–51; Garrett Power, "Deconstructing the Slums of Baltimore," in *From Mobtown to Charm City: New Perspectives on Baltimore's Past*, ed. Jessica I. Elfenbein, John R. Breihan, and Thomas L. Hollowak (Baltimore: Maryland Historical Society, 2002), 54; M. Ray Della Jr., "The Problem of Negro Labor in the 1850's," *Maryland Historical Magazine* 66, no. 1 (Spring 1971): 19. On William Watkins, see Leroy Graham, *Baltimore: The Nineteenth Century Black Capital* (Washington, DC: University Press of America, 1982), 93–94, 97–108; Martha S. Jones, *Birthright Citizens: A History of Race and Rights in Antebellum America* (New York: Cambridge University Press, 2018), 38–45.

60. *Sun*, 12 October 1844; *Sun*, 14 October 1844; Minute Book E, 14 January 1846; on frustration with arrangements at the Pratt Street Depot, see Minute Book E, 1 February 1844. On the expense of dual depots, see Minute Book E, 1 February 1844. On inconveniences for passengers, see *Sun*, 1 March 1850.

61. Minute Book G, 29 June 1852

62. Ibid.; Thomas Swann to Mayor and City Council of Baltimore, 15 July 1852, Box 91 [WPA 302], CCR; "An Ordinance relating to the Baltimore and Ohio Rail Road Company," No. 87, 16 July 1852, Box 95 [WPA 1318], CCR; this was then passed as Ord. No. 75, "An Ordinance relating to the Baltimore and Ohio Rail Road Company," approved 22 July 1852, in *Ordinances*, 72–73; *Sun*, 19 July 1852; Report of the Committee [on] Internal Improvements on the Petition of the Balto & Ohio Rail Road Co, 20 July 1852, Box 94 [WPA 788], CCR; *Sun*, 21 July 1852; Res. No. 175,

"Resolution to allow the Mayor to convey to the Baltimore and Ohio Rail-Road Company a lot of ground," approved 22 July 1852, in *Ordinances*, 151–152.

63. Land cost from *Sun*, 3 July 1852; see also *Sun*, 13 July 1852; Minute Book G, 29 June 1852. Clearing the land: *Sun*, 1 December 1852. On displacement within Baltimore: Power, "Deconstructing the Slums," 54. During the 1850s, Baltimore went from being a "place of refuge to one of repression" for African Americans, writes historian Christopher Phillips—see Phillips, *Freedom's Port*, 196–198, 201–206, 235–237 (quote on 236); see also Adam Malka, *The Men of Mobtown: Policing Baltimore in the Age of Slavery and Emancipation* (Chapel Hill: University of North Carolina Press, 2018), 116–121. On Watkins: Graham, *Baltimore*, 126; Kellie Carter Jackson, *Force and Freedom: Black Abolitionists and the Politics of Violence* (Philadelphia: University of Pennsylvania Press, 2019), 86–87, 102.

64. *AR* 26 (1852): 8. An expansion of the B&O's infrastructure would lead to further displacement for African Americans in the 1880s: Dennis Patrick Halpin, *A Brotherhood of Liberty: Black Reconstruction and Its Legacies in Baltimore, 1865–1920* (Philadelphia: University of Pennsylvania Press, 2019), 146.

65. *Sun*, 31 December 1852, 4 February 1853; Ele Bowen, *Rambles in the Path of the Steam-Horse. An Off-Hand Olla Podrida, Embracing a General Historical and Descriptive View of the Scenery, Agricultural and Mineral Resources, and Prominent Features of the Travelled Route from Baltimore to Harper's Ferry, Cumberland, Wheeling, Cincinnati, and Louisville* (Philadelphia: Wm. Bromwell and Wm. White Smith, 1855), 128–132; Mary Ellen Hayward and Frank R. Shivers Jr., eds., *The Architecture of Baltimore: An Illustrated History* (Baltimore: Johns Hopkins University Press, 2004), 82–83, 163–164; Carroll L. V. Meeks, *The Railroad Station: An Architectural History* (1956; New York: Dover Publications, 1995), 39–40, 43–46, 71–72; Randolph W. Chalfant, "Calvert Station: Its Structure and Significance," *Maryland Historical Magazine* 74, no. 1 (March 1979): 11–22, esp. 13–16. On the railroad station as a gateway and liminal space, see Wolfgang Schivelbusch, *The Railway Journey: Trans and Travel in the 19th Century*, trans. Anselm Hollo (New York: Urizen Books, 1979), ch. 11.

66. On Boston: Michael Rawson, *Eden on the Charles: The Making of Boston* (Cambridge, MA: Harvard University Press, 2010), 196–197; Carroll L. V. Meeks, "Depots in the City Plan," *Journal of the American Institute of Planners* 14, no. 2 (Spring, 1948): 6–7; *Colton's Map of Boston and Adjacent Cities* (New York: J. H. Colton & Co., 1856). New York: Kurt C. Schlichting, *Grand Central Terminal: Railroads, Engineering, and Architecture in New York City* (Baltimore: Johns Hopkins University Press, 2001), 30–38; Condit, *Port of New York*, 25, 76–77, 86–89. Philadelphia: Churella, *Pennsylvania Railroad*, 511–512.

67. The B&O's experiments laid the groundwork for electrification in other cities, including New York; they took place in 1895. See Condit, *Port of New York*, 188–200.

68. "Rights of the individual": Remonstrance against the Widening of Cecil Alley by Balt & Ohio Rail Road, Presented by Wm. Ridgely from 10th Ward, 11 May 1853, Box 96 [WPA 485], CCR; "entirely monopolized": Petition of Howard Darlington remonstrating against opening and widening Cecil Alley, 18 May 1853, Box 96 [WPA 486], CCR. See also Petition of Simon Martez praying the Council not to widen Cecil Alley from Little Montgomery Street to Ostend Street, 14 February 1853, Box 96 [WPA 487], CCR. Location of Cecil Alley from *Sun*, 31 December 1852. A counterpoint: Petition of George Warner Jr. asking permission to lay down certain rail road switches, 13 June 1853, Box 96 [WPA 488], CCR. None of these petitions references race; of the six signatories (of fifteen) whom I could track down in *Matchett's Baltimore Director for 1854–54* (Baltimore: Richard J. Matchett, 1853), two (William H. Woodyear [373] and Dan Stew-

art [366]) were listed in the "Colored Householders" section and four in the larger compendium of white households (Harmon Classon [62], Howard Darlington [78], George Gelback Jr. [115], J. S. Nicholas [227]).

69. *Sun*, 14 April 1853.

70. *Sun*, 17 May 1855.

71. *Sun*, 27 December 1855.

72. *Sun*, 11 March 1859.

73. *Sun*, 21 May 1859; *Sun*, 11 June 1859; John H. B. Latrobe to Wm. Prescott Smith, 23 May 1859 (Copy), Box 1, Folder 2, GPC.

74. *Sun*, 24 June 1859 (quotes); also *Sun*, 22 June 1859; *American*, 24 June 1859. An infant girl was maimed by a train on a street near Camden Station: Cochran & Stockridge Firm to Prest and Directors of B&O, 30 August 1859, Box 63, Folder 3136.1, GPC.

75. *AR* 33 (1859): 20.

76. *Sun*, 27 October 1875; see also, *Sun*, 19 May 1875, 2 June 1875. Lobbying: William Keyser to John W. Garrett, 23 July 1875, Box 1, Folder 2, GPC; John King Jr., Vice President of the B&O to John W. Garrett, 1 November 1875, Box 1, Folder 2, GPC. An earlier effort: "An Ordinance to close Conway Street between Howard and Eutaw Streets," passed 22 May 1861, Box 1, Folder 2, GPC. Quote from Petition in refference [sic] to the mode of Regulating the Cars of the Baltimore and Ohio R. Road at and near the Camden station Depot, 1868, Box 145 [WPA 229], CCR. See also William Robertson to John W. Garrett, 27 August 1869, Box 34 [WPA 2118], MC; Memorial respecting loading & unloading Cars in S. Eutaw Street, 2 July 1870, Box 156 [WPA 2210], CCR.

77. Nearly complete: *Sun*, 4 March 1864; central clock: *Sun*, 12 February 1857; another comment on the station's improvement can be seen in *Sun*, 25 May 1854. A late improvement (the decoration of the main hall): *Sun*, 18 May 1870. On Baltimore's railroad time: Stover, *Iron Road to the West*, 212.

78. *Sun*, 2 January 1866.

Chapter Six

1. On delivery: Minute Book H, 11 June 1856, 10 September 1856. On coal: Minute Book H, 14 October 1857. On dividend: Minute Book H, 17 December 1856. On journalists: Minute Book H, 8 July 1857. Brinkley's background: *Woods' Baltimore Directory for 1858–59* (Baltimore: John W. Woods, [1859?]), 99. All information concerning the composition of the board and the tenure of board members comes from G. F. May, *Chronological and Alphabetical Lists of Presidents and Directors, also Executive Officers and Heads of Various Departments of the Baltimore and Ohio Railroad Company, 1827–1929* (Baltimore: Office of the Secretary, Baltimore & Ohio, 1929), at the B&O Museum. I am indebted to Daniel Zink for locating this pamphlet.

2. On cronyism: *Sun*, 25 June 1855. Bribes: *Sun*, 17 November 1855; Minute Book H, 12 December 1855. Attacks on fellow board members: Copy of Resolution [of] Finance Committee, 16 May 1856, Box 63, RGFP; *Rules of Order for the Government of the Board of Directors of the Baltimore and Ohio Railroad Company* (Baltimore: James Lucas & Son, 1857).

3. City Directors of B&O to Mayor of Baltimore, 1858, Box 30 [WPA 35], MC; *American*, 24 July 1858; *Sun*, 10, 21 September 1858.

4. Scholars have found their accounts persuasive to varying degrees. Alfred D. Chandler Jr. famously argues that railroads became the first modern (meaning multifaceted and hierarchical) businesses "because they had to." The wide geographical scope of railroad operations and the

pressing decisions, both daily and for the long term, that had to be made necessitated the creation of modern corporate structure and facilitated the rise of the middle manager, who takes center stage in his analysis instead of the "part-time members of the board of directors"—see *The Visible Hand: The Managerial Revolution in American Business* (Cambridge, MA: Belknap Press of Harvard University Press, 1977), quotes on 120, 123. But as the sociologist Charles Perrow points out, the different path taken by European railways undercuts the claim that these changes were inevitable. The relevant question, he suggests, is not which system is more efficient but to whom the efficiencies accrue: *Organizing America: Wealth, Power, and the Origins of Corporate Capitalism* (Princeton, NJ: Princeton University Press, 2002). This position more closely accords with my findings in this chapter, which frames changes in railroad practices in the 1850s and 1860s as matters principally of the distribution of power. Private investors play a much larger role in this analysis than they do in Chandler's, likely because he assumes that the private nature of the company was already set by the 1850s. On the privatization of the railroad more generally in this period, see also James A. Ward, *Railroads and the Character of America, 1820–1887* (Knoxville: University of Tennessee Press, 1986), 136–139.

5. *Proceedings of the Individual Stockholders of the Baltimore and Ohio Rail Road Company, with the Report of the Committee of Stockholders, to whom the Annual Report of the President & Directors, dated October 1854, was referred* (Baltimore: John Murphy, 1854), 4–5. John W. Garrett later characterized these closed-door meetings as an opportunity to determine the "proper course" of action for the company and for their faction—*Sun*, "Special Meeting of the Balto. and Ohio Railroad," 19 March 1857.

6. *Proceedings of the Individual Stockholders*, 14–15, 17–20. See also *Sun*, 17 October 1854.

7. See the appendix for sources and methodology behind this group portrait of the post-1854 private directors.

8. *Sun*, 3 April 1855 (quotes). On McLean's D.C. background and Harvard education: *New-Bedford Mercury*, 9 September 1825; on McLean's occupation and address: *Matchett's Baltimore Director for 1855–56* (Baltimore: R. J. Matchett, 1855), 227. On William G. Harrison's career before assuming the presidency of the B&O: *Matchett's Baltimore Director for 1851* (Baltimore: R. J. Matchett, 1851), 119. On public directors' turnover, see the appendix.

9. *Sun*, 3 April 1855. McLean did not come to this idea on his own—the occasion for his remark was a proposal that had arisen in the city council to sell the city's shares in the B&O: Resolutions to sell Baltimore & Ohio RR Stock, 22 February 1855, Box 104, CCR; also, *Sun*, 5, 9 March 1855. Pennsylvania eventually sold the Main Line to the PRR for $7.5 million in 1857: *New York Times*, 26 July 1857. On the withdrawal of state support for internal improvements and the influx of municipal funding (though without municipal control), see Carter Goodrich, *Government Promotion of American Canals and Railroads, 1800–1890* (1960; Westport, CT: Greenwood Press, 1974), 74, 97–98, 162–164, 268 ($125 million); Louis Hartz, *Economic Policy and Democratic Thought: Pennsylvania, 1776–1860* (1948; Chicago: Quadrangle Books, 1968), 85–89; Harry H. Pierce, *Railroads of New York: A Study of Government Aid, 1826–1875* (Cambridge, MA: Harvard University Press, 1953), 18–21. An exception was Massachusetts, which launched a new, publicly aided western rail line in 1854; the commonwealth did not, however, strive to control the management of the railroads it supported: Edward Chase Kirkland, *Men, Cities, and Transportation: A Study in New England History, 1800–1920*, 2 vols. (Cambridge, MA: Harvard University Press, 1948), 1:324–326. This period also witnessed the first significant aid to the railroads from the national government in the form of the Land Grant Act of 1850, which yielded federal lands in several western states to support the development of rail networks: Zachary Callen, *Railroads*

and American Political Development: Infrastructure, Federalism, and State Building (Lawrence: University Press of Kansas, 2016), 153–156, 179–181.

10. "Legitimate owners" is from McLean's speech, *Sun,* 3 April 1855; *Report of the Directors Representing the City in the Baltimore & Ohio Rail Road Company, to the Mayor and City Council of Baltimore* (Baltimore: James Lucas & Son, 1855), 4, 13–17.

11. On stockjobbing and public responsibility: *Sun,* 2, 14 February 1854. The letters were signed by "Viator," actually Alexander Marshall of Virginia, who felt he was owed $50,000 for services rendered by the B&O in the state legislature at Richmond: [Alexander J. Marshall], *Baltimore and Ohio Rail Road Company. An Analysis of their Reports since 1848; their Misrepresentations Sifted & Exposed in a Series of Chapters, under the Signature of "Viator." By a Virginian* [Baltimore? 1854], chs. 1–4.

12. *Sun,* 3 April 1855. Vickers's occupation: *Matchett's Baltimore Director for 1855–56,* 352.

13. *Report of the Directors Representing the City,* 4.

14. For example: *Sun,* 14 December 1848; *Patriot* quoted in *Sun,* 16 October 1850.

15. *A Communication of the Stockholders of the Baltimore & Ohio Railroad Company, by a Stockholder* (Baltimore: Jos. Robinson, 1852), 3, 17.

16. *Sun,* 13 September 1853. See also Minute Book G, 12 April 1854; D. B. Major to the President and Directors of the Baltimore & Ohio Railroad Company (Copy), March 1854, Box 58, RGFP.

17. Mayor's Communication, January 1856, in *Ordinances,* A24.

18. *Sun,* 8 January 1848; Thomas Swann, "To the Stockholders of the Baltimore and Ohio Rail Road Company," [n.d.], p. 4, Box 3, Swann Collection. Charles Francis Adams Jr. later described this as a common practice among railroad corporations as they built their lines: see Adams, "The Railroad System" in *Chapters of Erie, and Other Essays* (Boston: James R. Osgood and Co., 1871), 399–400.

19. *Address and Report of a Select Committee of the Baltimore and Ohio Railroad Company: Also, a Letter from the President, Recommending Measures for the Immediate Prosecution of the Road to the Ohio River* (Baltimore: John D. Toy, 1848), 36, 27. The city government contemplated selling dividend stock in order to lower the municipal tax rate, but held off: *The City and the Baltimore and Ohio Rail Road Dividend Stock* (Baltimore: Murphy & Co., [1850]).

20. Edward Hungerford, *The Story of the Baltimore & Ohio Railroad, 1827–1927,* 2 vols. (New York: G. P. Putnam's Sons, 1928), 1:251; John F. Stover, *History of the Baltimore and Ohio Railroad* (West Lafayette, IN: Purdue University Press, 1987), 93–94.

21. Minute Book H, 10 December 1856.

22. Elected as stockholder director: J. J. Atkinson, Secretary of the Balt. & Ohio Railroad Co., to John W. Garrett, Esq., 12 July 1855, Box 61, RGFP. Garrett family background: Kathleen Waters Sander, *John W. Garrett and the Baltimore & Ohio Railroad* (Baltimore: Johns Hopkins University Press, 2017), 10–19, 24, 38–43, 48–56, 59–60, 103.

23. Sander, *John W. Garrett,* 60–64, 68–69 (quote on 62); Stover, *History of the Baltimore & Ohio Railroad,* 79–80; William Bruce Catton, "John W. Garrett of the Baltimore & Ohio: A Study in Seaport and Railroad Competition, 1820–1874" (PhD diss., Northwestern University, 1959), 63–64.

24. He was the chairman of the "Committee of Seven Stockholders"—see J. J. Atkinson, Treas., B&O RR Co., 18 October 1854, Box 60, RGFP; Copy of Letter from J. W. Garrett to J. J. Atkinson, Treas., B&O RR Co., 24 October 1854, Box 60, RGFP; Wm. G. Harrison, Pres. B&O RR Co to John W. Garrett, 25 October 1854, Box 60, RGFP.

25. *Sun*, 18 December 1856; Sander, *John W. Garrett*, 70–71.

26. *Sun*, "EXTRA DIVIDEND OF THE BALTIMORE AND OHIO R. R. CO.," 13 December 1856. There were several people named William Henry Norris living in Baltimore at this time, including a bank cashier and a lawyer; my guess is that this person was the attorney, because he later represented the B&O in the extra-dividend case—see *Sun*, "THE RAILROAD 'EXTRA DIVIDEND' CASE," 30 July 1859, and the appendix.

27. *Sun*, "THE EXTRA DIVIDEND," 17 December 1856.

28. *Sun*, 11 December 1856; see also *American*, 4 December and 11 December 1856.

29. Resolutions relative to Balt & Ohio Rail Road Company, 3 December 1856, Box 106 [WPA 740], CCR; *Sun*, 30 December 1856; *Sun*, "BALTIMORE AND OHIO RAILROAD—The Extra Dividend Question," 13 December 1856; *Sun*, 15 December 1856; *American*, 4 December 1856. Counterpoints: *Sun*, 31 December 1856; *Sun*, "The Extra Dividend," 1 January 1857.

30. *Sun*, 27 December 1856 and "The Extra Dividend," 1 January 1857.

31. First quote from "Majority and Minority Reports" in *Sun*, "The Extra Dividend," 2 January 1857; second from *Sun*, "The Baltimore and Ohio Railroad Co's Extra Dividend: Correspondence between Mayor Swann and the President of the Road," 3 January 1857.

32. Minute Book H, 17 December 1856. The city directors were censured by the council for their actions: Majority Report of Special Committee to whom was referred Communications of the Mayor &c Relating to Extra Dividend of Baltimore and Ohio Rail Road Company, 31 December 1856, Box 106 [WPA 746], CCR; *Sun*, 13 January 1857. See also *Sun*, "*The Baltimore and Ohio Railroad Extra Dividend*," 1 January 1857.

33. Initially Swann opposed the injunction, but he changed in his mind after the B&O refused to yield: *Sun*, 24 December 1856; for the resolution and injunction, see Resolutions relative to B&O RR Co, 22 December 1856, Box 106 [WPA 745], CCR; "Majority and Minority Reports" in *Sun*, "The Extra Dividend," 2 January 1857; *Sun*, "The Baltimore and Ohio Railroad Co's Extra Dividend: Correspondence Between Mayor Swann and the President of the Road," 3 January 1857; Res. No. 7, "Resolution directing the employment of additional Counsel in the case of the Mayor and City Council against the Baltimore and Ohio Railroad Company," approved 9 February 1857, in *Ordinances*, 109–110.

34. *The Mayor and City Council of Baltimore, vs. the Baltimore and Ohio Railroad Company: Containing the Bill and Answer, and the Exhibits referred to in the latter* (Baltimore: John Murphy & Co., 1857), 5–7, 9–10, 17; *Sun*, 12 January 1857; also, 8 January 1857.

35. The theories of shareholder value advanced by proponents of the Extra Dividend could be transplanted with little modification to the corporate boardrooms of the late twentieth century: see Karen Ho, *Liquidated: An Ethnography of Wall Street* (Durham, NC: Duke University Press, 2009).

36. By this time, some in the city council had decided the B&O was in a suitable financial position to declare the dividend anyway: Preamble and Resolution in relation to the Thirty Per Cent, or extra dividend of the Baltimore and Ohio Railroad Company, 17 July 1860, Box 118 [WPA 1031], CCR; Resolution of inquiry directed to Messrs. Dulaney & Meredith in relation to the Extra dividend of the B&O RR Co, 18 July 1860, Box 118 [WPA 1034], CCR; *Sun*, 18 July 1860; Preamble and Resolution relative to obtaining information in relation to the settlement of the suit between the city & B&O Rail Road, 19 July 1860, Box 118 [WPA 1035], CCR. The final decision and Garrett's response is written up in Baltimore & Ohio R.R. Company, *Extra Dividend Case. Statement made by the President to the Board of Directors, At their Meeting on the 12th September, 1860, with the Opinion of Messrs. Randall & Hagner, Concurred in by William Price,*

Esq., of counsel for the state of Maryland, in reference thereto (Baltimore: W. M. Innes, 1860). Also Stover, *History of the Baltimore & Ohio*, 95.

37. *AR* 34 (1860): 17–18.

38. Campbell Graham to Henry S. Garrett Jr., 26 May 1860, Box 71, RGFP; George W. Robinson to John W. Garrett, 12 July 1860, Box 71, RGFP; Campbell Graham to Henry S. Garrett, 3 August 1860, Box 71, RGFP. Garrett also arranged for a quiet sale of $150,000 in shares in order to avoid "a very serious decline in prices." Jno. W. Garrett to S. Brady, 24 May 1860, Box 71, RGFP.

39. George N. Moale to his Uncle (Unnamed), 27 March 1860, George Nicholas Moale Correspondence, 1857–1861, MS 2489, MdHS.

40. *Sun*, 30 December 1852.

41. *Sun*, 31 December 1856; also *American*, "The Locomotive Question," 1 January 1857.

42. *American*, "The Working Men and the Baltimore and Ohio Rail Road," 3 January 1857 (quote); *Sun*, 1 January 1857.

43. *Sun*, "MAMMOTH MACHINE SHOP," 8 January 1857. This article is signed "R.," who is almost certainly Ross Winans. On Ross Winans: Hungerford, *The Story of the Baltimore & Ohio Railroad*, 1:77–79, 1:228–232, 1:260–263, and ch. 5 in vol. 2; Mary Ellen Hayward, *Baltimore's Alley Houses: Homes for Working People since the 1780s* (Baltimore: Johns Hopkins University Press, 2008), 126, 138–139; James D. Dilts, *The Great Road: The Building of the Baltimore & Ohio, the Nation's First Railroad, 1828–1853* (Stanford, CA: Stanford University Press, 1993), 364–365.

44. *Papers relative to the recent Contracts for Motive Power, by the Baltimore and Ohio Rail Road Co. and the Reports of the Officers of the Different Departments on the Relative Advantages of the Winans Camel Engine, and the Ten Wheel Engine, for various Branches of their Service* (Baltimore: James Lucas & Son, 1857), 4–5, 9. Baltimore-based locomotive manufacturer Adam Denmead, one of Ross Winans' competitors, confirmed this story: *American*, "To the Editors of the American," 3 January 1857.

45. *American*, 6 January 1857.

46. Preamble and Resolution in relation to the Balto & Ohio Railroad Co, 24 November 1858, Box 110 [WPA 604], CCR; Hungerford, *Story of the Baltimore & Ohio*, 2:88–89.

47. William G. Thomas, *The Iron Way: Railroads, the Civil War, and the Making of Modern America* (New Haven, CT: Yale University Press, 2011), 45–51, 217 (table 5), 218 (table 6); Walter Licht, *Working for the Railroad: The Organization of Work in the Nineteenth Century* (Princeton, NJ: Princeton University Press, 1983), 13–14.

48. Extract from the Minutes of the Board of Directors of the Baltimore & Ohio Railroad Company, 14 January 1857, Box 64, RGFP; Sander, *John W. Garrett*, 72–73.

49. *American*, 30 April 1857.

50. *Sun*, 1 May 1857.

51. *Sun*, 2 May 1857 (quote); *Sun*, 4 May 1857; W. S. Woodside to Col. A. P. Shutt, 1 and 4 May 1857, Vertical File, MdHS.

52. Minute Book H, 13 May 1857, 10 June 1857.

53. *Sun*, 14 May 1857 (quotes); Minute Book H, 13 May 1857.

54. Minute Book H, 13 May 1857 (blacklist); Minute Book H, 9 December 1857 (prosecution); Felton quoted in Sander, *John W. Garrett*, 73.

55. *Sun*, 15 May 1857.

56. Tracy Matthew Melton, *Hanging Henry Gambrill: The Violent Career of Baltimore's Plug Uglies, 1854–1860* (Baltimore: Maryland Historical Society, 2005), 88–89; Matthew A. Crenson, *Baltimore: A Political History* (Baltimore: Johns Hopkins University Press, 2017), 204–205.

57. Crenson, *Baltimore*, 208–211, 223–230; Gary Lawson Browne, *Baltimore in the Nation, 1789–1861* (Chapel Hill: University of North Carolina Press, 1980), 208–212; Jean H. Baker, *Ambivalent Americans: The Know-Nothing Party in Maryland* (Baltimore: Johns Hopkins University Press, 1977); Frank Towers, "Violence as a Tool of Party Dominance: Election Riots and the Baltimore Know-Nothings, 1854–1860," *Maryland Historical Magazine* 93, no. 1 (March 1998): 4–37. On the violence of this era in urban history, see Mary P. Ryan, *Civic Wars: Democracy and Public Life in the American City during the Nineteenth Century* (Berkeley: University of California Press, 1997), ch. 4; David Grimsted, *American Mobbing, 1828–1861: Toward Civil War* (New York: Oxford University Press, 1998).

58. *American*, 1 July 1858.

59. *American*, "The Caucus Nominations for Railroad Directors," 24 January 1859 (quote); also *American*, "The City Railroad Directors," 24 January 1859; *Sun*, 14 May 1858.

60. On his influence within the Board and among the stockholders: A. H. Herr to John Garrett, 27 June 1856, Box 63, RGFP, and Wm. Henry Norris to John W. Garrett, 19 October 1856, Box 63, RGFP. President pro tem: C. Brooks to John W. Garrett, 2 December 1856, Box 64, RGFP.

61. Planting items in the press: H. D. Mears to John W. Garrett, 18 October 1856, Box 64, RGFP; voting against reporters' access: Minute Book H, 8 July 1857. This came on the heels of a series of controversies concerning newspaper access in which directors—principally though not exclusively public directors—sought to exclude journalists for fear, they said, of misrepresentation: Minute Book G, 13 June, 14 June, 21 June 1855; *Sun*, 21 June 1855 and 12 July 1855.

62. Anonymous to John W. Garrett, April 1858, Box 67, RGFP.

63. *Sun*, 12 November 1858; *Sun*, 13 November 1858; Resolution in reference to the Baltimore & Ohio RR, 13 November 1858, Box 110 [WPA 601], CCR; *American*, 3, 16 November 1858; *Sun*, 18 November 1858; Sander, *John W. Garrett*, 76.

64. Sander, *John W. Garrett*, 80, 83–85, 188–192.

65. *Sun*, 11 February 1860; [George R. Vickers], *Objections to Yielding to Northerners the Control of the Baltimore and Ohio Rail Road, on which depends the development of the Farms, Mines, Manufactures and Trade of the State of Maryland, by a Marylander* (Baltimore, 1860), 3.

66. *Sun*, 2 March 1860.

67. Preamble and Resolution in relation to the State and City interest in the Baltimore and Ohio Railroad Company, [1860], Box 118 [WPA 1030], CCR.

68. [Vickers], *Objections to Yielding to Northerners*, 3–5.

69. Ibid., 7–10, 16–20. See also the article by "Tocsin" in *Sun*, 13 February 1860.

70. Report of the Joint Standing Committee on internal improvements on the Mayor's Message in reference to the Directors of the Balto & Ohio Rail Road, 16 February 1864, Box 130 [WPA 751], CCR; *Sun*, 18 February 1864; on the 1867 efforts: *A Statement showing the effect that might be produced against the State of Maryland and City of Baltimore by the proposed increase of the Stockholder Directors in the Baltimore and Ohio R. R. Company, by a Marylander* [Baltimore, 1867].

71. Hartz, *Economic Policy and Democratic Thought*, 123–128, quote on 127; Albert J. Churella, *The Pennsylvania Railroad*, vol. 1, *Building an Empire, 1846–1917* (Philadelphia: University of Pennsylvania Press, 2013), 182; John Lauritz Larson, *Internal Improvement: National Public Works and the Promise of Popular Government in the Early United States* (Chapel Hill: University of North Carolina Press, 2001), 252–255.

72. *New York Times* quoted in *American*, 9 January 1860. On the destabilizing effect of the Panic of 1857: Chandler, *Visible Hand*, 126.

73. Evidence of these tactics and angry correspondence can be found in the Robert Garrett Family Papers at the Library of Congress. For example: L. S. Gordon, General Freight Agent for the B&O, to J. Edgar Thomson, 8 August 1856, Box 63, RGFP; J. Edgar Thomson to John W. Garrett, 5 November 1856, Box 64, RGFP; J. Edgar Thomson to John W. Garrett, 3 August 1857, Box 66, RGFP; J. Edgar Thomson to Chauncey Brooks, 31 July 1857, Box 65, RGFP; Calhoun & Cowton, Agents, to John W. Garrett, 6 August 1857, Box 66, RGFP.

74. M. Porter to John W. Garrett, 10 January 1857, Box 64, RGFP. The phrase "entangling alliances" is from Jefferson's "First Inaugural Address," delivered 4 March 1801, jeffersonpapers .princeton.edu/selected-documents/first-inaugural-address.

75. Circular to Agents and Connecting Lines, September 1858, Box 68, RGFP. On rate wars and public confidence, see also John W. Garrett to Chas. Moran, Pres., New York & Erie, 31 July 1857, Box 65, RGFP. Rate wars stimulated public opposition because they exacerbated discrimination against local shippers: J. Edgar Thomson to John W. Garrett, 21 April 1858, Box 67, RGFP.

76. Agreement between the New York Central, [New York & Erie], Pennsylvania Company and the Balto & Ohio Companies, 7 September 1857, 2–3, 6, Box 66, RGFP.

77. E. F. Fuller to John W. Garrett, 1 November 1858, Box 68, RGFP. For a similar complaint that came in on the same day, see Chas. Moran to J. W. Garrett, 1 November 1858, Box 68, RGFP.

78. L. M. Cole to J. W. Garrett, 21 October 1858, Box 68, RGFP; Louis L. Houpt to L. M. Cole, 1 October 1858, Box 68, RGFP. On the notional support for home markets: C. Brooks to President of Cleveland Convention, 27 September 1856, Box 63, RGFP. The struggles within the Pennsylvania Railroad and Thomson's rise to power fit much more neatly within the narrative of professionalization advanced by Chandler than the story of Garrett and the B&O does—see Churella, *Pennsylvania Railroad*, 125–149.

79. J. Edgar Thomson to John W. Garrett, 7 October 1858, Box 68, RGFP.

80. J. Edgar Thomson to John W. Garrett, 1 October 1858, Box 68, RGFP.

81. *Sun*, 20 May 1858.

82. *Annual Statement of Trade and Commerce of Baltimore, for the Year 1860. Office of the Baltimore Daily American*, 1 January 1861; shipping manifest: J. B. Ford to John W. Garrett, 4 October 1856, Box 65, RGFP. On the B&O's annual reports: Gary John Previts and William D. Samson, "Exploring the Contents of the Baltimore and Ohio Railroad Annual Reports, 1827–1856," *Accounting Historians Journal* 27, no. 1 (June 2000): 1-42.

83. *Sun*, 20 May 1858. The B&O reported gross earnings of $4,616,998.95 on the Main Stem for the fiscal year ending 30 September 1857: *Sun*, 20 October 1857.

84. [Vickers], *Objections to Yielding to Northerners*, 12–13, 23; see also Minute Book H, 9 September 1857.

85. "Cruel step-mother": *Memorial to the Baltimore and Ohio Railroad Company, and Reports thereupon of the Majority and the Minority of its Committee on Transportation & Machinery, concerning the charge for Delivery of Cars in the Streets of Baltimore, October, 1857* (Baltimore: John Murphy & Co., 1857), 4; "handmaid": *Daily Exchange*, 11 September 1860, reprinted in the *Sun*, 12 September 1860; "parricidal": [Vickers], *Objections to Yielding to Northerners*, 12. See also *Statement to the General Assembly of Maryland, Relative to the Charge of Local Transportation over the Baltimore and Ohio Rail Road. January 1860* [Baltimore: 1860]. On the hearings: Order of the House of Delegates to the Presidents of the Northern Central and B&O Railroads, 17 January 1860, Box 29, Folder 474, GPC; [Maryland], *Testimony taken before the Special Committee on the Baltimore and Ohio Railroad* [Annapolis: 1860].

86. Garrett quoted in *American*, 10 June 1859; also, *American*, 31 January 1859.

87. Resolution of the Corn and Flour Exchange, [1860], Box 29, Folder 474, GPC. See also J. M. Drill to John W. Garrett, 13 January 1860, Box 29, Folder 474, GPC; *Sun*, 21, 23 January 1860.

88. *Sun*, 27 January 1859; also, *Sun*, 11, 14, 21 January 1859.

89. [Maryland], *Testimony taken before the Special Committee on the Baltimore and Ohio Railroad* [Annapolis: 1860], 8, 11–12. Most of the other witnesses testifying were businessmen involved in some of Baltimore's principal industries, such as sugar and coffee imports. They all concurred that the B&O had discriminated in their favor.

90. Committee report and expression of "regret": [Maryland], [Document BB], *By the House of Delegates February 28th, 1860. Report of a Select Committee appointed by the House of Delegates of Maryland, to Inquire into Certain Charges made by Jas. E. Tyson against the Baltimore and Ohio Railroad Co* [Annapolis, MD, 1860], 2. The company itself later echoed this position: Minute Book I, 10 June 1863. The minority report commented on the need for discrimination: Report of the Minority of the Committee of the House of Delegates appointed to Inquire into the Charges of James E. Tyson, [1860], quote on 8–9, Box 29, Folder 474, GPC. The *Sun* agreed: 10 August 1860.

91. *American*, 22 November 1859 (on the "science" of railroad management); *American*, 28 January 1859 (on absolute discrimination). An example of absolute discrimination: Woods, Weeks & Co. to John W. Garrett, 30 March 1866, Box 29, Folder 474, GPC. See also *Sun*, 10 March 1868.

92. Mayor John Chapman to Second Branch of City Council, 22 June 1863, Box 126 [WPA 590], CCR.

93. On Philadelphia and eastern efforts to regulate railroad rates generally, see George H. Miller, *Railroads and the Granger Laws* (Madison: University of Wisconsin Press, 1971), 32–41; on opposition from New York City interests, see Lee Benson, *Merchants, Farmers, & Railroads: Railroad Regulation and New York Politics, 1850-1887* (Cambridge, MA: Harvard University Press, 1955), 10–16; on the Pittsburghers' laments, see Churella, *Pennsylvania Railroad*, 199–200. In Boston, merchants complained in the 1850s that rates on the Boston & Albany favored New York City, and the state saw an unsuccessful movement for pro-rata rates in the 1870s, but state-funded railroads linking Boston to the West had to, of necessity, connect with the New York Central: see Kirkland, *Men, Cities, and Transportation*, 1:152, 1:371–376.

94. *American Railway Times* reprinted in *American*, 31 January 1860; Miller, *Railroads and the Granger Laws*, 32–41; Frederick Merk, "Eastern Antecedents of the Grangers," *Agricultural History* 23, no. 1 (January 1949): 1–8.

95. William J. Novak, "The Public Utility Idea and the Origins of Modern Business Regulation," in *Corporations and American Democracy*, ed. Naomi R. Lamoreaux and Novak (Cambridge, MA: Harvard University Press, 2017), 139–176, esp. 160–171. On anti-urbanism among later rail reformers, see Elizabeth Sanders, *Roots of Reform: Farmers, Workers, and the American State, 1877-1917* (Chicago: University of Chicago Press, 1999), 194–195.

96. William Cronon places the fixed cost problem at the center of his analysis of railroad rates and thus his explanation of the spatial logic of railroad capital: *Nature's Metropolis: Chicago and the Great West* (New York: W. W. Norton, 1991), 84–87. See also Richard White, *Railroaded: The Transcontinentals and the Making of Modern America* (New York: W. W. Norton, 2011), 5–8; Miller, *Railroads and the Granger Laws*, 39; Merk, "Eastern Antecedents," 7–8. For a critical assessment of the fixed cost problem, see Gerald Berk, *Alternative Tracks: The Constitution of the American Industrial Order, 1865-1917* (Baltimore: Johns Hopkins University Press, 1994), ch. 3.

97. See, for example, political economist Henry Carey, who in 1865 dubbed rate discrim-

ination "The Railroad Question": Carey, "The Railroad Question," in *Miscellaneous Works of Henry C. Carey, with a Memoir by Dr. William Elder, and a Portrait* (Philadelphia: Henry Carey Baird & Co., 1883), 1:2–3. See also Berk, *Alternate Tracks*, esp. 13–14 and chs. 4–5.

98. *American*, 20 February 1860 (quote); also *American*, 14 February 1860 (on the movement in Pennsylvania); see *Sun*, 10 March 1868 for a resurgence of antidiscrimination legislation in New York.

99. H. J. Jewett, *Letter of H. J. Jewett, President of the Central Ohio Railroad Company, to the President and Directors of the Baltimore and Ohio Railroad Company, in regard to the Connection between the two Roads* (Baltimore: John F. Wiley, 1858), esp. 5–6; see also H. J. Jewett to J. W. Garrett, 26 February 1863, Box 8, B&O Business Letters; P. G. Van Winkle, *Letter to the President and Directors of the Baltimore and Ohio Railroad Company, from P. G. Van Winkle, President of the Northwestern Virginia Railroad Company* (Baltimore: John F. Wiley, 1858).

100. *Reports of the Majority and Minority of the Special Committee of the Baltimore & Ohio Railroad Co. appointed to Investigate its Financial Condition, General Line of Policy Heretofore Pursued, Etc. Presented at a Meeting of the Board, April 14, 1858* (Baltimore: William M. Innes, 1858), esp. 7–9, 16–22.

101. Robert Garrett & Sons dealt heavily in these bonds, as the RGFP in the Library of Congress shows. See, e.g., Johns Hopkins to R. Garrett & Sons, 3 March 1854, Box 58. On Garrett's role: Elias Fassett to John W. Garrett, 6, 11, 12 April 1858, Box 67; Campbell Graham to Henry S. Garrett Jr., 26 May 1860, Box 71. Outside observers suggested that the B&O's emphasis on through trade reflected the private directors' interest in funneling traffic to the Central: *Clipper* reprinted in Minute Book H, 12 May 1858.

102. John H. Done, Master of Transportation, to William G. Harrison, President of the B&O, 12 June 1854, Box 59, RGFP; see also W. Bollman, Master of Road to Wm. G. Harrison, President of the B&O, 7 June 1854, Box 59, RGFP.

103. James C. Clark to Henry Garrett, 5 February 1855, Box 60, RGFP; L. M. Cole to John W. Garrett, 1 April 1858, Box 67, RGFP.

104. Charles W. Russell to J. W. Garrett, 30 July 1860, Box 8, B&O Business Letters.

105. See for example Done to Harrison, 12 June 1854, Box 59, RGFP; Benjamin H. Latrobe to the President and Directors of the Balto & Ohio R Road Company, 6 July 1857, Box 65, RGFP. On the tendency toward consolidation: *Philadelphia Public Ledger*, 24 August 1869. On the formation of trunk line systems more generally, see John F. Stover, *Iron Road to the West: American Railroads in the 1850s* (New York: Columbia University Press, 1978), 119–122.

106. J. Edgar Thomson to John W. Garrett (Copy), 14 March 1863, Box 74, RGFP.

107. "Extract from the Minutes of the Board of Directors of the Baltimore & Ohio Railroad Company," 11 March 1863, Box 8, B&O Business Letters.

108. Report of the Joint Standing Committee on Internal Improvements in relation to the Injunction Lately laid by his Honor the Mayor to enjoin the Baltimore and Ohio Rail road Company from purchasing the First Mortgage Bonds of the Central Ohio Railroad, 19 March 1863, Box 127 [WPA 770], CCR.

109. Minority Report and Resolution in relation to the Mayor's Injunction to prevent the Officers of the Balto & Ohio R. R. from investing $1,500,000 in the 1st Mortgage Bonds of the Central Ohio R. R. Co, 23 March 1863, CCR.

110. *The Mayor & City Council of Baltimore, vs. The Baltimore & Ohio Rail Road Company. In the Circuit Court for Baltimore City. Injunction to Restrain the Defendants from Substituting themselves in place of the First Mortgagees of the Central Ohio Rail Road Co. for Complainants,*

William Price and Jno. L. Thomas, Esqs. For Defendants, John H. B. Latrobe, Esq. (Baltimore: John D. Toy, 1863), 42–43, 46, 49, 51, 53.

111. *The Mayor & City Council of Baltimore, vs. The Baltimore & Ohio,* 11, 20–21, 23, 60, 65–66. On Price's background, prominence, and other work: *Sun,* 24 October 1855, 27 May 1862 (sworn in as U.S.D.A.); Baltimore & Ohio R.R. Co., *Extra Dividend Case* (support for the extra dividend).

112. *The Mayor & City Council of Baltimore, vs. the Baltimore & Ohio,* 78–79.

113. Agreement with the Central Ohio Rail Road Co. re: assignment of first mortgage Bonds to the B&O RR Co., 9 April 1863, Box 8, B&O Business Letters. Garrett found the city's objections both as frustrating and as fruitless as their objections to the Extra Dividend seven years earlier: *American,* 13 March 1863.

114. *Sun,* 30 March 1865; John W. Garrett, *Address of John W. Garrett, on his Re-Election as President of the Baltimore & Ohio R. R. Co., On the 23d November, 1864 . . .* (Baltimore: Kelly & Piet, 1865), 8.

115. John Lee Chapman, Mayor's Message, 12 January 1864, in *Ordinances,* A24-A25. Later that year, the city began to arrange to transfer its interests in the NWV and the P&C to the B&O: John W. Garrett to Johns Hopkins, 23 May 1864, Box 10, B&O Business Letters; Minute Book I, 14 September 1864.

116. John Lee Chapman, Mayor's Message, 3 January 1865, in *Ordinances,* A19-A20. For other counterfactual speculations, see Chapman, Mayor's Message, 15 January 1866, in *Ordinances,* A25-A26; *Statement . . . Relative to the Charge of Local Transportation,* 10; Vickers, *Objections to Yielding to Northerners,* 11–15. On the coal question specifically, Garrett responded that the B&O's rates were the lowest that could be found in the country, but Chapman's argument had been that the railroad charged high rates relative to its expenses: *Sun,* 13 January 1865; Minute Book I, 8 February 1865.

117. Johnson quoted in *Memoranda Concerning Baltimore City and its Surroundings. Dedicated to the Western Editors who visit Baltimore on the Editorial Excursion over the Baltimore and Ohio Railroad, and its Western Connecting Lines, May and June, 1860* (Baltimore: W. M. Innes, 1860), 58.

Chapter Seven

1. George William Brown, *Baltimore and the Nineteenth of April, 1861* (1887; Baltimore: Johns Hopkins University Press, 2001), ch. 4. Gov. Hicks denied he had anything to do with the controversial decision to burn the bridges, while Mayor Brown protested it was done under Hicks's supervision: *Communication from the Mayor of Baltimore, with the Mayor and Board of Police of Baltimore City* (Frederick, MD: Elihu S. Riley, 1861), 2–4, 8. See also Robert J. Brugger, with the assistance of Cynthia Horsburgh Requardt, Robert I. Cottom Jr., and Mary Ellen Hayward, *Maryland: A Middle Temperament, 1634–1980* (Baltimore: Johns Hopkins University Press, 1988), 274–281; Barbara Jeanne Fields, *Slavery and Freedom on the Middle Ground: Maryland during the Nineteenth Century* (New Haven, CT: Yale University Press, 1985), 93–100; Festus P. Summers, *The Baltimore and Ohio in the Civil War* (New York: G. P. Putnam's Sons, 1939), 49–58. The mayor also asked Garrett to send the soldiers back to the state line: Mayor George William Brown to John W. Garrett, 19 April 1861, Box 72, RGFP.

2. On the consolidation of federal authority in this period: Richard Franklin Bensel, *Yankee Leviathan: The Origin of Central State Authority in America, 1859–1877* (New York: Cambridge

University Press, 1990); William J. Novak, "The Myth of the 'Weak' American State," *American Historical Review* 113, no. 3 (June 2008): 752–772; Brian Balogh, *A Government Out of Sight: The Mystery of National Authority in Nineteenth-Century America* (New York: Cambridge University Press, 2009); Mark R. Wilson, *The Business of Civil War: Military Mobilization and the State, 1861–1865* (Baltimore: Johns Hopkins University Press, 2006); Robert G. Angevine, *The Railroad and the State: War, Politics, and Technology in Nineteenth-Century America* (Stanford, CA: Stanford University Press, 2004); Richard White, *Railroaded: The Transcontinentals and the Making of Modern America* (New York: W. W. Norton, 2011). On the consolidation of corporate power during and after the Civil War: William G. Roy, *Socializing Capital: The Rise of the Large Industrial Corporation in America* (Princeton, NJ: Princeton University Press, 1997); Sean Patrick Adams, "Soulless Monsters and Iron Horses: The Civil War, Institutional Change, and American Capitalism," in *Capitalism Takes Command: The Social Transformation of Nineteenth-Century America*, ed. Michael Zakim and Gary J. Kornblith (Chicago: University of Chicago Press, 2012), 249–276.

3. John F. Dillon, *Commentaries on the Law of Municipal Corporations*, 3rd ed., rev. and enlarged (Boston: Little, Brown, and Co., 1881), x, 209. On the background of Dillon's rule and the common-law home arguments about home rule he superseded: Edwin A. Gere Jr., "Dillon's Rule and the Cooley Doctrine: Reflections of the Political Culture," *Journal of Urban History* 8, no. 3 (May 1982): 271–298; John G. Grumm and Russell D. Murphy, "Dillon's Rule Reconsidered," *Annals of the American Academy of Political and Social Science* 416, no. 1 (November 1974): 120–132, esp. 121–125; Stanley K. Schultz, *Constructing Urban Culture: American Cities and City Planning, 1800–1920* (Philadelphia: Temple University Press, 1989), ch. 4; Hendrik Hartog, *Public Property and Private Power: The Corporation of the City of New York in American Law, 1730–1870* (Ithaca, NY: Cornell University Press, 1983).

4. David Schuyler, *The New Urban Landscape: The Redefinition of City Form in Nineteenth-Century America* (Baltimore: Johns Hopkins University Press, 1986); Mary P. Ryan, *Civic Wars: Democracy and Public Life in the Nineteenth-Century City* (Berkeley: University of California Press, 1997); Sven Beckert, *Monied Metropolis: New York City and the Consolidation of the American Bourgeoisie, 1850–1896* (New York: Cambridge University Press, 2001); David M. Scobey, *Empire City: The Making and Meaning of the New York City Landscape* (Philadelphia: Temple University Press, 2002).

5. Gere, "Dillon's Rule," 273–276.

6. Ele Bowen, *Rambles in the Path of the Steam-Horse. An Off-Hand Olla Podrida, Embracing a General Historical and Descriptive View of the Scenery, Agricultural and Mineral Resources, and Prominent Features of the Travelled Route from Baltimore to Harper's Ferry, Cumberland, Wheeling, Cincinnati, and Louisville* (Philadelphia: Wm. Bromwell and Wm. White Smith, 1855), 321–322.

7. Kathleen Waters Sander, *John W. Garrett and the Baltimore & Ohio Railroad* (Baltimore: Johns Hopkins University Press, 2017), 115–117, 153, 155 (quote on 117); Edward Hungerford, *The Story of the Baltimore & Ohio Railroad, 1827–1927*, 2 vols. (New York & London: G. P. Putnam's Sons, 1928), 1:350–351; William Bruce Catton, "John W. Garrett of the Baltimore & Ohio: A Study in Seaport and Railroad Competition, 1820–1874" (PhD diss., Northwestern University, 1959), ch. 5. Garrett eagerly offered to assistance to both the federal and Virginia governments in suppressing John Brown's rebellion. The company later transported onlookers to witness Brown's execution: J. Lucius Davis to Baltimore & Ohio Railroad Co., 5 December 1859, Vertical File,

MdHS; *Sun*, 2 December 1859; *Sun*, 19 December 1860; Summers, *Baltimore and Ohio in the Civil War*, 45.

8. Quote from Anonymous to John W. Garrett, 19 April 1861, Box 72, RGFP. For other threats and petitions: Petition to John W. Garrett from Citizens of Frederick County, Virginia, 16 April 1861, Box 72, RGFP; C. L. M. Germin to John W. Garrett, 21 April 1861, Box 72, RGFP.

9. Summers, *Baltimore and Ohio in the Civil War*, 211–213.

10. G. P. Roman to John W. Garrett, 26 April 1861, Box 2, Folder 11, Baltimore & Ohio Railroad Collection, Smithsonian Museum; J. B. Ford to *Wheeling Daily Intelligencer*, 22 April 1861, Folder 1, J. B. Ford Legal Papers, A&M 1679, Special Collections, West Virginia University. Also see Ford's deposition from 1877 in the same folder, pp. 20A–22. On 514 miles: John W. Garrett, *Address of John W. Garrett, on his Re-Election as President of the Baltimore & Ohio R. R. Co., On the 23d November, 1864, sketching the policy and prospects of the company; together with the Remarks of the President on the Annual Message of the Mayor of Baltimore On the 11th January, 1865* (Baltimore: Kelly & Piet, 1865), 3. On the West Virginia constitutional convention: Sean Patrick Adams, *Old Dominion, Industrial Commonwealth: Coal, Politics, and Economy in Antebellum America* (Baltimore: Johns Hopkins University Press, 2004), 216.

11. Questions of loyalty: *New York Times*, 23 June 1861, 5; Lawrence Langston to Daniel C. Bruce (Copy), 19 September 1862, Box 73, RGFP. Garrett, a longtime Democrat, was asked to support the campaign against Lincoln's reelection, although it is unclear how he responded to these requests: J. Jones to John W. Garrett, 25 August 1863, Box 75, RGFP; R. W. Latham to Gov. Wm. Seward (Copy), 20 August 1864, Box 75, RGFP. Stanton quote: Secretary of War Commending Mr. Garrett to the Confidence of Maj. Gen. E. O. C. Ord, 12 July 1864, Box 75, RGFP. On Stanton's ties to the Central Ohio and RG&S, see Sander, *John W. Garrett*, 140.

12. William G. Thomas, *The Iron Way: Railroads, the Civil War, and the Making of Modern America* (New Haven, CT: Yale University Press, 2011), 69–78. See also Angevine, *Railroad and the State*.

13. Summers, *Baltimore & Ohio in the Civil War*, 165–180, 203; James McPherson, *Battle Cry of Freedom: The Civil War Era* (New York: Oxford University Press, 1988), 675.

14. The government originally agreed to pay local rates on all shipments, and then renegotiated and secured a 10 percent discount: White, *Railroaded*, 5–8.

15. Petersburgh *Express* quoted in *New York Times*, 30 September 1862, 4 (quote originally italicized); *Sun*, 13 November 1861; *AR* 36 (1862 [1864]); *Sun*, 24 September 1864; Summers, *The Baltimore and Ohio in the Civil War*, 109. On Jackson's raid: John E. Clark Jr. *Railroads in the Civil War: The Impact of Management on Victory and Defeat* (Baton Rouge: Louisiana State University Press, 2001), 37.

16. *Sun*, 26 November 1862 (quote); Summers, *Baltimore & Ohio in the Civil War*, 101–102.

17. Garrett, *Address of John W. Garrett, on his Re-Election as President*, 3.

18. John W. Garrett to Sec. of War Edwin Stanton, 24 March 1862, Box 10, B&O Business Letters.

19. John W. Garrett to E. M. Stanton, Secretary of War, 1 February 1864, Box 2, Folder 11, Baltimore & Ohio Railroad Collection, Smithsonian.

20. For example: D. S. Miles to J. W. Garrett, 12 April 1862, B&O Papers.

21. William Prescott Smith to Alexander H. Stephens (copy), 28 October 1865, Box 76, RGFP; on Davis, see Sander, *John W. Garrett*, 151, 171–173.

22. Maj. Gen. Lew Wallace to John W. Garrett, 18 June 1864, Box 70, Folder 4004, GPC.

23. John W. Garrett to the Board of Police, 26 May 1862, Box 36, Folder 562, GPC; General Dix Interrogation concerning Riots at Mt. Clare, 31 May 1862, Box 36, Folder 562, GPC. Garrett also used his power to exempt employees, including non-essential ones, from the draft: Thomas Perkins to John W. Garrett, 19 October 1862, Box 36, Folder 568.1, GPC.

24. *Sun*, 25, 26, 28 October 1861, 11 November 1861, 13, 17 December 1861.

25. [S. M. Felton], *Letter of the President of the Philadelphia, Wilmington & Baltimore Railroad Company to the Secretary of War, in reference to improved facilities of transportation between New York and Washington . . . and Letters and Papers showing the nature of the services rendered the Government by the aforesaid railroad at the breaking out of the rebellion* (Washington, DC: Henry Polkinhorn, 1862), 7, 15–16. See also Correspondence between Gen. M. C. Meigs and J. W. Garrett (Copy), 3 September 1862, Box 7, B&O Business Letters; Minute Book I, 13 November 1861. On wartime traffic jams in Philadelphia: Albert J. Churella, *The Pennsylvania Railroad*, vol. 1, *Building an Empire, 1846–1917* (Philadelphia: University of Pennsylvania Press, 2013), 297–301.

26. [Simon Cameron and John W. Garrett], *Correspondence between the Secretary of War and the President of the Baltimore and Ohio Railroad Company, in Relation to Additional Routes Between Washington & New York, and Improvements of the Established Railway Line* (Baltimore: John W. Woods, 1862), 8, 10. The city government praised Garrett for fighting these proposals: Resolution of the Mayor & City Council of Baltimore re: Metropolitan and Other Rail Roads, July 1863, Box 15, Folder 219.1, GPC; Minute Book I, 11 February 1863; Resolution complimentary to John W. Garrett, Esq., president of the B&O RR for his defense of the rights of the city, 4 March 1862, Box 124 [WPA 2316], CCR.

27. Howard Street and locomotives: Minute Book I, 12 February 1862; Ord. No. 12, "An Ordinance to authorize the construction of a new Rail Road Track on Howard street," approved 4 April 1862, in *Ordinances*, 21–22; radii: Ord. No. 72, "An ordinance to authorize the Baltimore and Ohio Railroad Company to enlarge the radii of the curves at President and Howard streets in the Pratt street track, in the city of Baltimore," approved 18 May 1864, in *Ordinances*, 59. Similar adjustments took place in Philadelphia: *Statement made by the Railroad Companies owning the lines between Washington and New York to the Postmaster General* (Washington, DC: Gideon & Pearson, 1863).

28. John Lee Chapman, Mayor's Message, 8 January 1863, in *Ordinances*, A23. Report of the Joint Standing Committee on Highways on the Petition of the Balt. & Ohio R. R. Co., 25 April 1864, Box 130 [WPA 604], CCR; Petition of the Baltimore & Ohio Railroad Company to the Mayor and City Council of Baltimore, [1864], Box 89, Folder 14116, GPC; John W. Garrett to Maj. Gen. John A. Dix, 1 May 1862, Box 26, Folder 380, GPC. On property holders' objections: Report of the Joint Standing Committee on Highways with an Ordinance Granting Certain Privileges to the Baltimore & Ohio R.R. Co, 7 March 1862, Box 124 [WPA 1005], CCR.

29. Statement of J. W. Garrett . . . made before the Committee on Military Affairs of the House of Representatives, at their request, in the Committee's Rooms at Washington, on the 25th of April, 1862, in opposition to the 'Proposition of the Metropolitan Railroad Company' to 'build a new road making direct communication between Washington City and New York.' 25 April 1862, Box 15, Folder 219.1, GPC.

30. *Journal of the First and Second Branches of the City Council*, 11 and 13 September 1865, Box 63, Folder 3137, GPC; John Lee Chapman, Mayor, to John W. Garrett, 29 September 1865, Box 63, Folder 3137, GPC; John Lee Chapman to First and Second Branches of City Council, 9 October 1865, Box 132 [WPA 377], CCR. Even during the War, supposed military justifications

were subject to council oversight; see John Lee Chapman to First Branch of City Council, 18 July 1864, Box 128 [WPA 539], CCR. Citizens of Canton Ave. petitioned to that effect; Remonstrance of Madison Wheedon & 126 others against laying a double track on Canton Avenue, 26 April 1864, Box 128 [WPA 177], CCR.

31. Letter from "A Tax Payer" to the Legislature of Maryland, 18 February 1864, Box 75, RGFP.

32. *Sun*, 21 October 1868 ("desperadoes"); *American*, 13 October 1868 for the initial report; *Sun*, 30 October 1868.

33. *Sun*, 21, 31 (quote) October 1868; for the *American*'s reaction, see 22, 24 October 1868, and coverage from 27 October to 2 November 1868.

34. L. M. Cole to John W. Garrett, 28 May 1868, Box 89, Folder 14116, GPC.

35. E.g., *Sun*, 28 September 1871, 6 February 1873, 17 May 1871.

36. *American*, 8, 17 January 1873.

37. Supplement to Revised Ordinance, Ch. 33 of 1858, being the Ordinance to enforce useful regulations &c., 7 October 1867, Box 144 [WPA 2313], CCR; Ord. No. 11, "Supplement to revised ordinance No. 33 of 1858, being the ordinance entitled 'An Ordinance to enforce useful regulations, to restrain certain evil practices therein mentioned, and to remove nuisance,'" approved 3 March 1868, in *Ordinances*, 39–40; *American*, 7 February 1868; *Sun*, 18 February, 19 November 1868, 31 August 1869.

38. On gradual shifts in railroad liability, see Barbara Y. Welke, *Recasting American Liberty: Gender, Race, Law and the Railroad Revolution, 1865–1920* (New York: Cambridge University Press, 2001).

39. *Sun*, 16 October 1860 (quote) and *Sun*, 15 October 1860. That Peter Banen is aged eleven is from a later record; in these articles he is listed as first twelve and then ten.

40. J. H. B. Latrobe to John W. Garrett, 30 January 1861, Box 63, Folder 3136.1, GPC. For other cases with similar liability issues, see *Sun*, 26 March 1868, 16 April 1868.

41. John E. Toole to W. P. Smith, 28 March 1866, Box 63, Folder 3136.2, GPC; on Smith's speeding arrest, see *Sun*, 27 February 1865; "countenances of the jury" and "was and is poor" is from John E. Toole to W. P. Smith, 31 March 1866, Box 63, Folder 3136.2, GPC.

42. John W. Garrett to J. H. B. Latrobe (Copy), 7 April 1866, Box 63, Folder 3136.2, GPC.

43. *New York Sunday Mercury*, 22 May 1870; also, *Sun*, 5 May 1875.

44. *Philadelphia Public Ledger*, 10 May 1870 (quotes); *New York Sunday Mercury*, 22 May 1870.

45. *Sun*, 22 April 1858, 17 May 1871.

46. *Philadelphia Public Ledger*, 16 April 1866; "Two-story": *Sun*, 10 April 1868; "depressed railway": *Sun*, 23 February 1872; *New York Sunday Mercury*, 18 December 1870; tunnel: *Sun*, 23 April 1872.

47. Dillon, *Commentaries*, 2:680, 2:698. Dillon conceded that railroads may be permissible in city space, but also reasserted the right of municipalities to regulate motive power; 2:706. See also *Philadelphia Public Ledger*, "The Control of Our Streets," 17 May 1871.

48. *Sun*, 5 May 1875.

49. *The Stranger's Guide in Baltimore and its Environs: Showing Strangers where to Go and what to See; The Centennial Exposition, Philadelphia, and Public Buildings, Washington, &c.* (Baltimore: John Murphy & Co., 1876), 10.

50. See Eric H. Monkkonen, *America Becomes Urban: The Development of U.S. Cities and Towns, 1780–1980* (Berkeley: University of California Press, 1988), esp. 4–5, 92–108, 161–167.

51. Churella, *Pennsylvania Railroad*, 356–357.

52. Ord. No. 37, "An Ordinance to authorize the Baltimore and Potomac Railroad Company to make certain uses of the streets in the city of Baltimore, in the construction of the said Railroad within the limits of the city," approved 29 May 1869, in *Ordinances*, 33–39, quotes on 34, 37; *American*, 26 April 1869, 7, 11 May 1869; *Sun*, 26 April 1869. The BCA houses a number of petitions that convey residents' fears about open cuts, particularly loss of mobility and damage to property; see the entries in CCR, Boxes 151–153, 173.

53. It was called "Union" because it was designed to accommodate several rail lines at once. The city endorsed the Union RR's bonds: Communication asking Endorsement of the Bonds of the Union Rail Road Co., 8 March 1867, Box 142 [WPA 1171], CCR; Report of the Joint Standing Committee on Internal Improvements on the Communication from Wethered Bros. and Nephews, James S. Garey & Sons, Howard Cole & Co. and Others; asking an endorsement of the bonds of the Union Rail Road Company, 20 May 1867, Box 142 [WPA 1419], CCR; *Sun*, 26 February 1868, 6 March 1872.

54. Union Minute Book, 24 September 1870, p.117, Union Railroad Company Minute Book, Accession No. 1807, B-48, Hagley Museum and Library, Wilmington, Delaware; *The Stranger's Guide in Baltimore and its Environs*, 10; *Sun*, 24 June 1870. As discussed below, the B&O opted not to participate in this project: *Sun*, 14 May 1869. On the B&O's dissent: *Sun*, 18 May 1870, 24, 30 June 1870, 24 August 1870. On completion to Canton: *Sun*, 25 February 1873. On times for transfer: *American*, 20 April 1874.

55. Petition of Isaac Cox and others asking that the terms of the ordinance granting certain privileges to Balto & Potomac RR be complied with, 30 March 1871, Box 162 [WPA 1752], CCR; Res. No. 206, "Preamble and resolution instructing the City Counsellor to take action to enforce provisions of ordinance granting privileges of streets to the Baltimore and Potomac Railroad Company," approved 12 June 1872, in *Ordinances*, 224–225. For "iron blockade": *Sun*, 21 June 1872.

56. For "dwarfed and contained": *Sun*, 26 June 1872; also *Sun*, 20 June, 12 July 1872; *American*, 19, 24 June 1872.

57. *Sun*, 22 April 1875; *American*, 1 October 1875. On new piers and grain elevators: *Sun*, 22 February 1875; Petition of Northern Central R Road to build Pier, 8 April 1876, Box 189 [WPA 994], CCR; *Sun*, 18 (Pennsylvania Station), 25 (Fulton Station), 27 (Bolton Depot) November 1873, 1 April 1875.

58. *Sun*, 21 November 1873 (quote), 23 July 1873.

59. Baltimore *Inquirer*, reprinted in *Sun*, 18 October 1873; *Sun*, 31 January 1874.

60. Minute Book J, 14 April 1869; *AR* 44 (1870 [1871]): 10; *Sun*, 17 June 1869, 30 July 1869, 4 February 1871. William P. Smith first proposed this method in 1860: W. P. Smith to John W. Garrett, 21 September 1860, Box 89, Folder 14116, GPC.

61. *Sun*, 24 March 1871, 21 November 1871; *The Stranger's Guide*, 12–13. It also gave the company peace of mind in a time of track removal efforts: Minute Book J, 13 March 1878.

62. *American*, 21 April 1869.

63. The (apparently unauthorized) flyer making these claims is referenced in *American*, 8 September 1873.

64. Flooding: *American*, 18 April 1874; noise: Balto & Potomac RR blowing steam whistles within city limits, 30 November 1875, Box 39 [WPA 551], MC.

65. *American*, 14 July 1873.

66. By enacting their urban vision in a space largely of their own making, the railroaders built what Henri Lefebvre might call a "space of representation," where imagined ideals take physical form: Lefebvre, *The Production of Space*, trans. Donald Nicholson-Smith (Malden, MA:

Blackwell Publishing, 1991). On the development of industrial districts, see Robert Lewis, *Chicago Made: Factory Networks in the Industrial Metropolis* (Chicago: University of Chicago Press, 2008).

67. *American*, 15 April 1874. The frog pond is defined in a dime novel: Anthony P. Morris, *Electro Pete, the Man of Fire: Or, the Wharf Rats of Locust Point* (New York: Beadle & Adams, 1884), 12, 12n.

68. J. M. Vernon to John W. Garrett, 23 October 1860, Box 91, Folder 16617, GPC.

69. Lars Maischak, *German Merchants in the Nineteenth-Century Atlantic* (New York: Cambridge University Press, 2013), 135–138, 149–151, 202–203.

70. *Sun*, "Letter from Europe," 6 August 1859.

71. J. Pearse to J. W. Garrett, 8 November 1860, Box 71, RGFP; J. M. Vernon to John W. Garrett, 23 October 1860, Box 91, Folder 16617, GPC; *Sun*, 20 December 1851. The *American* held this position even before the B&O had reached Cumberland: *American*, 21 July 1838, 1 September 1838.

72. On transatlantic steamers in Philadelphia: Churella, *The Pennsylvania Railroad*, 468–472.

73. Minute Book I, 13 September 1865; AR 39 (1865 [1867]): 10. Garrett first proposed transatlantic steamers in 1859: *Remarks of John W. Garrett, Esq., President, to the Board of Directors of the Baltimore & Ohio R. R. Co. regarding a Line of Steamships from Baltimore to Europe* (Baltimore: W. M. Innes, 1860), 3–4.

74. Minute Book J, 11 November 1874. Garrett blamed the losses on the ships' low capacity: AR 45 (1871): 6.

75. Minute Book I, 8 May 1866; John W. Garrett to Mayor and City Council of Baltimore, March 1867, Box 91, Unnumbered Folder, GPC; see also Minute Book I, 13 March 1867.

76. *Sun*, 26 March 1868; also 23, 24 March 1868; Res. No. 97, approved 21 March 1868, in *Ordinances*, 169–170.

77. Minute Book I, 12 February 1868.

78. John W. Garrett to Mayor and City Council of Baltimore, March 1867, Box 91, Unnumbered Folder, GPC; see also Minute Book I, 13 March 1867; Application of the B & O RR Co for the privilege to erect piers at Locust Point, with an Ordinance, 19 March 1867, Box 140 [WPA 761], CCR; *Sun*, 22 March 1867; Report of the Joint Standing Committee on Harbor in relation to Application of B&O RR C. to extend piers at Locust Point, 29 March 1867, Box 142 [WPA 1192], CCR; *Sun*, 12 April 1867.

79. AR 42 (1868 [1869]): 8; AR 43 (1869); AR 44 (1870 [1871]): 9–10; AR 47 (1873): 8, 15–16, 18; AR 49 (1875): 16–17; *Sun*, 22 March 1872; *Sun*, 9 May 1874; A. & H. W. Ellicott to John W. Garrett (Copy), 7 August 1863, Box 75, RGFP.

80. For the construction of new tracks, see, among others, Ord. No. 53, "An Ordinance to condemn and open Wells street, from the east side of Jackson street, Claggett street and a curved street 825 feet radius," approved 17 June 1869 in *Ordinances*, 56–57. "Gridironed" is from *Sun*, 23 May 1874.

81. Statement of Property in 17th Ward, B&O RR, 1877, Box 2 [WPA 2006], Miscellaneous Administrative Papers, RG41 S6, BCA.

82. Robert T. Banks, Mayor's Message, 21 January 1868 in *Ordinances*, A27; Wm. P. Campbell to John W. Garrett, 23 June 1873, Box 78, RGFP; *American*, 24 February 1873 (quote); *Sun*, 15 May 1872, 3 July 1874.

83. [Charles C. Bombaugh], *From Baltimore to Put-in-Bay, (Via the B. and O. R. R.) Being Letters Descriptive of the Third Annual Excursion of the Maryland Editorial Association, August,*

1871 (Annapolis: George Colton & Son, 1871), 7. See also *Sun*, 26 June 1869 for a similar reaction from the *Cincinnati Gazette*.

84. *Proceedings of Railway Meetings held in relation to the Baltimore & Ohio Railroad and Its Extensions, Branches and Connections, at Pittsburgh, Uniontown, Chicago, Louisville, and Elsewhere, and the Remarks of John W. Garrett, President, at those points* (s.l.: s.n., 1870), 19, 29–30.

85. *New York Times*, 27 December 1874, p.6.

86. *New York Times*, 31 August 1874, p.4; *Herald* quoted in *Sun*, 13 March 1874; also, *Sun*, 24 June 1867, 9 November 1872; Scobey, *Empire City*, 138–139.

87. *Sun*, 21 July 1869; "Terminal Facilities for Railroads," Newspaper Clipping, 11 February 1875, and "What is Said of Us at Boston," Newspaper Clipping, 13 February 1875, John Work Garrett I—Railroad and Personal Information, Box 17, Evergreen Library. $10 million figure: *New York Times*, 31 August 1874, 4. Cincinnatians similarly looked to Baltimore for a solution to their own congestion and transshipment problems: C. H. Kilgour to John W. Garrett, 27 February 1877, Box 70, Folder 4009, GPC.

88. *The Stranger's Guide*, 12–13 (quote on 13).

89. Morris, *Electro Pete*, 12.

90. *Sun*, 8 September 1871; Ord. No. 77, "An ordinance to alter the grade of certain streets in the city of Baltimore," approved 26 September 1868, in *Ordinances*, 118–119; see also Petition of the Philadelphia Rail road Company, 20 February 1866, Box 135 [WPA 1051], CCR; and Remonstrance of A & W. Denmead & Son and Thos. Booz & Bro and twenty six others, Property Owners, Against the laying of a double track on Boston street, 26 February 1866, Box 134 [WPA 774], CCR.

91. These arguments can be found in a number of petitions from the late 1860s and early 1870s. See, for example, Thos. McCusker & Others, A petition of remonstrance against the Baltimore & Ohio rail road laying a track on Wolf[e] Street, 25 June 1868.

92. Efforts to regulate the movement of animals through city streets: Ord. No. 49, "An ordinance to prohibit Cattle, Sheep or Hogs, being driven through Lexington street, between Eutaw and Charles, and on Fayette between Green and Gay streets, except between the hours of 9 P. M. and 5 A. M.," approved 22 April 1872, in *Ordinances*, 56; Ord. No. 64, "An ordinance to prohibit hogs and cattle from running at large within the city limits," approved 27 May 1872 in, in *Ordinances*, 78–79; Ord. No. 73, "An ordinance to prevent the driving of cattle, sheep or hogs through the streets, lanes or alleys of the City of Baltimore," approved 17 June 1874, in *Ordinances*, 84; *Sun*, 12 December 1874; *American*, 26 September 1873. A number of people tied this explicitly to concerns about urban tracks: *Sun*, 30 June 1870, 10 November 1874. This was part of a long conversation about animals in urban public space: see Catherine McNeur, "The 'Swinish Multitude': Controversies over Hogs in Antebellum New York City," *Journal of Urban History* 37, no. 5 (2011): 639–660.

93. Track removal: *Sun*, 2, 3 May 1871. Calls for track removal: Petition of Peter Zell & others asking removal of Rail Road track on North Howard Street, from Franklin to Richmond Market, 16 April 1850, Box 86 [WPA 381], CCR, BCA; R. M. Magnew, President of the B&S to the Mayor and City Council, 18 April 1850, Box 87 [WPA 553], CCR; Petition of Nathaniel T. Williams and Others, asking for the Construction of a Passenger Railway along the bed of Howard Street, 9 June 1859, Box 111 [WPA 219], CCR; Petition of Tenants on Howard St for Removing the Present Railway Track & Substituting Passenger Rail Way, 19 August 1859, Box 111 [WPA 221], CCR.

94. *Sun*, 17 August 1859; Remonstrance of P. P. Pendleton, D. Hinks & Co & others against the removal of the Rail Road Track in Howard St, 24 May 1859, Box 111 [WPA 222], CCR. (Signed

by 50). Report of the Joint Standing Committee on Highways with a resolution adverse to the removal of the present railway track on Howard Street, 19 August 1859, Box 113 [WPA 581], CCR. See also Petition of Martin Belt & Co & fourteen other Citizens against the Taking up the Rail Road Track on Howard St, 3 June 1859, Box 111 [WPA 220], CCR (Signed by 15); Remonstrance of James N. Keys and son and others to the removal of the present railway track on North Howard Street, 6 December 1859, Box 111 [WPA 141A], CCR (signed by 33). On ownership of the lines: Ord. No. 39, "An Ordinance relating to the Railroad Track on Howard street, between Pratt and Franklin streets," approved 10 June 1854, in *Ordinances*, 44; *Sun*, 30 May 1856.

95. There was another major campaign to remove the tracks in 1866, and this time only a minority of Howard street residents defended their vested interest in maintaining the system of tracks. They did so successfully, however: Petition of James M. Pouder and Others, Residents on North Howard St asking the removal of the Rail Road thereon, 2 April 1866, Box 135 [WPA 1014], CCR; Remonstrance of James Louge [*sic*] & others against the removal of the Rail Road Track on Howard St, 21 April 1866, Box 136 [WPA 1129], CCR; Report of the Joint Standing Committee on Highways in regard to removal of Rail Road Track on Howard Street, 12 July 1867, Box 142 [WPA 1309], CCR. John W. Garrett, speaking as a resident of Howard Street, defended the tracks two years later: John W. Garrett to Philip P. Pendleton, Stevenson & Sons, Stonebraker & Co., Samuel Elder & Co., Communication in regard to Rail Road track on Howard Street, 2 April 1868, Box 146 [WPA 454], CCR.

96. *Sun*, 17 June 1869; *American*, 28 April 1871. This was despite the opposition of nearly sixty firms and individuals: Remonstrance against the removal of rail-road Track on Howard Street, 24 March 1869, Box 151 [WPA 232], CCR. CCR, Box 163 (from 1871) contains a number of petitions that either call for or oppose a delay in removing the track. The final decision: Report of the Joint Standing Committee [on] Highways, in relation to the Track on Howard Street, 27 April 1871, Box 165 [WPA 2168], CCR.

97. *Sun*, 2, 3 May 1871.

98. *American*, 1 May 1871.

99. *American*, 2 May 1871.

100. For the Central, Eastern, and Monument petitions, see Petition of H. P. Cohn and Thirty five others, Praying the removal of the Railway on Central & Eastern Avenues and Monument and Bond Streets, 7 April 1872, Box 168 [WPA 807], CCR and eleven other petitions, WPA numbers 808 to 818, signed by approximately 349 people; each petition represented residents of one or two streets. For the Pratt, President, and Boston petitions, see Petition of King & Co., M. Friedmann and 30 others, praying the removal of Railway in Pratt, President and Boston Streets, and on Central Avenue, 15 April 1872, Box 169 [WPA 973], CCR, as well as WPA nos. 974 and 975, signed in total by ninety-nine people. Removal efforts on Pratt followed a successful campaign to ban locomotives from that street—*Sun*, 18 January 1873; *American*, 18 January 1873. Sixty cars a day: Removal of the Northern Central Railway Tracks on Monument Street and Central Avenue, 1875, Box 184 [WPA 973], CCR.

101. *Sun*, 29 April 1874.

102. A Petition in Relation to Rail Road Track, 3 February 1873, Box 175 [WPA 792], CCR. See also WPA 794, 797–799; *American*, 29 April 1874. Interestingly, railroad engineer Ross Winans favored Pratt Street track removal: *Sun*, 25 February 1873.

103. Petition of Gambrill & Co against removal of Pratt St Track, &c., 30 January 1873, Box 175 [WPA 791], CCR (quote). H. Straus & Bros. and others to Mayor and City Council, 30 March 1874, Box 179 [WPA 674], CCR; and A Petition remonstrating against taking up the Rail Road

track on Monument Street & Central Avenue, 7 April 1874, Box 179 [WPA 674], CCR; Petition opposing removal of track on Monument Street, 1875, Box 184 [WPA 972], CCR. About twelve petitions circulated in the form of Petition of R. J. McDaniel and 44 other Citizens of East Balto against the removal of rail road track from Monument St and Central Ave, 20 May 1874, Box 178 [WPA 671], CCR: signed in total by approximately 550 people and firms. See also *Sun*, 21 April 1874; Petition of J. J. Turner & Co., Stirling Alonso & Co., and 37 other Business Firms of Baltimore, against Removal of Tracks on Monument Street & Central Avenue, 25 May 1874, Box 179 [WPA 673], CCR. Two other entries under the same WPA number have forty-one and thirty-two signatures. See also: J. W. Osborn to Chs. A. Gambrill & Co., 27 January 1873, Box 173 [WPA 592], CCR.

104. [Henry James and Others to City Council], 12 May 1874, Box 179 [WPA 672], CCR.

105. *Sun*, 16 April 1874, 30 May 1874, 15 August 1874; Petition of Pastor and 89 Members of the St. Matthews German Church asking the removal of the Railway tracks from Central Avenue, 14 May 1874, Box 178 [WPA 559], CCR.

106. *Sun*, 21 May 1874.

107. Removal of the Northern Central Railway Tracks on Monument Street and Central Avenue, 1875, Box 184 [WPA 973], CCR.

108. *American*, 29 April 1874.

109. *Sun*, 19, 23 July 1873; *American*, 21 July 1873.

110. *Sun*, 23, 25 December 1873, 2 February 1874 (independent line).

111. *Sun*, 29 December 1873, 5, 7, 9 January 1874, 2 February 1874, 17 April 1874, for the resolution. Another rate war followed in 1875: *Sun*, 16, 22 February 1875, 14 June 1875.

112. William Cronon, *Nature's Metropolis: Chicago and the Great West* (New York: W. W. Norton, 1991); on the beginnings of the Chicago Branch: *Sun*, 15 May 1868. Chicago Extension announced: *Sun*, 1 June 1870. Flank movement and competition: *Sun*, 26 April 1871; also *Sun*, 22 April 1871, 28 September 1871. On the Saratoga Springs compact: Alfred D. Chandler Jr., *The Visible Hand: The Managerial Revolution in American Business* (Cambridge, MA: Belknap Press of Harvard University Press, 1977), 137–138.

113. *Sun*, 13 November 1874.

114. Quoted in *American*, 15 April 1871.

115. John W. Garrett, *The Great Railway Conflict. Remarks of John W. Garrett, President, made on April 14th, 1875, at the Regular Monthly Meeting of the Board of Directors of the Baltimore and Ohio R.R. Co. Printed by Order of the Board* (Baltimore: Sun, 1875), 8. Even New Yorkers seemed concerned: *Sun*, 8 August 1873, 20 February 1871; *New York Times*, 12 November 1874, p.6.

116. *AR* 50 (1876): 18; *Proceedings of the Meeting of the Four Atlantic Trunk Lines, held at the St. Nicholas Hotel, New York, May 22d and 23d, 1866, together with the Proceedings of the Convention held at Buffalo, New York, May 2nd, and at Indianapolis, Indiana, May 10th, 1866* (Baltimore: "The Printing Office," Sun Iron Building, 1866), 6. See also *Remarks of John W. Garrett, President, Embracing a Statement of the Necessity for and Advantages of an Additional and Competing First-Class Railway between Baltimore, Philadelphia and New York, Made on the 11th of January, 1871, at the Monthly Meeting of the Board of Directors of the Baltimore & Ohio Railroad Company, Printed by Order of the Board* (Baltimore: Sun Book and Job Printing Office, 1871), 4; E. A. Pearson to John W. Garrett, 22 November 1872, Box 78, RGFP.

117. *Sun*, 23, 28 February 1874, 19 July 1876.

118. *New York Times*, 28 November 1874, p. 3; *Philadelphia Press*, reprinted in *Sun*, 24 November 1874.

119. Sander, *John W. Garrett*, 210–211, 280; Hungerford, *The Story of the Baltimore & Ohio Railroad*, 2:196–197; John F. Stover, *History of the Baltimore and Ohio Railroad* (West Lafayette, IN: Purdue University Press, 1987), 166.

120. On congressional complaints: *Sun*, 9 January 1869; on rates: *National Intelligencer* quoted in *Sun*, 18 November 1868; see also *Sun*, 20 November 1868. Garrett insisted that rates to the West were the same from DC and Baltimore: *Address of John W. Garrett to the Board of Directors of the Baltimore & Ohio Railroad Co. upon his Re-Election as President of that Company, December, 1868* (Baltimore: John F. Wiley, 1868), 11.

121. *Sun*, 24 March 1865; *Address of John W. Garrett to the Board of Directors of the Baltimore & Ohio Railroad Company upon his Re-Election as President of that Company, December 1865* (Baltimore: "The Printing Office," Sun Iron Building, 1865), 9.

122. [Barzillai Marriott], *The Washington Conspiracy against the Railroad Interest of Maryland* [Washington, 1867], 2; *AR* 46 (1872); *Sun*, 13 February 1873.

123. Herbert Harwood Jr., *Impossible Challenge II: Baltimore to Washington and Harpers Ferry from 1828 to 1994* (Baltimore: Barnard, Roberts, 1994), 166.

124. E. M. Killough, *A History of the Western Maryland Railroad Company, including Biographies of the Presidents* (Baltimore, 1938), 66–67; *Sun*, 5 November 1867, 9 April 1869.

125. See, e.g., Mayor John Chapman to Second Branch of City Council, 22 June 1863, Box 126 [WPA 590], CCR; John Lee Chapman, Mayor's Message, 3 January 1865, in *Ordinances*, A19; Chapman, Mayor's Message, 15 January 1866, in *Ordinances*, A25-A26.

126. Minute Book I, 14 February 1866; on Chapman's putative ignorance: [Benjamin Henry Latrobe], *The Western Maryland Railroad and His Honor the Mayor of Baltimore, versus the Balt. & Ohio Railroad* (Baltimore, 1863), 4–5.

127. *Sun*, "The Mayor and the President of the Baltimore and Ohio Railroad Company," 20 February 1866; *Sun*, "The Resolutions of Censure," 20 February 1866; *Sun*, 28 February 1866.

128. On the PRR: John W. Garrett, *Address of John W. Garrett, on his Re-Election as President of the Baltimore & Ohio R. R. Co., On the 23d November, 1864, sketching the policy and prospects of the company; together with the Remarks of the President on the Annual Message of the Mayor of Baltimore On the 11th January, 1865* (Baltimore: Kelly & Piet, 1865), 11–12.

129. Application of the Western Maryland RR Co for an endorsement by the City of $200,000 of the Company's bonds to aid the completion of the Road, 29 November 1859, Box 111 [WPA 160A], CCR; *The Western Maryland Rail Road, Its Agricultural and Mineral Resources—Its Future Importance to the Trade of Baltimore—Necessity of its Speedy Completion—Its Bonds and Stock a Safe Investment* (Baltimore: John D. Toy, 1859).

130. John Lee Chapman, Mayor's Message, 3 January 1865, in *Ordinances*, A19-A21. On coal rates: John Lee Chapman, Mayor's Message, 15 January 1866, in *Ordinances*, A28-A33; Sherry H. Olson, *Baltimore: The Building of an American City*, rev. ed. (Baltimore: Johns Hopkins University Press, 1997), 158.

131. Remonstrance of Alfred Jenkins & others against the city of Baltimore Subscribing to the Capital stock of the Western Md Rail Road Co, 27 July 1866, Box 136 [WPA 1099], CCR; Total signatures across the anti-petitions: 514. Dozens more petitions are in the same box, under WPA nos. 1099, 1100, 1102, and 1103.

132. *American*, 3, 8 March 1866; Memorial in favor of the City subscribing $200,000 to the Stock of the Western Maryland Rail Road, 5 March 1866, Box 136 [WPA 1101], CCR, signed by 143. The total number of pro-WMd signatories including firms and citizens, was 891. Many more petitions are in the same box, WPA nos. 1102 and 1103.

NOTES TO PAGES 189-191

133. Report of the Joint Standing Committee on Internal Improvements with an Ordinance, 6 March 1866, Box 137 [WPA 1518], CCR; *Sun*, 8 March 1866; Ord. No. 16, "An ordinance to provide for the subscription, on the part of the Mayor and City Council of Baltimore, to four thousand shares of the capital stock of the Western Maryland Railroad Company, of the part value of fifty dollars each," approved 15 March 1866, in *Ordinances*, 15–17. On extra-dividend money: *Sun*, 5 November 1867.

134. Chapman out as mayor: *Sun*, 5 November 1867; investigations: *Sun*, 28 January 1868, 4 February 1868, 7 February 1868, 17 February 1868. *Sun*, 25 February 1868 (ouster); 3 April 1868 (new president). *Sun*, 16 April 1868 (investigation announced); James Hyde, Clerk of the First Branch to Mayor Robert T. Banks, 1 May 1868, Box 33 [WPA 156], MC; *Sun*, 2 May 1868 (details of the alleged corruption). Also—*Sun*, 1, 4 May 1868. *Sun*'s criticism: 20 June 1868. The pro-Republican *American* challenged the ouster of Chapman from the presidency: *American*, 2 May 1868. Chapman was the president of the WMd from 8 November 1866 to 2 April 1868. He was Mayor until 5 November 1867. See Killough, *History of the Western Maryland Railway Company*, 56, 66–67.

135. *Sun*, 25, 27 May 1869; WMd first asks for more aid in *Sun*, 1 April 1869. Hardly a year went by without further investment by the municipal government; see, e.g., Ord. No. 23, "An ordinance to authorize and direct the Commissioners of Finance of the City of Baltimore to invest the sum of three hundred and twenty thousand dollars in the . . . Western Maryland Railroad Company . . . ," approved 10 April 1873, in *Ordinances*, 37–38.

136. Councilmen (Bishop opposed, Price in favor) paraphrased in *Sun*, 13 June 1871. For the figure as of 1902, see Carter Goodrich, *Government Promotion of American Canals and Railroads, 1800–1890* (1960; Westport, CT: Greenwood Press, 1974), 238–239.

137. Dillon, *Commentaries*, 1:x, 185. On the Pennsylvania example—and the case of *Sharpless v. Philadelphia* (1853) in particular—see Louis Hartz, *Economic Policy and Democratic Thought: Pennsylvania, 1776–1860* (1948; Chicago: Quadrangle Books, 1968), 109–125. On New York: Harry H. Pierce, *Railroads of New York: A Study of Government Aid, 1826–1875* (Cambridge, MA: Harvard University Press, 1953), 26–37.

138. Sven Beckert, "Democracy in the Age of Capital," in *The Democratic Experiment: New Directions in American Political History*, ed. Meg Jacobs, William J. Novak, and Julian E. Zelizer (Princeton, NJ: Princeton University Press, 2003), 146–174; David Quigley, *Second Founding: New York City, Reconstruction, and the Making of American Democracy* (New York: Hill and Wang, 2004); "Taxpayers' Suits: A Survey and Summary," *Yale Law Journal* 69, no. 5 (April 1960): 895–924, esp. 898–907; Noam Maggor, *Brahmin Capitalism: Frontiers of Wealth and Populism in America's First Gilded Age* (Cambridge, MA: Harvard University Press, 2017), 58–74; Andrew Heath, *In Union There Is Strength: Philadelphia in an Age of Urban Consolidation* (Philadelphia: University of Pennsylvania Press, 2019), 207–210, 230–232.

139. *Sun*, 28 January 1868. The second quote is from the city register, but the *Sun* reprints it with express approval.

140. *American*, 2, 5, 11 October 1866; Matthew A. Crenson, *Baltimore: A Political History*. (Baltimore: Johns Hopkins University Press, 2017), 250–252, 258–260.

141. Robert T. Banks, Mayor's Message, 21 January 1868, in *Ordinances*, A5; Res. No. 81, "Preamble and resolutions extending a public reception and the hospitalities of the city to his excellency Andrew Johnson, President of the United States," approved 20 February 1869, in *Ordinances*, 126; Crenson, *Baltimore*, 266–267; Brugger, *Maryland*, 306; Dennis Patrick Halpin,

A Brotherhood of Liberty: Black Reconstruction and Its Legacies in Baltimore, 1865–1920 (Philadelphia: University of Pennsylvania Press, 2019), 16–17.

142. *American*, 3 May 1869 (quote); injunction: *Sun*, 13 March 1868, 1 July 1869, 27 November 1869; Crenson, *Baltimore*, 269–273.

143. *Sun*, 13 June 1870; see also a councilman's remark that "the citizens of Baltimore are getting tired of the question of railroads." *American*, 1 March 1870. On ever-mounting tax burdens: *Sun*, 8 April 1872.

144. *American*, 20 February 1868, 7 March 1870 (p. 1—"Western Maryland Railroad—Special Election on Tuesday"), 7 March 1870 (p. 2—"THE WESTERN MARYLAND RAILROAD LOAN") (quote), 8 March 1870. On the P&C, see for example Ord. No. 7, "An Ordinance to provide for the extension of the time of payment by the Pittsburg and Connellsville Railroad Company . . ." approved 19 June 1871, in *Ordinances*, 94–95; and Ord. No. 48, "A supplement to the ordinance of 1868 . . ." approved 13 April 1872, in *Ordinances*, 52–55.

145. *Sun*, 3 February 1870. See also *Sun*, 18, 21 February 1868, 11 March 1869; John W. Garrett to G. Harrison, 14 April 1869, Box 1, JWG Letterbooks; Petition Relative to the Virginia Valley Railroad, 27 April 1869, Box 152 [WPA 387], CCR.

146. For example: a fifth of the electorate voted to endorse $1.4 million in Western Maryland Railroad bonds in 1870 (7,037 in favor, 2,022 opposed)—*Sun*, 9 March 1870. Funding also was forthcoming for the Maryland Central, the Baltimore & Drum Point, and the Pittsburgh & Connellsville: *Sun*, 1 July 1868 (B&DP); *Sun*, 13 June 1870 and 17 October 1873 (MD Central); Mendes Cohen, President of the Pittsburgh, Washington and Baltimore Railroad, to Mayor Joshua Vansant, 12 June 1873, Box 174 [WPA 703], CCR (P&C). A rare exception was the Virginia Valley Railroad, supported by the B&O, the city council, and many businessmen, turned down at the polls by a margin of 1,750 votes: *Sun*, 16, 18 May 1870; Opinion of Merchants and Business Men of Balto in regard to V. R. R., 22 January 1873, Box 52 [WPA413], City Register Records, RG32 S1 Box 52, BCA. Six-million dollar figure from Goodrich, *Government Promotion*, 237–238.

147. Olson, *Baltimore*, 152.

148. This case revolved around the one exception to the B&O's tax-exempt status: a lien on one-fifth of the ticket price for every passenger on the Washington Branch, which had been exacted by the state government in 1832. The B&P, when it opened, was liable for property taxes but did not have to pay this fare tax, and so Garrett refused to pay as well. See John W. Garrett to F. C. Latrobe, Speaker of the House of Delegates, 25 January 1870, Box 2, JWG Letterbooks; *The Case of the Baltimore and Ohio Railroad Co.* [Baltimore: 1877]; Oden Bowie to John W. Garrett (Copy), 2 November 1871, Box 77, RGFP; Crenson, *Baltimore*, 295.

149. Chapman, Mayor's Message, 3 January 1863 in *Ordinances*, A21 (quote). For the $80,000 figure: Robert T. Banks, Mayor's Message, 21 January 1868 in *Ordinances*, A23; Banks, Mayor's Message, 19 January 1869 in *Ordinances*, A39.

150. *Memorial of the Baltimore and Ohio Railroad Company to the General Assembly of the State of Maryland. Printed by Order of the Board* (Baltimore: Sun Book and Job Printing Est., 1876), 10–12.

151. John Johnson Donaldson, *Speech of John J. Donaldson, of Howard County, on the Subject of the State of Maryland's Relations with the Baltimore & Ohio Railroad Company. Delivered in the House of Delegates, Thursday, March 9th, 1876* (Baltimore: William K. Boyle & Sons, 1876), 60–61. On reformulations of tax policy at the state and local levels, see Maggor, *Brahmin Capitalism*, 179–183.

152. Journalist—see Barzillai Marriott to John W. Garrett, 21 November 1858, Box 68, RGFP; and Marriott to Jno. W. Garrett, 3 January 1859, Box 69, RGFP. Everett: Edward Everett to [William P. Smith], 30 October 1859, Box 69, RGFP; Taney: R. B. Taney to J. W. Garrett, 4 January 1861, Box 72, RGFP; Hayes: R. B. Hayes to L. M. Cole, 17 January 1877, Box 79, RGFP. More thank you notes can be found in the RGFP in the folder for "January" of any given year in the 1860s and 1870s.

153. Edward Potts to John W. Garrett, 12 January 1877, Box 79, RGFP.

154. George W. Howard, *The Monumental City, its Past History and Present Resources* (Baltimore: J. D. Ehlers & Co., 1873), 290. Other paeans, from Garrett, the *Sun*, and others (including articles reprinted in the *Sun*): *Sun*, 5 June 1867, 8 February 1869, 24 August 1871, 1 December 1871, 11 April 1872, 10 December 1874; Garrett, *The Great Railway Conflict*, 8–9, 17; Minute Book J, 9 May 1877; Remarks of Mr. John W. Garrett, made before the Trustees of the Johns Hopkins University, at their meeting on Monday, October 6th, 1879, pp.21, 30–32, Box 85, RGFP. For historical reflections on the railroad: *Sun*, 26 January 1876, 29 April 1876; Herbert B. Adams, "Maryland's Influence upon Land Cessions to the United States, with Minor Papers on George Washington's Interest in Western Lands, the Potomac Company, and a National University," in *Johns Hopkins University Studies in Historical and Political Science*, ed. Herbert B. Adams, 3rd ser. (1877; Baltimore: Johns Hopkins University, 1885), 97–101; John H. B. Latrobe, *The Baltimore and Ohio Railroad. Personal Recollections. A Lecture, Delivered before the Maryland Institute, by John H. B. Latrobe, March 23d, 1868* (Baltimore: Sun Book and Job Printing, 1868).

155. N. Rufus Gill, Invitation [to] Prest. Johnson's Banquet, 9 March 1869, Box 77, RGFP.

156. Unknown to John W. Garrett, 1871, Box 77, RGFP; H. A. Jackson to John W. Garrett, 3 July 1872, Box 78, RGFP.

157. Report of a Speech by Mr. J. W. Garrett before a Comte., [1876], pp. [3, 18], Box 84, RGFP. The document is in a folder labeled "Robert Garrett, Addresses and Speeches," and though marked 1866 refers to events that took place after Johns Hopkins's death in 1873; 1876 is my best guess for this document's date.

158. "What Is Said of Us at Boston," Newspaper Clipping, 13 February 1875. The *Times* pointed to the "light" local taxation in Baltimore compared with New York—quoted in *Sun*, 26 December 1874.

159. *Sun*, 25 December 1873; Johns Hopkins University, *Official Circulars*, No. 1 (Baltimore: 1876), 1.

160. *Memorial of the Baltimore and Ohio Railroad Company to the General Assembly*; Minute Book J, 9 May 1877; Remarks of Mr. John W. Garrett (op. cit.).

161. Garrett, Reverdy Johnson, and Francis T. King were among the trustees with B&O connections. Johns Hopkins University, *Official Circulars*, 2, 3 (quote). A number of board members had backgrounds in city government, including ex-mayor George William Brown, but did not serve as city representatives. Background on the board members drawn from *Woods' City Directory of Baltimore* (Baltimore: John W. Woods, 1876): 87, 114, 163, 256, 303, 346, 589, 624. Also, Olson, *Baltimore*, 152. On Garrett's vision for the university: Sander, *John W. Garrett*, 209.

162. Colleen A. Dunlavy, *Politics and Industrialization: Early Railroads in the United States and Prussia* (Princeton: Princeton University Press, 1994), 239–243; Elizabeth Sanders, *Roots of Reform: Farmers, Workers, and the American State, 1877–1917* (Chicago: University of Chicago Press, 1999), 183–185; George H. Miller, *Railroads and the Granger Laws* (Madison: University of Wisconsin Press, 1977); White, *Railroaded*, 111–117.

163. See, for example, the title of this pamphlet critical of the power of private freight com-

panies: Oedipus [pseud.], *Truth without Fiction for the Consideration of the Community: Fiction without Truth, for the Recreation of Stockholders* (Boston, 1867). On safety: *Sun*, 17 April 1868.

164. *Sun*, 14 April 1873. Also, see *Sun*, "Corporations vs. People," 17 April 1871.

165. Charles Francis Adams Jr., "A Chapter of Erie," in *Chapters of Erie, and Other Essays* (Boston: James R. Osgood and Co., 1871), 12.

166. William J. Novak, "The Public Utility Idea and the Origins of Modern Business Regulation," in *Corporations and American Democracy*, ed. Naomi R. Lamoreaux and Novak (Cambridge, MA: Harvard University Press, 2017), 161–163.

167. Adams, "The Railroad System," in *Chapters of Erie*, 415. Other calls for state or national control: *Proceedings of the National Convention of the American Cheap Transportation Association (Name now changed to 'The American Board of Transportation and Commerce,'[)] Held at Association Hall, Richmond, Va. Commencing on the 1st December, 1874* (New York: F. H. Pinney & Co., 1875), 13, 17, 32; *Railway Economy of the Future* [Alabama, 1872], 7; *The National Convention of the American Cheap Transportation Association, Held at Washington, D.C., January 14–17, 1874* (Troy, NY: Whig Publishing, 1874), 3, 40.

Chapter Eight

1. *Sun*, "RAILROAD WAR IN MARYLAND," 21 July 1877.

2. Ibid.

3. Richard White, *The Republic for Which It Stands: The United States during Reconstruction and the Gilded Age, 1865–1896* (New York: Oxford University Press, 2017), 345–355; Albert J. Churella, *The Pennsylvania Railroad*, vol. 1, *Building an Empire, 1846–1917* (Philadelphia: University of Pennsylvania Press, 2013), 480–486; Robert V. Bruce, *1877: Year of Violence* (1959; Chicago: Ivan R. Dee, 1989), 253–260; Walter Licht, *Working for the Railroads: The Organization of Work in the Nineteenth Century* (Princeton, NJ: Princeton University Press, 1983).

4. Scholars have read the Great Strike both as a dramatic turning point in American history and as a manifestation of long-standing concerns about railroads, capitalism, and class. I see the strike as a culmination of a two-decade long consolidation of power by the private directors in the B&O but also suggest that it points to the future development of the railroad. On the turning point view: Bruce, *1877*; Philip S. Foner, *The Great Labor Uprising of 1877* (New York: Monad Press, 1977); Michael A. Bellesiles, *1877: America's Year of Living Violently* (New York: New Press, 2010). Emphases on continuity that place the strikes within broader shifts in class relations and urban history include Nick Salvatore, "Railroad Workers and the Great Strike of 1877," *Labor History* 21, no. 4 (September 1980): 522–545; David O. Stowell, *Streets, Railroads, and the Great Strike of 1877* (Chicago: University of Chicago Press, 1999); Brian P. Luskey, "Riot and Respectability: The Shifting Terrain of Class Language and Status in Baltimore during the Great Strike of 1877," *American Nineteenth Century History* 4, no. 3 (Fall 2003): 61–96; Stowell, introduction to *The Great Strikes of 1877*, ed. David O. Stowell (Urbana: University of Illinois Press, 2008), 1–14.

5. This division of labor is from Licht, *Working for the Railroads*.

6. "Appendix: Detailed Report of Casualties," in *AR* 29 (1855): 33–39. Most of the nonemployee accidents involved people being hit by trains either because they were crossing the track, were gathering loose coal from between the rails, or were trying to stowaway and slipped. This was the only comprehensive accident report I found.

7. See, e.g., Minute Book G, 9 June 1852, 21 January 1853, 9 February 1853.

8. Minute Book G, 11 September 1853, 12 October 1853, 14 December 1853.

9. Douglas Bly, U.S. Commissioner for the Manufacture of Artificial Legs, to John W. Garrett, 30 March 1865, Box 91, Folder 16137, GPC.

10. Mount Clare figure from George W. Howard, *The Monumental City, Its Past History and Present Resources* (Baltimore: J. D. Ehlers & Co., 1873), 289. Single-largest employer: William G. Thomas, *The Iron Way: Railroads, the Civil War, and the Making of Modern America* (New Haven, CT: Yale University Press, 2011), 45.

11. Minute Book H, 14 April 1858.

12. Minute Book H, 12 May 1858. The quote is the board's (accurate) representation of the *Clipper*'s position.

13. *Sun*, 9 January 1866. Initially around 200 walked off the job, joined by another 100 a day later; machinists in Piedmont and Grafton struck as well—see *Sun*, 10 January 1866.

14. Communication from the Machinists of the B&O RR Co setting forth the cause of their late strike, 2 February 1866, Box 136 [WPA 1140], CCR.

15. Reports: Resolution requesting the Directors in the B & O RR Co to enquire into Certain Difficulties, &c., 22 January 1866, Box 138 [WPA 1780], CCR; Reply to resolution passed Jan 22 in reference to the difficulty Between the B&O RR & its Employees, 26 January 1866, Box 136 [WPA 1137], CCR; Communication from Jno. F. Sharett, 29 January 1866, Box 136 [WPA 1138], CCR; Communication from Jno Henderson and Wm Evans, directors in relation to B&O RR & employees, 30 January 1866, Box 136 [WPA 1139], CCR; Resolution in relation to the Strike of the Machinists on the B&O RR, 8 February 1866, Box 138 [WPA 1781], CCR.

16. Minute Book I, 14 March 1866; *American*, 15 February 1866.

17. *Sun*, 29 December 1873.

18. *Sun*, 17 October 1873.

19. *Sun*, 3 December 1874.

20. *Sun*, 1 October 1875.

21. *Sun*, 2 November 1875.

22. *Sun*, 18 May 1876.

23. *Sun*, 9 December 1875.

24. *Sun*, 27 September 1876; see also *Sun*, 22 August 1876. For an example of the workforce's adjustability, see B&O vice president John King Jr.'s letter to Garrett, who was touring Europe, in 1873: 18 November 1873, Box 78, RGFP.

25. *Sun*, 12 August 1869.

26. Kathleen Waters Sander, *John W. Garrett and the Baltimore & Ohio Railroad* (Baltimore: Johns Hopkins University Press, 2017), 225, 228–233, Carnegie quoted on 232.

27. John W. Garrett to Master of Transportation, 6 July 1877, Box 2, JWG Letterbooks.

28. *Sun*, 27 June 1877.

29. No Title, 1877, Box 2, JWG Letterbooks.

30. Bruce, *1877*, 40 (quote), 63–65; Foner, *The Great Labor Uprising*, 20, 36; John F. Stover, *History of the Baltimore and Ohio Railroad* (West Lafayette, IN: Purdue University Press, 1987), 136.

31. *Martinsburg Independent*, 14 July 1877; Allan Pinkerton, *Strikers, Communists, Tramps and Detectives* (1878; New York: Arno Press and New York Times, 1969), 136.

32. *Sun*, "Baltimore and Ohio Railroad Strike," 17 July 1877 (quote); *Sun*, "LABOR TROUBLES AND DISTURBANCES," 17 July 1877.

33. *Sun*, "THE BALTIMORE AND OHIO R.R. STRIKE," 18 July 1877.

34. *American*, "THE RAILROAD STRIKERS," 21 July 1877 (quotes); *American*, "A RAILROAD STRIKE," 17 July 1877; Foner, *Great Labor Uprising*, 18. The engineer wrote in response to an editorial in the *American* that had suggested that the B&O was in fact trying "to do something in the way of philanthropy by cutting down wages and dividing up the work of moving its trains among a great many people in order to keep them in its service." *American*, "THE WRONG REMEDY," 19 July 1877.

35. *American*, "THE FIREMEN'S STRIKE," 18 July 1877.

36. *American*, "A RAILROAD STRIKE," 17 July 1877; *American*, "THE FIREMEN'S STRIKE," 20 July 1877 (quote); Foner, *Great Labor Uprising*, 18.

37. *Sun*, "A WAR ON THE RAILROADS," 20 July 1877.

38. *Sun*, "The Railroad Strike," 18 July 1877.

39. *American*, "THE WRONG REMEDY," 19 July 1877 (quotes). For an example of the paper's sympathy for the condition of the striking workers: "THE FIREMEN'S STRIKE," 18 July 1877. On the plight of B&O investors of limited means, particularly widows and orphans: "RAILROAD SHARES," 10 July 1877 (from before the strike); "THE DUTY OF THE HOUR," 24 July 1877; "THE TRAINS IN MOTION," 30 July 1877.

40. All papers quoted in *Sun*, "Comments of the Press," 19 July 1877.

41. *American*, "THE RAILROAD STRIKE," 27 July 1877.

42. *American*, "A WORD TO RAILROAD OFFICIALS," 26 July 1877. Moreover, the Pennsylvania sometimes paid its dividend in scrip: John King Jr. to John W. Garrett, 18 November 1873, Box 78, RGFP.

43. *American*, "THE FIREMEN'S STRIKE," 19 July 1877.

44. *American*, "A WORD TO THE STRIKERS," 25 July 1877; see also George C. Fulton, *American*, "PROTEST AGAINST THE STRIKERS," 25 July 1877.

45. *American*, "THE STRIKERS AT GRAFTON," 23 July 1877.

46. *Sun*, "The Situation at Martinsburg," 18 July 1877; *Sun*, "Midnight News from the Seat of War," 18 July 1877. Vandergriff's fatal wound: Pinkerton, *Strikers, Communists, Tramps and Detectives*, 155.

47. John W. Garrett to H. W. Matthews, 16 July 1877, Box 2, JWG Letterbooks. Garrett renewed this call the next day—John W. Garrett to John King Jr. (Copy), 17 July 1877, Box 14, Folder 197.7, GPC. See also E. A. Gallaher to John W. Garrett, 20 July 1877, Box 14, Folder 197.3, GPC.

48. John W. Garrett to Rutherford B. Hayes, 18 July 1877, Box 2, JWG Letterbooks.

49. John W. Garrett to Geo. W. McCrary, Sec. of War, 18 July 1877, Box 2, JWG Letterbooks; presidential proclamation quoted in *Martinsburg Independent*, 21 July 1877; John W. Garrett to William Keyser (Copy), 18 July 1877, Box 14, Folder 197.3, GPC (quote).

50. J. A. Dacus, *Annals of the Great Strikes in the United States: A Reliable History and Graphic Description of the Causes and Thrilling Events of the Labor Strikes and Riots of 1877* (1877; New York: Burt Franklin, 1969), 176 (quote), 42. On Jackson's precedent: Bruce, *1877*, 90–91. On the justification for deployment: Troy Rondinone, "'History Repeats Itself': The Civil War and the Meaning of Labor Conflict in the Late Nineteenth Century," *American Quarterly* 59, no. 2 (June 2007): 404–405.

51. Martinsburg *Independent* from 11 August 1877, quoted in William T. Doherty Jr., "Berkeley's Non-Revolution: Law and Order and the Great Railway Strike of 1877," *West Virginia History* 35, no. 4 (1974): 284. This is justified in *New York Times*, 11 August 1877, 4.

52. *Sun*, "The Baltimore and Ohio Strike," 20 July 1877.

53. *Sun*, "On the Way to the Front," 19 July 1877.

54. *Sun*, "Threatened Demonstration on the Ohio and Mississippi and Other Roads," 20 July 1877; *Sun*, "A WAR ON THE RAILROADS," 20 July 1877; *American*, "A GENERAL STRIKE," 20 July 1877.

55. John King Jr. to John W. Garrett, 17 July 1877, Box 14, Folder 197.3, GPC.

56. John King Jr. to John W. Garrett, 19 July 1877, Box 14, Folder 197.3, GPC; also, on police jurisdiction: *American*, "THE FIREMEN'S STRIKE," 18 July 1877.

57. *Sun*, "RAILROAD WAR IN MARYLAND," 21 July 1877. Herbert biographical info from Luskey, "Riots and Respectability," 67.

58. John King Jr. to John W. Garrett, 21 July 1877, Box 14, Folder 197.7, GPC. (There are three correspondences from King to Garrett stored in the same folder; this one has a time stamp of 12:00 p.m. and is the third of these communications.)

59. Ibid. Also, John W. Garrett to Wm. Keyser, re: Condolence for Mrs. Robert Garrett, 18 July 1877, Box 80, RGFP.

60. John King Jr. to John W. Garrett, 20 July 1877, Box 80, RGFP.

61. Stowell, *Streets, Railroads, and the Great Strike*. Northern Central tracks had been the target of removal campaigns in the mid-1870s. For continued operations of the NCRR—*American*, "Mob Spirit Abroad," 23 July 1877.

62. Andrew Anderson to John W. Garrett, 22 July 1877, Box 14, Folder 197.5, GPC.

63. Anonymous to John W. Garrett, 27 July 1877, Box 14, Folder 197.5, GPC. The *American* would later comment that during the strike "the colored people were peaceable and orderly." *American*, "THE COLORED PEOPLE AND THE STRIKE," 25 July 1877.

64. Quote from Jas. Reanry to John W. Garrett, 22 July 1877, Box 14, Folder 197.5, GPC; but see also *American*, [untitled], 23 July 1877, "The Railroad Troubles. A Plan for Settlement," 23 July 1877, "A WORD FOR CONCILIATION," 25 July 1877.

65. Anonymous to John W. Garrett, 21 July 1877, Box 14, Folder 197.5, GPC. See also Wm. H. Jolliffe to John W. Garrett, 22 July 1877, Box 80, RGFP. In the days after the riots, new militia companies formed rapidly—*American*, "PROGRESS OF THE STRIKE," 26 July 1877.

66. *American*, "PROTEST AGAINST THE STRIKERS," 25 July 1877.

67. King to Garrett, 21 July 1877, Box 14, Folder 197.7, GPC (first communiqué). See also Barbara Jeanne Fields, *Slavery and Freedom on the Middle Ground: Maryland during the Nineteenth Century* (New Haven, CT: Yale University Press, 1985), 194.

68. King to Garrett, 21 July 1877, Box 14, Folder 197.7, GPC (second communiqué). Locations of troop relocations from Pinkerton, *Strikers*, 196.

69. Andrew Anderson to John W. Garrett, 22 July 1877, Box 14, Folder 197.5, GPC.

70. *Sun*, "The Railroad Situation in Baltimore," 22 July 1877. Several days later, the *American* commented that "Camden Station is still a military garrison," "THE RAILROAD STRIKE," 25 July 1877.

71. *Sun*, "THE GREAT RAILROAD REVOLT," 22 July 1877.

72. *Sun*, "The Railroad and the Strike," 27 July 1877; *Sun*, "Workingmen's Meeting at Cross Street Hall," 28 July 1877 (quotes).

73. *Sun*, "The Speeches," 28 July 1877. On attitudes towards Chinese workers, see Richard White, *Railroaded: The Transcontinentals and the Making of Modern America* (New York: W. W. Norton, 2011), 293-314.

74. John W. Garrett to William Keyser (Copy), 28 July 1877, Box 14, Folder 197.7, GPC.

75. William Keyser to John W. Garrett, 29 July 1877, Box 14, Folder 197.7, GPC; *Sun*, "THE GREAT RAILROAD REVOLT," 28 July 1877.

76. *Sun*, "RESUMPTION OF RAILROAD TRAFFIC," 30 July 1877; *American*, "NEARING THE END," 30 July 1877.

77. *Sun*, "THE RAILROAD TRANSPORTATION TROUBLES," 31 July 1877.

78. William Keyser to John W. Garrett (Copy), 29 July 1877, Box 14, Folder 197.7, GPC. On continued trouble in West Virginia: John W. Garrett to John King Jr. (Copy), 30 July 1877, Box 14, Folder 197.7, GPC.

79. *Sun*, "Railroad Combination Against Trades' Unions," 22 July 1877.

80. Thomas A. Scott to John W. Garrett (Telegraph), 24 July 1877, Box 14, Folder 197.4, GPC; Garrett replied the same day that he was "in entire accord" with these views: John W. Garrett to Thomas A. Scott, 24 July 1877, Box 14, Folder 197.6, GPC. See also Thomas A. Scott to John W. Garrett, 25 July 1877, Box 14, Folder 197.5, GPC.

81. Andrew Anderson, Asst. to Prest., to J. T. Crow, Esq., Editor of the *Sun*, 25 July 1877, Box 2, JWG Letterbooks.

82. Sander, *John W. Garrett*, 269–270.

83. *Sun*, "Cause and Effect— *The Right Policy*," 24 July 1877.

84. *Sun*, "The Need for a Speedy Adjustment," 25 July 1877; Fields, *Slavery and Freedom*, 198.

85. *Sun*, "Labor and Capital," 7 August 1877.

86. *Sun*, "The Distribution of Labor," 25 July 1877. Allan Pinkerton argued that the market made it impossible for wages or capital to be out of balance: Pinkerton, *Strikers*, 16.

87. *American*, "SURPLUS LABOR," 30 July 1877.

88. *Sun*, "The Blockade Must Be Raised," 26 July 1877; see also *American*, "A FEW PLAIN WORDS," 27 July 1877.

89. *American*, "THE SITUATION," 27 July 1877; also *American*, "THE STRIKERS AND THE LABORING CLASSES," 25 July 1877.

90. Quoted in *Sun*, "RESUMPTION OF RAILROAD TRAFFIC," 30 July 1877. The *Sun* responded with a more negative valence, arguing that the telegraph and railroad had here been used to spread "more rapidly the contagion of disorder and revolt in the late riots." *Sun*, "The Spread of Moral Contagion," 1 August 1877.

91. Thomas A. Scott, "The Recent Strikes," *North American Review* 125, no. 258 (September– October 1877): 356; White, *Republic for Which It Stands*, 347–348.

92. Edgar T. Welles, of Gatling Gun Co., to John W. Garrett, 24 August 1877, Box 14, Folder 197.7, GPC.

93. Welles to Garrett, 24 August 1877.

94. *AR* 51 (1877).

Conclusion

1. Edward Hungerford, *The Story of the Baltimore & Ohio Railroad, 1827–1927*, 2 vols. (New York: G. P. Putnam's Sons, 1928), 2:180–183; John F. Stover, *History of the Baltimore and Ohio Railroad* (West Lafayette, IN: Purdue University Press, 1987), 141, 165–166, 173–175.

2. Hungerford, *Story of the Baltimore & Ohio*, 2:196–197; Kathleen Waters Sander, *John W. Garrett and the Baltimore & Ohio Railroad* (Baltimore: Johns Hopkins University Press, 2017), 304.

3. Sander, *John W. Garrett*, 245–246, 257–259, 278–279; William Bruce Catton, "John W. Garrett of the Baltimore & Ohio: A Study in Seaport and Railroad Competition, 1820–1874." Ph.D. Diss., Northwestern University, 1959, 395–398; Sherry H. Olson, *Baltimore: The Building*

of an American City, rev. ed. (Baltimore: Johns Hopkins University Press, 1997), 152–153; Stover, *History of the Baltimore and Ohio*, 156, 164–165.

4. Sander, *John W. Garrett*, 304–308; Stover, *History of the Baltimore and Ohio*, 377.

5. Matthew A. Crenson, *Baltimore: A Political History* (Baltimore: Johns Hopkins University Press, 2017), 314–315, quote on 315; Stover, *History of the Baltimore and Ohio*, 176.

6. Olson, *Baltimore*, 242–243; Stover, *History of the Baltimore and Ohio*, 176–178, 180–199.

7. Olson, *Baltimore*, 237–241; Crenson, *Baltimore*, 310–312.

8. E.g., Leon Fink, *The Long Gilded Age: American Capitalism and the Lessons of a New World Order* (Philadelphia: University of Pennsylvania Press, 2015), 148–149; Richard White, *Railroaded: The Transcontinentals and the Making of Modern America* (New York: W. W. Norton, 2011), xxxii–xxxiv.

9. Naomi R. Lamoreaux, *The Great Merger Movement in American Business, 1895–1904* (New York: Cambridge University Press, 1985); Martin J. Sklar, *The Corporate Reconstruction of American Capitalism, 1890–1916* (New York: Cambridge University Press, 1988); Lamoreaux and William J. Novak, eds., *Corporations and American Democracy* (Cambridge, MA: Harvard University Press, 2017).

10. Maryland Department of Transportation, Port Administration, Port Information: https://mpa.maryland.gov/Pages/port-information.aspx.

11. Kevin Rector, "FRA Picks Plan to Replace Problematic Amtrak Tunnel Beneath Baltimore after Years-Long Review," *Baltimore Sun*, 31 March 2017, https://www.baltimoresun.com/bs-md -ci-bp-tunnel-study-20170331-story.html. Opposition to this plan invokes concerns reminiscent of those that accompanied the initial construction of the tunnel: see Hallie Miller, "Protestors Rally against Proposed Baltimore and Potomac Tunnel Project Diesel Vent outside Elementary School," *Baltimore Sun*, 4 September 2018, https://www.baltimoresun.com/news/maryland /baltimore-city/bs-md-ci-amtrak-tunnel-replacement-20180904-story.html.

12. See Raymond A. Mohl, "Stop the Road: Freeway Revolts in American Cities," *Journal of Urban History* 30, no. 5 (July 2004): 674–706; Michael P. McCarthy, "Baltimore's Highway Wars Revisited," *Maryland Historical Magazine* 93, no. 2 (Summer 1998): 136–157.

Index

A "c," "f," "n," or "t" following a page number indicates a caption, figure, endnote, or table respectively. All streets are in Baltimore.